S0-BMR-234

4-3-98

	DATE DUE	
FEB 0 4 1999		

The Morgade Library
Martin County Library System
5851 SE Community Drive
Stuart, FL 34997

Amazon Journal

AMAZON JOURNAL

Dispatches from a
Vanishing Frontier

Geoffrey O'Connor

A DUTTON BOOK

MARTIN COUNTY LIBRARY SYSTEM
Cummings Library / Palm City Branch
Palm City, Florida 34990

DUTTON
Published by the Penguin Group
Penguin Putnam Inc., 375 Hudson Street,
New York, New York 10014, U.S.A.
Penguin Books Ltd, 27 Wrights Lane, London W8 5TZ, England
Penguin Books Australia Ltd, Ringwood, Victoria, Australia
Penguin Books Canada Ltd, 10 Alcorn Avenue,
Toronto, Ontario, Canada M4V 3B2
Penguin Books (N.Z.) Ltd, 182–190 Wairau Road,
Auckland 10, New Zealand

Penguin Books Ltd, Registered Offices:
Harmondsworth, Middlesex, England

First published by Dutton, an imprint of Dutton Signet,
a member of Penguin Putnam Inc.

First Printing, September, 1997
10 9 8 7 6 5 4 3 2 1

Copyright © Realis Pictures, Inc., 1997
All rights reserved

 REGISTERED TRADEMARK—MARCA REGISTRADA

Library of Congress Cataloging-in-Publication Data:
O'Conner, Geoffrey.
    Amazon journal : dispatches from a vanishing frontier / Geoffrey O'Connor.
        p.   cm.
    Includes index.
    ISBN 0-525-94113-4 (alk. paper)
    1. Environmental degradation—Amazon River Region.
2. Environmental degradation—Brazil.
GE160.A685O26   1997
333.75'137'09811—dc21   97-23611
                                                                          CIP

Printed in the United States of America
Set in Goudy
Designed by Eve L. Kirch

Without limiting the rights under copyright reserved above, no part of this publication may be reproduced, stored in or introduced into a retrieval system, or transmitted, in any form, or by any means (electronic, mechanical, photocopying,
recording, or otherwise), without the prior written permission of both the copyright
owner and the above publisher of this book.

This book is printed on acid-free paper. ∞

*For my mother and late father
for their love and their courage,
and for the people of Amazonia
who trusted me with their stories.*

A question is like a knife that slices through the stage backdrop and gives us a look at what lies hidden behind it.
—Milan Kundera

fron•tier (frun-**teer**). 1. the land border of a country. 2. the edge of settled territory, facing the wilderness. 3. the limit of what is known in a subject.
—*Oxford American Dictionary*

1

A qui," says the miner Sebastião, motioning with his hand to the jungle off to our left. He is directing us towards a small opening in the trees just a few yards from the airstrip. We descend into dense tropical forest, a chopper passes overhead, the dirt path becomes narrow and slippery, still wet from last night's rain. I look to my right, where I see a wall of vines twisting around trees the size of high-rise buildings. They stretch upward into the sky, their leaves creating a lush green ceiling made translucent by the bright sunlight. As we follow the path, it veers sharply to the left. Then twenty yards in front of us there is a clearing where I can see a maloca, a massive thatched hut, conical, open at the center to release smoke. The communal house of the Yanomami Indians, it can hold up to one hundred people—families living together in a circle, husbands and wives and children sleeping in hammocks, each nuclear unit with its own fireplace but sharing the game brought in from the day's hunt, the fish caught in a local stream, the fruit and vegetables gathered from a nearby garden.

As we walk towards the maloca a young Yanomami man stumbles from the dark interior and vomits just outside the entrance. Upon seeing us approach, a younger Indian woman, terrified, runs off around the side of the communal house and disappears.

More helicopters are now passing above us, swirling dust

that sweeps through our clothes and hair. I am walking directly behind the mining entrepreneur Sebastião, carrying my video camera, which I'm beginning to think is probably indistinguishable from a gun as far as most of the Yanomami Indians are concerned. And guns are a problem here, or so some human rights activists have been saying. Rumors of conflicts between Indians and miners have been getting back to the cities: four dead and mutilated Indian bodies left here on this jungle airstrip just a year ago, two miners murdered in a retaliatory attack, another six Indians shot and killed at Homosxhi village. And diseases, that's the other rumor, contagious epidemics passing from village to village, brought in by the miners and left to take their fatal toll on the native population. If the rumors are true, then another nightmare page has been written in the history of Indian societies in the Americas, isolated indigenous populations succumbing to disease and armed conflict resulting from the rapid expansion of a lawless frontier. Gold, again, is the catalyst turning this world upside down: nature overwhelmed by technology, faces and bodies contorted by panic and culture shock, rules and logic thrown to the wayside. This is the Amazon's frontier in 1989.

Amidst all this *confusão*, as the Brazilians call it, Sebastião is trying to maintain the pretense of a formal press junket. As the right-hand man of a powerful gold miner, his job is to watch over us during our stay in the forest. This whole trip is part of an elaborate scheme concocted by his boss, José Altino Machado, to convince Brazil and, in my case, the international press that the illegal presence of forty-five thousand miners in Yanomami territory can be justified—that the Yanomami "like" the miners and want them to stay. And Sebastião is determined to prove it even if these initial reactions of the Yanomami provide evidence to the contrary. He is, he says, going to introduce us to some Yanomami who will support what the miners have been saying all along: that their presence is improving the Indians' lives.

Sebastião is a hawk-eyed man in his mid-thirties with a pencil-thin mustache and coiffed brown hair. Even in the forest he continues to wear his city attire: shiny brown patent leather shoes, gray synthetic pants, a matching shirt in pale gray and brown paisley. These clothes cling to his body like a disco outfit from the 1970s. There is something comic about him, but sinister as well. Walking up the landing strip en route to this village, he told my Brazilian soundman, Mario "the Wolf" Salgado, that he would kill a Brazilian TV crew accompanying us if they made a "bad" report about the situation here. This crew was flown in on a separate plane to do a documentary for Rede Manchete, Brazil's second largest television network. Mario is now relating the story, whispering to me in English, as we walk along the side of the maloca. *Would he really kill them?* I think. *Would he kill me? He's got to be joking.* But as I look at Mario I can tell he is concerned. That severe crease in his forehead is now reappearing, a dead giveaway that the Wolf is worried. We have both heard the stories about the criminal elements that make up the miners' population. Perhaps my cultural distance allows me to take it a little more lightly. Perhaps this is one of the pluses of what I call the "gringo factor"—the naivete that got me here in the first place.

We continue walking around the maloca, the young Yanomami man still throwing up in the vegetation adjacent to the communal house. I go through my checklist of the diseases most commonly contracted by isolated indigenous populations. Measles, malaria, smallpox, influenza. Which ones have vomiting as a symptom? Then too, I have heard that the rivers are polluted by mercury used in mining. The miners aren't drinking the water but has anyone told the Indians? Or perhaps it's the alcohol. Some Catholic missionaries are claiming that several Yanomami have died from overdoses of *cachaça*, a sugarcane drink, given to them by the miners in exchange for food and, in some cases, Indian women.

Sebastião is now looking anxious. We've been stopped at the entrance to the maloca by João Davi, a young Yanomami man who looks to be in his twenties, wearing shorts and a T-shirt with an image of Charlie Chaplin on the front. Clothing is often the most obvious sign of contact with our world. The shorts traditionally used to come from the missionaries, but the practice has been appropriated by the miners. They are offered as part of what the Brazilian Indian agency, FUNAI,* calls the "attraction" process: a way of gaining favor with the Indians, getting them to come out of the forest and into contact with "white" society. (This can take bizarre forms. As we stand outside the entrance to the maloca, two Yanomami women, bare chested and with long thin pieces of wood extending from their chins, approach wearing men's underwear on backwards. As they pass by us, they quicken their pace, ushering their children into the dark entrance of the communal house.) These "gifts" of clothing are just one part of what anthropologists call the "middle ground," the relationship of reciprocity that is established between our world and theirs. The attraction is often initiated through gifts, but eventually—once there is a period of sustained contact—this relationship becomes based on exchange or barter as we attempt to integrate them into the ways of our world. And that is when things can get complicated, where misunderstandings can take place. If there is a breach of trust and honesty, the middle ground can quickly degenerate into a tangled relationship clouded in deceit and deception. Violence very often becomes the final arbitrator. A lack of shared cultural cues and of a thorough understanding of each other's languages diminishes the potential for negotiation. That's the scary part. It's what makes the middle ground a precarious environment, a sociological terrain where human behavior is often seen in its rawest form, a place where anything can happen.

The Yanomami man standing before us and confronting Sebastião, this João Davi, is one of his society's middlemen, an ad hoc cultural diplomat called on by local leaders to negotiate their people's relationship with the invading army of gold miners. He was not randomly selected but chosen because he has certain skills that facilitate his encounters with Brazilian society. He knows how to wear the white man's clothes. He

---

*FUNAI is the acronym for the Fundacão National do Indio. This government agency provides medical and educational services to the Indians and oversees their relations with the national society.

also speaks broken Portuguese. His hair is styled more like the miners' than the traditional Yanomami bowl cut depicted in various anthropology texts. And he is not afraid to take on Sebastião.

"No one can enter with cameras," he says.

But this is part of Sebastião's tour and he doesn't want "his" journalists to miss it. We were brought here to see that the Yanomami still lead their traditional life. And that they are happy that the gold miners are here. And, as he and other miners have said on numerous occasions, that it is the Indians who invited the miners into the area.

At Sebastião's suggestion I hand my camera to Mario and enter the maloca with the woman reporter from TV Manchete. It is pitch black. One hole in the center of this vast cone-shaped structure supplies the light, a beam of sun that cuts directly through the darkness to illuminate a spot approximately three feet in diameter. A little dust adds texture to the beam, which falls on a square but indistinguishable object about twenty yards away. Various people are now screaming in the Yanomami language from the far reaches of this large circular room. Yanoman, as it is called, is a language I don't understand and one that perhaps only a dozen people outside their culture speak. I pass a man in a hammock, emaciated and coughing, his eyes watery and lifeless. I start to run another mental check—malaria, influenza—but my mind is fixated on this object under the light.

Sebastião lingers at the entrance, trying to convince João Davi that he should speak in front of the cameras. Looking back, I see their silhouettes in the doorway gesticulating passionately, probably working out the parameters of their troubled middle ground.

Now I am getting closer to this object in the center of the room. Crossing the dirt floor, I concentrate on trying to make my presence unthreatening, thinking that I can somehow distinguish myself from the gold miners. *Will they understand the word* jornalista? *Where do I go from there? How do smiles translate in their culture?* A small naked child, wobbly legged and disoriented, appears before me. Here, I tell myself, is an opportunity for a "baby friendly moment," a chance to ingratiate myself with the locals, a ploy borrowed from politicians but one I've used extensively in my documentary work with different cultures across the planet. The basic message: *I like children too. Trust me. I'm human.* I smile at the child and extend my hand but he is quickly snatched away by a young mother who disappears into the cool darkness to join dozens of others who have sought solace from the scorching heat of the equator's midday sun.

The village chatter level reaches a loud, intolerable pitch. Now I have done it, I've probably reconfirmed what these Indians have always thought: that the white man is a baby-snatching monster sent down by evil spirits in giant birdlike helicopters to wreak havoc on their population. If someone were to suddenly plant an ax in the back of my head, I wouldn't be surprised. "Not a very smart move," I mumble to myself as I proceed through the darkness. Then, just five feet in front of me is the object that has drawn me into the depths of their communal house.

It is a gas stove—the type you would have in a small economy-size apartment—with torn metal hoses protruding from the back, somehow left abandoned in this fantastic structure, a strange anomaly in this traditional village. Was it traded for a piece of land? Or perhaps given by the gold miners as a joke? None of what has happened today seems to make any sense, each event just another absurd piece of what is quickly becoming an indecipherable puzzle.

"*Oi, Jefferson!*" Sebastião screams from across the room, inciting more clamor from the surrounding Indians. "*Volta.*" Come on back, he is saying, standing at the entrance and waving his arm in a gesture intended to lure me from the darkness.

Jefferson is the name I have come to use in the Amazon—a suggestion of the Wolf, who usually does the introductions. Geoff or Geoffrey doesn't translate well in Portuguese but Jefferson is a gringo name familiar to Brazilians. It seems that there were quite a few Confederate Jeffersons who opted to travel to Brazil rather than accept rule by the Yankees after the Civil War. They carved out their niche in the south of the country. There's even a town in the state of São Paulo called Americana where they settled.

Gringos were more readily accepted back then. We weren't considered a serious threat. It was only later that the U.S. Congress debated occupying the Amazon as part of their effort to promote the Monroe Doctrine. The Portuguese monarchy still dominated the Amazon Basin in the nineteenth century. That was before the United States became a global power, before gunboat diplomacy brought American troops to Nicaragua, Panama, and the Dominican Republic, before clandestine quasi-government operations helped to undermine governments in Guatamala and Chile and, some say, Brazil. Now attitudes have changed. Gringos buying property anywhere in Brazil are looked on with suspicion. Gringos with an interest in the Amazon come under even closer scrutiny. Anyone could be a CIA agent or a representative of American multinationals. The disinformation campaigns are effective. One's reputation is fragile. Since I did my first documentary here in 1987 I have worked hard to keep a low profile: I'm always accompanied by a Brazilian soundman and never open my mouth unless it's absolutely necessary. But inevitably the gringo stands out and can easily get caught in the complex North-South dynamic that has been building between Brazil and the United States for the past two centuries, one that is tainted not just by superpower politics but also by the economic inequities and cultural confusions existing between our two countries. American banks currently hold the Brazilian economy hostage to a longstanding debt while our television culture for years has been exported into their living rooms. Generations of young Brazilians have been raised watching dubbed versions of American television fantasies like *Bewitched* and *I Dream of Jeannie*. American music, magazines, and products increasingly dominate the life of youth in Brazil, creating an uneasy balance with their own vibrant tropical culture.

And now the Brazilians are being told by the world that the Amazon must be protected because it is a critical component of the earth's environment. More conspiracy rhetoric, say the miners. Just another way for foreigners to take control of our country.

journal entry
Paapiú Airstrip
2/23/89

Here are some facts from initial conversations I've had with the miners. Cokes cost five dollars apiece and many of the men are buying them with gold dust. Planes are flying constantly with estimates at two hundred and fifty landings and takeoffs per day.

Over lunch a group of angry pilots confronted the Wolf and me with a copy of Time Magazine. They wanted to know why Americans were getting involved faces into the affairs of their country. I explained I was here to listen to both sides, that I wasn't Time Magazine. The Wolf—once again the lifesaver—diluted the tension with some jokes.

It must be 105 degrees in the sun. I'm just hoping my camera holds up in this insane tropical heat.

As I step back into the light of day it becomes clear that the interview has been denied. Sebastião has failed in his first task as a part-time press agent. The problem is, as Mario explains to me, that none of the Yanomami will talk to him. Not a soul. But he is prepared. He has brought Marcelo from the city, an orphaned Yanomami boy of eighteen years who traveled with us in the back of the cargo plane. He's someone who spent his first year in a Yanomami village before being whisked away to the Brazilian capital by an Indian Agency employee. Just before we flew in to the jungle, a woman with a pair of sixties bee-eyed sunglasses and bleached blond hair—possibly the wife of a miner—stood on the airstrip in Boa Vista instructing Marcelo on how he has to tell Brazilian people the "truth" about the Yanomami situation. That "the Indians like the miners." This is a phrase I have already heard a half dozen times in the last twenty-four hours: Os *indios adoram os garimpeiros*. This was not a conversation but a lecture, each word a further assertion of the power that this white woman felt she could exert over an Indian. Whether it is true or not that "the Indians adore the miners," it is becoming part of the focus of my story and the hurdle I will have to overcome if I want to accurately document this collision of cultures.

How the miners found Marcelo I do not know. What I do know is that they give him free rides into the jungle and that he is one of a number of Indians that they are grooming as part of their campaign. He is someone who could serve as a spokesperson to the outside world, who can speak Portuguese but understands very little Yanoman. He could tell the media what the gold miners want the Indians to say. Someone they could manipulate. Someone they could control. A token Indian. An invaluable instrument in their campaign to stay in the forest and tap one of the world's last unexplored regions of mineral wealth.

Sebastião grabs Marcelo by the shoulder and sits him in front of the maloca, telling him to speak to the press, which in this case is the crew from TV Manchete. The director from Manchete, like myself, has been promised exclusive access to gold mining sites by the mining leaders. We are the first television cameras to be allowed into Yanomami territory since the gold rush began two and half years ago. Their camera starts rolling. Mine doesn't. I've tried to be a diplomat, but I refuse to be manipulated by the miners. I sit watching this clumsy photo opportunity unfold—the way the miners have orchestrated the event for the cameras and the way the Manchete crew is complying with Sebastião. Are they being diplomatic? Is this the story they are going to tell? Is this the story I came here to document?

The director tells the cameraman to pan down from the top of the maloca to Marcelo. Connection: traditional house, Indian face. If you had seen this whole thing set up you'd know the pieces don't fit but, properly executed, the puzzle comes together. The journalists have their story ("Yes," Marcelo tells them, "it would be good if the Indians could work with the miners") and the gold miner has controlled the situation.

Mythmaking in action. Reality relegated to another dimension, an obstacle that need not interfere with meeting the deadline of a breaking news story.

Happy with his work, Sebastião retreats several yards away to a small makeshift hut. I sit crouched with Mario behind the Machete crew wondering if I should waste tape and precious battery power on this ridiculous scene. Instead I wander over to the hut, where our press agent is in the middle of an argument with his local Indian contact João Davi. They are having a heated discussion about landing rights, something the miners have told me about in the city—one of the ways they say they are helping the Indians, introducing them to the white man's economy, providing them with a little surplus cash, getting them used to the "civilized" way of doing things.

The shack is tiny and the light inadequate. But I have found what I came here to cover: interaction. The meeting of two worlds, the coming together of these wildcat miners and the Indians, the establishment of a middle ground. This is an encounter that has been played out throughout this part of the world since the Portuguese explorer Pedro Cabral first stepped on the shores of Brazil's western coast in the year 1500 and convinced the coastal Indians to cut down brazilwood trees for export back to Portugal.

I hit two small switches and the camera is up, the little gray screen of my eyepiece quickly snapping into focus. I am behind Sebastião, who sits with his back to me. The Wolf steps into the shack and positions his shotgun microphone dangerously close to the ceiling, which is a tangled mesh of branches and large leaves now faded brown by the equatorial sun. Seated opposite Sebastião on a plank is João Davi. He is agitated, bouncing nervously on the flimsy board. I'm having difficulty getting a frame because the camera keeps knocking against the roof. But I am rolling. My grasp of Portuguese is limited but I am able to understand the general drift of the argument.

"After, after, they always say they will pay after," says João Davi. "When the planes land here in Paapiú, they have to pay. The planes land, they pay. But all they are doing is talking and lying to the Indians."

Sebastião is now aware that we have entered the shack and looks over his shoulder. I play the stupid gringo and keep rolling, trying to ignore the unnerving sensation caused by his penetrating glance. Sebastião turns back to João Davi. Reverting to the role of press agent, he makes another attempt at asserting his position, hoping to establish once and for all that the miners have been welcomed here as if they were heroes from a liberating army, saviors who come in the name of progress and civilization.

"It is good, no? You want the gold miners to continue to work here," he says.

"Let's just take care of this situation first, okay?" responds João Davi.

"Okay, okay," says Sebastião.

João Davi stares at Sebastião angrily, tired of being manipulated, tired of being "talked at" rather than conversed with. The conversation falls into a momentary lull. Sebastião sits slump-shouldered, probably contemplating his next move. This is undoubtedly not the type of scene he had in mind when he brought these TV crews into the forest. He needs to change tacks and make one last attempt at burnishing the image of the gold miners.

"If our chief was here," says João Davi, "I could ask him what he thinks. But I am alone here, what can I do?"

"You don't have the authority to speak?"

"No, I don't. Our chief is in Boa Vista being treated for a sickness."

"Is he sick? What does he have?"

"He has malaria."

"When you lived here by yourselves, you used to get malaria, didn't you?"

Here it is, the moment of truth, the critical point in the debate being waged in the cities: whether the presence of the gold prospectors has had an impact on the health of the Yanomami. Small bouts of violence can be explained away as an inevitable consequence of frontier expansion. But proof that a malaria epidemic is under way—one introduced by the miners—would have terrible consequences for their efforts to whitewash this gold rush.

"No, we *never* had malaria before," says João Davi.

Sebastião turns and stares back at me with a vicious look, an evil eye meant to intimidate. It does. I turn off the camera and the scene dissolves. João Davi disappears through an opening in the back of the hut, leaving Sebastião staring at his shiny shoes and bouncing alone on the plank of wood. No one moves. Not a word is spoken. There is just the piercing squeak of the wobbling wood. Sebastião has made a fool of himself and I have found a critical hook for my story. Faits accomplis. I'm not about to erase the tape. That part I don't think needs explaining.

"*Então?*" I say with a gringo smile: "So what now?"

Sebastião stands, glances at Mario, and walks past us. I look at Mario, who looks right back, his head shaking, his eyes still and tense. This is the first time I have seen the Wolf at a loss for words. I walk outside and he follows. As we head back towards the airstrip, Sebastião, no longer sulking, ignores us. He spends his time joking with the crew from TV Manchete. The message is obvious: we have not played by the rules of the game, therefore he is going to make us pay for it.

Mario walks head down, chin to his chest, kicking the dirt. At times like this I feel sorry for the Wolf, a born fatalist who somehow manages to muster the motivation to go on these trips with me. I wonder if he knew what he was getting into. I did try to explain the nature of this story, but then again I didn't really know what to expect. He's probably asking himself why he let this stupid gringo talk him into coming out to this corner of the Amazon's frontier. He's also probably calculating the extra days he'll now be away from his girlfriend in Rio. But I have been with him in these kinds of situations before. I know he'll come out with it.

"We now have *confusão*," says the Wolf as we walk alone.

"Confusion?" I ask.

"Yes. Mixed up. You call it a meese."

"You mean a mess."

"Yes, that is what I said."

"You think we will also have trouble."

"Yes. Trouble also."

"Will Sebastião kill us?"

"No. He will kill *you*," he says. "You are the gringo."

The Wolf spits on the ground and takes a drink from one of our water bottles. He shoots me a blank stare, then lets forth a lunatic chuckle. I get the joke and begin to lose it myself, my body suddenly convulsed with belly laughs. I laugh so hard that it hurts, but there is also a sense of relief that comes with the laughter. Humor is a great facilitator in places like this, different from naivete but equally effective. It smooths the rough edges of tense and tricky situations. It allows you to forget for a moment the obstacles being faced. It gives you time to consider the next step in your plan. I just wish I had a plan.

2

I've always been a bit of a wanderer, but this trip into the Brazilian Amazon looks to be pushing things to the edge: two degrees from the equator, a malaria epidemic possibly under way, precarious air travel, a story no television news agency seems interested in running, and a population of gold miners whose criminal past is common knowledge to everyone including the local branch of the federal police. It is late February of 1989. I think the date is the twenty-third. I am beginning to loose track. We were held up in Boa Vista for several days before we got permission to fly in here. I arrived just this morning hoping to make a documentary on what is happening to the Yanomami Indians, the largest unacculturated indigenous society in this hemisphere. This was a gamble but one that I had convinced myself was worth taking. I read the appropriate books, consulted other journalists and anthropologists, persuaded the gold miners to take me in, then bought my plane tickets. But now the whole scheme seems to have backfired, so I can add self-deception to that list of great facilitators that got me into this mess in the first place.

In truth I am beginning to think that my decision to document this gold rush is just another stage in the mind game I've been playing most of my life: put myself out on the limb, use impulse rather than logic as the compass by which to chart my course, then let the story unfold. In years past this let-it-happen-as-it-may philosophy cloaked itself in various guises. When I was nineteen it took the form of the Rastafarian credo Positive Vibrations which I picked up as a college dropout living with dreadlocked hill dwellers in Jamaica's Blue Mountains just outside Port Antonio. A few years later in Europe I was swept up by Sartre's "self-surpassing" existentialism as the justifying philosophical wellspring for reckless romances, bar brawls, and many a lonely roadside hour spent trying to put together the unresolved chapters of my young life. Traveling through a dozen countries over a two-year period I tried to escape the soft confines of my middle-class upbringing, hoping that the experience of the tougher side of life would bring spiritual salvation. To drop headfirst into any unknown adventure was the inevitable course my life took during that period of cathartic soul-searching. On various trips to Carcassonne, Killarney, Istanbul, or Marrakesh, I would pass my time trying to decipher the cultures I encountered, seizing on images that seemed to define the place and my experience in it. In the south of France it was those old women dressed in black with their strong, knobby hands wrinkled and weathered from years of hard work in the fields. Or outside Izmir it was those village cafes patronized only by burly Turkish men with dark sandpaper beards, an enclave unto its own which informed you immediately about the sex roles of that culture. In each country I became obsessed by these details and the way they reveal the dynamics of the larger culture. My visual take on the world was actually defining itself, but I was too caught up in the moment to realize what was going on.

I remember sleeping one night in the park in Belgrade and waking to the sound of folk dancing in the morning. To my left was a young man in his late teens, his black hair disheveled and his clothes dirty and unkempt. He was standing next to a bedroll and peering through the same bushes I had used as my shelter the night before. He spoke neither French nor English, the only two languages in which I had any fluency. But we shared bread and chocolate and found a few words in common, enough to have a rudimentary conversation. The cluster of low-lying brush where we had awoken separated us from the spectacle of Yugoslavians dancing before us. I was an outsider. I had a reason to be sequestered on the periphery. But I couldn't understand why he too felt the need to stay hidden behind these bushes. As we searched for other ways to exchange our thoughts he pointed to himself and said "Croat." He then pointed to the people dancing in the distance and uttered the word "Serb." The image of Yugoslavia that had been exported to the West, as a controlled and orderly society, was suddenly broken by this dynamic of ethnicity; our ready acceptance of their government propaganda had overshadowed the complex underpinnings of culture and ethnic identity as determinant forces in the rise and fall of nation-states. When the Croats and Serbs went to war two decades later, this brief encounter, this personal and specific incident, became for me the defining image for understanding the conflict. I knew then that in the future I would depend on moments like these to interpret the world.

During those years in Europe I visited with relatives and started to piece together the stories from my parents' past. My mother, born to an American father and French mother, had come as a young woman to the United States from France after World War II. My father likewise had immigrated to America, from Ireland, with his parents as a young boy. For my two brothers, my sister, and myself, our childhood tales were of the Nazis taking over my mother's house outside Paris, of her and her sister and my grandmother living in a kitchen for three years. She told us stories of German soldiers committing suicide in the backyard rather than face the prospect of being sent to the Russian front, and of girlhood friends arrested for participation in the Resistance. The accounts on the Irish side were filled with family lore about my radical grandfather who made two trips to the United States with his wife and son, each time barely escaping the grasp of the British military. On their second journey they decided to stay, and my father grew up in an enclave of immigrants in Manhattan's Yorkville. This was a time when the Irish and Italians were the exploited immigrant class. It was they who filled the prisons, panhandled on the streets, and ran illegal liquor franchises during Prohibition. But the lucky ones—like my grandfather—were able to find jobs. He became a bus driver in Manhattan and later a union organizer. Over the years, through sheer will and determination, he and a generation of his countrymen made Irish ethnicity a force to be reckoned with in New York City politics. My father, in turn, carried out the dream of his immigrant father. He became a doctor and set out to define a place for himself in an Anglo-Saxon Protestant world that had, up until then, excluded the Irish.

These family stories with their repeating theme of cultural conflict were the prism through which I came to look at life. When I returned to the United States in the late 1970s, I got a degree in anthropology and set out over the next two decades on a journey of shooting and directing documentaries. After those years of intently watching encounters between people, looking through the lens was second nature; my obsessive interest in the details of human behavior had become focused and transformed in the manipulation of moving pictures.

The stories I was drawn to were those of cultures and societies at a breaking point: Puerto Rican street gangs in the decaying South Bronx, West Virginia steelworkers trying to save their hometown factory from bottom-line Wall Street economics, Vietnamese immigrants seeking refuge in Middle America, the Soviet Union during perestroika, Panama before the fall of Noriega, and Japanese society amidst its explosive economic boom of the mid-1980s.

However, in 1987 my work took a sudden geographic shift when I did a story about a priest under death threat who lived on the perimeter of the Amazon's frontier. It was there that I first heard about a gold rush taking place on Indian lands deep in the interior of the rain forest. This was a part of the world I had always wanted to travel to, a blank space on the map that seemed to fulfill my continuing need to immerse myself in exotic cultures in foreign terrains. If you wanted to "get lost" there seemed to be no better place than that giant green expanse called the heart of the Amazon, a region where roadways had failed to penetrate, and towns and cities were still the distant dreams of urban planners.

But there was also a more focused and serious side to my interest in this part of the world. The more I researched the story, the more unbelievable it appeared to be: one billion dollars worth of gold was leaving Yanomami territory every year, yet the Brazilian government was not intervening nor, it seemed, was anyone reporting on it. When I contacted various international news agencies, I was told that the story was not newsworthy enough to warrant an assignment: "Nobody cares about Indians in the Amazon," one executive producer said to me as he stood up abruptly, signaling the end of our meeting. "But thanks for coming by." So I did what any self-respecting freelance journalist would do: I ignored the opinions of colleagues and set off at my own expense to cover the story.

I remembered enough from my college history courses to know that a gold rush of this magnitude on Indian lands was going to have devastating consequences. It was a sociological time bomb waiting to explode. So I spent the next year and a half researching the story, immersing myself in the history of the region and the cultures that inhabit the forests. I picked up another freelance assignment, as a cameraman shooting a documentary in a small frontier town about a union leader named Chico Mendes. My grasp of the language was improving, and I was beginning to understand Brazilian culture. Then I set off for Yanomami territory, where I have quickly learned that no research could have prepared me for the clash of cultures I have encountered. Hopefully in the coming week I will be able to gather enough material to document this gold rush, yet I already know that there is a larger story unfolding here, a story I find myself drawn to in ways that are difficult to explain. Amidst all the chaos and insanity of this strange, edgy world, I feel a rush of excitement that I have never experienced anywhere else. *Predictable* is the last word that anyone would apply to the Amazon's frontier. Yet it's precisely its unpredictability that I find most seductive.

3

The Wolf walks up the steps of a ramshackle plywood house sitting under a high canopy of trees. He pushes his way through the screen door without introducing himself. I follow, my television camera dangling from a shoulder strap, exhausted from Sebastião's lunatic press tour at the Yanomami village near the airstrip. This house is just one of a number of makeshift structures bordering the Paapiú runway, which has become the center of operations for five hundred gold miners occupying an area of forest that until recently had been the exclusive domain of three hundred Yanomami Indians.

The wobbly structure we've just entered is known among the miners as the Goldmazon house, the home and headquarters of a wildcat mining entrepreneur by the name of Elton Kronholt. Elton is a large, amiable guy with a striking resemblance to Jackie Gleason. He is also known to be one of the richest gold miners in the Amazon. We met him at a press conference in Boa Vista several days ago, and he immediately extended an invitation to stay at his house in Yanomami territory. Such a gesture of hospitality took me by surprise, in light of his posturing as a militant renegade and die-hard xenophobe. In countless press reports Elton has spoken vehemently about the international environmentalist conspiracy to take over the Amazon. To back up his outspoken opinions he carries a gun made of gold, a weapon he has threatened to use against foreign intruders, particularly those who don't agree with his opinions. Recently his photo appeared in the well-known Brazilian news-magazine *Veja*. He is pictured standing on top of a cluster of logs at night, wearing a trenchcoat and a weird Sherlock Holmes hat, his eyes fixed on some distant point in the darkness and his precious pistol extended before him. The caption quotes him: "I am not going to be a zookeeper for the Americans."

As we step into the front room of this little house with its low, crooked ceiling, I have the impression we've walked into the middle of a Sam Shepard play. Everyone is hyped up, a little on edge. The floorboards bend and creak under our feet. Helicopters whirl above us every few minutes as they take off from a nearby launch pad, transporting equipment and prospectors farther into the jungle. Each time the screen door slams, it announces the entrance of yet another quirky character in this strange little stage play, more misfits from Brazil's interior seeking fortune and salvation in this expansive green hell. There is Ana, a big-boned woman in her late teens who is constantly teased by the others for being an Indian. Her features resemble those of the Macuxi, a local indigenous group contacted by Brazilian society more than a century ago, but she denies any kinship. She is the housekeeper. Then there is Artur, a plump gay man in his mid-twenties who is the cook. He walks about in an open short-sleeved shirt and bikini bathing suit talking incessantly about his crushes on various miners who have appeared that day at the encampment, just some of the two hundred men said to be arriving daily in Yanomami territory. A few minutes after our arrival Artur pulls me outside and insists that I take a photo of him so that *gatos americanos*, sexy American men, "can see what a real Brazilian man looks like." He jumps into an open-air shower a few yards from the house and wets down his flabby frame. The yard surrounding me is a mess of wood shards and jagged tree stumps that have been haphazardly cleared by miners with chain saws and axes. I stand outside checking the exposure of my little Olympus and looking around for an appropriate background. Artur emerges from the shower, hair slicked back, soaking wet, glistening in the afternoon sun. He suddenly strikes a body-builder pose amidst the severed stumps and shredded wood. The shot is both pathetic and comic but I take it anyway. This little photo opportunity is simply an innocent, fleeting moment in the fantasy of sexual prowess and promiscuity that seems to dominate Artur's life here in the forest. Besides, I like Artur. His vulnerability and sense of humor provide a relief from the rugged macho culture of gold prospectors and frontier entrepreneurs. To Artur's credit, there is nothing mercenary or cruel about what he is doing. If anything, the joke is on him and he knows it.

This shot is very different from the other, more troubling, photographic encounters I have had today when the miners would grab an Indian and force him or her to strike a pose in front of my camera. Normally I shut the camera down during such scenes, but today I made certain to grab the images because they are a part of this story, posed moments that have as much validity as my documentary coverage of the airstrips and the few interviews I have conducted so far. This environment is unlike any I have ever worked in. This gold rush is not simply about the assertion of power by one group over another. That story I have documented before in New York and Central America and elsewhere when the police, the military, and the paramilitary used force and intimidation to control and subjugate a population whose actions challenged the status quo. That story is one-dimensional. There is a clear delineation between good and evil. But here there is something more complicated taking place, a game of manipulation being acted out that remains hidden behind the layers of cultural differences separating the Indians' world from my own. To not film contrived moments would limit my understanding of the story unfolding here. In this story it is not just what people do and say that is important but how they consciously choose to act in front of the camera. I look for messages in their performances, hoping that in the process I might discover some answers.

"Is it good?" Artur asks through his teeth without breaking his smile. Then suddenly he twists his torso to the right and thrusts his curled arms above his shoulders in a vain attempt at a more seductive pose. I can hear him gasping for breath as he sucks his stomach in.

"It's perfect," I tell him. "The *gatos* are going to love it back in the States."

The shutter clicks. Artur remains frozen for a moment, then breaks his stance with an ecstatic little cry. As he returns to the shower to towel down, I go back into the house, where I find the Wolf chatting up Ana. In the background an intense young man with short, curly dark hair sits listening to the blaring garble of a ham radio spewing out directions to incoming pilots and ad hoc news reports of murders and accidents from various airstrips in the forest. The Wolf introduces him. His name is Martins and he is the person responsible for supervising Elton's operation at Paapiú. Artur comes in and brushes by me, bestowing a lingering, lascivious glance. "Ciao, Jefferson," he says. He walks into a small room at the back of the house and slams the crooked door of rough wood planks.

As I look about the little abode I am struck by a quality this crazy group of people seem to share. They are all very nice, but there is a sadness about them, as if they are all a little lost. Perhaps this characteristic provides a cohesive bond for their eclectic community of misfits. That and the likelihood that there is nothing left for them back home. Money, or lack of it, I have come to learn, is not the only force that propels people to the Amazon's frontier. These are individuals attracted to life on the edge. So far in my conversations with many of the miners on this airstrip I have found that living in the dense tropical forest is a preferred choice over a more civilized existence in the interior country's towns and cities. It provides an escape from broken marriages, bad romances, perhaps even the complications of a criminal past. "The Amazon," an anthropologist friend of mine once said, "is like a psychiatrist's couch. It attracts a lot of people from a lot of different places, trying to work things out." I can see it in their eyes and those of my colleagues as well, other anthropologists and journalists with whom I have worked over the years. On this trip and the others I have caught a glimpse of it in my own reflection in a mirror, a piece of glass, the window of a beat-up Cessna. A little bit of that intensity. A desire to immerse myself in some new unexplored corner of the earth, hoping that perhaps here I will find the answer, the experience that will finally soothe my soul, allowing me to return to the norm of existence with a family, a fixed schedule, a pattern to life. Maybe after I've done my time I will be able to give up the harried journalist's existence that has provided a seemingly worthy excuse for not coming to terms with my own life. But for now there is the task of completing this documentary and dealing with the inhabitants of this airstrip. Their unpredictable nature has made this part of the stay amusing at the very least.

"*Artur sai*"—Artur is leaving—I hear announced from behind me in a whisper as Artur comes back into the front room in a flowered shirt and matching shorts, reeking of cologne. He picks up a bag from the counter and sashays out of the house, slamming the front door for added effect.

"I'm like the old shoe that fits anywhere," the Wolf says about himself. He is a man who often gets his clichés mixed up, an endearing characteristic that also manages to add an extra layer of truth to the observations he makes. But what I appreciate most about him is that he's adaptable and comfortable in almost any environment. In situations like these he is at his best: drinking, playing cards, flirting with the plump Macuxi girl, swapping recipes with Artur, putting everyone at ease in the wisecracking manner of the *carioca*, the native son of Rio de Janeiro, that seductive coastal city whose inhabitants are known throughout Brazil as disarming charmers and incorrigible womanizers. Thanks to the Wolf we have quickly settled into relaxed relations with the various occupants of the house: Artur, Ana, Martins, and a fourth person named Guilherme, a scruffy middle-aged mechanic with curly brown hair, small dark eyes, and a beer barrel of a belly. Guilherme worked the oil fields of the Middle East in the early 1980s and was brought here by gold mine owners to service the hydraulic pumps that power their jungle mining operation. We are accepted into this circle at the Goldmazon house in part because we help to break the monotony that has descended on them after six continuous months in the forest. But there is a second, perhaps more significant, factor facilitating our entry into the group. We have brought with us food that is hard to come by in this corner of the world: large cans of tuna fish and sardines, pasta, canned meat, cookies, and coffee.

Sharing—whether you are with Indians, missionaries, or miners—is the key code of conduct in the forest. The underlying message is simple: if you don't share or participate in an equitable exchange of what you have, then you will inevitably fight over it. And if you fight over things on the frontier, chances are you will lose everything or kill somebody or be killed yourself. If you do kill, it is understood that you are submitting yourself not to the hands of formal justice but to vendetta, the code that rules in most of the towns, cities, and miners' encampments in the Amazon—the uneasy glue that holds together the rickety social structure of the frontier. The circumstances in which these scenarios unfold start simply but can quickly erupt in chaos and violence.

One such scenario: a group of Yanomami give bananas to a miner who promises to give them a dozen machetes. The miner then ignores the Indians' persistent requests for compensation. After several weeks the Indians, frustrated, decide to raid the miners' encampments and take what is owed to them. Undetected, they steal pots, pans, machetes, and mirrors and retreat to their village. To exact revenge—to maintain their control of the forest—the miners wait outside the village and kill two Indians who have set off on a hunt. The Indians in turn exact revenge by killing three miners. There are no intermediaries, no institutions of justice to negotiate differences. This is the undiluted power of vendetta invoked as the result of a mismanaged exchange.

Here in Yanomami territory the miners say that, among themselves, there are two to three killings a week in the hundred or so mining airstrips scattered throughout Indian lands. Most of those murders stem from disputes over the division of profits. In other parts of the frontier, however, violence is most commonly the result of conflicts over land. In the last twenty years sixteen hundred nuns, priests, lawyers, union leaders, and local politicians have been assassinated in the Amazon with only twenty-six trials and fourteen convictions. The majority of those murdered died defending the rights of desperate Amazon migrants who for decades have come to this region seeking arable parcels of rain forest for subsistence farming. Some of the poor—there are an estimated 12 million people without land in Brazil—manage to claim small plots for themselves, but others have chosen to follow the perilous life of squatters rather than subject themselves as peons to the medieval conditions that await them as laborers on large estates. Ironically, miners and missionaries both affirm that the gold camps are filled with former gunslingers known as *pistoleiros* who were hired by large ranchers to exact vengeance in disputes over land. I am sure that is true (no one denies there is a significant criminal element here), but these camps are predominantly inhabited by the impoverished of Amazonia—part of an army of three hundred thousand miners—many of whom would prefer to be working the land rather than toiling in the forest. Out of frustration they have given up the dream of owning their own plots of land and come here to pursue *a droga*, the term used by many to describe the crazed and intoxicated state that overcomes people in pursuit of gold.

———

Earlier today at the landing strip, a local Indian Agency employee described to me an incident that brought violence to this community of Yanomami. Almost a year ago a Yanomami man shot and killed two gold prospectors in a drunken dispute near the airstrip. The miners retaliated by abducting and killing four Indians. They chopped their bodies to pieces and left them on the runway not far from one of the Yanomami villages. More than revenge on behalf of the dead, this was an act calculated to terrorize the living, adding to the Yanomamis' long-standing fear of outsiders abducting their women. And it has been effective. The Indians, particularly the women, seem paralyzed by fright each time they must cross the landing strip. Their faces contract in horrific grimaces whenever I, or anyone from outside their culture, try to approach them. The Indian Agency official also told me that after the murders the governor of this territory (the region has yet to become a state) sent in a federal policeman to supervise the area. The policeman, however, spent most of his time searching for gold in mining pits rather than trying to maintain order in this reckless frontier community.

After dinner I retire to my hammock strung up on the front porch next to the room of the mechanic Guilherme. As I secure the knots and prepare to sleep, Guilherme sits near a small kerosene lamp talking to his dog and touching it gently on its back and sides. Much of his day was spent being choppered in to various mining sites to repair the hydraulic pumps that run constantly in the pits. In the evenings Guilherme hangs around the house sipping coffee and trying to seduce the housekeeper Ana. I can tell that he has spent a lot of time in foreign countries: he is more comfortable than the others in my presence. To him I am not so much an item of curiosity as a potential source of entertainment.

"Are you going to go out there to piss in the night?" he says to me as I begin to undress.

"Maybe."

"Make sure you bring a lighter."

"You mean a flashlight, a *lanterna*, not an *acendedor*, a lighter," I say as I mime the action of striking a Bic lighter. (I'm once again succumbing to the tourist ritual of acting out what I am trying to say, something I always promised myself I wouldn't do.)

"No, no." He laughs. "A lighter."

"Why a lighter?"

"Because of the vampire bats." He pauses a moment to let this sink in. "It's the only way to get them off. You have to put the flame right up next to them." He lights his Bic. The dog, startled, makes a sudden movement.

"*Sério.* You are serious, yes?"

"Sure," he says. "Look at what happened to him last night."

Guilherme now turns on a *lanterna*, a flashlight, and shows me the dozen deep, bloody scars on the back and sides of his dog. There is a pained and terrified look on the animal's face and a sick grin on the face of his owner.

"If you don't scare them away with the flame," he warns me, "they will just sit there sucking into you, drawing out the blood."

I'm speechless. "Thanks," I say finally.

As Guilherme pats his dog, he stares at me for a moment. He then breaks out in a big smile—a sign of contentment, I take it, that he has managed to sufficiently upset his gringo visitor. I say good night and settle into my hammock.

Looking up above the tree line of the forest I can see the vampire bats as they crisscross the sky in sharp, rapid semi-circles, a strange web of violent and chaotic silhouettes, disturbingly reminiscent of the way life unfolds in this corner of the world.

4

The Yanomami didn't always inhabit these forests. Some historians believe they are descendants of the first Asiatic populations that traveled across the Bering Straits during the Ice Age and headed down into the Americas twenty thousand years ago. The theory is that for generation after generation these peoples moved closer and closer to the lower, flatter parts of what is now the Brazilian Amazon. Anthropologists call them lowland Indians. Highland Indians can be found in the mountains of Peru, Colombia, and Ecuador. In North America we had the Plains Indians, the Pueblos, and Coastal societies. Separate cultures, economies, and belief systems. These were worlds unto themselves. In the land now known as Brazil, entire societies have lived for centuries sequestered in the forest, occasionally bumping up against each other, sometimes in conflict, sometimes with a mutual sense of awe that there are others out there sharing the forest, surviving in this plentiful but hostile environment. The specific climate, geographic location, and ecosystem of each of these groups in the Americas has necessitated a different cultural development. Today an estimated one hundred seventy different Indian societies live throughout the Amazon Basin in Brazil. And many of these societies, not just the Yanomami, continue to be threatened by the encroachment of the civilized world on their once isolated communities.

Indian populations in the Amazon can be roughly classified into five linguistic subgroups: the Ge-speaking people, the Tupi, the Panoan, the Carib, and the Arawak. Although sharing similar language bases, Amazonian societies have developed in relative isolation, giving each a specific culture, language, and genetic makeup. The Yanomami, like many of the lowland populations in the Amazon, have developed extremely efficient forms of ecological adaptation. A mix of hunting, slash-and-burn agriculture, and the gathering of products from the forest kept them completely self-sufficient for centuries—until their first contacts with white explorers. Then the big picture began to change, and with it their ancient worldview. The start of the gold rush in 1987 forced the Yanomami to come to terms with the sheer numbers of the white man, a strange people who by the tens of thousands descend to earth in giant metal birds and who employ noisy machines to carry them everywhere, to bring light to their houses, to give energy to the orange hoses and hydraulic pumps tearing apart the once pristine riverbanks of this part of the forest. (The Yanomami refer to the miners as "wild pigs snorting in the mud" because of the way they press their bodies into the sides of rivers as they search the embankments for gold.)

When white missionaries, anthropologists, and Indian Agency employees first began to live among the Yanomami in the early 1960s, the Indians believed that these strangers communicated with each other by utilizing the same supernatural songs that their shamans used to communicate with the spirit world during ritual chants. They would watch the white men talk all day into boxes called radios: a man would sit there speaking, then a voice would come out of the radio. It only made sense that these strange white men were employing a form of communication that the Yanomami were familiar with. But with time the high-tech logic of Western European societies started to become incorporated into the worldview of the Yanomami and radios are now understood to be devices of communication. Still there are vast dimensions of reality and experience that the Yanomami could not share with us and we cannot share with them. And to assume we can is a dangerous proposition. Because the moment we presume that there are no differences between their world and ours, that twenty thousand years' separation has no lasting import and is only a minor obstacle to social interaction, at that moment misunderstandings take place.

In Yanomami territory and throughout the Brazilian Amazon, differences of culture and language exacerbate problems: a miner might believe that a young Indian girl has been promised to him by a village elder, or an Indian man may assume that he is to get ten times more in an exchange than was actually offered. Such misunderstandings often have brutal, even fatal, consequences because there are no shared cultural or institutional means of mediating conflict. In the case of the murders at Paapiú, no one knows what prompted all the violence. Perhaps it was a fight about a woman or an argument over the runway landing fees that had been promised to the Indians.

Each time I hear such stories I think how many similar misunderstandings must have been reenacted in the history of contact between Indians and Western European explorers in this hemisphere. And I wonder, can we ever hope to really comprehend a society so different from our own? To do so we must make a giant leap into another cultural landscape, must completely immerse ourselves over a period of years in the logic of a separate world dependent not on the high-tech functioning of cities and towns but on an intimate relation with the plants, the animals, and the rivers of an untouched tropical forest. It is unfortunately a leap few of us are willing to make, and so we go along, as we have for centuries, blindly interacting with a people whom we don't really understand, creating that intermediate but tenuous space called the middle ground. There are some anthropologists who have referred to societies such as the Yanomami as our contemporary ancestors. I think it is best to simply recognize these people as our equals operating on a separate plane. It's safer that way for everyone involved: miners, environmentalists, journalists, and all the rest of us who have decided to enter this forest, a land where the predominant logic and rhetoric of our Western world suddenly become ineffective—at times an obstacle—in our efforts to relate to the indigenous inhabitants.

So when did we outsiders come into the picture? That is still a debate in anthropology circles. Some Yanomami have not yet seen—despite the gold mining invasion—the face of an outsider, the mythical "white man." Yet the influences of the Western European world more than a century ago penetrated even the most isolated areas. Machetes, knives, fishhooks, pots, pans, mirrors, and even guns have reached distant areas through an elaborate trade network joining approximately 350 villages. While anthropologists working with the Yanomami have their theoretical differences, all seem to agree that these Indians are fanatical traders, looking to exchange almost anything for valued objects from the outside world. Like most cultures, including my own, these are a people always on the lookout for a good deal.

The first documented cases of contact with the Yanomami were by Portuguese explorers in the late eighteenth century. But it was not until the 1910s that the Yanomami experienced a period of sustained contact with rubber tappers, the Indian Protection Service (FUNAI's predecessor), and missionaries who had navigated small, lightweight boats up the intricate waterways of Yanomami territory, carrying them over waterfalls so that they could penetrate this remote part of the northwest Amazon. It was these natural barriers (*cachoeiras* the waterfalls are called in Portuguese) that protected the Yanomami from the large boats that over the past three centuries had already penetrated most points of the lower Amazonian river systems. But the most persistent explorers were getting through in smaller boats, and the goods they were carrying attracted some Yanomami communities closer to the rivers. These Indians were seeking trade items that could be bartered back in the forest, machetes to clear gardens or to be presented as gifts in the elaborate seasonal visits that take place between villages. However, in spite of these points of contact, the Yanomami have historically enjoyed only brief periods of limited interaction with small numbers of outsiders. They eluded the

Portuguese slave raids of the seventeenth and eighteenth centuries which depopulated villages bordering the Amazon, leaving behind epidemic disease that killed off the majority of the remaining inhabitants. The Yanomami also escaped the attentions of Jesuit priests in the sixteenth century who, with the help of the Portuguese government, tried to "civilize" the Indians of Amazonia by luring them into regimented evangelical communities organized like jungle communes. The work was done collectively but the land and the assignation of labor tasks was strictly controlled by the clergy. Although considered a liberal alternative to slavery, these disciplined Catholic compounds—at one time the Jesuits had set up over sixty of them along the Amazon's riverbanks—were responsible for the obliteration of native languages, customs, and traditional shamanistic practices.

But miraculously over a period of five centuries the Yanomami managed to maintain their indigenous worldview—including a dimension embraced by many other lowland Indian societies before contact with Portuguese colonizers or Brazilian nationals. These Indians believed they were the first people, the center of the universe. The creation myths of most lowland Amerindian societies are constructed in such a way as to position their own culture at the point of origin of the world. The particular manner in which a society's creation takes place changes with the mythology of each culture. But what didn't change was that the first people were *their* people, and that the world—or what they knew to be the world—evolved from them.

By the 1950s, however, the increasing presence of outsiders could no longer be ignored. It was obvious that there were more types of people in the world than just the other Amerindian societies—"the real foreigners" the Yanomami call them—who had been their neighbors and, at times, enemies in the past. These new people were a type of *napë*, or non-Yanomami, who had entered their universe: these were called *kraiwa*, the white people. The exact size of their population and their intentions were still unclear. Contact was limited and controlled by certain intermediaries: missionaries, anthropologists, an occasional group of rubber tappers, and the country's Indian

Protection Service. They arrived by canoes and planes and, in most cases, seemed to be friendly. Slowly they started to be incorporated into the Indians' belief system. Today the Yanomami shamans give a simple explanation for the appearance of these people: the *kraiwa* are descendants of the Yanomami. Their arrival on earth is ascribed to a breach of the ritual seclusion of a young couple in a menstruation hut, a common practice in Yanomami villages. Couples often marry very young. When the girl has her first menstruation, she and her husband are secluded in a small temporary hut just outside the village, where they are required to remain over the course of a week. Food is brought to them by relatives. Instead of using their hands to eat, they must use a stick. They may speak only in a whisper and then only to their closest relatives. In the eyes of the Yanomami this form of ritual seclusion protects the village from the dangerous effects of menstrual blood, which, if exposed to members of the community, has the power to make the world collapse.

"A very long time ago" a fight broke out during a village festival. Two Yanomami shamans who had passed the morning taking the ritual drug yakuana now stood facing each other, reeling back and forth on their heels, overcome by the yakuana's powers. They had spent the preceding hour blowing small bits of the hallucinogenic substance into each other's nostrils with a long thin reed resembling a blowgun. Somehow an argument had broken out between them, and they were now in the village center, a crowd of neighbors and relatives forming as they prepared to face off in a bout of chest pounding.

On this day one of the sisters of the two combatants was sequestered with her husband in a menstruation hut located just outside the village. As the pounding match began, it soon became clear that the young woman's brother was to receive a terrible beating, yet he stubbornly refused to surrender. Quickly his mother came to the hut and pleaded with her son-in-law to intervene in her son's defense. With each blow that landed, the old mother wailed and begged her son-in-law to leave the ritual seclusion and defend his suffering relative. Each time he refused. But eventually the hysterical pleas of both his wife and his mother-in-law became unbearable. With great hesitation the young husband emerged from the menstruation hut and intervened in his brother-in-law's defense.

Suddenly the sky turned dark and a tidal wave surged up from the foot of a nearby hill. A wall of water swept through the forest, knocking down villagers and carrying off their bodies. Those Yanomami who escaped by fleeing to the forest were transformed into deer and jaguars. Those who tried to climb to safety in trees were turned into termite nests and sloths. Still others were overpowered and eaten by giant otters and caimans. The bloody remnants of the carnage mixed with the water and created a red foam that traveled through the forest and became the river Catrimani. This bloody foam was carried downstream to that place on the distant horizon where the sky meets the earth, the land that is home to Remori, the immortal hero of the Yanomami people.

There at the edge of the earth Remori stepped in front of the waters and directed them into the underworld beneath the earth's surface. Leaning over the bloody river, he gathered the red foam into his hands and molded it into the form of human beings. He then placed his mouth against it and spoke into the foam a sound like "Rerererere," a sound similar to that which the white men make when they speak into their radios. These words of Remori suddenly brought life to the foam, creating human figures which he placed down on the side of the riverbank. When these figures began to speak they uttered the language of the white people and this is how Remori brought white people into the world.

Until this time Remori had been the only "foreigner" the Yanomami had known, a spirit-being able to fly through the air as the white people do today. It was he who gave the white people radios, machetes, pots, and pans and told them to return to the Yanomami lands carrying these objects as gifts. "These things you will give away among the people there," Remori said to the white people as he set them down on the riverbank. "You shall go then where you came from and take gifts back to your people who remained there."

Ever since this time, white people created by Remori have continued to visit the Yanomami, the people from whom they were originally created.

This mythic tale of the arrival of white people has been told in different versions throughout Yanomami territory. Each time, the shaman recounting it will transform it slightly so as to incorporate the specific geographic and cultural details of the region in which it is told. Where one shaman will refer to the Caltrimani River another might refer to the Pacu or the Jundia. In one version the whites return in canoes, in another in airplanes. To this degree myth is active, not static; it tracks the changes taking place in the larger society and incorporates them into the telling of the tales. It is their historical record.

Our history works the same way. It is also steeped in its own mythology, particularly those histories that recount our contact with indigenous populations. The one being told at present by gold miners in Brazil extols the rugged frontier explorer advancing steadily into an untamed forest with the aid of new technological breakthroughs. The Indians' myths and our own are struck from different molds, but they have a common impetus: each attempts to explain the place of the other in the forest.

In Brazil in the 1980s Yanomami territory became an area of renewed interest for wildcat gold miners as a result of recent advances in satellite photography and the availability of affordable lightweight aircraft. The first photographs of Amazonia were made by the Brazilian Radar Institute (RADAM) in the 1960s. On Yanomami lands they detected large deposits of gold and cassiterite, the latter an extremely valuable mineral substance which is the prime source of tin. During this time frontier entrepreneurs like José Altino Machado were anxious to lay claim to the mineral deposits before corporations had tied up all the exploration contracts with the military government.

In fact a cat and mouse game between mineral extraction companies and freelance gold prospectors had been going on in the Amazon for some time, and Machado was an expert gamesman. He was considered by many to be the quintessential Brazilian pioneer of this new era of exploration. He was a pilot who had made a small fortune working other gold sites in Amazonia and had now focused on the last unexplored regions of the rain forest as a new challenge. Not only was he a shrewd frontier explorer but he was also an articulate, charismatic man in his mid-forties whose weathered good looks helped to make him a favorite of the Brazilian press. Although he was often in front of the cameras, the tall, dark-haired José Altino dressed simply; jeans, lightweight shirts, and green aviator glasses were the staples of his attire. He stayed regularly at the Hotel Tropical in Boa Vista but also maintained homes in Manaus and Brasília. As one of the region's most successful pilots and mine owners, he was easily elected president of a loose confederation of 300,000 gold miners known as the Syndicate of Gold Miners in the Legal Amazon or, in its Portuguese acronym, USAGAL. Although he had recently vacated this post, he continued to be quoted regularly in the press as the region's most influential mining leader.

In his comments to the media Machado, like the Yanomami shamans, practiced his own particular version of mythmaking. He always depicted the Brazilian prospector as the "little man" or the "real Brazilian" who had been denied a role in a society that had become increasingly dominated by big government and uncaring corporate interests. In various meetings I had with José Altino he referred to himself as antimilitary, antigovernment, and a free market "anarchist" who did not want anyone telling him how he and his fellow miners should conduct explorations in Amazonia. "You can't have laws created by a civilization that occupies the south of the country applied to those who live in Amazonia, because these laws are incompatible and even impossible of being carried out," he told an audience of businessmen in São Paulo when I first met him. For José Altino the Indians were merely an obstacle to his efforts, a people who existed "on the periphery of the white man's economy." During one meeting in Rio de Janeiro he told me he considered himself a disciple of Aristotle, adding that in the Amazon traditional concepts of authority don't exist because "nature itself determines the course of society." I can only assume he was referring to the Aristotelian concept of "mutatis mutandis" where the acquisition of goods from the environment is categorized as "natural" and therefore not to be altered by society. Aristotle went so far as to include piracy in this category because pirates, like hunters, "simply live the life that their needs compel them to." In this sense some of Aristotle's writings provided a perfect model for José Altino to create his own myth justifying the occupation of Yanomami lands by Brazilian miners—an act of piracy in its own right. But perhaps the part of Aristotle that José Altino forgot to read was the chapter recounting the story of the King of Phrygia known as Midas, who found that "because of the inordinate greed of his prayer everything that was set before him turned to gold." Midas eventually starved to death, unable to eat any food set before him. The sad king is now a relic of Western European history. The fate of José Altino and his forty-five thousand miners is still to be determined.

During the 1970s and early 1980s Machado and several other mining entrepreneurs began to position themselves at the forefront of efforts to establish wildcat gold mining operations on Yanomami lands. Slowly and carefully they made periodic incursions into Yanomami territory, testing the reactions of the region's inhabitants as well as the local branches of the federal police.

In October of 1980 Ottomar Pinto da Souza, then governor of Roraima, sent in planeloads of prospectors to Yanomami lands just fifty kilometers from a large Indian community in the area known as the Serra dos Surucucus. Very quickly a measles epidemic broke out and twenty-seven Indians died. The Catholic Church and an alliance of anthropologists protested the invasion. Medical teams were sent in and three thousand miners were expelled. For a few years the situation was under control.

Then in 1984 a presidential decree gave mining companies the right to prospect on Indians lands. José Altino, fearful that freelance Brazilian miners were going to be excluded from reaping profits, went into action. In February of 1985 he flew dozens of gold miners in his own planes to a semiabandoned airstrip near the Venezuelan border. Once on the ground, he led an expedition of prospectors back to the Serra dos Suru-cucus, one of the areas the recently released radar photographs had confirmed as being rich in gold and cassiterite. It was also one of the most densely populated parts of Yanomami territory and the same area that Ottomar Pinto da Souza had invaded five years earlier. José Altino's strategy was to start a de facto gold rush before the mining companies could have their contracts approved by the military government. According to a Yanomami leader by the name of Davi Kopenawa, José Altino and his fellow miners took the extra precaution of wearing military fatigues and describing their group to local villagers as being part of an army expedition. But the Brazilian armed forces, tipped off by Kopenawa and local missionaries, soon arrived on the scene. They apprehended José Altino and his group, though not before the miners had hacked their way through the bush and discovered for themselves extensive mineral deposits. Although José Altino was never charged with impersonating a military official, he was arrested on February 13, 1985, for illegally entering Indian lands. He claims he was arrested not because he was breaking the law but simply because he and his men represented a threat to large mining concerns like the Paranapanema Group. His sentence was twenty-six days in jail, a ritual baptism for a frontier renegade determined to continue penetrating Indian lands, drawing on the mineral wealth that he claimed belonged to the Brazilian people.

These invasions by José Altino and Ottomar Pinto confirmed the worst fears of Brazilian human rights activists: there was an untapped fast-buck El Dorado just sitting out there in the rain forest.

But during this period new obstacles emerged to threaten José Altino's campaign for wildcat mineral exploration in Yanomami territory. Democracy, after two decades of military rule, was returning to Brazil. Frustrated by their own reckless economic mismanagement, the generals had decided to give the government back to the people. A new constitution was in the process of being established and, for the first time, institutions of justice were slowly gaining a foothold in the previously lawless terrain of Brazil's frontier. Nongovernmental organizations throughout the country—seizing the momentum of activism that arrived with this new period of democracy—were publicly protesting on behalf of the poor as well as the nation's indigenous populations. José Altino and his fellow miners found themselves working against a clock: the country's new constitution was to take effect in 1988 and the pro-Indian lobby had entered into preliminary negotiations extremely well organized. Machado's response was to continue to use the press to promulgate his vision of the rain forest as "a separate universe, accountable to the laws of nature but not to politics." Looked at in the context of Brazilian history, José Altino Machado's political maneuvering simply followed a formula for success that had been established in the nineteenth century by Brazilian pioneers known as *bandeirantes*: stay ahead of the institutions of the state, make your own laws, and get out with the profits before the state holds you accountable for your actions. This strategy (now repackaged by José Altino with an Aristotelian slant) had always worked along the Amazon's frontier. He wasn't about to change his ways nor was he willing to tolerate growing international protests—particularly by celebrities—about the burning of the rain forest and the displacement of the region's indigenous people. "If Sting shows up here," he once told me, "I will personally cut off his ponytail and send him on the first plane back to England."

By the time I entered Yanomami territory in 1989, the miners' occupation of Indian land had become an established fact and José Altino was moving forward with his agenda for frontier expansion. Recently he had won the support of the newest local governor, Romero Juca, who now backed the miners. He was simultaneously proposing in the press that the Yanomami "be put onto a reservation instead of taking out the forty-five thousand miners who are already there." He seemed unstoppable and the plight of the Indians a lost cause.

"What is the biggest obstacle you face now?" I asked him outside the Hotel Tropical in Boa Vista one afternoon. As I finished my question I focused my attention on trying to see behind the dark green lenses of his aviator glasses. A glint of golden sunlight just barely exposed the pupils of his eyes.

"My biggest obstacle now?" He paused to take a drag on his cigarette. A small smile creased his leathery face. I knew from our various encounters that this was the kind of moment he enjoyed. "The international press," he responded as smoke billowed from his mouth. He then slapped my back to accentuate the joke's-on-me tone of this little power-play riposte.

As I watched him walk into the hotel, I thought how brilliantly he had manipulated both the press and the government to create a smoke screen around those forty-five thousand miners out there in the forest, an army of peons toiling away in the shadow of sad King Midas. And I wondered if, or how much, he was also manipulating me.

5

"*Peixes e arroz à troca por as bananas.*" Fish and rice in exchange for bananas, says a man called Vivi who is standing inside a makeshift cafe and supply store constructed from cast-off pieces of wood and covered by a blue tarp. This establishment is just one of a half dozen rickety enterprises that hug the periphery of the landing strip. They supply miners and pilots with food, fuel, and radio transmissions either back to Boa Vista or to one of the other encampments in the forest. Farther on behind this shack, another twenty yards or so, the edge of the rain forest starts to creep in—a fifty-foot wall of green tropical trees and entangled vines which have to be beaten back each month with machetes and chain saws.

As we step off the runway, a small Cessna jostles past us, the rear section waggling precariously as the plane makes its way down the muddy track, the pilot revving the engine and testing the propellers prior to takeoff. When the sound of the plane drifts into the distance I lift the camera to my shoulder and nod to the Wolf to start recording sound.

It feels good to enter the shade after a brutal morning in the equatorial sun. We've been sprinting up and down the landing strip getting images of the details that make up the miners' operation in the forest: a Brazilian flag mounted on a makeshift pole; miners, laden with supplies, trekking off to the forest; dozens of planes and helicopters coming and going. Now here, just outside the store and shaded by the trees, I can get a closer look at Vivi. His powerful arms bulge out from his polyester short-sleeved shirt, the buttons opened halfway down to expose the black mass of hair sprouting from his bearlike chest. He has a large head and dark, deep-socketed eyes. At approximately forty years of age, Vivi has succumbed to considerable baldness. He compensates for it by obsessively pasting his errant hair onto the top of his shiny round head.

I focus the camera on Vivi standing at the entrance of his makeshift store looking at three Yanomami women shuffling about nervously in front of him. *"O que você quer?"*—So what is it you want?—he asks in a tone of voice that seems more like a command than a question.

The women's clothes are dirty and torn, the once colorful patterns of their dresses are now undistinguishable under the layer of grime that covers them. They are probably hand-me-downs given by missionaries who used to occupy this airstrip, or maybe they were gained in a trade for bananas or corn with some local miners. The women, small in stature like most of the Yanomami, all appear to be in their twenties. They have strong arms, large muscular shoulders, and sturdy legs. According to what I have read, they can deftly handle an ax or trek twenty miles through the forest in a single day. Their lives are spent cultivating the gardens, fetching hefty baskets of firewood, and toting water jugs from nearby rivers and streams. All of this work is done while they tend to their children, very often carrying infants in tree-bark slings as they go about their tasks. Among these three women a few young boys, no older than six or seven, hover with tiny bows and arrows clasped tightly in their hands. The eyes of the women—probably the boys' mothers—shift about as if they expect to be struck at any moment. Occasionally they reposition their young children in their slings in what I am assuming is a more protective position.

A miner seated at a table at the back of the cafe starts cackling hysterically. He then cries out: *"Elas têm medo!"*—These women are scared!

Vivi goes to the rear of the store and I move a little closer, ducking under the thick blue tarp that serves as a roof, turning the camera around on the Indian women. "What is it that you want?" Vivi says again to them from behind me. The women shout Portuguese words—*peixe, arroz*—as their children group around them in what may be a circle of defense.

I turn the camera back on Vivi who, now aware of the photographic eye, quickly fixes a few dangling strands of hair. He gives the women a plastic bag of rice with some pieces of fish thrown in.

Begging has now become part of life for these women, a chore that they have learned to incorporate into their daily routines. With the rivers polluted and increasing numbers of hunters getting sick, the prospect of getting enough fish or game by traditional means has become remote. The scenes of begging I've witnessed over the last two days confirm the worst fears of health officials in the cities: malnutrition will go hand in hand with malaria in decimating this once healthy Indian population.

I pull my eye away from the camera to check the larger scene, then enter back into the black-and-white images of my viewfinder, panning the camera from Vivi to the Yanomami women still standing at the entrance. I focus in on a young boy about five years old who is being carried in a bark sling on the back of his mother. His drab brown hair is thinning and falling out, his legs look like sticks: common indicators of a severely deficient diet. He stares at me as his mother turns to leave, his almond-shaped eyes fixed on the strange being with a bizarre metallic object attached to its shoulder. The boy's face has that deadpan look so commonly found in the adopt-a-poor-child ads in magazines in the United States and Europe. His mother continues walking, glancing behind her to see if anyone is following. I've now become accustomed to blank stares and phobic reactions, this last one mild in comparison to a woman yesterday who threatened me with an ax when I tried to take her picture on an isolated pathway. She scared the life out of me. She seemed to be hysterical with anger and rage. I have no idea what I would have done if she came after me with that ax. Fortunately, her husband appeared and calmed her down.

Lesson learned: in the last two days I've realized that my feeble attempts at introducing myself as a journalist—thereby distinguishing myself from the miners—have failed. That categorization means nothing to the Yanomami. I am a white man just like Vivi, and there is no way of getting around it. To these Indians the miners and I are simply a people to be kept at arm's length except for the occasional exchange of food and products. I can only assume that they see us as beings from another planet. We appear and disappear with a seemingly endless supply of metal objects, tearing away at the earth, taking pictures of them (do they even understand what that means?), sometimes giving them a token ax, knife, or piece of clothing. While working in the midst of their forest we kill and maim in pursuit of *ouro*, gold, a substance that for them has no value. We destroy their riverbeds and pollute their water. Then we return to the sky in our birdlike containers powered by strange loud rotating wings, scaring away the game animals on which they depend for food. This is as surreal an environment as I've ever seen. It makes me wonder if the Indians have a name for hell on earth.

I know now that negotiating this middle ground between their world and ours is the real challenge to documenting this story. I was naive to think that I could come in here with some rough phrases in Portuguese and a few icebreaker techniques that had passed the test in other cultures. This society is vastly different from any I have seen before. I had hoped to be here with an anthropologist, but the handful who know the Yanomami and speak their language feared breaking Brazilian law by entering the area. They were heeding the military's advisories that this "national security zone" should be off limits to all unauthorized personnel. I don't have authorization—but then again, neither do the forty-five thousand miners who now inhabit these forests. As much as I feel I am in over my head, I am still glad I made the trip. Someone needs to be documenting this gold rush and the havoc it is leaving in its wake.

I follow the women and the children with my camera as they climb up the the rocky slope leading to the runway. The little boys now stop and raise their bows and arrows, aiming at us as if they are about to shoot. In unison they let out a small war cry, a reminder that they too find this predicament intolerable: their mothers reduced to beggars, an army of men occupying their forest, a strange man here in front of them pointing provocatively with a long piece of glass attached to a metal box.

Vivi smiles at the children's gesture of defiance. He shakes his head, then turns towards me, waiting for his time on camera. His hair has managed to stay in place this time and there's a smile on his face.

I pan back to the women rushing off down the airstrip, hugging the periphery of the red dirt track, careful to avoid the path of another plane landing at a hundred and twenty miles per hour. As the aircraft buzzes by, I can see a group of miners huddled together in the back, another group brought in from the city to stake their claim to the untold riches lying below the floors of this forest.

"Why don't you go there at the Raimundo Nemen, man?" Vivi asks. "There is the right place for you to go and make a report. The Indians there are really wild ones. You will see lots of Indians if you go over there."

As he speaks, a clump of dirty unprocessed gold bounces about on his chest. It is suspended from a thick chain, also of gold. Its combined value is enough to make a down payment on a house. Such gaudy displays of wealth are de rigueur for those who have made it. Other varieties include Rolexes, gold bracelets, large diamond rings, new cars, and young blond girlfriends, dozens of whom can be found lounging at poolside in minuscule bikinis at Boa Vista's Hotel Tropical, awaiting the return of their jungle entrepreneurs. These ostentatious symbols—including the women—are meant to impress. Impact takes precedence over style, and gestures can be extreme. Recently in a crowded Boa Vista restaurant I asked Edem Barbosa, a wealthy mine owner, for his telephone number in São Paulo in order to do a follow-up interview. He wrote it out for me on a twenty-dollar bill, passing it across the table as if this were a common business practice. "Sorry I don't have a card," he said. He then turned his hand over and showed me a ring with a large sparkling diamond. "It's worth twenty thousand dollars," he said. "U.S. dollars. No joking." He then offered to lend me his condominium in Bahia if I wanted to use it for a vacation in the winter. I copied the number off the twenty-dollar bill and handed it back to him. I didn't like the suggestion implicit in his gesture: another act of seduction, this time the gold miner buying off the journalist. I found Edem amusing but I was also wary. He was part of what the Brazilians refer to as their mafiosi: a legion of loan sharks and wheeler-dealers who have made billions in Brazil's black market, an unbridled "parallel economy" said to be as strong as, if not stronger than, the legitimate national economy currently racked by hyperinflation and massive debt. The uncontrolled gold rush was just another opportunity to add to their riches and not pay taxes. A common sight at the airports here is mine owners with attaché cases chained to the wrists, cases filled with money heading off to the more "civilized" parts of the country.

"Um momentinho, Vivi," I say, interrupting him to get a close-up of the nugget on his chest.

Vivi takes my interest in this symbol as his cue to give me a little background. "I not just a store owner," he says. "You see, I am also a pilot."

"Uh-huh." I struggle to say the bare minimum for fear that my speaking will shake the camera.

"I'm one of the first pilots to fly this area," he adds. "I've got a plane and a helicopter. I can show them to you if you want."

I am having trouble finding a focus point for these chunks of gold. Then, just when I have the image I want, Vivi hands me a slab of dried beef jerky, which he thrusts towards the camera, ruining my shot. I am forced to pan up to him. I assume that was his intention. He seems used to being in control.

"I can take you to see wild Indians," he says. "Don't worry. I am an expert pilot. No crashes. I promise."

Vivi is the classic unsolicited interview, a real character. I can just let the camera roll, interjecting a question here or there to keep him talking. Each phrase, gesture, and detail of his behavior provides me with further insights into what this man represents in the context of the gold rush.

"Those are real savage Indians they have over there," he offers again without any prompting. "It's about forty minutes' flying time from here. Those are the Indians who have never seen people before. They're angry, really angry. I flew over their village in my helicopter, and they all ran away. Do you understand? Angry like you can't believe. You have got to see it. There is no way to have contact with them. You come close and they run away."

I have heard rumors about such expeditions—miners in copters hovering above the Yanomami villages, the propellers acting like a high-tech tornado, blowing out the fires, sending the Indians' few possessions flying in all directions. An act of distraction for some bored prospectors but another instance of terror for these once isolated people. I never thought the rumors were true but, having met Vivi, I am beginning to change my mind.

Vivi takes another bite of beef jerky. When his mouth is sufficiently full, he repeats, "Wild ones, really wild. I'll take you. You got to see it."

"I appreciate your offer, Vivi, but we have enough to see here at Paapiú."

"Okay," he says and heads into the back of the store to talk to someone calling from Boa Vista on the radio.

After changing batteries we position Vivi by his white Cessna out on the runway. It is time to add a little variety to his backdrop. If I have too many shots in one locale, I'll never be able to cut together a sequence. Before we start Vivi fixes his hair, checks his collar, then adjusts his necklace of gold. The Wolf gives me a quick summary of what he was saying while I was off changing the batteries. I check my scribbled notes for the next question.

"What about the relationship between the Indians and the miners?" I ask from behind the camera.

"The Indians love the miners," Vivi says, glancing back to the store where some of his friends have congregated. "Before the miners arrived, the Indians lived their lives inside the jungle, they lived their normal life, but now they have more comfort, they have more food."

Within the close-up framing I'm using, I can see men milling about in the background sorting through orange hoses, blue tarps, and Yamaha generators, essential bits of equipment to be transported by helicopter to other mining sites. I slowly zoom back, opening up the lens, the background becoming less prominent as the gestures of Vivi's hands begin to play in the foreground. The slab of gold sits prominently displayed on his chest in the center of the frame.

Vivi is enjoying the attention. "And the gold miners bring them progress also; we bring plenty of food, clothing, all the things they need." Vivi pauses a beat, takes a quick breath, then continues as flawlessly as a late night talk-show host. "Here as you saw we try to give them whatever we can. We never leave them in a hard time. We always give them something so they don't hate us and, like that, we get along fine."

He has given me a perfect summation of the miners' position. I shut down the camera, making a mental note of how much battery power we will have for shots in the morning. A minute later we leave Vivi standing by his store and head off across the airstrip in the direction of the Goldmazon house. As we climb up on the runway I can hear him talking to his friends. "I'm going to be shown on television abroad," he says. "I'm going to be famous."

We cross the airstrip and grab another shot of a plane about to take off in the late afternoon light. *Two hundred and fifty planes passing through here daily*, I remind myself. I need these images to tell my story. I'll get them tomorrow.

From deep within the forest we can already hear the sounds of cicadas. Walking along the path, I watch the trees turn from green to blue to black as the day becomes night. By the time we return to the Goldmazon house a blanket of stars has risen up in the sky and the tree line of the forest has passed into silhouette. During the evenings here there is some movement on the runway and in the miners' encampments but no one in his right mind roams out there in the forest unarmed and alone. It is the unconquerable ones, the snakes and jaguars, who rule by night. And it is the jaguar who is the ultimate power, that mythic being that many Indian groups believe to be part man, part animal. It alone can instill fear in the people Vivi likes to refer to as "savages." Once I heard an entire Indian village shrieking in the early hours of the morning upon the arrival of a jaguar.

After a great deal of commotion, the unruly beast made its way back into the forest. The next day the village elders recounted for the awestruck younger generation the details of the animal's prowess: its ability to leap incredible distances, its razor-sharp teeth, its lightning-fast reflexes. On another occasion I saw a group of Indian hunters, armed with shotguns, stop dead in their tracks at the first sign of a jaguar's presence. Fresh pawprints on the side of an embankment showed where the animal had leaped approximately fifteen feet from a log that traversed the river. We stayed absolutely quiet for half an hour, careful not to attract the animal's attention. "We're in their house now," a gold miner once said to me when we ventured deep into the forest. "That is something you simply have to respect."

"Jefferson, vamos à pista!" a voice calls to me—Jefferson, let's go to the airstrip.

I awake to the sight of Artur standing at my side, his face grossly distorted by the mosquito netting of my military-issue hammock. It is night but somehow still bright, probably a full moon, judging by the strong burst of light hitting him from behind. Off in the distance, from the direction of the airstrip, I can hear music and men laughing.

"Não quero, Artur. Eu quero dormir agora."—I don't want to, Artur. I want to sleep now.

"Olha, Jefferson"—Look at this—and he proceeds to model his outfit for this night's adventures, tiptoeing in little half circles on the front porch of the Goldmazon house. His getup consists of a straw hat frayed at the edges, a pair of tight, low-cut white shorts, and a matching white T-shirt that has been slashed from top to bottom in a series of vertical slits exposing the soft, flabby flesh of Artur's chest and stomach.

Mario passes by, entering the house hand in hand with a female companion, one of two women who work as cooks in the miners' encampments. He stops momentarily to look. "Give the man a break, Artur," says the Wolf in Portuguese as he turns and walks into the house, his girlfriend giggling behind him.

Artur blows me a kiss, then disappears into the night. "Ciao, gringo," he says as the slapping sound of his flip-flops mixes with that of the cicadas.

6

Behind Vivi's jocular macho banter about the Indians is the prototypical Western European's struggle to figure out the degree of "Indianness" of the indigenous people he encounters. "Those are real savage Indians they have over there," he told me. Yet I wondered, if they were the "real savage Indians" over there, then what type of Indians were the women in rags standing before us?

In the days that followed I did learn more about these women: they put on dresses only when they expected to be in contact with the miners, and they had learned a few phrases of Portuguese so as to scrape together some food for their families. These were ad hoc changes made to adapt to the rapidly changing circumstances of their environment. Although their outward appearance had become dramatically transformed, they had not yet abandoned the culture and language base they shared with those "real savage Indians" Vivi was referring to. Vivi was confused about the Indians he was encountering. And it was a confusion I understood. Making a distinction between different types of Indians was one of the problems I first encountered when I started working in the Amazon.

Before I entered Yanomami territory I probably had a dozen meetings with anthropologists in Brazil who had worked among the Indians but were now banned from returning during the gold rush. By this time I had gotten the miners to agree to take me in, and I had decided to ignore the military's restrictions. I just needed to determine which part of Yanomami territory I wanted to visit.

During our discussions I would point to various villages on a map, asking my informants whether or not the native inhabitants were "wearing any clothing." The eyes of my academic sources would usually twitch and flicker as I pressed this question. Commonly there was a moment of hesitation as I watched them collect their thoughts. I had obviously hit a raw nerve. Yet they were kind enough to explain to me what I might expect to find in a particular region: whether the villagers wore clothes, how long they had been in contact with missionaries or Indian agencies officials, and what might happen if I showed up in a community without the traditional escort of an anthropologist or a native guide. They were accustomed to this line of questioning. They had made a career out of explaining the world of indigenous people (or what little they knew of it) to the outsiders. I was not the first person to inquire whether the Indians wore clothing and I would not be the last. Like Vivi I was simply approaching this trip from the frame of reference of my culture. I was only doing what outsiders have always done in their attempts to understand Indians. I was trying to determine the extent of their acculturation by relying on external indicators. Vivi and I are essentially occupying the same boat as we attempt to navigate the complicated waters of this middle-ground world. But there is one difference: he and I are paddling in opposite directions.

Vivi, following in the tradition of the conquistadores and frontier pioneers, is someone who is intent on civilizing the Indians by *bringing them progress*. I, on the other hand, am trying to understand these native peoples by *bringing them sympathy*. My goal is not to change them but, through my work, to help them preserve their culture. This dichotomy among "whites" is not unusual and, in fact, can be considered part of a process or phenomenon that has been acted out in many periods of contact between Western European explorers and indigenous populations in the Americas. Even Christopher Columbus was scourged by a conscientious Dominican cleric and biographer by the name of Bartolomé de Las Casas whose opinions and observations often ran counter to those of the great Italian nav-igator. Columbus wrote, just after he had made first contact with the people he mistakenly called Indians:

> I saw a kind of peninsula with six huts. It could be made into an island in two days, though I feel no need to do this, for these people are totally unskilled in arms, as your Majesties will learn from seven whom I had captured and taken aboard to learn our language and to take them to Spain. But, should your Majesties command it, all the inhabitants could be taken away to Castile, or made slaves on the island. With fifty men we could subjugate them all and make them do whatever we want.

These sentiments of Columbus were later criticized by Las Casas who, when writing about the explorer, went to great pains to point out

> how far the Admiral was from the proper observation of divine and natural law, and how little he understood the duty of the King and the Queen and himself toward these natives, as he so lightly could say that they might take all these Indians, the natural inhabitants of these lands, to Castile or make them slaves on their own island, etc. This was very far from the purpose of God and His Church, to whom his voyage and the discovery of all this world and everything in and about it should have been dedicated.

Although we were separated by five centuries, Vivi and I and Las Casas and Columbus were in fact on the same voyage; we were descendants of Western European cultures who had found ourselves swept up in a quest for gold bringing us into contact for the first time with isolated Indian societies and a culture vastly different from our own. What separated us as Western Europeans into two opposing groups was what Las Casas referred to as "the proper observation" or what I have come to call the vision of the Indian. He didn't think Columbus had an accurate understanding of who the Indians really were or how they should be treated. I have the same criticism of Vivi. I cannot understand how he is able look at the cultural degradation taking place before him not as an outcome of his actions but as the responsibility of the Indians themselves. I believe that, like Columbus, his way of observing the Indians allows him to proceed with his conquest of their forest. In his mind his actions are justified: he is doing them good, helping the Indians in his own way.

It is a refrain I have heard from countless miners as well as politicians and pundits in the frontier states and federal capitals. I once interviewed a Brazilian congressman named João Fagundes, who told me that if Indians were dying of malaria in Yanomami territory it was not because the miners were bringing it into the forest but because this was a society where "starvation and bad nutrition" were common factors of everyday life. On another occasion, at the height of the gold mining invasion in Yanomami territory, Brazil's Indian Agency released alarming statistics about the numbers of Indians dying daily as a result of diseases such as malaria. In response to this announcement, the mining leader Machado offered me his own theories on Yanomami society. Sitting in his modern high-rise apartment in Brasília, he gave his interpretation of their culture which led neatly into a scenario wherein the miner is once again the savior. He cited a litany of statistics about the low birth rate of the Yanomami, which he claimed was "the lowest in the world." He informed me that thirty-five to forty percent of the women die in childbirth, a figure that is refuted by anthropologists, one of whom told me that he had seen only two such deaths in the two decades he has worked among the Yanomami. When I brought up the matter of "white" diseases among the Indians as reported by the Indian Agency, José Altino went off into an angry tirade about how "the Yanomami man never works. . . . The persons who build the houses, carry the loads and the children are the women. So the loss of the women is a fundamental loss to the tribe."

Certainly these sentiments are in part a smoke screen of

rhetoric intended to hide the agenda of the miners. But I have come to believe that José Altino, his political allies, and other miners believe what they are saying. They are expressing their vision of the Indian based on their limited contact with these cultures and on what they want to see. That is, if a glass can be half empty or half full depending on how you look at it, so too can the Indian be portrayed as a depraved savage or an inno- cent victim, obstacle to progress or saviour of the rain forest. It all depends on the view an individual chooses to take.

Adding to the complicated vision of the Indian is the fact that, under Brazilian law, indigenous people are "wards of the state." This bizarre and seemingly condescending categorization ironically is defended by activist lawyers and indigenous leaders alike. It is the one legal device they have at hand to distinguish Indians from the "citizens" of the national society, who, for the most part, are descendants of Portuguese colonialists, European and Asian immigrants, and African slaves. Wards are not sub- ject to the same laws, but they are also not allowed to vote and their rights have to be mediated through the government's Indian agency known as FUNAI. Because the state is their guardian, they are also guaranteed—at least on paper—medical care and education provided by the Brazilian government. And perhaps most important, they have certain inalienable rights to the land they have traditionally occupied. Brazil's 1988 consti- tution, established after twenty-four years of military rule, rep- resented a major victory for a well-organized coalition of Brazilian human rights activists, liberal politicians, lawyers, and a significant number of indigenous leaders who had learned how to negotiate the labyrinthine, futuristic hallways of the nation's federal capitol in Brasília. They played on the mythology of the national connection to and responsibility for the Indian. And they won some major battles including guaran- teeing—again, at least on paper—indigenous people's right to the lands they've inhabited since time immemorial.

What they were not able to control, however, were the "mineral or subsoil rights"—the extremely valuable gold, cassi- terite, and titanium that sit below the surface of Indian territories and are, according to the constitution, owned by the national society of Brazil. True, only under special circumstances can these lands be mined, and only with the government's supervision. But men like José Altino, Sebastião, and Elton Kronholt have seized upon this reference to subsoil rights in the constitution to justify their illegal incursions into Yanomami territory. They claim that men like Vivi and the forty-five thousand other miners who have descended on Yanomami lands are entitled to this mineral wealth because it belongs to the citizens of Brazil. The result of the dispute is that, by the time of my arrival, Brazil has for two years been a messy political quagmire overseen by a hapless José Sarney, an octogenarian politician who inherited the presidency after the charismatic and popular Tancredo Neves died of a mysterious disease just two weeks after taking office. Neves had enjoyed a landslide victory in an indirect election presided over by an electoral college handpicked by the dictatorship. Yet he was still the first president since 1964 who was not directly appointed by the military junta. But he had also brought with him, as part of a package of political compromises he needed to get elected, Sarney—a man no one expected would ever rise to power, a compromise appointee who has found himself in the middle of a political minefield pitting the Brazilian government—which refuses to take action to stop the gold rush—against a handful of politicians, lawyers, and activists who are calling the invasion unconstitutional, inhumane, and potentially genocidal.

This classification of the Indian as having a separate status—living in the country but not a citizen—remains a highly politicized concept. In the two decades prior to the 1987 constitutional hearings, Brazil's interior ministry was pushing for the "emancipation" of the natives so that they could be "integrated" into Brazilian society. Free from the tutelage of the Indian Agency, it was argued, they could be incorporated at a faster pace into Brazilian society. But, as the pro-Indian lobby understood, once they entered the state of being "acculturated" they would lose the rights to their land

and be moved into Indian settlements. For this reason indigenous leaders and their sympathetic lobbyists have fought to maintain the classification of Indians as wards of the state, a legal status that highlights their unique cultural and historical legacies. But frontier politicians and pioneers see the distinction chiefly as an obstacle to their claims that the Amazon belongs to the citizens of Brazil. From their point of view, if they can establish that indigenous peoples are Brazilian citizens, then they can nullify the Indians' unique legal status and with it their claims to eighteen percent of the Amazon's land or eleven percent of the national territory of Brazil. No wonder many miners and frontier politicians take almost any opportunity to attack the Indian Agency's credibility. They would like nothing better than to see it abolished. I have frequently been told by miners in Yanomami territory that they, in fact, are the ones helping the Indians with food and medicine and not the Indian Agency. "The Indian Agency," José Altino says, "has the reputation in Brazil as knowing the Indians less than anyone else, particularly in the Amazon."

One of the core points of debate between these two groups is the degree of an indigenous person's "Indianness." The frontier congressman João Fagundes once gave me an elaborate version of his vision of the Brazilian Indian as someone who "already likes to watch TV, he already likes to go to the hospital, he already doesn't cure himself with the resources of biodiversity the jungle offers. He is not the primitive Indian." Fagundes's definition of the Indian fit conveniently into his plan to develop zones of economic activity inside Yanomami territory, thereby legalizing the presence of miners. He assured me that "there isn't this primitive Indian that the international press is concerned about. This primitive Indian doesn't exist."

The problem is that such assessments are based on external indicators: the way people dress, or dance, the houses they live in, whether they have a bank account or can drive a car. They don't take into consideration the worldview of a society, its customs, the way its members make their livelihood, or how they perceive themselves in relation to other cultures. All these things are the below-the-surface factors that are critical in determining the identity of an indigenous group—the difficult-to-discern cultural characteristics that have historically complicated the interactions between the white man, who assumes he knows what an Indian is, and the Indian populations themselves. This dynamic was probably at work when Columbus wrote in his journal:

> I gave them a thousand pretty things in order to get their affection and make them want to become Christians. I hope to win them to the love and service of your Highness and of the Spanish nation, and make them collect and give us the things which they possess in abundance and which we need. . . . They believe that power and goodness are housed in the sky and they are absolutely convinced that I come from the sky with these ships and men.

Today, as in Columbus's time, ideology and perception have become intertwined as convenient, flexible frames of reference for justifying the economic imperatives of the particular colonial or national societies ruling over the indigenous populations of this hemisphere. The Uruguayan writer Eduardo Galeano put it succinctly when he wrote in 1973 that "the Indians have suffered, and continue to suffer, the curse of their own wealth; that is the drama of all of Latin America." Undoubtedly it can be argued that there were very different social, political, and economic forces that drove Columbus to the Caribbean, Custer to the American West, and Brazilian miners into the Amazon. But what can't be denied is that gold was a key catalyst for their expeditions and that they shared a vision of themselves as superior beings motivated by a higher purpose, bringing progress and civilization to a backward and deprived people. That is the history, and the story we have told to our children and grandchildren, of the conquest of the Americas—a tale steeped in the mythology of the Western world with its people depicted as being swept up in a developmental trajectory that began in ancient Greece, continued through the Enlightenment, and blossomed in the Industrial Revolution. As the anthropologist Eric Wolf points out, this vision of the world is

> misleading, first, because it turns history into a moral success story, a race in time in which each runner of the race passes on the torch of liberty to the next relay. History is thus converted into a tale about the furtherance of virtue, about how the virtuous win out over the bad guys. Frequently, this turns into a story of how the winners prove that they are virtuous and good by winning. If history is the working out of a moral purpose in time, then those who lay claim to that purpose are by that fact the predilect agents of history.

Who are the predilect agents of history? The chosen ones, the righteous, the ones who "bring them progress" as Vivi says, those who convince themselves that they are part of a "manifest destiny," that they are carrying out their ventures in the name of a civilized Christian God. On an expedition into the Black Hills in 1873 a Lieutenant James Calhoun, serving under General George Armstrong Custer, wrote:

> the hives of industry will take the place of dirty wigwams. Civilization will ere long reign supreme and throw heathen barbarianism into oblivion. Seminaries of learning will raise their proud cupolas far above the canopy of Indian lodges, and Christian temples will elevate their lofty spires upward towards the azure sky while places of heathen mythology will sink to rise no more. This will be a period of true happiness.

Shortly after the discovery of gold in the Black Hills, with its attendant trumpeting of the arrival of an American El Dorado, an editorial in the Chicago newspaper *Inter Ocean* declared the "red man . . . is but an episode in the advance of the Caucasian. He must decrease that the new comers grow in wealth." In this same period the U.S. Congress in a report entitled "The Condition of the Indian Tribes" attempted to explain the destruction of Indian societies as simply "the irrepressible conflict between a superior and inferior race when brought in the presence of each other." The battle cry of that period was Manifest Destiny, which, as promulgated by Washington policy makers, portrayed Europeans and their descendants as being "willed by destiny" to expand westward. One of the many frontier groups to take up the call was a coalition of pioneers in Cheyenne, Wyoming, known as the Big Horn Association. They proclaimed that

> the rich and beautiful valleys of Wyoming are destined for the occupancy and sustenance of the Anglo-Saxon race. The wealth that for untold ages has lain hidden beneath the snow-capped mountains has been placed there by Providence to reward the brave spirits whose lot it is to compose the advance-guard of civilization. . . . The destiny of aborigines is written in characters not to be mistaken. The same inscrutable Arbitrator that decreed the downfall of Rome has pronounced the doom of extinction upon the red men of America.

But what are the consequences of the advance of civilization? It is estimated that at the time of the arrival of Columbus, the territory that now comprises the United States was inhabited by some two to ten million Indians. By 1865 that number has been reduced to only three hundred thousand.

The statistics on the conquest and colonization of Brazil were, and continue to be, equally startling. Since the Portuguese explorer Pedro Cabral arrived in Brazil in 1500 the population of indigenous groups has been reduced from four million to just over two hundred thousand. In this century alone eighty-seven Indian tribes have become extinct.

The extent to which warfare, slavery, and starvation contributed to these statistics varied in both Brazil and North America. The U.S. military did carry out extensive military campaigns against indigenous peoples in the nineteenth century and earlier but their impact, in comparison to other factors, has been grossly overplayed by the popular image of cowboys fighting Indians in Hollywood movies. The most dev-

astating of all forces in the Western Hemisphere has been outside diseases transmitted by Europeans to indigenous societies.
In North America such diseases were responsible for ninety
percent of all deaths of native peoples between 1492 and 1900.
As early as 1514 a smallpox epidemic swept through the native
populations of Panama. In succeeding decades waves of
cholera, tuberculosis, scarlet fever, measles, and influenza devastated indigenous societies throughout the Americas. A little-
mentioned fact, substantiated in the 1867 Congressional
Report on the Condition of the Indian Tribes, is that one of the
biggest killers of indigenous societies in the nineteenth-century
American West was "venereal disease, particularly secondary
syphilis" transmitted by the white man to Indians of this hemisphere—a dirty secret of our legacy that popular historians have
chosen to delete in their accounts.

But the last five centuries of conquest have not gone without
condemnations by outraged witnesses from our world sympathetic to the plight of native peoples. There have always been
clerics, journalists, and soldiers, people who came into sustained contact with indigenous societies and learned to look at
them with a perspective different from that of the dominant
society. I recounted earlier the scathing critiques of Columbus
by his chronicler Las Casas, but there were others throughout
the centuries who documented and objected to the abysmal
treatment of indigenous societies by pioneers and conquerors.
Among them was the mythic trapper, guide, and soldier of the
American West, Colonel Kit Carson, who spent more than
forty years living among North American Indians in both
peacetime and war. In 1865 he delivered lengthy testimony
before a U.S. congressional committee on what he perceived as
the origin of the conflicts between whites and Indians. "As a
general thing the difficulties arise from aggressions on the part
of the whites," he stated. "The whites are always cursing the
Indians, and are not willing to do them justice." He went on to
detail how cultural misunderstandings are often the catalyst for
violent conflicts. A journalist accompanying Carson on one of
his final expeditions wrote for the New York *World* that "we are

goading the Indians to madness by invading their hallowed grounds, and throwing open to them the avenues leading to a terrible revenge whose cost would far outweigh any scientific or political benefit possible to be extracted from such an expedition under the most favorable circumstances."

In Brazil in the twentieth century there has been an unprecedented outcry by individuals and associations working in support of indigenous peoples. The most famous of them all was Colonel Cândido Rondon, who in 1910 founded the Indian Protection Service and inspired generations of Brazilians after him to maintain some institutional form to mediate between their society and the indigenous populations of their country.

For me the most poignant of all of these sympathetic reactions was that of an anonymous sixteenth-century deserter from the French army. In the ruins of an abandoned outpost deep in the wilderness of the New World, he left behind an epigram carved into a plank of wood. It read: WE ARE ALL SAVAGES.

7

Bad news often comes when you least expect it.

We spent the early morning getting establishing shots of the runway under a clear blue sky. Each image was crisp and sharp in the brilliant light. The arrivals and takeoffs of the planes appeared to be perfectly choreographed for my camera. Everything has gone so well, we have covered the scene in half the time expected.

Ready to move on, we have gathered our equipment from the Goldmazon house and begun making our way to the airstrip to meet Sebastião. He agreed late yesterday to fly us to a mining site so that we could see the operations of one of the most profitable gold pits in the area. But now across the airfield he is walking briskly toward a prop plane with the crew from TV Manchete. He glances in our direction, then enters the aircraft and shuts the door. As the engine starts, the Wolf and I both stop in our tracks, struck by the realization that there is no point in going any further. There will be no goodbyes. No opportunity for discussion. No handclasps or pats on the shoulder. This is a de facto desertion. We've lost. He's won. I probably should have shut off the camera the other day.

As the plane jogs down the runway, I turn to the Wolf and watch his chin fall suddenly against his chest and his shoulders cave inwards. I ready myself to catch him before he falls, but I remember that he loves to indulge himself in theatrics at such moments.

Sebastião's plane lifts off with a mechanical roar, disappearing quickly over the jagged stretch of blue-green forest at the end of the runway. We catch a glimpse of him in the small side window of the Cessna as it soars above the empty shells of crashed planes littering this part of the airstrip. He stares down at us like some cruel Greek god on a quick jaunt back to the heavens. The message is clear: he has punished us for questioning his omnipotent powers.

I turn to the Wolf to gauge his mood. He begins kicking the dust, and making a clicking sound with his tongue. It is my cue to begin speaking. I suggest we splurge on a meal of meat, beans, and five-dollar Cokes. A small smile appears at the corner of his mouth. He doesn't speak but bobs his head up and down. I interpret this as some primal signal of affirmation. We head off to the lunch shack beside the runway.

After lunch, the Wolf's spirits restored, we begin negotiating our way out of here, aided by a few cartons of Hollywood cigarettes. A young man who runs a helicopter supply store allows us to use his radio to communicate back to Boa Vista. We contact the mining leader José Altino who originally arranged for our trip into the forest. We inform him that his people haven't kept their end of the bargain and we still need to be taken to the second mining site.

"I need shots of the gold pits to make my story work," I reiterate to the Wolf who translates for the kid at the radio who relays the message back to a guy in Boa Vista sitting at a radio receiver who, by phone, is passing the message to José Altino. I can barely understand any of the Portuguese spoken during these transmissions but, judging from the Wolf's upbeat appearance, the tide may be turning in our favor. Occasionally I make out the standard response of "*Positivo*" but that's about it. The rest is a strange garbled mess, as if I were listening to a chicken being slaughtered through a megaphone. *There's got to be a better way to do this,* I think to myself. *Something is going to get lost in translation. We're going to be here forever.* Then the kid at the radio turns to us. "You will have your answer tomorrow," he says. Mario gives him another carton of Hollywoods. I'm doubtful.

The next day I am cleaning the equipment when the Wolf comes back from the radio shack. We have gotten a message that José Altino has arranged for a pilot named Roberto to drop us at a mining site called Baiano Formiga or "The Little Ant from Bahia." The plane is supposed to be here within an hour. According to the message, once we arrive there we will be able to spend several hours filming before returning to the state capital. José Altino told me about Baiano Formiga when we were back in Boa Vista. It's one of the largest gold pits in the region. "A place where the Indians are working side by side with the miners. Actually sharing the profits. This you must see!" he said, all excited as if he were describing an interethnic Shangri-la rather than this era's El Dorado. I can't, however, shake the feeling that there is something odd about this part of our journey. Although I am pleased, I don't understand why José Altino is continuing to help us. Just yesterday our part of the press junket was ostentatiously terminated by Sebastião. Certainly José Altino spoke to him. He must know by now that their game of trying to control the truth hasn't been working, that I've been refusing to play by their rules. So why then is he facilitating this trip farther into the forest? Maybe there are in fact Indians and miners working collaboratively at Baiano Formiga? That could be true. I am willing to suspend judgment for now. The delays have hurt: I'm short on money and time and I can't leave without shots of a gold pit. Without those I can't tell the story of the gold rush.

Roberto flies us into Baiano Formiga as promised, unannounced, just past noon, banking in over an abandoned, partially destroyed Yanomami village and touching down on an earthen landing strip. As the little Cessna bounces along, a few miners emerge from the half dozen makeshift shacks. As in Paapiú these are men looking for distraction, hoping to find something to break the monotony of life in the forest. Most of them are bare chested, in soccer shorts, with scraggly beards and thick thighs made sturdy by long hikes through the mountains laden like pack mules with food and equipment.

I already know a little bit about this place and I can tell a lot from looking around. The landing strip and environs have been constructed more recently than those at Paapiú. There's less activity, less evidence of attempts to beat back the jungle. The tall trees of the forest loom over the airstrip: it's claustrophobic here. We're farther into the forest, farther away from the flights heading directly to and from the local capital, farther from any direct line of communication with a developed society.

As we get out of the plane, I am struck by the immediate impression that the forest is engulfing us. The humidity, oppressive as ever, is counterbalanced by a cool stream of air wafting in from the jungle, surrounding us and providing—for the moment—a sense of relief from the heat. An echo reverberates through the trees as our pilot Roberto revs his engine for takeoff. He has promised to come for us in two to three hours, cautioning us to be careful, not to ruffle any more feathers.

This last-minute warning adds to the ominous sense I already have of this place. There is no mistaking it: this is really the frontier. No missionaries, no restaurants, and no Indian Agency employees. In plain fact, the collection of mines surrounding Baiano Formiga have the worst reputation of all the gold pits in the region. No one talks about it much, but most miners say they don't want to work here. The bosses are considered ruthless and dictatorial. More than a few murders are reported to have taken place in and around this encampment. Roberto wouldn't answer any questions on the flight in. Yet he smiles now as he passes, safe in his Cessna. Happy, I guess, to get the hell out of here. Perhaps also amused at the dumbfounded expression on my face. *What next?* I have been asking myself since we touched down. Here I quickly realize my style of stumbling about the periphery of a story—searching for a way in—is not going to work. There's not enough time. I need to be more focused than at Paapiú. I can't leave as much to chance.

I pick up the camera and send the Wolf to find out who is in charge. Meanwhile I start with cover shots of the airstrip.

Through my lens the runway looks as if it had been ripped out of the rain forest. Half of a mountain in the background has been razed, leaving a hillside of felled trees lying in zigzag patterns in the distance. In the foreground solemn and weary miners wearing shorts, T-shirts, and hiking boots carry huge lengths of orange tubing as they pass en route to one of several mines in the area. These men are the *formigas* or ants, another generation of South American peons once again chasing a dream of riches in a remote unconquered terrain. With high-powered hoses they prospect the mineral-rich embankments of the region's innumerable waterways, snakelike tributaries that twist and turn through the rain forest as they descend towards the great and mighty Amazon. The fat orange hoses carried by the *formigas* are components of an elaborate procedure called hydraulic mining. It is all part of the age-old business of sifting through the earth in the hope of discovering precious metals. In this new era, though, Yamaha generators and filtration tanks and high-powered hoses have replaced the primitive process of panning by hand. Here it is as if the Medieval Age and the Industrial Age have suddenly become fused: paradise for those who own the mines but purgatory for those who are forced to work them. Most of these men have recently come from the gold rush at Serra Pelada in the southern part of the state of Pará. There a giant *garimpo* or mining pit became the center of activity for an army of eighty thousand fortune seekers. But in the mid-eighties Serra Pelada ran dry and in desperation more than half of those gold-seeking migrants set off for Yanomami territory. Here they have carved out their own place in Brazilian history, making this gold rush the largest ever to take place on Indian lands.

We start by interviewing the Colonel, one of the *donos* or mine bosses who share in the profits from several *garimpos* in the area. Just a few minutes ago, he pulled the Wolf aside to speak to him, Brazilian to Brazilian, as I went about getting cover shots of this lonely airstrip operation. I know enough to know that, at times like this, it's important to stay out of the way, to let go of my tendency to be the control freak and remember that the Wolf is brilliant when it comes to getting people to cooperate. After their brief tête-à-tête Mario returns with his interpretation of their little encounter: if we are going to film here at Baiano Formiga, then we had better respect the local hierarchy and start our filming with the Colonel.

"Do the right thing," he pleads. "Interview him. *Calmamente*," he adds for emphasis.

As I look at Mario's sorry face I can tell it is time to get out of here. These long days in the jungle have eroded his confidence in me and my dubious enterprise. My status is quickly plummeting: the dumb gringo has become the dangerous gringo, a liability in a place like this, a lot more than he bargained for. I don't blame Mario, though. Our life has not been easy recently. We have both passed our birthdays here, commemorated only with snapshots on the airstrip: sunburnt, bearded burnouts looking homesick and weary. He is now having severe *saudades*, heartaches, for his city of Rio and the girlfriend who awaits him. I am suffering less, perhaps because this is my project, perhaps because there is less for me to go back to. Sure, I keep telling myself I will settle down after the next assignment, straighten out my personal life, "get it all together." But already I sense a problem with that plan. The Amazon has the makings of an obsession: there are too many good stories to tell, too many fantastic vistas to take in, too many ways to get lost.

For the interview we position the Colonel with the airstrip in the background. He is a proud ex–military officer in his late forties, but the soft years of civilian life are starting to show around his midsection. When he speaks he pulls in his stomach, forcing his chest out in a pose that could found at any Veterans of Foreign Wars function in any part of the U.S. But just as we are about to begin, the Wolf starts to have trouble with his equipment. There is static coming through one of the cables.

I smile at the Colonel, trying once again to smooth over one of those uncomfortable moments before an interview, that time when the subject wonders what he is going to say and you wonder what you are going to ask. Avoiding his eyes, I look across the runway at a group of miners standing outside a one-story shack watching us. The Colonel, however, doesn't pay them any attention. It's his hour of glory.

The Wolf has switched cables but now we must wait for an

aircraft to land, another small prop Cessna built for four but carrying ten miners. I wonder for a moment if the Aeronautics Association, or Brazil's equivalent, has checked out the over-crowding of these planes. Then I remind myself that no one has investigated anything out here. This is the frontier. People—Indians and miners alike—often disappear without question. "Anything can happen in the forest" is the common refrain.

"The gold miner is a common man just like any other Brazilian citizen. The gold miner is an anonymous hero. He is a struggler. Nothing stops him," says the Colonel, rattling off this litany as if reading from a Teleprompter.

"I consider the gold miner to be a frontiersman, a discoverer of new wealth, new heritage," he says. "The gold miner works with his heart and soul. Many times the gold miner gets sick but he doesn't go back home without meeting his objective."

I have seen only one Indian since we arrived, a young boy walking arm in arm with another miner, the first sign so far of a relaxed relationship between the two groups. Perhaps José Altino is right? Perhaps the miners are working side by side with the Indians? I ask the Colonel about this, but he tells me without hesitating that the "average Indian won't work more than two hours before he quits."

"What kind of future can the Indians have, working together with the miners?" I ask.

"We have to begin approaching more and more Indians. We have to colonize this area. We have to teach them how to work," he says, suddenly inspired by this line of questioning. "We have to do something with them. The Indians have to work as well for the success of the country."

The Colonel goes on to tell us that there have never been any Indians working in the mines as far as he knows.

His statements make me wonder what José Altino could have been talking about. Didn't he believe that I would ask this question when I arrived here? Perhaps he simply forgot to call ahead and arrange to have a few token Yanomami working the pits? Perhaps he thought a lone gringo with a video camera was nothing to worry about? Maybe I am just part of some larger scheme he has concocted, a pawn who has yet to meet his destiny. But there is no time to obsess over these details. I need to cover the story, get the facts, and get out. I'll worry about the details when I am back in New York.

"I don't have any more questions," I tell the Colonel as I look over at Mario, who is smiling and looking content for the first time in a while. The Colonel, for his part, also seems satisfied. I congratulate myself on being politic and we move on.

The Colonel escorts us down to the end of the airstrip where we can see several mining pits—great ugly holes in which a dozen men, dwarfed by their environs, do in fact resemble ants. Off in the distance a line of trees, two hundred feet tall, make up the forest's new perimeter. According to the Colonel, there are approximately twenty-five pits like this one in the area, producing a combined total of six kilos of gold per day, at a world market value of half a million dollars per week. He takes us to one of the largest and most productive mines. We pass a group of men with chain saws and torches, cutting and burning, clearing ground for more barracks to house the hundreds of new miners arriving daily, impoverished pilgrims who have substituted gold for God as the path to a more fortunate life.

Standing on the perimeter of one pit, I have the impression I am looking down into a football stadium that has sunk into the earth. We knock off a couple of wide shots to establish its size, then descend the slippery slope barefoot with a minimum of equipment—an extra tape, extra battery, that's it. As we search for footholds in the mud, our arms flail about, grabbing desperately for broken roots to check our slide. The camera bounces precariously at my hip, a constant reminder that a sudden tumble could put an end to the entire film. Our steps are short and precise, each one calculated to get a few feet ahead to the next position. I look back up at the Colonel, who smiles and waves. The Wolf curses in a low voice, just loud enough for me to get the joke. I now become aware of my own breath gasping for air in the humid midday heat. I think about the heart attack my father had when he was just a few years older than I am now, then assure myself his fate will not be mine. Halfway down I begin to wonder whether there might have been an easier way to do this. But after seventy-five feet, the terrain suddenly begins to level off. I can now stand upright.

Down here the dimensions and details are different. It resembles a devastated lunar crater. Everything is awash in the light brown mud splattered from the riverbanks by the high-powered hoses. Two large tree trunks, recently torn from the earth, sit lopsided in front of me. A miner, eyes vacant, covered in dirt from head to toe, slowly wades past through a pool of water, showing no recognition of our presence. This is the land of the walking wounded, a mud-caked hell on earth where men are so far beyond the point of exhaustion that a simple hello is visibly difficult. Most of them just blink at you as if a wave or gesture entails too much effort in this dreadful heat.

In the middle of the pit portable Yamaha generators sit vibrating continuously on wooden platforms. The tiny, powerful machines drive the hydraulic pumps and give off a deafening noise permeating every corner of this devastated landscape. The miners who control the hoses seem to be in a hypnotic trance as they twist and turn, their bodies wrestling the blast of the jet spray. Mud flies everywhere as other men, barefoot, walk up and down the sluiceways kicking free the debris that disrupts the murky effluence.

Up on top of the embankment the *donos* in clean clothes stalk the perimeter, clipboards in hand, overseeing operations. They are the ones who originally discovered the sites, purchased the equipment, then transported the miners into the forest at a cost of eight hundred dollars to be taken out of each man's share of profits. The take from the extracted gold is seventy percent for the owners and thirty percent for those working the pits. The workers buy food, supplies, and medicine at the company store at prices that are five times what they would be in Boa Vista. There are no unions out here, no police to resolve conflicts, only the owners who resemble nothing so much as modern-day feudal barons ruling over little forest fiefdoms.

We talk to one José Rodrigues, an old, gap-toothed worker with a sunken face and gray whiskers. He provides us with a little background on his fellow miners in the pits. I start to scribble a series of notes and questions, listening with one ear to Mario's rough translations. The men here are refugees from the poverty of Brazil's northeast, the dark-eyed sons of peasant farmers who worked as indentured servants at the turn of the century. Many of them have recently left jobs as field hands for patrons because they couldn't support their families on two-dollar-a-day wages. Most have several children whom they don't see for a year or two at a time. They have come here in the expectation of a better income, six times their normal wages as field hands. José is the oldest in the group, the one who seems to have the most experience in the mines. Seasoned men like him become de facto leaders who make the deals with the bosses and speak for the group as a whole. They also act as father figures and go-betweens for younger men—some as young as seventeen—who are spending their first time away from home, learning the ropes, and dealing with the boredom, fatigue, and loneliness of work shifts that can last for six months straight.

I flip on the camera as José continues to describe his life at Baiano Formiga. He pauses, a sudden sadness coming over him as he talks about his home.

"God knows that there is suffering back in our cities, in the streets. But here in the bush, there is always rain during the day and then the heat, dealing with the mud, the water, ninety days of working without stopping. It's difficult to tolerate this life."

José is standing in a muddy stream of runoff from the mining. As he speaks he makes small circles with his feet, breaking free the rocks and soil sediments and allowing the water to flow freely into filtration tanks. Every action here is directed towards sifting and cleaning, all of it part of the painstaking effort to uncover each and every ounce of gold.

"We tolerate it because of the money. If it wasn't for the money believe me we wouldn't be here." José stops for a moment and looks down at his feet as if he is mustering the strength for his next statement. "You can't imagine what it is like at night with the cold and the rain," he says. "Much of the time we go without sleep."

We pause for a minute to change tapes. I look around at José and the others. I try to grasp what he has said and what that means for his life and that of the others. I consider doing other interviews, but the Colonel is now motioning for us to meet him on the other side of the pit.

We say our goodbyes to José and the half-dozen lost souls moving aimlessly on this strange, ravaged landscape. "*De nada*," José says—It was nothing—turning back to his work, his bare feet wading through the small man-made river, his entire body caked in a thin layer of dried brown mud.

Climbing out of the pit is easier, the camera balancing steadily on my back, the footholds now simple to find in the incline. We reach the Colonel in a matter of minutes and he take us to the filtration tanks where the gold is separated from other soil sediments. He says that the miners here do not use mercury to separate the gold from soil sediments—a process that is illegal in Brazil—yet downriver at Paapiú the miners told me they are afraid to drink the water coming from this direction. It is common knowledge that everyone uses mercury to process the gold, though no one will admit to doing it. At the filtration tank a twenty-four-hour guard stands posted to prevent raids by neighboring miners.

A man comes up and speaks to the Colonel and then heads off to one of the pits. The Colonel quickens his pace, hurrying us along on our tour. A soft rain is beginning to fall. A little thunder rumbles in the distance. After a minute the Colonel informs us that one of the *donos* has asked to meet with us. It seems he wants to discuss the focus of our intended report. Mario turns and glances back at me. That telltale crease has reappeared on his forehead. The Colonel has stopped talking to us. A cool breeze arrives with the approaching rain. I check my watch. Roberto should be arriving in a half hour.

We approach a small wooden building adjacent to the airstrip and I tell the Wolf to go on in. I figure he will be able to smooth-talk this *dono* pretty easily. Meanwhile, the rain has let up and I want to knock off a few more shots.

I work quickly, trying to get the last material I need to make the sequence work. A helicopter passes overhead, and I pan and tilt as it speeds off into the forest. The pilot dips his chopper right at me as he passes by, intentionally ruining my shot. Now more men with more rubber hoses trot by and I grab other images that I missed before, these from a low angle and using a wider lens. Another plane lands and I zoom out, revealing the airstrip. I've got it covered, so I power down.

Moments later I step into an office with Mario standing in front of a desk and a man introduced to me as Mr. Mineiro sitting behind it. Mineiro translates as a man from the state of Minas Gerais—or simply as miner. Mr. Mineiro is a small man in his late thirties with curly blond hair, the obligatory gold chain hanging from his neck. Behind his desk an automatic rifle stands just out of reach. As I position myself against a side wall, I am immediately struck by the tension in Mario's eyes. Something is going wrong. I take it his standard jokes and small talk haven't broken the ice with this *dono*. I begin to think that I underestimated the seriousness of this request for a discussion. Mario fidgets nervously with his sound cables and explains that Mr. Mineiro is confused about what we are doing here. Mineiro now begins directing his comments to me. When a young and very pretty woman—his girlfriend, I assume—walks through the office with a young child following, he asks her to close the door, which I had deliberately left open. He rambles on incoherently about the ecologists' plot to stop the work of the gold miners. He talks at me but never looks me in the eye. His voice becomes tense, almost inaudible, as he starts talking about *Time* magazine and the North American press. "Regarding the ecology, the gold miners don't destroy, don't burn the forest," he says, raising his voice in order to be heard over the chain saws blaring across the way.

I check my watch and realize that if our pilot comes and doesn't see us on the airstrip, he will leave right away. Pilots here don't fly at night. There are no identifiable landmarks to stand out in the darkness, making aviation an impossible task.

Suddenly Mineiro slams his fist down on the desk, an action not called for by anything he is saying. He continues rambling but still doesn't look into anyone's eyes. "The gold miners' interest is gold. They get gold and leave the rest. The gold miners don't destroy anything." I consider asking him about those H-bomb craters we just walked through, but I don't want to get provocative. Besides, he is sitting too close to that rifle.

It is obvious to me that we have stumbled upon a psychopath. The longer we let him get worked up, the better the chance we will miss our flight back to Boa Vista. I interrupt Mineiro in midsentence. Mario turns and looks at me as if I too am crazy. His eyes, now bulging and imploring, are locked dead on mine.

"I think we should do an interview with Mr. Mineiro," I suggest to Mario in English as I open the door to the office. *"Quer fazer uma entrevista, Senhor Mineiro?"*—Do you want to be interviewed, Mr. Mineiro?—I say to him in my halting Portuguese. Mario pauses, then translates again just to be certain Mineiro has understood our request.

When I exit, the Wolf is right behind me. "Let's get out of here," he whispers in English as we shuffle our way across the dirt runway.

Mineiro follows us, thankfully leaving behind the rifle. With both his hands he adjusts the gold chain hanging from his neck as he catches up to us on the airstrip: even the insane can be vain.

We set Mineiro up in front of a plane, instructing him to simply say what is on his mind. I can see the tables turning slowly, the intimidating Mr. Mineiro somehow neutralized a little bit out here in the open, the electronic gaze of the camera helping to pacify his troubled soul. Perhaps this is part of what I've come to call "the Hi-Mom, phenomenon"—the need of anyone, including lunatics like Mineiro, to look good in front of the camera because maybe their mothers will see them. This is partly a joke, but at such times I begin to believe that this theory is true. Somehow television and its images have become more than a means of communication. They have established a presence in our consciousness: a strange mirror reflecting back to us our dreams and myths, and perhaps even the discerning eyes of our mothers and fathers. Maybe it is because we have all grown up with a television in our homes, and it has become like a relative you just don't want to offend. Whatever the case, I am grateful for its special power at times like this.

"*Tudo bem, Senhor Mineiro?*"—Is everything okay, Mr. Mineiro?—I say to him as I hit the start button on the camera.

He stares at the ground, then recommences his ranting. I do a slow dance from right to left, trying to catch his eyes in the perspective of the lens. The Wolf is recording sound, keeping one eye on the sky in expectation of our plane.

Five minutes into Mineiro's incoherent interview, a small Cessna bounces to a halt on the dusty runway; our pilot Roberto has returned. The camera clicks off, we say our good-byes to Mineiro and take off.

Once in the air I ask Roberto again about the *donos* and rumors of murder at Baiano Formiga. He just smiles, refusing to comment, abiding by another of the unspoken rules of this land: Don't make enemies of your clients, especially these characters. I glance down at a pint bottle filled with gold dust lodged near the landing gear. Silence is not without compensation. Roberto knows what he is doing.

I look out the window and see a Yanomami maloca, a little circular dot sitting almost imperceptible in the green forest. I think of the Indians' side of the story, the one I wasn't able to get on this trip, the one I will need to get if I want to have a complete understanding of what is really happening here. So far I've heard only the miners' side with its convoluted ideology of half-truths trumpeted by a battalion of men who, I believe, are obstinately refusing to see what is taking place around them. Certainly I have enough material to knock out a few news reports on the miners' gold rush. Those are plain facts. We can see them. That's journalism. But there are more complicated levels to this story. There is something going on here that has less to do with what we see and more to do with the way we are seeing it. It's as if there is an elusive truth that wavers between their world and ours—a truth that belongs to neither one of us but we each claim as our own.

8

journal entry
Conçeição do Araguaia
August 8, 1987

I arrived at 5:00 pm and was met at the airport by Father Ricardo. He was accompanied by a tall tough-looking theology student from Imperatriz. Ricardo immediately starts telling me about the two peasants murdered in the last three days. He expects that there will be more violence by the end of the week.

We took a long road into town and fireworks broke out in the background as we talked. A quick turn of my head had both the priest and the student laughing.

Once in town Ricardo couldn't drop me at the hotel because it is owned by one of the local ranchers, and he says he is afraid of being shot. This information triggered something in me. After I got to my room, I started feeling flipped out and was talking to myself. It hit me that I had spent the afternoon driving around with some guy on a death list. I didn't sleep, but by daybreak I was settled down and ready to cover this story.

* * *

"Don't go on that road to Trevo" is what João Moreira's godmother remembers telling him before he headed off into town and never came back.

João Moreira was an impoverished peasant and father of eight in a country where 120 million people live below the poverty line. He and his family were just a few of the estimated eight million people in Brazil who had migrated into the country's rain forest since 1966. These dirt-poor migrants began arriving in droves after the dictator General Castelo Branco initiated Operation Amazonia, the first of several ill-conceived plans under the military regime to "open up" and develop the Amazon. General Geisel's approach was essentially a military operation to "integrate" the Amazon with the more developed and heavily populated southern half of the country. A special branch of government known as the Superintendency for Amazonian Development, or SUDAM, was put in place to oversee the expansion of the frontier. It was during this period that liberal tax incentives were given to corporations and wealthy individuals to foster cattle ranching in the region. However, the real catalyst to migration came in 1970 when a newly appointed military dictator, General Emílio Garrastazú Médici, initiated a "penetration scheme" into the Amazon whereby an extensive highway system would be built as part of an official government policy to populate the region with economic refugees from the drought-stricken region of northeast Brazil. During this time the country's Indian Agency was put into the hands of a group of colonels who were mandated to begin turning indigenous populations into "normal" people. Over the next fifteen years 9,300 miles of railways lines, 1,850 miles of paved roads, 8,700 miles of dirt roads, and General Médici's dream scheme, the gigantic 2,700-mile Transamazon Highway, were constructed to create an infrastructure for immigration and economic development.

As part of their initiative for resettling the poor, Médici's government reserved a six-mile stretch of land on each side of the Transamazon Highway so that migrant families could start a new life. João Moreira, his wife, and his young children were part of a wave of landless people who—responding to the

General's well-publicized plan—took advantage of these new roads to settle in the southern part of the state of Pará. As with many of the peasants who were traveling to this region, the dreams of the Moreira family were modest: a small plot of land, some cattle, and enough cash from a season's crops to put meals on the table and pay for life's essentials.

But within their first decade these projects created a number of problems unforeseen by the military dictators and their functionaries who ran SUDAM. Hundreds of previously untouched Indian tribes were suddenly thrown into contact with Brazilian highway workers, and many of them soon died off from disease. The work of cutting through the forest was also much more difficult and labor-intensive than had originally been expected. Stronger and more powerful tractors and bulldozers were needed. The budget for the operation quickly doubled in size. Then as Brazil's dictators scrambled for international financing, a third serious problem began to emerge: open war between the ranchers, the *fazendeiros*, and the landless peasants who had come to claim their promised plots of land.

In part these violent disputes could be traced back to the land distribution strategies of SUDAM. While the military government had promised free plots to the nation's poor, it was simultaneously giving huge tax incentives for the creation of large-scale farms and cattle ranches. As thousands of immigrants poured into the region, the competition for available plots reached fever pitch. The problem was exacerbated by corruption and mismanagement on the part of SUDAM. Because of bribery, shoddy record keeping, and a generally disorganized settlement process, plots that had been settled for a number of years by peasants were also being assigned to large landowners and corporations. With the possibility of obtaining any land from the government diminishing, many of these desperate migrants became *posseiros*, peasant squatters who, in accordance with Brazilian law, were claiming areas of large estates that were not actively being cultivated. If the *posseiros* could prove that they had been working the land for five years, then they were legally entitled to claim it as their own. If they settled an untilled area of rain forest for a year and a day, they could also claim it as their own. But as land speculators continued to buy more and larger plots, there was a surge in the number of land-title conflicts between peasant populations and *fazendeiros*. With no effective justice system in place, the cattle ranchers and peasants resorted to violence and terrorism to settle their disputes. The region that had once been a dream land for João Moreira and his family was transformed in a few short years into a land rife with violence and terrorism—an area with the worst human rights record in all of rural Brazil.

To understand poverty in the Amazon, it is necessary to look at the larger picture of land ownership in all of Brazil. Two percent of the people control sixty percent of the land, while close to seventy percent of the poor families have no title to property. The estates of some of the large ranchers are so extensive that you can drive for hours and never leave their property. A survey of 340 of the largest ranches in the Amazon totaled 183,397 square miles—an area larger than the state of California. Slavery and debt servitude are also common. And for decades there has been almost no judicial infrastructure in most frontier communities.

The problems of social injustice and severe discrepancies in wealth, so evident in the Amazon, have led to organized attempts at revolution in other Latin American countries such as Chile, Argentina, Bolivia, Uruguay, and Paraguay. Yet in recent Brazilian history there has not been an armed insurgency movement with the exception of a Maoist campaign in the south of Pará in the early 1970s. This Guerrilha do Araguaia was a band of eighty revolutionaries who had split off from the Brazilian Communist Party in 1969 and fled into the backlands of Pará in hopes of fomenting an armed insurrection. Their model might have been Fidel Castro's Twenty-sixth of July Movement but their fate was closer to Che Guevara's disastrous peasant revolt in Bolivia. They had not foreseen two major obstacles: the weakness of their support among the peasantry and the severity of the government's opposition. General Médici responded to the news of the Guerrilha do Araguaia by transforming Operation Amazonia into a full-scale military endeavor. Twenty-five thousand troops were sent in to root out the ragtag revolutionaries. Roadblocks were everywhere. For three years the military controlled the region. Peasant houses were routinely searched and any arms—even the simplest hunting rifle—confiscated. At the end of the campaign two thousand people had been killed. When the armed forces finally abandoned the area, there was still no effective judicial infrastructure to carry out the law. As the decade progressed, land disputes began to increase and conflicts became more extreme. Impoverished farmers like João Moreira now found themselves increasingly pulled into small-scale wars pitting a loose alliance of landless *posseiros* against the big ranchers and their hired *pistoleiros*.

When he arrived in this region João had been one of the lucky people to be given a plot of land by SUDAM. He built a small wooden house and was able to raise his family on the meager yield of his cultivated fields and the revenue brought by a small herd of cattle. But as is common in the region, he encountered trouble when his two eldest sons were ready to marry. It is customary among Brazilian peasants for a father to subdivide his plots at the time of a son's marriage. But João had no land to spare, so he settled his children on some uncultivated acreage that, it turned out, was also being claimed by a cattle rancher referred to locally as Doctor Jundir. Who actually had the legal right to this land has never been settled, but the invocation of brutal violence to resolve the dispute has been well documented. Soon after João Moreira had settled his sons on the new plot, he began to hear rumors that *pistoleiros* were pursuing him. "Sometimes a car passed by," his godmother told me when I arrived at his house the day after his death, "and he would say, 'the man passed by but he didn't see me.' But that day he was caught." The killers—the family believes there were two of them—were waiting in some low scrub by the side of the road as night fell on this quiet peasant community. They had taken precautions. The area was populated; João Moreira was well liked; gunfire would have alarmed the community. They had armed themselves with thick pieces of wood.

The Wolf and I drove out to João's small settlement in a beat-up Chevy I had hired along with a driver named Amori.

This was August of 1987, the first time I had ever been in the
Amazon. It was also right in the middle of "the burning
season," the driest time of the year, when the forest was being
torched by cattle ranchers to clear land for pasture. Small
farmers also burned off their meager plots then as part of their
slash-and-burn agriculture. There was smoke everywhere.
Driving along, we could see huge trees in flame; occasionally
they would burst and crumble, their limbs shooting out sparks
as they hit the ground. I remember the forest floor as one long
stretch of crisp black ash—a medieval vision of a desolate hell.
The air in the car was too stifling if we rolled up the windows,
so we wore bandanas around our mouths to cut down on the
intake of dust and smoke. I draped my shirt over my camera,
hoping to protect it from all the ashen fallout. I never thought
about getting a shot of the fires. I didn't understand their significance. I had come here to focus on human rights.

When we knew we were close to João Moreira's home we
stopped in the small town to ask directions. But the locals were
hesitant to tell us where the Moreiras lived. It took them a
while to believe that a journalist from North America would be
interested in the story of a peasant killed in their little town. I
remember a poster of Tina Turner hanging from the wall—
bizarre juxtaposition, I thought.

The townspeople were typical of many frontier communities
in that they didn't trust outsiders. Pistoleiros were most often
strangers brought in from out of state, killers with no links to
the towns in which they murdered. But the Wolf persisted. He
answered their questions and gave lengthy explanations of our
intentions. Eventually we gained the confidence of a shop-
keeper who directed us to João Moreira's house not far from the
cluster of stores that comprised the town's center. There we
learned that the burial had taken place the day before. We
found a family in a great deal of pain. The youngest daughter
was catatonic with grief. As we introduced ourselves she stood
in the front yard chewing on the base of her thumb. An old
woman who identified herself as João's godmother was only
able to muster a few barely comprehensible phrases before she

would break down in tears. But one of the oldest sons, Clecio, had a different reaction to his father's death. He was outraged. He wanted to talk about it. So he took us to the site of his father's murder.

Clecio believed João Moreira was caught off guard as he came down the dusty road on his way to town. On each side barbed-wire fence enclosed a field of tall grass. "It was there," he said, pointing to the field. "It was there that they must have been hiding."

Clecio thought the first blow, to his father's head, knocked him down. Then, he explained, the killers must have cracked open his skull with the hard wooden planks. As we followed a trail of blood, Clecio described to us how the assassins probably dragged his father's body four hundred feet into a nearby field to finish the job. "They destroyed his whole face," he told us as we walked about filming the scene of the crime, the flies swirling frantically around the remnants of thick blood still stuck to the tall grass at the roadside.

I stopped to get a shot of a small wooden cross erected by his children. His name and the date of his murder were crudely inscribed on the wood with red and blue paint.

"They pierced his eyes so that no one would recognize him," Clecio said as I panned the camera from the cross to the blood still staining the dirt roadway. "He was identified by his boots, because by looking at the body no one could tell that it was my father."

I remember Clecio's phrases coming in short spurts as he tried hard to fight back the emotion of the loss of his father. "It was Jundir, the landowner of the Bela Vista estate, who sent the killer over here. He was the one who paid somebody to do the job," he said. "They picked on him because he was the biggest *posseiro* around here. They tortured him and they killed him. They tortured him a lot."

I had left Conceição do Araguaia early that morning in the hope of arriving before the burial. If you want to sell a violence story to television you need to have corpses. That's the way it works, or so I was told. "Don't come home without one," a news editor warned me over the phone before I left. "If you want me to run that story, I gotta have a body," he reiterated in the I've-seen-it-all tone common to assignment editors. So I made the effort to "get the body." But this was the Amazon. Corpses decompose quickly. João had been buried the same day that he had been found; not even Clecio had a chance to see his father before the funeral took place. By the time I arrived the police had done a cursory investigation which consisted of stopping by the house to ask the family a few questions. No one was holding the body for an autopsy. Besides, there wasn't a morgue.

After spending the day with João's family I returned to my base in Conceição do Araguaia where, over the next few days, another five peasants involved in land disputes were killed. They were all buried before we could get to them, though there was one whose burial had been substantially delayed, intentionally. In this case the *pistoleiros* were keeping watch over the victim's body so that it couldn't be recovered and properly laid to rest. They wanted it to rot in the tropical heat so that the victim's friends and family would eventually find only a decaying cadaver infested with maggots. This was part of their tactics of intimidation, and it was effective. His friends and family were obsessed with getting to the body. It was as if the continued abuse of the body of the victim had become a means of furthering the impact of the *pistoleiros'* violence. They were torturing the living. I've never seen anything like it. It made me understand how violence could become an art form.

Although I never did get my shot of João's disfigured body, a Catholic nun named Sister Tarcísia had taken a black-and-white photo of João in an open casket, his face bloody and punctured, his youngest daughter standing beside him, her hands placed delicately on the edge of the casket, her face registering shock. I eventually used this still shot in a news report I did back in the States. The news editor never complained. The testimony of Clecio and his family had been so powerful that no one seemed to notice. For all his I've-seen-it-all pretensions, my editor was actually moved by the story.

A report on the João Moreira murder case was filed with Amnesty International by Father Ricardo Rezende, a local Franciscan priest whose best friend, a fellow clergyman named

Father Josimo Tavares, had been killed the previous year by a *pistoleiro*. Rezende—as I had found out on my first day here— was on a *lista negra* or blacklist of those to be killed. Padre Ricardo, as he is referred to by the locals, is one of those hand-some priests over whom old ladies swoon at parishes every-where. He has long, curly black hair and a thick mustache that is stylish in this region of Brazil. He is also one of the hundreds of politicized priests inspired by liberation theology and working in the Amazon. He divides his time between minis-tering to the spiritual needs of the people and advising them on legal matters regarding land conflicts. His small office, cluttered with papers and folders, is located on one of the dusty back streets of Conçeição do Araguaia. The battered metal filing cabinets lining the walls are filled with reports on murders that have never been brought to trial. "Eighteen-year-old Leonilde Resplande was raped by eighteen *pistoleiros* and burned alive in front of her husband who was then also killed," he told me one afternoon as I filmed him behind his desk. "The group of *pis-toleiros* who killed them were commanded by Sebastião da Teresona and included the three Guedes brothers who were in prison for three weeks and then set free."

In the few hours I spent with Rezende he pulled dozens of photographs out of his files: bodies burned, decapitated, and, almost always, beaten beyond recognition. It was clear that murder in the south of Pará had become part of a strange and terrifying ritual. And as Rezende put it, "The violence here has a pedagogical trait: to kill isn't enough, it also terrorizes those who remain alive."

A year later I took an assignment as a cameraman which brought me to another violent locale in the Brazilian Amazon. This was the state of Acre where a well-organized movement of *seringueiros* or rubber tappers was involved in conflicts with local cattle ranchers. I had been hired to shoot a documentary on sustainable development produced by an independent film-maker named Miranda Smith. She had brought along her own soundman, an amiable, low-key fellow called Dudu. For ten days she and Dudu and I followed the daily life of one of the region's most popular union leaders, a man who had already escaped six assassination attempts. This was Francisco "Chico" Mendes, a forty-three-year-old self-educated union leader whose precarious life now necessitated the constant presence of two machine-gun-toting policemen. Unlike João Moreira's, however, Chico's death would not go unnoticed. It would dramatically change the face of politics in the Amazon.

"**W**e cannot tolerate the threats of the gunmen with all these police around," Chico said as he ate lunch with his two children, his wife, Ilzamar, and a half-dozen other rubber tappers at the long wooden table in his kitchen. He was a handsome man with wavy dark hair and hefty forearms. The pupils of his eyes were deep black. His face, although round and puffy, still maintained the exuberance of a young boy.

Chico had grown up in the forest outside the small backwater town of Xapuri. He was the son of rubber tappers, one of eighteen children. "There's not much to do in the forest," a rubber tapper had told me the day before when I asked him why families in this area were so big. He then informed me that he had sired twenty-five children of his own, all with the same woman. A big smile stretched across his face as he took in my awestruck reaction. "Have you thought about contacting the Guinness Book of World Records?" I asked as Dudu patiently translated. The man's face went blank. He had no idea what I was talking about. Dudu began to laugh. "It is time for you to realize, Jefferson, that you are in another world." That was November of 1988. I was still learning about life on the frontier.

The atmosphere in Chico's house that day had been lighthearted and celebratory. It was election day in Xapuri and Chico and his friends were anticipating a victory for the left-wing *Partido dos Trabalhadores*, or Workers' Party. The PT was started by a combative autoworker named Luís Inácio "Lula" da Silva who, earlier on, had been a supporter of the rubber tappers' movement in Acre. As I watched Chico that day, I found it hard to believe that this was a man who lived under the constant threat of assassination. He seemed relaxed and happy, as if he didn't have a care in the world. But as I came to learn, Chico was good at keeping up appearances. He needed to be. It was part of his job. He was the leader of Xapuri's local union of rubber tappers. If he showed fear the union would fall apart. The intimidation practiced by his enemies would have paid off.

Besides, he had a plan that, he told friends, was going to get him out of the corner that he had been backed into. He was going to get to the killers before they got to him—not with violence but with justice. He had found out that Darly Alves da Silva, the local cattle rancher threatening his life, was wanted for murder in the state of Paraná. Chico was determined to have justice exacted in a region little known for it. He intended to put away the man whose reputation for brutal violence posed a threat not just to his own person and livelihood but to the entire rubber tappers' movement. On learning of the outstanding indictment against Darly, Chico had contacted local prosecutors, the federal police, and even the governor, urging them to take action against Darly. "I believe in God," he told his uncle Amaro during this period. "And I'm going to take hold of God and drive these bad people away." He assured the friends and family who had been concerned about his welfare that it was just a matter of time before Darly was put away. He seemed to believe it, so we all did.

But this day, when someone at the table mentioned Darly's name, the entire mood changed. It was as if the spirit of Death had suddenly entered through an open window, lingering among the living, letting them know that it was close by. Through my camera I could see the fear working its way into Chico's face. I knew then that behind the upbeat facade was a man in fact frightened, not just by the threats of a sociopathic killer, but also by the impotence or indifference of the frontier judicial system. As I would find out later, Chico's pleas to the local prosecutor, the federal police, and the governor had gone unheeded. His fate was being left to the violent vicissitudes of life on the frontier.

Darly Alves da Silva owned a ten-thousand-acre estate known as Fazenda Paraná located on the outskirts of Xapuri. There he lived with his wife, three mistresses, thirty children, and a dozen ranch hands whom the locals considered to be part-time *pistoleiros*. Early in the year he had been involved in a bitter dispute with Chico and his union over a contested piece of forest known as the Seringal da Cachoeira. The government land agency, INCRA, had intervened and decided in favor of the rubber tappers. This was an unprecedented victory for the forest workers, one they hoped to build on in years to come. As part of the compromise agreement Darly was compensated for his disputed tracts of rain forest. Publicly Darly said he was satisfied with the settlement but, according to local rumor, he was privately set on vengeance. The protracted conflict between himself and Chico prior to the settlement had reached ever more unbridled levels of machismo, which carried over to related conflicts between the rubber tappers and other cattle ranchers. In the spring of 1988 two adolescents participating in a rubber tappers' demonstration were shot. Several weeks later another friend of the rubber tappers' union, a church monitor and Workers' Party candidate, was murdered outside his home. Chico was certain that Darly, and a son of his by the name of Darci, were behind the killings. The rubber tappers believed the actions were part of a campaign of intimidation intended to destabilize the union movement before it was able to capitalize on growing domestic support. Perhaps most important, the rubber tappers' victory at Seringal Cachoeira represented a serious setback to cattle ranchers intent on developing the same tracts of pristine forest that Chico and his men were working to preserve.

In the weeks before our arrival rumors of Chico's imminent death had been increasingly circulating on an elaborate grapevine of friends and relatives in Xapuri. According to the warnings trickling in, ten thousand dollars had been anted by a group of cattle ranchers as a reward to Chico's assassin. A deadline had also been set: Chico was to be killed by Christmas. That was just four weeks away. Friends of his had told us that *pistoleiros* and cattle ranchers had started appearing regularly at Chico's house at all hours of the day and night. These visits were part of their intimidation tactics and they soon spread to other locales—his union headquarters, his favorite little coffee stand—each time subjecting him to the evil eye. This is a look sociopaths specialize in, a look so venomous it manages to penetrate the very depths of one's soul.

I have been on the receiving end of such evil eyes in Brazil and elsewhere in Latin America on more than a few occasions. My first came courtesy of a goon in Guatemala City, one of the two-dollar-a-day killers hired by death squads to carry out their dirty deeds. He had been waiting for me outside my hotel as I loaded my equipment into a van one morning. He looked straight into my eyes with such intensity, it was as if he was trying to give me an intimation of my own death. Although it was my first experience with such looks, I knew what it was— and I knew why. It took me hours to recover. I was in Guatemala doing a human rights story on the atrocities perpetrated against that country's peasant populations, most of whom are descendants of Mayan Indians. Someone had reported our presence in the city paper the day before: we had filmed a body found on the roadside, the hands chopped off at the wrists and a scrawled message left that read, "More to come." Clearly, someone felt that we had gone too far in gathering the details of this story. A decision had been made to intimidate us, hence the visit from the goon. But there was more. That afternoon in a remote hilltop village we found ourselves suddenly surrounded by five jeeps with mirrored windows. The intimidation phase had intensified to terrorization. A dozen men emerged with sidearms and rifles. Once again they simply stared. No words. No threatening gestures. Then after a few minutes they climbed back in their jeeps and disappeared into the mountains. We left two days later, our story over. We were foreign journalists. We could do that.

Chico could also have left, yet he chose to stay. "I have a moral commitment to myself," he told us in an interview that morning. "I cannot leave this fight even if one sunny day I am struck by an assassin's bullet."

In these last weeks of Chico's life his family and friends became increasingly concerned. They wanted him to heed the warnings circulating through Xapuri, but he wouldn't listen. He was a hardened political animal. He had confronted and beaten more formidable opponents. He wasn't about to back down to Darly's threats. On two occasions Chico had taken on the military junta and won, once in the 1970s and then again in the 1980s. In both cases he had been accused of fomenting dissent against the government, an offense for which people could "disappear" or, if convicted, draw a jail term of up to thirty years. Chico was imprisoned and tortured but did receive a trial. "I was lucky to have some good lawyers," he told us. He won both cases and continued his organizing work with the rubber tappers. And now he assured us that "for the first time there has arrived here a military commander who has an interest in putting in prison the hired gunmen. The judge of the judicial district also has an interest in jailing the gunmen," he said. "Yet the higher levels of government neither permit nor provide the conditions for them to jail the gunmen. This is a grave problem."

"Were they all there including Darly?" Chico asked the man sitting next to him at lunch that day.

"Yes, they were all there," said the man.

Chico's wife, Ilzamar, an exotic beauty sixteen years younger than he, pulled her lush mane of dark hair back over her shoulder and looked up from her plate of rice, beans, and meat. The clatter of the dishes came to a halt. "When I was there I saw them," she said. "They were gathered together plotting something."

Chico's eyes went blank while his wife recounted the story of seeing Darly that morning. He stared off into the distance, past the wooden shutters of that cramped little room, lost in thought, perhaps imagining the unimaginable: how and when his life would come to an end. *Would it be a "sunny day"? Who would find him? What would become of his children?*

How, one asks, did Chico find himself in this predicament? The answer is rooted in the history of the forest reserves in his home state of Acre, a frontier region that shares a border with Bolivia.

Acre had seen a wave of settlement during the military government's "economic miracle" of the late 1970s. But before the peasants and cattle ranchers arrived there, the state had been populated by men like Chico's father, immigrants from the northeast who came to live among the Indians and tap the rubber trees for latex to be sold back in the cities. From the turn of the century until World War II latex collecting had enjoyed an economic boom, particularly for the rubber barons of the region who had profited enormously from contracts with the Ford Motor Company. But by the 1970s the world economy had changed drastically. Rubber was being produced more cheaply and abundantly in the Orient. The bottom had fallen out of the Brazilian market and rural land barons had abandoned the region, leaving the forests to the tappers.

Freed from the exploitive practices of these feudal patrons, the rubber tappers managed to support themselves by selling the latex and Brazil nuts they collected in the forest. But then the arrival of cattle ranchers, encouraged by government tax incentives to settle the area, threatened the reserves in which the rubber tappers made their living. By the late seventies, violent confrontations between the *seringeiros* and cattle ranchers were escalating. The military government intervened on occasion, but usually on behalf of the cattle ranchers.

During this period the rubber tappers developed a series of sophisticated techniques for combatting the destructive encroachments of cattle ranchers. They held *empates*, or pacifist demonstrations, in the rain forest. They would surround a group of workers sent in to clear the land, and try to show them the destructive implications of their action—how it was ruining not only the local economy but the forest on which they all depended. With time the *empates* became a powerful organizing tool, frustrating the attempts of cattle ranchers to cut down the forest. The Seringal had been the site of a decade-long struggle of the rubber tappers in which numerous *empates* had taken place. The success of the tappers began to gain wider recognition from national politicians and international environmentalists, journalists, and filmmakers.

"Without international support, without the international press, without the international environmentalist organizations," Chico said in our interview that morning, "we would still not have a single reserve."

Yet as the rubber tappers' tactics became more effective, attacks against their membership increased. By 1988, Chico's local union of a thousand men had lost ten of its leaders to assassination, three of them in the last year alone. Pressure by Amnesty International had forced the military police to provide bodyguards for Chico, but his friends and family were still worried. Xapuri was a remote backwater town. There was still no full-time prosecutor, and for a decade there had been no judge. This absence of a judicial infrastructure had, as in southern Pará, ensured a culture of lawlessness. Local cattle ranchers knew they ran little risk of prosecution for violent acts. Although Chico repeatedly requested the federal police to intervene on his behalf, nothing was done. Darly Alves da Silva remained free and the threats of death continued to circulate along the Xapuri grapevine.

"Either the police will have to take care of this problem or we will," he said that afternoon at the kitchen table. Chico was opposed to using violence for political change, but he was not against picking up a pistol to defend his own life.

After lunch that day I went to the front room of his modest three-room house to change the battery on my camera. The streets were still busy with people going to the polls. They were also rife with tension. Two truckloads of heavily armed soldiers had been brought in from a nearby post following rumors that a local candidate was trying to rig the elections; they blanketed the streets, guarding the voting booths and town hall, with bayonets mounted and machine guns at the ready. Ever since Darly's name had been uttered at lunch, Chico appeared distracted and nervous. He was now pacing around the house while his family cleared the table. As I pulled the used battery from my camera I looked up and saw Chico surveying the street through his front window. Suddenly he moved to the cupboard, pulled out a small pistol, checked its chamber, and returned to the window. Kneeling there in my dim corner, I could feel my adrenaline rushing, the senses of touch and sound disappearing as the world suddenly switched into slow motion. I stared at the old pistol by his side, my camera resting on my knees and my mind scanning for the next move. *What about the battery?* I

asked myself. *I need to get the shot.* Yet I couldn't move. Chico
stood perfectly still for a moment, his free hand signaling to me
not to move. Here I was supposed to be the distant observer and
not one of the victims, and he had broken the sacred space
between journalist and subject and pulled me into his life: it all
happened that fast. Then he simply turned back to the cupboard, replaced the gun behind some books, and walked quietly
out of the room. Once again I became conscious of the camera
on my lap, the sounds of his friends and family, the job I had
been sent here to do. I looked out on the street. There was no
one there. That morning Chico had said he was becoming
increasingly worried by the thought that his "enemies will get
one of my children, or kidnap someone in my family." He reiterated, however, that although he did not fear for his own life,
he still didn't want to die. "After death we are useless," he had
told some friends lately. "Living people achieve things—
corpses nothing."

Contrary to what he thought, Chico wasn't killed on a
"sunny day." It happened at night, just two days before the
Christmas deadline. As he stepped into his backyard on a hot,
muggy evening, two figures emerged from the bushes. The shot
was fired at close range with a 20-gauge shotgun—eleven pieces
of lead tearing through his lungs, sending him careening back
into his kitchen, where his wife was making dinner. There he
tumbled into the arms of one of his bodyguards and slowly bled
to death in the cramped hallway of his tiny three-room house.
"They've killed Chico!" his wife cried out as she ran into the
streets in search of help. He was buried on Christmas Day.

In the weeks following his murder, Chico's name appeared
on the front page of almost every major newspaper in the
United States, France, England, Italy, Spain, Japan, and Germany. His international "friends" had made certain that the
world would recognize his death. Hollywood producers and
stars—spurred on by eco-conscious spouses, colleagues, and the
mounting volume of this big-story reporting—quickly began
vying for the rights to Chico's life. They courted his widow
Ilzamar in the United States and sent development "execs" on
jets to the jungle to meet other members of his family as well as

his union. Robert Redford and Warner Brothers eventually spent over a million dollars in two separate deals purchasing the identity of a man who had left this earth with no more than a hundred dollars to his name.

The irony was that Chico's story was not much different from that of João Moreira or any of the thousands of other labor leaders, lawyers, and church workers who had been gunned down, tortured, threatened with death in towns and cities throughout the Amazon. What distinguished Chico's death from those others was the time and place. The world was ready for—indeed, desperately needed—a human face to attach to the rain forest cause. The international media lost no time in transforming him into a mythic being, a "Gandhi" of the rain forest, in the words of *Time* magazine. But what was left out of the postmortem eulogizing of Mendes was that he was—in essence and in his own eyes—a left-wing union organizer. He had been schooled as a child by a Communist political refugee who sought asylum in the forests of Acre after a military junta had put his life in jeopardy. When I filmed Chico on election day he was actively campaigning for the electorate's support of the left-wing Workers' Party. Just two years earlier he had named his son Sandino, after the Nicaraguan revolutionary who had led a successful peasant uprising against American marines in 1927. His daughter, Elenira, had been named after Elenira Rezende (no relation to Ricardo), the first woman to die among the Guerrilha do Araguaia in João Moreira's home state of Pará. Although Chico had a closer alliance to Marx than to Gandhi, the whitewashing of journalists and environmentalists and politicians had managed to eliminate that part of his persona from world consciousness, paving the way for global acceptance of a new type of hero. Hollywood deals were being closed. Book contracts were signed. Big-name casting choices were circulating in the popular press. Chico Mendes had become the world's first eco-martyr.

9

As I go to unlock the door to my room at Altamira's Hotel Americana, it suddenly swings open. Startled, I step back into the hallway and watch as two tall, scantily clad European women—English is my guess—emerge, their faces covered in circular black patterns vaguely resembling the traditional designs of the Kayapo Indians. The women both drop over-stuffed suitcases on the hallway carpet, raising a small cloud of dust which eventually settles against the light green baseboard of the shabby corridor.

My "trusted" companion the Wolf, here with me on another trip to the rain forest, approaches from the opposite end of the hallway. One look at these exotic beings and he stops short of the doorway, his shoulder bag of batteries and tapes and microphones hitting the floor with a deafening *clunk*. An old fluorescent fixture hanging above him flickers as if suddenly short-circuiting from errant electrical impulses emanating from his body. I watch his forehead crease spasmodically and his lips move frantically as he struggles to utter a coherent opening line in English.

The taller one, statuesque and stately in that British way, glances up at us and pauses for a moment, puzzled as she tries to figure out what we're doing there.

"Oh, sorry. We'll be out in a minute," she says as she and her friend turn and go back into the room, our room, the one the hotel manager just said was ready for us.

"Is there something or anything I can help you with?" says the Wolf, following them inside. I stand there, amused, but also a little startled by the presence of these strange creatures. No more than two months after the death of Chico Mendes, the Amazon appears to be a very different place.

Coming in from the airport a bald, ruddy-faced taxi driver with powerful, hairy arms held his steering wheel in a vise grip as he maneuvered around traffic and dodged potholes while giving us the breakdown of what was taking place in this depressed city of 38,000 inhabitants on the banks of the Xingú River. Six hundred Indians, one hundred international journalists, and a couple of hundred other *ambientalistas*, environmentalists, from Europe, the United States, and Brazil had descended on this backwater town for the Altamira Encounter, an event touted as the largest conference on the environment ever to take place in the Amazon.

"Brigitte Bardot will be here tomorrow," he added. "Sting, Prince Charles, and the King of Sweden are supposed to arrive today." The car swerved, he blasted the horn, and a man riding a mule cursed at us as we sped by.

After passing through the rocky streets of Altamira's outskirts, we came upon the smooth macadam boulevards leading to the center of town. They were crowded with the horse-drawn carts of peasants who had come to sell their produce in the central market. Down the side streets I could see groups of Indians in traditional dress from various Amazonian tribes. Some were carrying bows and arrows, other had only their mahogany war clubs. Most had their faces painted in traditional designs. Interspersed in the streets among the Indians were sunburnt North Americans and Europeans. These were wearing pieces of urban-hip lightweight jungle wear, carrying cameras and shoulder bags, their necks craning left and right as they tried to catch glimpses of the Indians while being careful not to tumble headfirst into the muddy trenches flanking the boulevards of this town known to most of Brazil as a strategic truck stop on the Transamazon Highway.

I wasn't surprised by what I saw coming in from the airport but these *turistas* in our hotel room are another story. The Wolf and I have arrived here a day late. I called ahead saying I would pay for the night but that the hotel should please hold on to our room. In the interim, the manager rented it to these women but forgot to tell us that they were still there. He did remember, however, to pocket their fee and ours, double payment for the night.

As I watch the two women—now accompanied by the Wolf—gather their remaining belongings, I begin to realize that I am not psychologically prepared for this type of "encounter," much less for Prince Charles, Brigitte Bardot, or the King of Sweden. I consider myself a serious journalist. My three trips to the Amazon were spent with small tribes, peasant squatters, or the men and women who extracted latex from the forest's trees. Those were stories with discernible issues that could be dissected in the black-and-white terms of statistics and legal precedents. But these young women (and the people I passed on the streets on the way in) represent a new social phenomenon: they are eco-activists from Europe and North America arriving in Brazil in support of the Indian cause. Perhaps what scares me most is that I could be considered one of them. I have entered a new realm, one that I am beginning to realize will necessitate a new perspective.

But the Wolf—suddenly transformed into Sir Walter Raleigh—has other concerns. "Where will you be staying now?" he asks the English women in his softest, most sincere tone as I pull him away by the back of his jacket. They break into smiles as they pick up their belongings. I can tell this little tug-of-war between us is only adding to his charm. As they walk away down the stairwell laughing, they bestow upon us a final "ciao" and disappear around the corner.

The Wolf throws himself against the wall. "There is no cure for my disease," he mutters. "I am a dead man."

"Patience," I tell him. "I think maybe you need more patience."

"Yes," he says. "Maybe I will try that." He then pauses to reflect on his words. "But I don't think it will work."

We enter the room and start organizing our equipment for a shoot. I test the camera while the Wolf stuffs day bags with tapes, batteries, cables, and some energy bars I brought from home. I check the schedule of events for the conference. We're already an hour late.

The cab driver lets us out a few hundred yards from Altamira's Civic Center. Working our way through the dense crowd, we pass some graffiti scribbled on the side of a building: CHICO MENDES DIED FOR OUR SINS. This crudely scrawled epitaph signals that Chico has joined the ranks of Che and Sandino; soon others will be naming their children after him. We continue dodging bystanders and vendors outside the Civic Center and soon we are inside a small arena of gray cinder block packed to the rafters with five thousand people. An aluminum ceiling soars a hundred yards above us. Television and still photographers blanket the perimeter of the stage area. Protest signs hang from rafters: STOP KILLING THE YANOMAMI and SAVE AMAZONIA and PEOPLE OF THE FOREST UNITE. I can hear bits of Italian, English, Japanese, and German being spoken all about me. The air is stifling but the atmosphere of the crowd is electrified by this incredible gathering of peoples. Groups of Indians—maybe six hundred—sit in tribal clusters in front of the makeshift podium and stage. The rest of the room is packed with journalists, environmentalists, politicians, and an odd assortment of observers. Some are academics, but there also appear to be representatives of the right-wing UDR, the Rural Democratic Union, a cattle ranchers' organization with questionable ties to incidents of rural violence in Amazonia. Many people have blamed them for Chico Mendes's assassination. I read in the paper this morning that yesterday they rode through town on horseback toting guns and placards in a show of support for the government's controversial dam scheme.

This proposed Kararaó hydroelectric station—a $5.8-billion project entailing the construction of forty-seven dams in the central Amazon—would flood an estimated 480 square miles of land. Even if only five of the proposed dams were built, the flooding would produce the largest artificially created body of water in the world. Environmentalists and Indian leaders are contending that the entire dam scheme would result in the displacement of nine thousand indigenous people in the surrounding area. The dam's supporters, however, claim its construction would be a critical catalyst to the local economy. Power is a major problem for this region: there is at least one blackout a day. And the infusion of capital would bring jobs to a marginalized frontier proletariat that feels it has been betrayed by the power brokers in Rio, São Paulo, and Brasília, the same ones who promised that the "opening" of the Amazon would solve their financial woes. The controversy surrounding the dam scheme has linked Altamira's impoverished classes with its local entrepreneurs. The Indians to them simply represent an obstacle to the region's economic advancement. Altamira has therefore become the focus of a showdown, a kind of Amazonian *High Noon* in which developers are facing off against activist Indians and their sympathetic eco-allies.

Seated at the table on the podium is a roundish Brazilian man in a green short-sleeved shirt, with a moon face and sleepy eyes. He is holding a microphone and explaining something in Portuguese to the audience. His words are almost incomprehensible to me, echo-chamber acoustics compounding the problem of a bad public address system. I check my watch and the schedule of speakers. He must be José Antônio Lopes, the engineer for the government's dam scheme. The Wolf gives me a rough translation of what he is saying, something about how the dams won't have a negative impact on the lives of the Indians. As he speaks I scan the auditorium looking for a place where we can cover the action.

Back at the podium a Kayapo woman steps towards Lopes from the crowd with a machete raised in her hand, screaming in the high-pitched wail of her native tongue. Senhor Lopes sits transfixed as the woman approaches, his arms resting on the wooden table, his hands folded delicately on his wrists. She is about five feet tall, heavy set, wearing black Jockey shorts, her breasts covered by two thick strands of red and blue beads. Her hair is long and dark, and there is a small rectangular shaved patch at the peak of her forehead. Unlike the gringa imposters this morning, this woman is the real thing, unmistakably

Kayapo. The machete in her right hand is a good two feet long. As she stands now in front of Senhor Lopes she continues screaming, punctuating her message by slamming the handle of the machete on the wooden table.

Things are off to a good start, I tell myself, half guilty at the exploitive nature of this thought. The problem is, I am still not in position for a shot.

Each time the woman hits the table it reverberates through the now silent auditorium as five thousand people hold their breath. Are they about to see a brutal beheading? Or maybe just a ritualized temper tantrum? The photojournalists below us twist away at their lenses, desperate to find the right focal length. They jostle, elbows extended, protecting their space, in anticipation of the perfect moment. The clicks of cameras are interspersed with curses in French, Portuguese, and English, as fists hit rib cages and hips swish left and right in a fight for steady ground.

The woman's machete lifts higher after her last gesture and then plunges down towards the man's neck. Several people gasp and turn away, but the majority of the crowd simply stare. With a sudden but slight twist of her wrist, the Kayapo woman flattens the blade and lays it flush against the side of Lopes's soft, blubbery face, delivering a little pat on the cheek, a harmless taste of hardened steel—ritual transformed into spectacle at a conference promising to be much more interesting than I could ever have imagined.

While the Wolf and I weave our way towards the podium, I do a quick breakdown of the crowd. There's an Indian with a boom box just in front of me taping the speeches; a Brazilian kid, maybe ten years old, works the audience selling ice cream; a couple of young U.S. print journalists scribble away in reporter notebooks as three local girls eye them from the periphery of the crowd. The rest of the room is reduced to a whirl of bodies and blurred faces as I try to get to the stage before I miss the next big moment in this surreal scene. My pangs of conscience have disappeared as the priorities of get-the-shot have taken all-consuming precedence. The crowd releases another burst of applause. The cluster of bodies packed near the podium eases, but the arms of photographers still fill the air, holding their cameras and clicking away, desperately snatching images.

A space opens before us. We push past a phalanx of Brazilian soldiers armed with pistols and dressed in baggy green fatigues. They stand like plastic toys against the cinder-block wall. It must be cooler there, I think to myself as I suck in the thick, acrid scent of the crowd: an unusual mix of ranch-hand sweat and European colognes with a hint of the ochre paste the Indians use to paint their bodies. I turn the camera on as we near the stage, stepping up onto a small space in a back corner. It is cramped, but I am close enough to get a shot. The "security man" stationed on the podium smiles at me and rolls his eyes, a signal that if I am crazy enough to attempt what I am doing, then he is just going to go ahead and let me do it. It is at times like this that I love working in Brazil, a land where bending the rules is a way of life: *o jeitinho brasileiro* they call it here—the Brazilian way.

Catching me off guard, the Kayapo woman returns to the podium. I am rolling now and zoom in on her face for a focus point as Lopes braces himself defiantly for another impassioned aria of contempt, her hatred for the whites spewing out unrestrained as the crowd watches in delight.

The dam scheme is yet another part of a continuing legacy of reckless development that has characterized large-scale projects in this region. But now, after two decades (and the setback of the Mendes assassination), the tables appear to be turning. In a powerful initial display of bravado, this young Kayapo woman has quickly confirmed the expectations of the international politicians and environmentalists assembled here: Chico was not a lone Amazonian phenomenon—the Indians of Brazil also have the requisite amount of savvy and courage to mount a campaign of resistence against the Brazilian government and the international lending institutions that threaten tropical forests and the people who inhabit them. And, if we can trust our taxi driver, there is more to come. The celebrities have yet to show.

The Kayapo woman begins again to shout and gesture with

the machete. I wonder whether this time she's going for his jugular. Suddenly she backs away and returns to the crowd as a young Kayapo man on the podium named Paulinho Payakan steps forward and grabs the microphone from the bemused Lopes. "*Obrigado*"—thank you—Payakan says to Lopes, who leans back looking relieved for the moment to be out of the spotlight. Payakan is wearing the traditional Kayapo headdress of blue and red parakeet feathers, a matching necklace of beads, no shirt, and a colorful pair of red and yellow surfer swim shorts. He smiles down at Lopes while simultaneously extending a hand to quiet the crowd.

At this point another Kayapo man leaps up from the audience, passing the woman with the machete as she takes a seat. This is "Colonel Pombo" (Colonel Pigeon), a powerful—some say Machiavellian—Kayapo leader who is also a consummate showman. He begins dancing about in front of the stage with a spear in his hand, gesturing violently with his weapon and derisively screaming out the name of the Kararáo Dam, one of the proposed dams that would flood his people's territory. A round of camera flashes goes off as he thrusts his spear into air and then back towards the ground as if he is single-handedly fighting off an onslaught of rival warriors. After thirty seconds of this traditional tirade he returns to his seat. The auditorium is silent. The audience members don't really know what they just saw.

"That was a war cry," Payakan says, simultaneously smiling with the ease of a trained orator. The crowd responds with applause. Each of Payakan's words and gestures now triggers a new flurry of camera flashes from local stringers for *Newsweek*, Reuters, *Time*, and dozens of other Brazilian and international news organizations. "It's the traditional war cry of the Kayapo people," Payakan adds, surveying the room, smiling and making eye contact with the audience even as he squints at the television lights. His words have given context to what would otherwise have remained an impressive but impenetrable display of native ritual. For an audience eager to understand the Indians' world, every little insight is appreciated. Payakan knows intuitively that this is true of a certain type of white people. He is a

master at navigating the middle ground between their world
and ours.

Paulinho Payakan organized Altamira with the help of several Brazilian nongovernmental organizations as part of the
Indians' initiative in the new global movement to save the rain
forest. In recent months he has emerged as the preeminent
figure in a growing alliance of Indian societies in the Brazilian
Amazon. His Portuguese is fluent. His manner among Brazilians
is confident and, at times, self-consciously condescending. His
years of contact with the whites have taught him how to play
their game.

"And what about the Indian?" Payakan continues. "Is it in
ten years that the Indian will be wiped out? Is it in ten years
that the Indian will no longer have a place to live in Brazil?"

Payakan looks down accusingly on the dam scheme engineer
as the audience obliges with more applause. Lopes stares off
into the distance, his face a mix of sulkiness and confusion; he's
probably wondering why he accepted the invitation to speak
here in the first place. Perhaps he and his superiors never
thought that the Indians could possibly pull off an event like
this. That is understandable. Lopes and his colleagues gained
power during the dictatorship, when pushing through such initiatives wasn't a problem. But this is a new democratic era, and
they are being obliged to play by the rules of a participatory
democracy.

Payakan, the son of an important chief from the village of
A'ukre, was sent away as a young boy to be educated by Jesuit
missionaries in a small town near Altamira. After school he
didn't return to his village but went to work for the Brazilian
Indian Agency as a guide and translator for *sertanistas*, those
daring Indian Agency employees who were sent into the forest
to make contact with and pacify isolated indigenous populations. After a few years with these groups, Payakan hired on
with work teams in the construction of the Transamazon
Highway. There too he worked as a guide and translator, liter-
ally paving the way for whites to enter the forest. Eventually he
quit, reportedly dismayed by the negative impact the highway
was having on the Indian communities. Recruited again by the

Indian Agency, he then became the first Kayapo to act as a government functionary at a village outpost. He was stationed in the village of Gorotire, a community that in centuries past had had hostile relations with his native village of A'ukre. As a government representative he began negotiations with local loggers and miners who had connived their way onto Kayapo lands. In an unprecedented agreement he forced them to pay a meaningful percentage of their profits to the Indians instead of the pittance that had been allotted on a sporadic basis. He also insisted that the Kayapo leaders divide the profits equally among the members of their community. To effect this he created a communal bank account. While his negotiations with the Brazilian entrepreneurs were appreciated, his attempt at redistributing wealth was received with bitter resentment by the traditional Kayapo hierarchy, who railed against his interference in their affairs. They wanted to do as they always had done: reserve the majority of the wealth for themselves and dispense the rest as they saw fit. Payakan was eventually forced out of Gorotire in an uncomfortable power struggle. However, his efforts had caught the attention of the regional director of the Brazilian Indian Agency. He was sent to the city of Belém, where he worked for the area supervisor, overseeing the relations of the Brazilian government with all the Kayapo villages scattered through a section of rain forest stretching from the state of Mato Grosso to the southern part of the state of Pará. He was the Agency's troubleshooter, responsible for four thousand Kayapo in fourteen villages. He made certain that medical supplies were delivered, that profits were returned for the sale of products, and that the children were being educated. These trips gave him regular access to all the Kayapo communities and their leaders. He made new alliances, patched up old conflicts, and served as a critical link between the Kayapo and the ever-encroaching outside world. He was a new Kayapo leader of a new era, politically savvy, in touch with a broad constituency but with no constricting allegiance to any one village—a factor that would both help him and hurt him in the years to come.

As Payakan confers in front of the podium with a few members of the Xavante tribe, I step off the stage and into a crowd of photographers. They are firing off shots at a dozen Kayapo warriors standing like stoics with war clubs and bows and arrows. The Indians pose compliantly at the direction of the photographers, who are eager to manipulate the Kayapo into the expected, sanctioned image of the native warrior—more evidence of the way reality is often jettisoned by my colleagues as they rush to collect archetypal images, images bearing a closer resemblance to museum displays than to the real people standing before us. This little bit of mise-en-scène is not simply about getting a good angle. My fellow image makers are not content with the Indians as they are; they want them to conform to the tired, unquestioned icons that haven't changed much since Columbus's time. Lost to these photos are the ambiguities and subtle possibilities of an unanticipated moment, the magic that can make a simple photograph into a work of art.

The Kayapo, for their part, seem inured to the barrage of camera flashes; they absorb them as if they are part of the price of admission. Their complicity (I am assuming) is part of a calculated dimension of the Altamira Encounter, an attempt to win over the media, and hence the Brazilian and international public, in their efforts to block the dam construction project.

Looking back into the center of the crowd, I spot amidst a group of Indians a young Kayapo man holding a video camera and focusing it on the podium. He is Kuben'i of Gorotire, the Kayapo videographer who, I've been told, has been given the job of documenting this event. As I am jostled about by my fellow photographers I wonder about the images he is taking, whether they differ from mine and those of my colleagues. Perhaps if I saw his images they might tell me something about the Indian's perspective on the world. Then maybe it would be easier to understand what is happening here at Altamira, an event that appears to be a fusion of indigenous ritual and Brazilian *carnaval*.

Behind Kuben'i I can see faces of dozens of different nationalities, all aglow in the energy of the moment. These people, most of them environmental and human rights activists, have seized upon the momentum of the death of Chico Mendes and embraced this new cast of heroes who have suddenly been thrust—or thrust themselves—center stage in the movement to save the rain forest. *Woodstock in Amazonia*, I think. *Indians as ecological saviors. Where is this all headed?* I make my way towards the exit for a breath of fresh air. Mulling over the confusing tidbits of today's events, I find myself at a loss to make sense of those strange *turistas* at the hotel and this ritualized beheading of an Electronorte representative. But by the time I reach the bright glare of the Amazon's midday I recognize that there is more going on here than can ever be grasped in a cursory journalistic survey, that only by looking back to the past can I hope to understand the perplexing pieces of this curious puzzle.

10

The Kayapo have arrived at this unique moment in history through a slow and difficult process of adaptation to the white man's world. Part of the linguistic group known as the Ge-speaking people, they live in the low forests and savannah of the south-central Amazon between the Araguaia and Iriri Rivers. For three centuries their reputation in Brazil has been similar to that of the Apache of the American West: fierce fighters with the potential for horrifying brutality. Their relations with Portuguese colonialists and, later, Brazilian citizens have been characterized by periods of warfare with occasional episodes of peaceful coexistence. Since the Kayapo were "pacified" or brought under the control of the Brazilian government in the 1950s, the murders and kidnappings of poachers, miners, loggers, and settlers have occurred less frequently. But unlike the Apache, the Kayapo have managed to survive until this day with most of their traditional culture intact.

The word *Kayapo* is derived from the language of the Tupi Indians and means *como macao*, monkeylike. In the eighteenth and nineteenth centuries, Portuguese colonialists used this epithet to encapsulate a broad cross section of indigenous groups who today are referred to as the southern and northern Kayapo. The former include the Paraná and the Kreen-Akrore peoples, who in the last two centuries inhabited the region that today geographically corresponds to the Brazilian state of Goais. Their societies bore the brunt of contacts with Portuguese colonialists, who through massacre and disease devastated the Kayapo numbers, leaving behind small pockets of populations who migrated to the protective reserves of the Xingú Park. They unwittingly acted as a human buffer zone for the northern Kayapo, who currently inhabit the region of northern Mato Grosso and southern Pará. By bearing the brunt of the first waves of colonial contact, the southern Kayapo permitted their neighbors to the north to live in relative isolation until well into the twentieth century.

It was Portuguese slave raiders who first contacted the southern Kayapo in the late eighteenth century, when they invaded the Indians' forest seeking bodies to work the sugarcane plantations and gold mines that formed the backbone of the colonial economy. During this time small groups of Kayapo were pacified with gifts of metal products and promises of transcendent miracles by the white man's Christian God. Indians who were enticed into the cities were often baptized en masse, delighting the colonial clerics who had been assigned the responsibility of tending the Indian flocks along the frontier. But by the middle of the eighteenth century Queen Maria I of Portugal began supporting a government plan to resettle the Southern Kayapo into "model villages" outside of the city of Goias. These settlements were to be overseen by her colonial administration. The role of the Church was being restricted. It had become too powerful in the view of the Portuguese crown, particularly as it related to Indian affairs. Government was now responsible for "civilizing the savages."

During this period colonial administrators had the good fortune to have the services of an extraordinary Kayapo woman by the name of Daiawa. In 1781 her father had been one of the first southern Kayapo leaders to accept the rule of the Portuguese colonialists when, with Daiawa in tow, he was persuaded to settle near Goias. Daiawa was baptized and the educated by the local authorities. She took the name da Cunha (which had been that of the local governor) and grew up to be a devout Christian and the willing subject of the local authorities. As a young woman she married a white soldier, and in 1808 she began a successful career luring hundreds of Kayapo from the forest with promises of gifts, Christian benevolence, and resettlement in model communities. In spite of Daiawa's success, the majority of the Kayapo—particularly those in the northern regions—resisted pacification. And as the numbers of the colonialists grew, the southern Kayapo fled westward across the Araguaia River into an area of savannah and low-level forest larger than the size of Scotland, an area that today comprises the territories of Mekragnoti, Rapôt, Kararaó, Cateté, and the Area Indigena Kayapo. Refusing to succumb to the rule of the white man, these Indians terrorized Portuguese settlers who encroached on their lands by staging daring assaults on local fortresses, roadways, and pioneer communities. Their combination of guerrilla warfare tactics and the skillful use of traditional weapons gave them a substantial edge over the colonialists with their clumsy armaments and scant knowledge of the forest.

In 1831 the colonial government's efforts to control the southern Kayapo suffered a serious blow when Daiawa died of hunger and exhaustion during an expedition to some uncontacted Indian villages. For the next several decades Kayapo encounters with white society were limited to raids on settlers and rubber tappers in order to obtain firearms and other manufactured products. For a time the Kayapo allied themselves with runaway African slaves, strengthening their numbers in their attacks on the Portuguese colonialists. Those southern Kayapo who had been lured into model villages over the last few decades were suffering from the neglect of their colonial administrators. Historical records of this period are filled with accounts of starvation, forced labor, and widespread death by disease among the southern Kayapo. While some of the Indians were lucky enough to flee back into the forest, those that remained intermarried with local whites or passed their last days living in small thatched huts—their former model villages having been usurped by Portuguese pioneers. In just a few decades Queen Maria's dream of an ideal Indian community had ended in complete failure. Once again, white society was at a loss for an alternative to armed conflict and enforced pacification. Yet as the frontier expanded, Portuguese colonialists were forced to contend with the region's indigenous populations. It was in this period that the northern Kayapo first began to come in contact with colonial society.

The failure of the government administrators opened the way once again for missionaries to try their hand at pacifying the Kayapo. At the turn of the twentieth century a French priest named Gil Vilanova established a mission for Indian children, which he called Conceição do Araguaia. Vilanova had conducted three different expeditions into the unexplored region of the northern Kayapo in the 1890s. Traveling by boat along the western banks of the Araguaia River, he had managed to establish ongoing contact with a group of Indians living in a village he called Pau d'Arco. Over the course of the decade he convinced the village elders to send their children to a missionary school that had been established by Vilanova and a fellow French cleric, Guillaume Vigneau. The Indians' parents were permitted to construct a modest village nearby and to visit the children on a regular basis. For almost a decade Vilanova and Vigneau were successful in slowly introducing Portuguese culture to small bands of the northern Kayapo still living east of the Araguaia River. But then both clerics succumbed to an epidemic of malaria. New Church administrators were unprepared and unqualified to carry on the work of these dedicated priests. The mission closed. Yet Vilanova and Vigneau's limited success helped to preserve a role for missionaries in the sphere of Indian affairs in Brazil. From the turn of the century onwards Protestant and Catholic emissaries would be allowed to establish small missions in remote corners of the rain forest. Proselytizing, educating, and administering medical care would become their sole mandates. More complicated questions of the Indians' relationship with the larger society of Brazil were, as of 1910, to be decided by the Indian Protection Service (SPI) under the direction of its founder, Colonel Cândido Rondon.

As a Brazilian military officer Colonel Rondon had supervised the exploration of the Amazon's frontier and other remote areas for a period of twenty years. In the course of his career he and teams of young military officers mapped more than fifty thousand square miles of rain forest, laid out some fourteen hundred miles of telegraph line, discovered twelve new rivers, and came into contact with hundreds of previously isolated Indian societies. During these decades of unprecedented exploration, Rondon began lobbying the Brazilian government to create an organization to protect such Indian societies.

Indeed, frontier violence was not the only threat to the Indians. In the cities of Rio de Janeiro and São Paulo academics and legislators were calling for the eradication of indigenous peoples in order to facilitate economic expansion. They often cited the precedent of U.S. government intervention in the American West as their model. Rondon, however, had been inspired by the writings of the French philosopher Auguste Comte and his guiding altruistic principle Live for One's Neighbor. He had developed his Indian Protection Service in direct opposition to those political and economic forces intent on genocide. The guiding motto of the SPI became "Die if necessary, but never kill." Working under the Ministry of Agriculture, the new agency's mandate as of 1910 was to protect the Indians from starvation, contact diseases, poverty, and exploitation by whites along the frontier. Its teams often spent months at a time in the forest before first contact was made. Rondon was determined to alter the tragic history of contacts between Western European explorers and indigenous populations.

By the time SPI teams approached the lands of the northern Kayapo, there were already dramatic changes taking place within their communities which set the stage for a new period of rapprochement between white society and indigenous villages in the states of Mato Grosso and Pará. Violent internecine battles had been breaking out between the Kayapo of Gorotire and the people of Mekragnoti, a group whose name translates as "people who paint their upper faces with red urucum." Then as the Mekragnoti moved westward fleeing the encroachment of outsiders, they came into conflict with the "people with shaved heads" or Kreen-Akrore and other southern Kayapo tribes as well as Brazilian rubber tappers who had been traveling the Araguaia River.

During this period the northern Kayapo stepped up their raids against Brazilian settlers, seizing as bounty high-powered Winchester rifles, which they used against their indigenous adversaries as well as Brazilian pioneers. The Indians' new arms combined with their fierce warrior traditions made them a major obstacle to government efforts at frontier expansion. The SPI stepped up their efforts to pacify the northern Kayapo by increasing the number and amount of gifts offered to the Indians. Peace eventually came about because the Indians found it easier to attain metal products, ammunition, and glass beads through sustained contacts with the Indian Protection Service than by plundering local pioneers. Throughout the 1930s and 1940s SPI teams were able to set up outposts in a number of Kayapo communities through the steady distribution of gifts to the Indians. But it was not until the 1950s that these ferocious warriors were officially pacified, setting the stage for a new era of dependency on Brazilian society.

But pacification was not without problems. Increased contact with white society brought new diseases. Violent internal schisms also continued to flare up between various Indian communities. The Indian population began to dwindle rapidly. One of the first villages contacted in the 1930s, Gorotire, saw its numbers decline from well over eight hundred inhabitants to barely one hundred in just a few years. During this era, missionaries and SPI officials worked to suppress the Indians' culture by giving them clothes, proselytizing among them, and moving their families into Brazilian-style houses. Throughout the country this official SPI policy of deculturation and the devastating impact of contact diseases led to population loss among Brazilian Indians, from one million in 1900 to less than 200,000 in 1957. In that time eighty-seven different Indian societies simply disappeared, either killed off by disease or assimilated into the mainstream of Brazilian society.

For the surviving communities, particularly the Kayapo, corruption within the SPI was becoming a major problem. SPI employees, drafted from the impoverished classes and paid a pittance, often acted as middlemen in the sale of the Kayapo's Brazil nuts to merchants in nearby towns and cities. They frequently pocketed large parts of the Indians' profits or made false claims that the harvest had been destroyed or lost in transport to urban areas. Even more scandalous activities on the part of SPI employees were exposed in 1968, when Brazil's attorney general Jader Figueiredo investigated the Agency's activities. In addition to widespread corruption Figueiredo charged SPI employees with acts of enslavement, sadism, and several different massacres carried out in collusion with frontier pioneers. Of 700 people in employment at the SPI at the time of the investigation, 134 were charged with crimes and 238 were dismissed from their jobs. One former head of the SPI, a Major Luís Neves, had amassed an astounding record of abuse and misconduct. He was accused of forty different crimes including several murders of indigenous people, the illegal sale of Indian lands, and the embezzlement of $300,000 of SPI funds. The northern Kayapo, like most indigenous groups contacted during this era, had little or no recourse against such crimes. They had almost no understanding of Portuguese, scant knowledge of the legal system, and few allies within the larger society of Brazil. Although the attorney general promised to clean up the SPI, the Indians found themselves caught in a double-edged predicament. To change the course of their destiny would mean rejecting Brazilian society, the very source of the food and medicines upon which they had become dependent for survival.

Meanwhile, in spite of persistent efforts at acculturation on the part of SPI employees and missionaries, the Kayapo managed to preserve many of their traditional customs. And their cultural resistance was to prove their salvation. Elaborate naming and initiation rituals continued to be performed with the changes in the seasons. Myths—"things that take a long time to tell"—were still passed down from generation to generation. Small wooden plates known as "lip plugs" were inserted into the lower lip, a tradition of ornamentation practiced exclusively by the men. Some groups maintained the Kayapo hair style of long hair with a shaved forehead. Many women still painted their bodies in traditional Kayapo designs but kept them hidden beneath their "Brazilian" clothes. These traditions and rituals retained by the Kayapo were not a self-conscious expression of their culture but remained in effect because "they had always been done that way." In fact, as with many Indian societies before contact, the Kayapo knew only one culture, their culture. That other societies had specific rituals and customs was not something they had been conscious of: their way of life was simply the way life was, the way it had always been.

Resilient as they were, however, even these age-old traditions were by the early 1960s succumbing to the powerful influences of contact and acculturation. The Kayapo had reached a crisis point. Their cultural foundation was slipping away, while it seemed unlikely that they would ever secure a foothold in Brazilian society. But then a new group of outsiders appeared, transforming the northern Kayapo's relationship with the larger world and with their own traditional culture.

The first of this new group of whites, sympathetic whites, had arrived in their villages in the 1950s. Decidedly different from the intolerant missionaries, miners, and corrupt Indian Agency employees who had dominated Kayapo encounters with outsiders in the past, the newcomers didn't seek to transform the Indians into supplicant subjects. These people—anthropologists, filmmakers, musicologists, botanists, and environmentally concerned individuals—were interested in Kayapo culture as a valid and valuable entity, as something to be appreciated, preserved, and reflected upon. By the 1960s they began arriving in the Indian villages in increasing numbers, rattling off endless questions, taking thousands of still and moving pictures, and recording the Indians' ceremonial chants. They accompanied hunters on week-long forays in the forest and permitted the Indian women to paint their white-skinned bodies with traditional designs. These whites were spending tremendous amounts of time and money documenting a way of life that, up until then, had been denigrated, abused, and rejected by previous generations of outsiders. All of which prompted the Kayapo to look at their own culture in a different context, to see their status in Brazilian society as separate rather than subordinate.

As the years passed, and the encounters and explorations continued, the impact on the Kayapo consciousness became indelible. Once the Indians started seeing their culture as a specific entity distinguishable from Brazilian society, they soon began to identify themselves not just as Kayapo but as "Indios"—people, whose worldview, history, and tradition lay in closer proximity to that of other Amerindian societies than

to the lately dominant culture of Brazilians and their white predecessors, the Portuguese colonialists.

The Indians also came to understand that being Kayapo—
practicing traditional dances or oratory, adorning themselves
with body paints, participating in initiation rituals—was something that attracted these sympathetic whites and consequently
would provide revenue for their communities. In the barter
process, beads and manufactured goods and medicines could be
obtained in exchange for the outsiders' access to life in their
villages. The Kayapo had found a way to manipulate outsiders
rather than be manipulated by them. They had uncovered the
key to asserting power vis-à-vis the outside world.

In years to come, the northern Kayapo would learn to apply
this new power dynamic in the larger field of Brazilian and
international politics. And, as fate would have it, their efforts
would coincide with the global movement that had taken off in
the 1980s to save the rain forest. Suddenly they found themselves making common cause with hundreds of thousands of
outsiders who in turn were being led by their own political,
environmental, and media ideologues. This new generation of
whites, like those who arrived in the 1960s, expressed a passionate interest in helping the Kayapo in their quest for cultural
survival. They wanted to "save" the Indians.

However, the Kayapo were already defending their identity
vigorously. In the 1970s a warrior and political leader named
Raoni had emerged in the forefront of the society's new relationship with white society. He was from the generation before
Payakan—someone who, according to Kayapo custom, is
respectfully called Payakan's "uncle" to signify his status as an
elder. Unlike the younger leader, Raoni did not have a childhood influenced by the teachings of Jesuit missionaries or an
early career spent working for wages in various frontier enterprises and administrations. Raoni had grown up in the forest,
living a life steeped in the traditions of Kayapo culture and
indigenous community politics. Also unlike Payakan, whose
negotiating strategy reflected a hybridization of white and
Indian society, Raoni remained confrontational, acutely sensi-

tive to the legacy of conflict with white society that had been passed down through the generations.

"My father told me it has already begun, the white man has come here to take our land," Raoni explained to me the first time I interviewed him at Altamira. "He said to me, 'They have come to take our land and then when they are finished with our land, they will destroy us also.' "

Raoni's emergence as one of the Kayapo's most powerful leaders came shortly after the disreputable Indian Protection Service was replaced by the new administrative branch of government known as the National Foundation for the Indian (FUNAI). On paper the new agency's mandate was more far-reaching than that of the SPI. It purported to be interested not just in protecting Indians but in preserving their traditional culture and lands, two elements only recently recognized as being essential for safeguarding indigenous peoples from the devastating consequences of the contact experience.

Then, just two years after FUNAI was created, General Emílio Médici was named president by the military junta that had seized power in 1964. As one of his initiatives to transform the country, General Médici introduced a grandiose scheme to open up the Amazon for development through the construction of extensive roadways. In furtherance of this plan the General appointed a new head of FUNAI, General Bandeira de Mello, to bring the mandate of the agency into conformity with the country's new economic imperatives. Almost overnight the emphasis of the Agency's work shifted from preservation to integration. "Ethnic minorities such as the Indian," General Bandeira de Mello said during this era, "must be oriented to a well-defined planning process, taking into account their participation in national progress and integration as producers of goods."

What this new regime of generals was not aware of was that their rise to power had been simultaneous with the emergence of a new generation of Kayapo leaders. Men like Payakan and Raoni, schooled in the ways of Westerners and embraced by a new generation of sympathethic whites, were now able, as their ancestors had not been, to confront the aggressions of outsiders.

This was a generation no longer interested in being pacified. They wanted contact with the whites on their own terms.

As a young adult Raoni became friends with Orlando and Cláudio Villas Bôas, two brothers whose exploits and calls to action captured the imagination of the Brazilian public in the same way that Colonel Rondon had done a generation earlier. They had first entered the territory of the northern Kayapo as part of a government survey team in the 1940s. Working outside the structure of the Indian Protection Service, these sympathetic whites successfully championed the cause of Amazonian Indians by convincing the country's government to develop protective legislation to assure the preservation of indigenous populations. The work of these fraternal *indigenistas* became the genesis of the creation of FUNAI two decades later. In their frequent encounters with Raoni they taught the young warrior Portuguese, instructed him in Brazilian politics, and helped to shepherd him through the complex web of the country's Indian Protection Service, and later FUNAI, and the state and national political machines. When in the 1950s the Villas Bôas brothers established the first protective reserve for Brazilian Indians in the Xingú Park, Raoni became one of its earliest administrators. By the 1960s these combined experiences had allowed Raoni to make a name for himself as a powerful political figure both within his community and in neighboring Kayapo villages. He had direct access to the Villas Bôas brothers, the Indians' closest and most supportive allies, and he had become recognized as someone who could be relied on to effectively assert the needs of his community within the larger world of Brazilian society. All through this time, however, Raoni continued to live in his native village of Porori, solidifying his role as a traditional leader in Kayapo society. His power was derived from a tradition of alliance building that starts within one's community and extends into neighboring villages through a web of kinship ties, historical allegiances, and intervillage exchanges.

Raoni's role as preeminent in the sphere of national politics was launched when a feeder road of General Médici's Transamazon Highway reached the territory of the northern Kayapo in 1971. The roadway, BR-080, cut dangerously close to his native village of Porori located in the northern reaches of the Xingú Park. Suddenly Raoni and his fellow villagers found themselves without the protective jungle barrier that for five centuries had been their primary safeguard against hostile incursions. Their response, developed under the leadership of Raoni, combined warrior tactics of centuries past with a shrewd understanding of the workings of the Brazilian media. Choosing not to engage in outright confrontations with highway workers, Raoni and some of his fellow villagers headed south into the Xingú Park, where they established the community of Kretire. A second group traveled north, where they established the village of Jarina in Mekragnoti territory. From these new bases, warriors began raiding and killing highway workers as well as any white settlers, miners, and poachers who entered their territory. Over the next decade dozens of people were murdered or taken hostage, securing for the northern Kayapo the reputation as one of the most warlike indigenous populations in the Amazon.

During this era of revived guerrilla tactics, the northern Kayapo also began to attract the attention of the national society and its media. The most high-profile event of this era was the "War of the Barge" in the early 1980s. Outraged that the Brazilian government was charging a toll for a roadway traversing their lands, Raoni and dozens of Kayapo warriors attacked a ferryboat outpost along the Xingú River, killing the boat's captain known as "Ze de Radio." The ferry had been established to transport cars and trucks across the Xingú River, which traversed BR-080. In seizing control of the barge, Raoni hoped to convince the Brazilian government to hand over operation of the ferryboat to the Indians so as to give them complete control of its revenues. To strengthen their bargaining position the Indians kidnapped local Indian Agency officials as well as several high-level government bureaucrats who had been flown in from Brasilia as part of a negotiating team. For a period of four weeks Raoni's dramatic guerrilla tactics held the nation spellbound. He frequently appeared on television adeptly negotiating his people's position in exchange for the lives of the hostages. In the end he emerged victorious, giving the Indians control not only of the ferry but of its revenues as well. Raoni's brilliant mix of guerrilla tactics and media-savvy public relations had pushed the Kayapo into a new era of encounters with white society, one in which the camera—and the Kayapo's knowledge of how to use it—had become an extremely effective weapon.

During most of the 1980s Raoni dominated his people's encounters with the outside world. His witty, candid, and irreverent assessments on television of the military government as "idiots" and "animals" won him praise among liberal intellectuals and activists who welcomed any form of dissenting critique of the military regime. His role as one of Brazil's emergent indigenous leaders was crystalized on celluloid when a Belgian rock promoter named Jean-Pierre Dutilleux decided to make a film about him entitled *Raoni*. Its extensive international exposure contributed to the burgeoning press he was already receiving in Brazil. These factors—combined with his distinctive lip plug and his daring political stances—had, by the middle of the decade, made Raoni a household name synonymous with the indigenous rights struggle.

Throughout the same period Payakan continued to work for the country's frontier administrations, quietly attempting to improve his people's lot from within the world of white society. He married a young Kayapo woman named Irekran and started a family. They divided their time between the urban centers of Payakan's administrative assignments and the Kayapo villages where he served as an outpost official. His contacts with his community were extensive, yet superficial in the traditional Kayapo sense: he still had no deep roots in any one village. His power was relative, based more on his ability to deliver on the white man's promises than on his own standing as a leader within the community. Raoni, on the other hand, continued to spend most of his time in the forest. After the War of the Barge, he reunited the villages of Jarina and Mentukire into one community, which became known as Kapot. In traditional Kayapo fashion this move expanded his base of power by increasing the size of his village. Although he shared authority with a cross section of traditional elders, he was recognized by all as the principal spokesperson in their people's encounters with the larger society of Brazil. Nowhere was this role more evident than at the hearings on the new Brazilian constitution in 1987.

But it was also there that Payakan began to assert himself in the sphere of radical indigenous politics that Raoni had spear-headed throughout the late 1970s and 1980s. Suddenly two generations of Kayapo were coming together under the tutelage of individuals who exemplified two styles of leadership. Raoni personified the quintessential Kayapo warrior: aggressive, combative, and afraid of no one. Payakan by contrast was the harbinger of a new era. He was smooth-talking and diplomatic. Where Raoni didn't hesitate to phrase his arguments in confrontational rhetoric, Payakan would say, "Violence, guns, and threats didn't solve anyone's problems. What solves problems is making yourself seen and heard." In combination these two leaders furthered the Kayapo cause by fusing their distinctive leadership roles. Working in alliance with Brazilian human rights activists and politicians, they managed to successfully assert their political agenda in a new era of democratic rule.

No event in the twentieth century carried greater weight for the future of Brazil's indigenous people than the hearings surrounding the establishment of the new Brazilian constitution. The military dictatorship had ground to a halt just two years earlier, its aged leaders no longer interested in commandeering a country they had driven into bankruptcy. A "new Brazil" was now being established, and talks on the fine points of legislation regarding Indians began in 1987 and continued into February 1988. By June 1988 there was a pitched battle between conservative members of Congress (many from the Amazonian states) and their more liberal opponents concerning the decrees on Indian rights that were coming up for approval. Participating in this debate (though not in the actual voting) was an unprecedented alliance of Indian leaders and supporters who included, among others, human rights activists, ethnologists, academics, and church leaders. Although Payakan was actively a part of Kayapo actions surrounding the debate on this constitutional mandate known as Decree 266, it was Raoni who was still the principal spokesperson for his people.

In an event that has become part of Brazilian political folklore, Raoni—supported by dozens of Kayapo warriors—staged an occupation of a congressional caucus chamber and held court for an array of television and print reporters on the eve of the critical vote on Decree 266. This proposed provision of congressional legislation was intended to guarantee Indians living within Brazil an array of rights not available to them under prior constitutions. Raoni's daring move could easily have backfired. But with characteristic flair Raoni succeeded in dominating the discussion of indigenous rights and presenting his case in clearly identifiable but emotionally charged terms. "The president of the Indian Agency, he thinks we are stupid," he told reporters as he displayed a map of Kayapo territory. "Where are our children and grandchildren going to live? I am not going to tolerate the way things are today. The Kayapo have their own rights. [President] Sarney is stupid. I don't like stupid people. I like nice people."

The next day Decree 266 was approved. For the first time in Brazil's history the country's constitution protected the languages, beliefs, and customs of all indigenous people as well as their inalienable right to their traditional lands. Perhaps most important, the decree granted that "Indians, the communities and organizations are legitimate parties capable of suing in defense of their rights and interests." While still maintaining their status as wards of the state, this legal entitlement to sue on their own behalf meant that Indians were no longer dependent on the Indian Agency to defend them in the judicial system. They could even file claims against the Indian Agency if they chose to do so. For the Kayapo at least, the days of absolute dependency appeared to be part of the past.

It could be said that Raoni's storming of the Congress was merely symbolic, as it came weeks after the discussions in which the fine print of Decree 266 had been analyzed and debated. Yet it cannot be denied that his action sent a message to Congress and the public at large that Indians in Brazil would no longer remain in the forest as their fate was being decided in the cities. Although not recognized as citizens, the indigenous people of Brazil could participate in the decision-making process affecting their lives. The passage of Decree 266 set the stage for a new era wherein indigenous people could hold government administrations accountable for transgressions of the law. This would have been unheard of in the time of Colonel Rondon.

One of the first people to test the limits of Brazil's new democratic spirit was Paulinho Payakan who, shortly after the constitutional hearings, traveled to the United States to speak at a conference on tropical forest conservation at the University of Southern Florida. There he gave a rather perfunctory account of the importance of the rain forest from the indigenous perspective. But when he proceeded north to Washington, trouble began.

At a World Bank meeting Payakan, accompanied by a fellow Kayapo leader named Kubei and an American ethnobotanist named Daryl Posey, spoke out critically about Brazil's plan to create a massive hydroelectric scheme on Indian lands. Payakan for his part knew all too well the government's intentions. He had served as a guide and translator for survey teams that had traveled the entire region in exploratory stages of the project. His views represented an informed indigenous perspective on the negative impact of the dam scheme on the Indian peoples of Brazil.

World Bank officials, to their credit, were open to hearing it. Kubei and Payakan were fortunate in the timing of their visit. For a decade the Bank had been reevaluating its criteria for guaranteeing international loans. The officials assembled at this meeting were aware that prior Bank support of Operation Amazonia and subsequent Amazon development schemes had caused problems, to say the least. They couldn't overlook the fact that between 1964 and 1971 the U.S. government and its various lending institutions had provided Brazil with $3.5 billion in bilateral aid and international loans, many of them directed towards the Amazon—and that by 1972 Brazil had surpassed all other countries as the major debtor nation to the Bank. Nowhere was the role of the World Bank and the Inter-American Bank more apparent than in the $400 million provided for highway construction in the Amazon between 1968 and 1972. After several international scandals the World Bank had become uncomfortably aware that Brazil's military dictatorship and its local frontier governments had consistently ignored long-standing warnings regarding the lethal consequences of uncontrolled contact with isolated Indian societies. Several European newspapers had uncovered cases of brutal genocide against Brazil's Indians. The SPI scandal of the late 1960s and subsequent investigations by international journalists had tarnished the image of the World Bank. Even within Brazil the country's Indian Agency had been referred to by then–Attorney General Figueiredo as "a den of corruption and indiscriminate killings." To make matters worse, many journalists filing Amazon stories made a direct connection between World Bank funding and the roadways that had brought ruthless pioneers and corrupt administrators to the Brazilian frontier. Perhaps the most scathing of all critiques was Shelton Davis's landmark study *Victims of the Miracle*, which in 1977 systematically documented the relationship between cases of genocide against Indians and World Bank financing of frontier expansion projects. Subsequently, damage control had become a priority in Bank decision making, and hearing the testimony of affected forest dwellers fit conveniently into its new agenda for evaluating loans.

Although no final decision was reached during Payakan's visit to Washington, news of the unprecedented meeting sent shock waves throughout Brazil. When Kubei, Posey, and Payakan returned to Brazil they were charged by the attorney general with defaming the national image. This was big news and made all the major newspapers: the crime was punishable by one to three years in jail or expulsion from the country. Just a few months after Raoni's success at the constitutional hearings, his "nephew" was now in the nation's spotlight. And Payakan took to his role with the zeal of an ambitious understudy.

Posey, Payakan, and Kubei hired a local lawyer to defend them. Then, in what was fast becoming a Kayapo tradition, Payakan added another dimension to his defense strategy. On the day he was to appear in court, he and Kubei showed up in the port city of Belém accompanied by two hundred Kayapo warriors armed with war clubs and bows and arrows. They threatened and harassed military guards who surrounded the courthouse as the judge and his assistants barricaded themselves inside. Blocking off the street, the Indians then lined up in four rows of twenty, chanting in unison and performing a traditional Kayapo dance. The local press was mesmerized. Photojournalists and television crews fell over themselves attempting to capture these extraordinary images. During breaks between ceremonial dances and the ritualized berating of the military police, Payakan placed a map on an easel in the middle of the street and gave impromptu lectures to the tribesmen on the impact of the dam scheme and his motives for appearing before the World Bank. Adding to the array of photogenic images was Payakan in traditional face paint and dress documenting the event with his own video camera so that those villagers remaining in the forest could see what their fellow Kayapo were doing in the cities.

All in all, the event showed that the Kayapo's years of interacting with sympathetic whites had made them acutely aware of what types of images would work in their favor with the public at large. And it didn't hurt that Payakan—the event's master of ceremonies—exhibited a flair for public relations that surpassed even that of his uncle Raoni who, although in attendance, kept a very low profile during the course of the day's events.

In the months following the Belém demonstration there were no further hearings in the Brazilian courts regarding the charges against Payakan, Kubei, and Posey. During that period, Payakan was busy making plans for what became known as the Altamira Encounter. Once that event got started, the charges mysteriously disappeared in the Brazilian courts.

11

"Get us six *frangos* to go," squeaks the walkie-talkie as the production assistant steps up to the counter of a local Altamira restaurant. He's wearing Ray•Ban sunglasses, a green Benetton shirt, long khaki shorts, and a spotlessly clean pair of Nike Airs. "Roger that," he responds. To his mouth he raises a clear plastic container of Evian water—just one bottle, rumor has it, from several cases flown into Altamira from the States by a Hollywood film crew.

The Wolf and I are sitting here taking a break from Day Three of the Encounter. We're trying to restore our energy before we subject ourselves to another round of international camera jostling. Beside us lie the remnants of a small feast of meat, beans, and rice that was consumed in a matter of minutes. We stopped only to swat the flies or take sips from our Guarana sodas. Before pushing on to dessert and coffee, we are soaking in a little of the atmosphere, trying to get a feel for what this town is really like. Scattered about the restaurant taking their noontime meals are a cross section of indigenous leaders, some with traditional headdresses, others adorned only with ceremonial paint. They all wear the requisite bathing suit; this year's fashion leans towards brightly colored surfer shorts. Around wooden tables they sit huddled in distinct ethnic clusters—representatives of the Xavante, Kayapo, and Panara people. There doesn't seem to be much mixing among them, which is perhaps an indication of language differences and their own cultural barriers rather than any history of conflict between their societies. The intertribal battles of the past have dissipated in recent years as, one by one, these groups have come to recognize themselves as *Indios* and started to ally themselves in opposition to the national society of Brazil. Slowly they have begun referring to other Indians as their "relatives" while still characterizing most whites as a group not to be trusted.

Above us an old wooden ceiling fan spins, wobbling precariously, providing the vague semblance of a soothing little breeze. Tables and chairs screech against the concrete floor as other Indians arrive to join the groups already seated. From a transistor radio off in the kitchen we can hear the scratchy sounds of Brazilian country music mixed with the chatter of the restaurant staff; it's not exactly my favorite style of music but it provides a welcome relief from the endless conference speeches which, after two long days, seem to have blended together into an indistinguishable litany of ecological woes. So far in this Encounter I have been pummeled, threatened, and kicked at least two dozen times. I am not eager to get back to it, and this guy with the *frango* order is a sufficiently amusing distraction to justify lingering over our meal a few minutes longer. I get a lot from moments like these, incidents that don't make their way into the reports I file or the documentaries I knock out back in New York. They tell me a lot about the nature of this traffic jam involving Western and indigenous cultures. Certainly both groups share an avowed desire to "save the forest" but what I find puzzling is that, beyond this one factor, there is no reason these disparate groups should come together: no link, no ties, just a catchy idea that has swept up the world and me along with it. For now I am content not to figure it out but simply to soak it in. I sit here fascinated by the way the Indians stare blankly at the young man as he jokes with his colleagues on the walkie-talkie and, for his part, the way Mr. Frango-To-Go cannot separate himself from his techno-toy and settle into the atmosphere of the room. He uncomfortably surveys his surroundings as he rambles on into his portable squawk box about what he is seeing in the restaurant as if he's an astronaut, nervous but excited by his new discovery, reporting back to planet Earth after touching down on an alien terrain.

In the last two days there have been two or three people who have spoken out in support of the government's position on the hydroelectric project and the massive destruction it would entail. But, as would be expected, the majority of the speakers have condemned it. One of the project's proponents, Brazil's environmental secretary Fernando Mesquita, was booed off the podium this morning as he tried to lecture the Indians and the audience on how they should behave at their own conference. Mesquita appears to be an honest man in a difficult place: he has been asked to undo overnight the ecological crisis created by twenty years of trying to develop the Amazon. But he has made the classic mistake of the stereotypical bureaucrat: he preaches to his audience of indigenous leaders rather than conversing with them, betraying an assumption that the white man's words carry greater weight therefore the Indians should simply sit back and listen. What Mesquita obviously hasn't realized is that this is a new era. The balance of power has changed. The Indians are "empowered" (as one anthropologist said today) by their alliance with international environmentalists and their welcoming reception in institutions of power like the World Bank and the U.S. Congress. In fairness to Mesquita, his manner of speaking to the Indians is not exclusive to representatives of government. Even the most well-intentioned sympathetic whites—and there are plenty of them at this event—can be condescending and patronizing in their efforts to "help these people" as opposed to keeping them in their place. Each is an assertion of power and each can be dangerous. Here, however, no one seems to be concerned about such details. Everything is happening too fast. Everyone is swept up in the moment, and the "cause."

One interesting fact I noted today is that the number of representatives of various Indian societies attending the conference—the Kraho, the Xavante, the Kreen-Akrore—has suddenly dropped. They too must be getting bored. There were fewer men marching into the convention center this morning as they sung tribal chants. It was easier to get a shot. I wasn't spending as much time tripping over my camera-laden cohorts. One of my anthropologist sources told me that the Indians are spending more time at their makeshift village on the outskirts of town. He suggested rather surreptitiously over breakfast that I take a trip out there this afternoon. I assumed I was being passed a lead on something exclusive, which is a most welcome gesture considering that this conference appears to be grinding to a halt. I can tell by the nighttime banter in the bars that my journalist and filmmaker friends have the same concern: we are all searching for a new take on the old story, hoping to justify our presence in this pleasant backwater town for just a few more days.

Certainly, the arrival of a few celebrities would spice things up. Mr. Frango-To-Go standing before us does bear witness that at least one Hollywood contingent has graced us with its presence. But there is still no sign of a marketable celebrity. Those of us who are "capturing" the images here know that "celebs"— real ones—can provide the picture-perfect moments that will be the big sellers back on the home turf: Brigitte Bardot with a headdress, Prince Charles gesturing defiantly with a war club, the King of Sweden twostepping to the beat of the Kayapo Corn Dance. As freelancers we can sell such images to the entertainment shows and journals while hoping to slip in a few "artsy" shots or ethnographic sequences to market to the more "serious" broadcasters and publications. Most of us detest this approach, but that's the way it is if you are working without a contract: the glitz and glamour pay the way for the committed work of the freelancer interested in stories that are deemed too political or too offbeat. I have paid for a few of my trips down here already with magazine pieces about Brazilian music, the soap opera industry, and a profile of Xuxa, the platinum-haired former Playboy playmate and onetime girlfriend of the soccer player Pelé who wears micro-miniskirts and talks nonstop four hours a day as the hostess of Brazil's most popular children's show. That's an "easy sell," as they say in the entertainment industry. Tales of political violence are more problematic.

"No one cares about sixteen hundred people who have been

assassinated in the Amazon," a high-powered television executive told me just a few months ago. He was trying to usher me
out of a producer's office as I was pitching a story on the deaths
of rural leaders in the Amazon over a two-decade period. This
was three months before Chico Mendes was killed. The 1,600
other nuns, priests, lawyers, and labor leaders who had been
murdered in the rain forest were people this executive did not
consider newsworthy. But Chico's story, and the way it crossed
over into the international arena, had an unusual twist. After
his death someone else bestowed upon him what I call "the
aura of significance" by putting him in the news and thereby
making him worthy of news coverage. He appeared in print
before getting on television, a progression that is becoming
increasingly prevalent. Marlise Simons from the *New York
Times* wrote a front-page story on his assassination within forty-
eight hours of his death, catapulting his story onto the desks of
television news editors in this country and abroad. Only then
did his story have credibility.

That's often the way television journalism functions these
days. News bureaus around the world have closed down, so very
few people are doing original reporting from the field. The
length of foreign news stories is being cut in half with the
explanation that "no one is interested." What replaces them
are softer puff pieces, celebrity profiles, and voyeuristic tabloid
violence that attempt to present themselves as "serious" news
because there is a "serious" side to the stories, often involving
rape, murder, child molestation, divorce, drugs, drinking, a
celebrity, a politician, a prostitute, or any combination thereof.
So America's view of the world is turning myopic as a new generation of media executives struggles frantically to "give the
American public what they want" or perhaps, more accurately,
what it perceives the American people want. The corporate
heads are tired of losing dollars on the news business and are
trying to turn a profit by adding some glitz, glamour, and, let's
be honest, voyeurism. At the end of the day it's about money.
Foreign news stories get the lowest priority.

And that's where freelancers come in. Increasingly, foreign
coverage of obscure stories is brought in by stringers reporting

from regions of the world where they have a special interest. But selling such a story is not an easy proposition. It's not just about convincing the news bureau that the issue you've documented is newsworthy in its own right. You usually have to do more. One ploy is to convince the prospective buyers that their competition wants it as well—that someone *else* considers it newsworthy and they risk getting scooped. Another option is to tip off your colleagues in the print world to the same story. You then wait for their coverage to appear in the *New York Times*, the *Washington Post*, or *Time* magazine. When you go in the next day and make your pitch, bingo, you've got your sale. Still, it's only the big foreign stories that are guaranteed coverage these days: the fall of the Berlin Wall, Tien-an-men Square, Mandela's release from prison. Those stories are safe. They are easily identifiable and they are on the agendas of the competition. What gets lost, and what we are losing as a nation, are the smaller stories that put us in touch with real people in remote regions.

But I shouldn't complain. The Amazon is now "hot" and I am lucky to have the exposure and access that I currently have. News editors will take my calls; I can even call collect from these little frontier towns. The fact that I delivered the Chico Mendes story has put me on the rosters of several news organizations. Even so, as a stringer, I am considered a good source of stories but not someone to be absolutely trusted. "Are you an environmentalist?" or "Did you set up that shot?" are questions I have been asked more than once. And for all the recent inroads I have made, no one in the United States seems interested in this unprecedented meeting of Indians in the Amazon. But I'm not going to be deterred by their reactions. One thing I have learned is that freelancers live and die by their instincts. You follow your hunches until one pays off. Then your access to the remote and exotic suddenly becomes marketable. You can then pay off your bills and have the satisfaction of seeing your once unnewsworthy story now in the spotlight. That is, until the next big story comes along.

Mr. Frango-To-Go exits with his order and we finish our

meal with a *cafezinho* or "little coffee," an Amazonian amphet-
amine version of espresso that does a little more than simply
"recharge the batteries." I can feel it pumping its way through
my system as the Wolf and I exit the tiny cinder-block restaurant, stepping out into one of Altamira's narrow back streets.
Suddenly we are enveloped by a dense mass of soft, warm
humidity. A light rain is blowing in from the west and, above us,
the sky has turned gray. The rain and light have transformed the
color of the dusty clay road into a dark, rich red. The Wolf has
gone down the street in search of a taxi and I stand here
guarding the equipment under a torn blue canopy flapping in
the breeze. I watch the pattern of the rain as it hits the street,
sweeping left and then right in tandem with the bursts of the
wind. Above me the palm trees are bending sideways as their
long green leaves twist and spin backwards. An emaciated old
Indian man on a beat-up bicycle appears suddenly from around
the corner wearing only a headdress, bathing suit, and flip-flops.
He bounces by, flashing a crooked smile and giving me the
thumbs-up sign, the universal salutation used throughout Brazil
but particularly common in the Amazon. Another gust of wind
arrives, sweeping away all sound except the *rickety-rack-rickety-
rack* cadence of the bicycle's chain. Returning his attention to
the road, the old man swerves to dodge a large puddle of brown
water in the middle of the dirt roadway. His bike tips but then
he steadies it miraculously with a quick jerk. Just as another
burst of wind comes tumbling down the street, the old man disappears around the corner. There remains before me only a row
of colorful one-story houses on a little back street totally abandoned by those who have sought protection from the oncoming
storm and the heat and humidity of the Amazon's midday. I
pull my poncho out of my camera bag and cover the equipment
as another powerful burst of wind sweeps down, this time
bringing with it a sheet of heavy rain. I stand with my feet on
the corners of the poncho to hold it in place. For just a minute
the manic insanity of the last few days disappears. There is only
a pleasant calm. I search my camera bag for my journal, hoping
to jot down a few impressions. But then the Wolf pulls around
the corner in a little four-door taxi, the car stereo blasting out

Gilberto Gil's latest pop-funk-samba hit O *Eterno Deus Mudança*, "The Eternal God of Change." *"We feel what the people feel,"* sings Gil. *"The people want to scream."*

12

Driving out of town on a two-lane blacktop, our taxi finally clears the blinding sheets of thick gray rain that have swept over us since we left town. As the *motorista* Manoel clicks off the wipers and throws the car into high gear, the last rivulets of water disappear from the windshield to reveal a vista of blue sky and swirling white clouds. This view has an almost cinematic effect, as if it's part of a projected landscape, shifting ever so slightly in time with the beat of the car stereo. *"Terras, povos diferentes— outros sonhos pra sonhar."* "Different lands, different peoples— other dreams to be dreamed," Gil's voice cries out from the radio as Mario and Manoel exchange banter in the front seat and my mind drifts off into the surrounding countryside.

Where the road meets the horizon, a rainbow cuts a broad arch across the sky, slowly dissolving into one of the larger clouds. Zipping by on our left and right is the high green grass of a cattle ranch set back behind crudely constructed barbwire fences with crooked tree limbs serving as posts. I can see small groups of cows grazing in the fields a few hundred yards in the distance as our little Ford taxi picks up speed, the macadam highway now shiny from the recent shower. Scattered across the pastureland are the tall, thick charcoal shells of once massive Amazonian trees: this part of the state of Pará was the front line of Amazon development in the 1960s and 1970s, one of the first regions to get torched in the push to tame the forest.

Manoel taps his horn as we zoom by an old peasant walking barefoot, carrying a machete and wearing just a pair of torn and dirty pants. His body, or what's left of it, is an emaciated shell of sun-dried skin clinging uncomfortably close to the bony frame of his shoulders and rib cage. In the rearview mirror I catch a glimpse of him as his tired hand rises slowly, acknowledging the passing presence of our air-conditioned vehicle. This modest car is worth more money than he will ever make in a lifetime, just another of the mind-boggling discrepancies of wealth in this country, a nation that has the greatest division between rich and poor of any in the Western Hemisphere. The numbers of the indigent grow daily as the economy spirals downward, caught in a relentless cycle of hyperinflation and recession: more crime, more violence, more children on the street each day; more people losing their land, and those landless then crowding into the cities to take up residence in the shanty-towns, the *favelas*, that spill across the hillsides of Rio or the outlying parts of São Paulo. Eventually the poverty of the cities becomes unbearable, forcing legions of the poor out into the Amazon in a last-chance crusade for economic salvation. Most of these Amazon migrants, like the old man now disappearing over the horizon, will die as they were born: destitute and desperate in a land of unrealized dreams.

"*Está por aqui, gentes*"—It's just near here, people—says the driver as we turn right off the highway and bounce down a dirt road heading in the direction of a Catholic mission where the Indians have established their temporary village during the Encounter. This area has, up until now, been spared our attention: off limits to anyone with a camera. But someone has decided to open it up to the media, and so we have come in search of more images to tell our stories. The driver lowers the music and we pull into the Church complex, where the atmosphere in the parking lot is much like that at a college stadium before the big game. Car doors open and close as people, mostly environmentalists and journalists, rush excitedly towards the large iron gates of the mission entrance. Our car inches forward; the people who swarm around the car appear decapitated in my partially obstructed view. They are dressed in an array of bright-colored shorts and shirts and they tote cameras, tape recorders, and pocket-sized notebooks en route to their next assignment. In the front seat the Wolf and Manoel lower their windows and a wave of the Amazon's hot humid air sweeps into the car. They deliver to the bystanders a mix of heavily accented expletives and lighthearted jokes designed to negotiate our way through the crowd. But it's too dense. The Wolf and I get out and proceed on foot.

As we pass through the large iron gates, we enter what is best described as an Amazon theme park. The Indians are encamped in a large courtyard in which stand a dozen hastily constructed shacks like those put up by hunters for temporary shelter. There are no walls to these structures, just roofs of thatched leaves suspended on sticks for protection from the rain. Men, women, and children—mostly Kayapo, it seems—are scattered about the area occupying themselves in a variety of activities. They are carrying out what, under normal circumstances, would be the simple rituals of daily life: women cleaning the carcasses of animals brought in from the hunt and cooking them over a fire, a group of men in the midst of a discussion, a young child adding an extra layer of palm leaves to a rickety roof. Surrounding various clusters of Indians are groups of photojournalists fighting among themselves to get their best camera angles against the sharp rays of the afternoon light. They push and shove, struggling to frame out any hint of the modern world. These photos are designed to place the Indians in their "natural setting." They eliminate the cars in the background or the box radio sitting in the foreground, all the details that connect the Indians with our world.

The atmosphere is strange—weird and wired. It's as if an entire wax museum of lowland Indian peoples has suddenly come to life and the attendant tourists—cameras at the ready—are swooping down upon them in a vigilante act of anthropological documentation. I take a moment to check my battery. The Wolf and I then enter the throng.

We step past a cluster of television crews filming an old Kayapo man sitting and weaving a headdress. Beyond them I have a clear shot of the Englishwoman I met on my first day at the Hotel Americana. She's getting a touch-up to her face and long, thin black lines are being added to each arm. There is an air of serene contentment about her, as if I've caught her in the midst of a blissful conversion: Botticelli's Venus suddenly transformed into a New Age goddess. I can tell the Wolf is distracted because the boom pole has drifted into the shot. I clear my throat. He recovers and retrieves the pole just enough for me to get the shot. We then move on. As I look about the encampment I can see that there are more than just a few of these individuals caught up in the joyous frenzy of bonding with the Indians. Somehow, like mushrooms, dozens of them seem to have popped up spontaneously after the heavy rains. A few feet behind the New Age Botticelli is an American television producer who, judging from her face paint, also seems to be surrendering to the spirit of the moment. As she poses for a picture taken by her friend, I pivot to document this little scene: I pan from the picture taker to the subject posed, hands on hips, in front of a thatched hut. Slowly I zoom in, creating a frame that is the equivalent of a snapshot. "For my mother," the producer says as my lens homes in to a stop exactly timed to match the shutter click of her friend's Nikon. The sound of that still camera joins the cacophony of whirling gears and shutter snaps coming from the hundreds of other Canons and Leicas and Olympuses firing off around us.

I change my camera battery, but before I can move on to the next image the Wolf taps me on the shoulder, calls time-out by placing his hands in the shape of a T, and points down at the cables falling out of his mixer: he needs time to unravel this mess. Disengaging the cable that joins his mixer to the camera, the Wolf heads back to the equipment bags we have left sitting next to a tree a few feet away. I turn on the camera's automatic microphone so that I can work independently.

Looking up, I notice that near one of the larger thatched huts there are a half dozen television and film crews lining up their tripods in what looks like a preparation for a press conference. I ask an English colleague what's going on.

"Sting's coming, man," he says without looking up from his

camera. "You better get your spot or you'll be covering it from on top of one of these rickety huts."

I see that three more crews have arrived in the few seconds it has taken him to divulge this information. The buzz that has permeated this little village since we first entered is now getting frenzied in expectation of the arrival of a commodity more marketable than a forest dweller returning home with a day's catch. This is a rock star, an icon of our own.

The British are the ones who are really getting hysterical here. Sting, the pop-star-turned-activist, is a hometown boy. This means potentially big sales for freelancers and major career points for television producers who can work his image—perhaps even an interview—into their satellite newscasts. However, my British colleagues' unaccustomed exposure to equatorial sun has turned their cherubic white complexions to dark shades of crimson, adding a demonic aspect to their already questionable demeanor.

"Back off," shouts a burly Englishman as he pushes his assistant to the side and locks his camera into its safety plate, then in a violent thrust mounts it on top of the tripod. Behind him I can see a Kayapo boy watching, startled at the behavior of this angry stranger with a face the color of blood. *Who here is "civilized"? I ask myself. Is it us with our steel instruments and stressed-out schedules? Or is it these Indians with their war clubs, lip plugs, and drug-induced shamanistic rituals?* This little episode of pushing, shoving, and screaming is probably as incomprehensible to this young boy as some of the Kayapo "war cries" that we witnessed yesterday back in the Civic Center. I imagine that it must only confirm the stereotypes of the white man that have become a part of the folklore of his world. Such tales are passed from village to village and from generation to generation: that the white man drinks too much, that he is greedy and violent, that he is the one who does not know how to live by a civilized code of conduct. In a weird way I am thankful for little dramas like this one. They allow me to take a step back and look beyond my own culture. For a few seconds I can, through the boy's eyes, get a glimpse of our world. And a scary place it must be.

Suddenly the boy's head snaps to the side and his eyes lock on a group of still photographers who have just abandoned a cluster of Indians like a school of sharks suddenly departing from a feeding frenzy. The journalists move in the direction of an approaching mob—mostly Indians—who are surging in from the front gates, a tassel of blond hair bouncing among them, a sign perhaps that Sting has arrived.

The scene quickly descends into bedlam. Payakan is out in front of the pack accompanied by a half dozen Kayapo who are using war clubs like crowbars to push their way through the crowd of adoring groupies and anxious photojournalists. A short white woman with a French accent and bright red lines painted across her face is closely following the group, shouting Sting's name and holding an autograph book in her hand. I stand my ground against the wave of bodies that rises up around me. When I am at its center I start to backpedal, slowly keeping pace with the momentum of the mob. In spite of the pushing and shoving, I am able to get a good twenty-second shot of this frenetic scene. The image works in that it is immediately comprehensible to an international audience: the rock star arrives in the Amazon and encounters the same chaos and clamor he is confronted with on world tours. But I will need other images if I want to put together a report. So I circle the perimeter of the mob in the hope of rejoining the crews lined up in front of the larger thatched hut.

As I sprint around the side I glance to my left and spot the Wolf in deep conversation with a beautiful dark-haired Brazilian woman, her back against a tree and my trusted soundman leaning close to her. Unfortunately for me, the Wolf is exactly where I left him and the cables he had gone to straighten out remain lying by his side—somehow more confused than ever—in a tangle of branches and leaves.

I whistle a few times, trying to get his attention. Then, unable to break away from the crowd, I call out urgently for the tripod. I am embarrassed by the shrillness of my voice; it sounds like the last panicked plea of a drowning man. Beside me I can see the Kayapo boy staring up, his eyes confused and questioning, an unfortunate confirmation that I too have joined the demonic and incomprensible world of the other, crimson-faced white man.

"Wolf, I need the tripod!" I call out again in a tone intended to be less strident.

Ever so slowly he glances in my direction, blinking to acknowledge my request but careful not to break his composure or allow his friend to move away from the tree. I can tell by the tilt of his head and his sleepy-eyed expression that he is at a critical juncture in one of his delicate negotiations. I have heard various versions of this routine on different trips to the Amazon: "Where will you be later?" "Do you live with your parents?" "Do you want to have dinner with me and my friends?"

I can feel my anger at the Wolf swelling as the mob of journalists surges forward, crowding the already limited space we have to cover this event. Without a tripod I will have to do it handheld, which will make the shoot a backbreaking task. I caution myself not to react too angrily to the ways of the Wolf. This is the manner in which things get done in Brazil, the way in which life unfolds; to question it is to go against the rhythm of the culture. The gringo option, an in-your-face confrontation, would be absolute suicide. I've learned that in the past. Brazilians simply shut down when faced with hostile Americans who believe that angry rages in tropical cultures can get them what they want. Besides, I tell myself, there is probably a logic to what the Wolf is doing; I just can't see it. There have been countless times on other trips when his Don Juan antics have paid off in the long run. This woman probably works for Varig airlines and will be a key contact when we try to leave without a reservation.

"Okay, can we get started please," says a young Indian man in Western dress, his accent revealing a perfect command of American English. Immediately he repeats his instructions in Portuguese in hopes of settling the anxious crowd. His name is Jorge Terena, and he has received a college education in the States funded by the American missionaries who worked among his people, the Terenas, when he was a young boy.

Sting has now positioned himself in the circle of cameras. He looks nervous as he glances about, head tilted, scanning the crowd. He has a blond ponytail, blue eyes, and strikingly hand-some features mitigated by a sharp, pointy nose. He is wearing an earth-color combination of green pants and boots and a red and green patterned shirt. This eco-conscious fashion fusion allows the rock star to blend in with his indigenous entourage yet distinguish himself from the motley array of brightly colored anthropologists, journalists, and Indian wanna-bes who have descended upon him. The rumor floating among the journalists is that Sting is here to announce the formation of a foundation to help save the rain forest. And, not surprisingly, he is doing it in collaboration with Raoni, who has just appeared by his side and set off another flurry of photos. The elderly Kayapo leader, conspicuously absent from the early part of Payakan's confer-ence, has now managed to steal the limelight from his nephew. Payakan might be able to muster the support of environmental-ists and politicians, but Raoni has come up with a rock star, a figure from the world of the new whites who has the power to raise millions of dollars while consistently attracting the atten-tion of the international press. In the last few days there has been talk of internal dissension between these two Kayapo leaders. But here, at least for those of us on the outside, they appear to be getting along.

As Jorge Terena tries to settle the crowd, Sting takes a few moments to pose for the press. But he appears ill at ease in this setting. It's as if the serious environmentalist within him is uncomfortable inhabiting the body of the rock legend. Perhaps this is the trade-off whenever fame is used to proselytize for a cause. There is a confusing set of signals being sent that, in this case, seem to confuse even the sender.

Sting's collaborator in the foundation project, the filmmaker Jean Pierre Dutilleux, quiets the crowd. Sting whispers some-thing to Raoni, laughs to himself, and takes a step forward to meet the press.

"I spent a day yesterday with some Kayapo in the jungle and realized that I was in Paradise," says Sting. "That I was in the Garden of Eden." He pauses, takes another nervous breath, and continues.

"If that culture is destroyed, then the world loses something that is invaluable," he says. "I also think that by saving the Indians, you save the rain forest. They are the gardeners of the forest. So we have to protect them to protect the forest."

Sting waits while Terena translates and there is another round of photos. Click: there's Sting with his arm around Raoni. More clicks and a flurry of flashes: Sting, Dutilleux, and Raoni standing and talking.

"What is it you are trying to do?" shouts an English reporter from behind me.

"I am here to speak for my own people," Sting quickly shouts out so as to avoid being deluged by more questions. "We want to help save the rain forest. We want to try and declare a huge National Park in the center of the Amazon. We need funds to do it. We need a few million dollars. I'm confident we can raise it with Raoni's help."

Sting's statements are again translated into Portuguese as he, Raoni, and Dutilleux, arms draped around one another, stand together for another round of photo opportunities. All of these images have been set against the picturesque background of the largest of the Indians' thatched huts. It gives the scene "local color" and provides a high point in an expertly orchestrated press junket. In spite of his initial anxiousness Sting now seems content with the attention of the press.

The Wolf finally arrives with the tripod. "Getting through that crowd was really difficult," he says.

"What was her name?"

"Who?"

I look up at him for a moment as I fix the tripod. "Mario, my friend. Please show me some respect."

"Yes. This is true. Respect is important," he says. He pauses as if to reflect on this concept, on the girl, or both. "Angela is her name," he says finally.

"I am happy for you," I say, then laugh as I lock the camera in and return to my shot.

The rock star rambles on for another fifteen minutes, giving details of his plans to establish boundaries around the part of Kayapo land known as Mekragnoti territory. He has recorded an "appeal," he says, in seven languages. A worldwide tour has been planned with Raoni to get the message out. He peppers his statements with assurances that his new foundation will be working "with" Brazilians, that this is "a Brazilian initiative," that it won't be like "North Americans trying to tell the Brazilians what to do."

Sting is proving himself to be a savvy diplomat. These declarations are aimed at many of the journalists here, particularly the Brazilians, who are suspicious of the Englishman's intentions. The legacy of outsiders interested in the Amazon triggers immediate feelings of xenophobia: Teddy Roosevelt raised eyebrows when he arrived here in 1913 and Henry Ford received a similar reception in 1926. The Midwestern megacapitalist had indeed come to exploit the Amazon's rubber trees, while the rough-riding naturalist claimed he was simply interested in writing about the region's flora and fauna. More recently, in 1967, the American billionaire Daniel Ludwig shocked Brazilians when, during the military dictatorship, he bought a section of the Amazon forest the size of Austria. He then spent tens of millions of dollars over two decades on an ambitious project to harvest lumber from rapid-growth trees imported from Asia. Rumors quickly began to circulate that the entire operation was actually a covert U.S. military base. The project eventually collapsed and Ludwig left the Amazon. Sting, now playing the humble rock star, says he doesn't want to exploit it but only "save it." Yet the Brazilian journalists want to know exactly what that means. In spite of his disclaimer, Sting's plans could easily be interpreted as imperialistic, just another European or American telling the Brazilians what they should be doing with their country. Even if he is well intentioned (and the jury is still out) his proposal—and it is a bold one—treads on sensitive ground for Brazil, a country beset by pressing economic woes to which, some feel, the Amazon's untapped wealth holds the solution.

"It's a Brazilian problem to be solved by Brazilians," Sting repeats in the final moments of the press conference. "I just want to help the Brazilians solve their problems."

When the speeches are done, a group of Kayapo begin performing a traditional dance in honor of Sting. They line up in single file, forming a snakelike pattern consisting of about thirty men. Suddenly they break into one of the ceremonial Kayapo songs. As they sing the line advances, the men lurching forward, shuffling one foot in front of the other, their backs bent and slightly arched. Their movements are powerful and dramatic. But within two minutes this beautiful ritual is aborted: the crush of cameramen has made it impossible for the Kayapo to complete the dance's intricate pattern. Leaving the crowd, the Wolf and I linger on the outskirts of the village, hoping to grab a few more shots before heading back to the Hotel Americana. I then spot a cluster of photographers at the far end of the encampment. We wander over in that direction. I always find the peripheral scenes most telling at such events, so it is not surprising that we have stumbled upon the most fascinating moment of the day.

The group of photojournalists is surrounding a Kayapo woman—her face painted red—who is holding a young boy. The pose is strikingly like that of a Madonna and Child. Enriching the iconography of the scene, she also holds a machete raised defiantly—a gesture calling to mind images of left-wing revolutionaries from the 1960s: Che riding into Havana on the top of a truck, a heavily armed Black Panther on the steps of a government building. The photographers standing in front of her are calling out instructions, telling her to raise the machete a little higher or tilt it slightly this way or that. Payakan, who has been standing off to the side, begins to insert himself into this scene, working with the journalists to make certain they are able to get the exact pose they desire. He takes the woman gently by the elbow and turns her to face the sun. He suggests that she lift the child up a little higher. I walk about the scene grabbing close-ups of the woman, long shots and profiles of the photographers, and every shot possible of Payakan as he works his mise-en-scene. The Wolf, following behind me with boom pole extended, is doing an excellent job, careful not to allow any shadows to fall across the images I am gathering. When Payakan steps back, the cameras fire away at their creation perfected with his collaboration: an archetypal New Age icon, an Amazon Woman for a new era. She—or the image they created of her—is part caring mother, part fearless warrior ready and poised in the new global fight to save the rain forest. But what she really represents is a resurrected icon, a descendant of the original Amazon. This mythological figure of a "man-killing" warrior who seduces and then murders her male opponents was made famous by Herodotus in the fifth century B.C., recounted by Virgil in the first century B.C., and then transported to Brazil by the Spanish explorer Francisco de Orellana in 1541. It was Orellana who applied the misnomer to a group of Tapuya Indians with whom he fought during his four-thousand-mile expedition up what was thenceforth called the Amazon River. He referred to the Tapuya as Amazons because, he noted, the women fought side by side with the men. Today's reappearance of the woman-warrior image attests to the residual power of ancient myths.

Certainly there is an innocent side to this impromptu photo opportunity. Many of my colleagues did not get a shot of the woman with the machete in the Civic Center, the defining image of the Altamira Encounter, so they are now trying to save their jobs by capturing an approximation. Payakan is only trying to help by acting as a cultural interlocutor, a position he has become accustomed to over the last two decades. Before he arrived, this poor woman was surrounded by a pack of overeager journalists shouting instructions in Portuguese, a language probably incomprehensible to her. Payakan has simply interceded, translated, and made some suggestions of his own.

As the Wolf and I move about this scene, it becomes clear to me why I have been feeling an odd disconnectedness ever since I got to Altamira. Something is haywire. To participate in such photographic encounters is like entering a strange dimension of time and space, a state of being both real and unreal. For me these illusory moments have come to define my experience at Altamira. I find myself increasingly drawn to documenting images of my fellow photographers and filmmakers who in turn are grappling with their perceptions of the Indians, churning out these approximations in a mad rush to circulate them to an unsuspecting outside world. It's no wonder that I am often asked, "Are there still really Amazon women in the Amazon?"

Images such as this Madonna with Machete will simply add to the long list of cloudy perceptions that have come to dominate the middle ground between our two worlds.

For the photographers "capturing" this scene it is not important who the Amazon Woman really is. She is only a token as fake as wooden cigar-store Indians, celluloid savages, the noble profiles on nickels, and the potent indigenous symbols borrowed by athletic teams in my part of the world. But what makes this scene fascinating is that Payakan is colluding in the fabrication of the images of his people. He is in fact seducing the media while they in turn are seducing his people: this is a complex, double-edged deal that even the desperate Dr. Faust would have taken time to consider.

Perhaps this is the only way that mass movements can be organized for change, by galvanizing a shared sense of *communitas* through the creation of attractive and identifiable images. Perhaps I should relax and let myself get swept up in the euphoric flow. Isn't that what happened in the sixties? People underwent spontaneous transformations and got in touch with another way of life. Here the Kayapo's efforts do appear to be paying off. They've clearly won the support of the international press, which will make the World Bank think twice about granting the Brazilian government a loan for the Kararaó hydroelectric project. No indigenous group has ever been able to galvanize so much support for one of its causes; this is a truly historic event. Yet somehow as I document the scene I can't escape the feeling that such moments are going to come back and haunt us all someday: Payakan, the journalists, and all those who have made "saving the rain forests" their cause of the day.

The uneasy feeling—the disconnectedness—is reinforced as I focus in close-up on one of the last images of the day. As I look through the lens I am struck by something I didn't notice before. It is the face of the young Kayapo child cradled in his mother's arm as they remain standing in front of the photographers. The expression on his face is one of absolute horror. It appears no one has asked him if he wants to participate in the insanity surrounding him. I steady myself and focus in on his face, and I wonder what will become of this new generation of Kayapo. _____

On my last night in Altamira I leave the Wolf sleeping at the hotel and walk to the Posto Telefônico, a building with a bank of phones for domestic and international calls. I want to contact Patricia Monte-Môr, my friend and researcher in Rio, and also my office in New York, so that I can begin laying the groundwork for selling a story on the Altamira Encounter. If I can ship my tapes back to the States in two days, the story will still be fresh. Any longer and I will probably be beaten by the competition.

I ask directions from an old man with a stubby beard, pushing a dilapidated wooden cart filled with cardboard and pieces of metal.

"*Onde fica a telefônica?*"—Where is the telephone bureau?—I manage to say in another of my pathetic attempts to pronounce this beautiful language.

"*Direto,*" he assures me with a crooked smile as he points down the street. "*Tudo direto.*" Straight ahead.

At this time of night the only illumination on the town's back streets is the bluish light emanating from television sets which spills out from the doors and windows of one-story houses. The old man turns back to his cart and walks on, mumbling to himself so low I can't make out what he is saying. As I pass by a few of the houses I hear the quiet calls of young girls in darkened doorways. "Pssst, pssst," they whisper. "*Gato, vem aqui.*" Cat, come here—playful, seductive advances like these are common in backwater towns. The occasional gringo passing through can represent a ticket out for a desperate young woman or a profitable evening for the professional hooker.

I remind myself not to get involved with either one. Not again. On one of my first trips to the Amazon I spent a wild evening at a nightclub in the backstreets of Belém. My friend Thomas and I had met three young women who were beautiful and fun. We bought them drinks. I spoke my broken Portuguese. We danced and joked all night. It was very casual and friendly, simply a group of young people out having some fun.

Then the negotiations began: How much were we going to pay for sleeping with them tonight? Which motel were we going to take them to? Who was going to pay for the taxi home? I was caught off guard, feeling like the naive gringo. I had not realized that I had been carousing with a group of professional hookers; that had never entered my mind. I had been around the world and back. I thought I could spot a prostitute in any city. But here prostitution is not as cold a transaction as what takes place in cities like New York and London and Paris where street-smart pros working the sidewalks negotiate their deals in a matter of seconds. Here it works differently. There is more seduction involved.

Now as I continue down this side street I hear footsteps behind me, slow and deliberate: stiletto heels on the cobblestones. As I come near the pool of light from the Posto Telefônico I turn and face the person who has been following me: a beautiful dark-haired girl in her early twenties with a curvaceous body packed tightly into a low-cut, silky black dress.

"*Eu quero ser tua mulher*"—I want to be your woman—she says, quickly stepping in front of me as I start towards the stairs of the white brick building. From the corner of my eye I can see two men and a woman talking on the top step. They stop and stare. Up close the smell of her perfume is strong and sweet, as if its power has been enhanced by this dense humid air.

"*Eu não quero,*" I say—I don't want to.

"*Não quero dinheiro.*" I don't want money.

"*Não, obrigado.*" No, thank you.

I move to step around her but she grabs my wrist, clamping down hard, her fingernails cutting into my skin. "*Não quero dinheiro,*" she repeats.

"*Entendo mas não quero.*" I understand, but I am not interested.

Pulling my hand free, I walk up the steps of the Posto Telefônico. Her strength caught me off guard, the experience confusing yet erotic in a way which also caught me by surprise. As I enter the crowded building I decide to call a woman I started seeing just before leaving on this trip. It's been a while since I thought about my home and those parts of my life I left behind. Looking back I can see Ms. High Heels standing in the shadows, her body swaying precariously as she tries to balance in those stilettos on the rocky street. I think about this thing called seduction and how it seems to be so much a part of the fabric of life here. It manages to infuse almost every human interaction—including the reckless economic expansion of the frontier: the bartering, the exchanges, the "courtship" of the missionaries, the interviews of the journalists, the photographic moments, the "teams of attraction." In a land where people want so much and have so little, seduction is a force to be reckoned with.

13

Documentation

journal entry
New York City
1990

Some facts I need to remember:

—*from 1985 to 1990 under the Presidency of José Sarney
inflation in the Brazilian economy rose from 200 percent a year
to 2,000 percent a year. 66 percent of all Brazilians are
classified as poor.*
—*in 1988 two hundred and forty thousand cases of malaria were
reported in the state of Roraima. That number represents 20
percent of the country's population.*
—*900,000 Indians live in all of Amazonia.*
—*the number of Indians in Brazil is 220,000 or .2 percent of the
country's population.*

In 1988 DNPM geologists at the Belem residency, who have more
regular contact with garimpos and garimpeiros than any other
formal-sector mining professionals, estimated 1987 garimpo production at around 120 metric tons of gold. . . . Historically, this
level of production matches and even surpasses the great nine-

teenth-century gold rushes. California from 1848 to 1856 produced an average of 80 tons of gold annually, while the Klondyke
produced a total of 42 tons between 1896 and 1900.

—David Cleary,
Anatomy of the Amazon Gold Rush (1990)

"You know gold ain't like stone in a riverbed. It don't cry out to be
picked up. You got to know how to recognize it. And finding it
ain't all. Not by a long shot. You got to know how to tickle it so
she'll come out laughing."

—Walter Huston, in the film
The Treasure of the Sierra Madre (1948)

In 1939, Lucy Young, a member of the Wintu tribe of northern
California, told a local historian her life story. . . . Mrs. Young
describes her family's terrible experiences during the gold rush
itself. The gold rushers and homesteaders who flooded into California then were responsible for murdering over fifty thousand
Native Americans between 1848 and 1870 alone.

—*Native American Testimony,*
Peter Nabokov, ed. (1991)

Our Lord in his goodness guide me that I may find this gold.

—Christopher Columbus, December 23, 1492

We are exterminating the Indian and doing so in the worst possible
way—by convincing ourselves that we are great humanists,
extending over the Indians wings of protection. . . . This is how you
can interpret all the humanity we have been imposing on the Indian.

—Orlando Villas Bôas

If you can persuade yourself that people who stand in your way are
savages, you can rationalize gunning them down and forcing them
to adapt to your purposes.

—David Maybury-Lewis, "Societies on the Brink,"
Harvard Magazine, 1977

The conquest of the earth, which mostly means the taking it away from those who have a different complexion or slightly flatter noses than ourselves, is not a pretty thing when you look into it too much. What redeems it is the idea only. An idea at the back of it; not a sentimental pretence but an idea; and an unsentimental belief in the idea—something you can set up, and bow down before, and offer a sacrifice to. . . .

—Joseph Conrad,
Heart of Darkness (1902)

"I am honored to be your guest here, and you have treated me kindly," I answer. "I believe that the forest is yours. But the white man has no real home. He is lost in a world that he doesn't understand. He has ceased to communicate with the spirits of the earth and the forest, the river and the air. So he is alone.

"Unhappy, he searches for happiness, and when he sees happiness in others, he become angry and wants to destroy it because inside he is empty. I am not a politician, I am only a singer, but many people listen to me. I promise you that whenever I can speak on your behalf, I will do so. I shall tell your story to whomever I can because you are the protectors of the forest, and if the forest dies, so does the earth. Even a white man can understand this."

Raoni looks content.

—Sting, quoted in "Primal Sting," *Vogue*, 1988

The Indian . . . stands free and unconstrained in Nature, is her inhabitant and not her guest, and wears her easily and gracefully. But civilized man has the habits of the house. His house is a prison.

—Henry David Thoreau, *Journal*, April 26, 1841

Their innocence is as great as Adam's.

—Pedro Alvares Cabral, "discoverer" of Brazil, 1500

Virtuous principals, ideological purity, willingness to die heroically for cherished ideals are no more than white fantasies. Indigenist activists who cultivate such an image do not seem to realize that by demanding it of the Indians they are, in fact, creating a perfection model of the honorable, incorruptible Westerner. The

contrast between the martyr Indian and the sold-out Indian is a
facsimile of the contrast between the honest white and the corrupt
white.
> —Alcida Ramos,
> "The Hyperreal Indian," *Critique of Anthropology* (1994)

This is what happens when the white man destroys. This was a
palm tree rich in fruits. . . . The smoke . . . it's going up in the air
to be carried to who knows what other people. . . . We've been
considered criminals by the government of our country. We took a
trip to Washington at the beginning of this year to help the government of Brazil to preserve our forests. Instead of thanking us,
the government accuses us of being criminals. This is the kind of
deforestation that is committed by the white man.
   And this is another way that white men destroy. This is a mine.
> —Paulinho Payakan, commentary to slide show,
> in Elaine Dewar, *Cloak of Green* (1995)

The nakedness of the inhabitants seemed to be protected by the
grassy velvetiness of the outside walls and the fringe of palm trees:
when the natives slipped out of their huts, it was as if they were
divesting themselves of giant ostrich-feather wraps. . . . It was as if
an entire civilization were conspiring in a single, passionate affec-
tion for the shapes, substances and colours of life.
> —Claude Lévi-Strauss,
> *Tristes Tropiques* (1955)

They have been fashioned very little by the human mind, and are
still very close to their original naturalness. The laws of nature still
rule them, very little corrupted by ours. . . . I am sorry that
Lycurgus and Plato did not know of them; for it seems to me that
what we actually see in these nations surpasses not only all the
pictures in which the poets have idealized the golden age and all
their inventions in imagining a happy state of man . . . there is no
sort of traffic, no knowledge of political superiority, no custom of
servitude, no riches or poverty, no contracts, no succession, no
partitions, no occupations but leisure ones, no care for any but
common kinship, no clothes, no agriculture, no metal, no use of

wine or wheat. The very words that signify lying, treachery, dis-simulation, avarice, envy, belittling, pardon—unheard of. How far from this perfection would he find the republic that he imagined: *Men fresh sprung from the gods.*

—Michel de Montaigne,
"Of Cannibals," *Essays* (1578–80)

It is thus extremely naive to look for ethnology among the Savages or in some Third World—it is here, everywhere, in the metropolis, among the whites, in a world completely catalogued and analysed and then *artificially revived as though real,* in a world of simulation: of the hallucination of truth, of blackmail by the real, of the murder and historical (hysterical) retrospection of every symbolic form—a murder whose first victims were, noblesse oblige, the Sav-ages, but which for a long time now has been extended to all Western societies.

—Jean Baudrillard,
The Process of Simulation (1983)

At the end of 1989, the deputy Helio Campos, renowned for his hatred of the Indians, indulged in obvious scaremongering, which seemed designed to influence military officers in the security forces. He said that the Yanomami and other Indian groups prac-ticed a type of 'tribal socialism,' and that to create large reserves for them on the country's border could be 'the first step towards dismembering these areas from the rest of the country.' He thus proposed that no Indian reserves should be created within 150 kilometers of the frontier and that all Indians living within this zone should be relocated elsewhere in Brazil. Anthropologists and others in Brazil immediately denounced this scheme as 'premedi-tated genocide' and it was eventually dropped.

—Sue Branford and Oriel Glock,
The Last Frontier: Fighting Over Land in the Amazon (1985)

The white men in the East are like birds. They are hatching out their eggs every year and there is not enough room in the East and they must go elsewhere; and they come west, as you have seen them coming for the last few years. And they are still coming, and will come until they overrun all of this country: and you can't prevent it. . . . Everything is decided in Washington by the majority, and these people come out west and see that the Indians have a big body of land they are not using, and they say, "We want that land."

—General George Crook,
during treaty hearings regarding the
Great Sioux Reservation, 1889

This is a promise that I can strongly make: we are going to create a policy of integrating the Indian population into the Brazilian society as rapidly as possible. . . . We think that the ideals of preserving the Indian population within its own "habitat" are very beautiful but unrealistic.

—Mauricio Rangel Reis, Brazil's minister of the interior, 1974

While Mr. Reagan said in Moscow that he was willing to hear the Indians out, he also said: "Maybe we made a mistake. Maybe we should not have humored them in wanting to stay in that kind of primitive life style. Maybe we should have said: 'No, come join us. Be citizens along with the rest of us.' "

—Julie Johnson, *New York Times*, Dec. 13, 1988

The Navahos, squaws, and children ran in all directions and were shot and bayoneted. . . . I then marched out to the east side of the post; there I saw a soldier murdering two little children and a woman. . . . After the massacre there were no more Indians to be seen about the post with the exception of a few squaws, favorites of the officers. The commanding officer endeavored to make peace again with the Navahos by sending some of the favorite squaws to talk with the chiefs; but the only satisfaction the squaws received was a good flogging.

—Captain Nicholas Hodt, 1861, quoted in Dee Brown,
Bury My Heart at Wounded Knee (1970)

journal entry
Rio de Janeiro
August 1988

Questions to be asked of the Yanomami:
—Who is getting sick? Has anything happened to the women?
Have they been shot? Have they tried to protect themselves?
Why haven't they retreated? Are they selling game? Are their
gardens being raided?

But when we reached the waters off Spain, around two hundred of
these Indians died, I believe because of the unaccustomed air,
which is colder than theirs. We cast them into the sea. . . . We dis-
embarked all the slaves, half of whom were sick.

—Christopher Columbus

It will be found, by the united testimony of all that this disease
[gonorrhea brought by whites], more than all other diseases, and
perhaps more than all other causes, is the active agent of destruction of the Indian race.

Senator James R. Doolittle, "Condition of Indian Tribes," U.S.
Congressional Report, 1867

Most Indian tribes "never had a word for Devil until Columbus
landed," [Mary Louise Defender-Wilson, a Northern Sioux] said.
"We have many words to describe a bear. But it wasn't until
Columbus arrived that he brought the Devil."

—*New York Times*, December 13, 1988

One group is coming to Plinio's village just north of here in a few
days. They said they were interested and wanted to hear more about
God. One village, Bocalahudumteri, did not receive them well at all.
They indicated to Roberto that the foreigners were actually the spirits
of dead yanomama that had come back again. Bruce Hartman was
formerly a yanomama that was shot with an arrow and God rubbed
his flesh in some mysterious manner and he came back to life again. I
am also a spirit. They say it is quite obvious because I don't have any

hair on my forehead. Francisco, too, is a spirit. This is quite evident to them because his teeth are loose. (They have never seen anyone with false teeth.) Roberto was telling me how Francisco had eaten a banana and dropped the peeling on the ground. One of the Indians called a small boy and said, "Throw this spirit's banana peeling away."
> —Keith Wardlaw, in the New Tribes Mission journal,
> *Brown Gold*, 1968

In the Amazon, a rubber boom that began in the mid-nineteenth century sent thousands of people up previously uncharted rivers in search of the native rubber tree. . . . When Indians refused to surrender to gradual assimilation, they were targeted for more rapid extermination by grim killers known as *bugreiros*. On one occasion, a German ethnologist, Gustav von Koenigswald, reported that a *bugreiro* "poisoned with strychnine the pools of drinking water of a Kaingang village . . . causing the deaths of some two thousand Indians of all ages." At different times, *bugreiros* organized for the exclusive purpose of hunting Indians.
> —Alan Riding, review of John Hemming's *Amazon Frontier*,
> *New York Times Book Review*, January 31, 1988

Mr. Reagan also drew criticism from some Indian groups for saying in the Soviet Union that a large number of American Indians had become "very wealthy" because the reservations were an oil-producing land. "And you can get very rich pumping oil," Mr. Reagan had said, speaking at Moscow State University.

Today the President, asked if he regretted having mentioned the American Indians' "primitive life style," replied: "I don't recall saying that."
> —Julie Johnson, *New York Times*, December 13, 1988

This country was a lot better off when the Indians were running it.
> —Vine Deloria, Jr., *New York Times Magazine*, March 3, 1970

The Wish to Be an Indian
If only I were an Indian, instantly alert, and on a racing horse, leaning against the wind.
> —Franz Kafka

journal entry
Blue Mountain Lake, New York
1990

Conquest becomes a necessity because the mechanisms of
exchange of the indigenous society are too complex, too time-
consuming to co-exist with the agenda of the outsider. That's why
we have always believed that they must learn our ways and
succumb to our desires.

What the Europeans sought on the coast was, above all, sea-otter
pelts. Between 1785 and 1825, some 330 recorded vessels revisited
the coast. . . . Sea-otter skins were obtained, at first, in return for
iron and tobacco, molasses and muskets. The native American
traders were mostly "chiefs" who mobilized their followers and personal contacts to deliver the otter skins, and whose power grew
concomitantly with the development of trade.
          —Eric R. Wolf, *Europe and the People Without History* (1982)

They . . . brought us parrots and balls of cotton and spears and
many other things, which they exchanged for the glass beads and
hawk's bells. They willingly traded everything they owned. . . .
They were well built, with good bodies and handsome features. . . .
They do not bear arms, and do not know them, for I showed them
a sword, they took it by the edge and cut themselves out of igno-
rance. They have no iron. Their spears are made of cane. . . . They
would make fine servants.
                    —Christopher Columbus, *Log,* 1492

We shall . . . show how our facts contribute to a general theory of
obligation. . . . One gives away what is in reality a part of one's
nature and substance, while to receive something is to receive a
part of someone's spiritual essence. . . . Whatever it is, food, possession, women, children or ritual, it retains a magical and religious hold over the recipient. The thing given is not inert. It is
alive and often personified.
                         —Marcel Mauss, *The Gift* (1925)

Diverse peoples adjust their differences through what amounts to a process of creative, and often expedient misunderstandings. People try to persuade others who are different from themselves by appealing to what they perceive to be the values and practices of those others. They often misinterpret and distort both the values and the practices of those they deal with, but from these misunder-standings arise new meanings and through them new practices— the shared meanings and practices of the middle ground.
—Richard White, *The Middle Ground: Indians, Empires and Republics in the Great Lakes Region, 1650–1815* (1991)

When there is an invasion of Indian territory—and usually it is an illegal one—the Indian for me is really a victim of the non-Indian. But from the moment that the Indian attacks he become the cruel Indian, the one who doesn't deserve anything, right? So what I am saying is for them to continue being victims—that is the best policy for the Indian—to avoid aggression.
—one Senhor Sigfrido, Brazilian Indian Agency employee, to Waiapi Indians complaining of gold miners on their land, 1989

se•duce (si-**doos**) *v*. . . . 1. to persuade (especially into wrong-doing) by offering temptations, *was seduced into betraying his country*. 2. to tempt (a person) into sexual intercourse.
—*Oxford American Dictionary*

Natives were sold to buy wine, oil, vinegar, salt pork, items of clothing, a horse, or whatever else the butcher and his men imag-ined they might need. A man would be invited to choose from among fifty or a hundred young girls the one he most fancied, and she would then be handed over in exchange for an *arroba* of wine or oil or vinegar, or for a side of pork.
—Bartolomé de Las Casas,
A Short Account of the Destruction of the West Indies (1559, published 1875)

The Scythians could not understand what was happening and were at a loss to know where the marauders had come from, as their dress, speech, and nationality were strange to them. . . . The Amazons used to scatter and go off to some little distance in ones and twos to ease themselves, and the Scythians when they noticed this followed suit; until one of them, coming upon an Amazon girl all by herself, began to make advances to her. She nothing loth, gave him what he wanted. . . . The young man then left her and told the others what had happened, and on the next day took a friend to the same spot, where he found his Amazon waiting for him and another one with her. Having learnt of their success, the rest of the young Scythians soon succeeded in getting the Amazons to submit to their wishes.

—Herodotus, "The Amazons," *Histories*, c. 446 B.C.

Did you sleep with any of the Indian women?
    —question repeatedly asked of the author by men and women
        in North America, Europe, and Brazil

ex•ot•ic (ig-zot-ik) *adj.* 1. (of plants, words, or fashions) introduced from abroad, not native. 2. striking and attractive through being colorful or unusual. **ex•ot´i•cal•ly** *adv.* **ex•ot•ic•cism** (ig-zot-ĭ-siz-ĕm) *n.* **exotic dancer**, a striptease dancer.

—*Oxford American Dictionary*

> *Lo, the poor Indian! whose untutor'd mind*
> *Sees God in clouds, or hears him in the wind:*
> *His soul proud Science never taught to stray*
> *Far as the solar walk or milky way;*
> *Yet simple Nature to his hope has giv'n,*
> *Behind the cloud-topp'd hill, an humbler heav'n.*

—Alexander Pope, *An Essay on Man*, 1733–4

It is my wish that nothing My Lord the King, my daughter the Princess, and my son the Prince may do, or allow to be done, shall bring any harm to the Indians living either on islands or terra firma, to either their persons or property. Indeed, they shall see to it that these peoples are treated in a just and kindly fashion.

—Queen Isabella of Spain (1451–1504),
last will and testament

The violence in the countryside is, in its essence, the result of an unjust agrarian structure that, besides generating tensions and deaths for possession and use of the land, constitutes the heart of the problem of accelerating urban growth.
—Antonio Cabrera, Brazil's minister of agriculture and agrarian reform, June 17, 1991

Fifty peasant squatters were rounded up from various estates and from the villages of Monte Sato and Parauna, Pará state, and detained by military police on one of the estates without judicial warrant. Some of the peasants, including children, were bound with rope, many beaten with rifle butts and sticks, two women were raped, and an attempt was made to rape a twelve-year-old girl; all were threatened with summary execution, some forced to eat human and animal excrement, thorns, and lighted cigarettes; some had bottles forced down their throats, and others were subjected to additional degrading and cruel treatment.
—Human Rights Watch, *The Struggle for Land in Brazil* (1992)

Scholars agree that Indians were a particular target when the army broke the peasant revolt in El Salvador in 1932. Some 30,000 people are believed to have been killed, many of them indigenous. The great majority of the Indians who survived abandoned their communities and traditional dress to avoid summary execution, and from then on no longer spoke indigenous languages in public.
—Amnesty International, *The Americas: Human Rights Violations Against Indigenous Peoples* (1992)

The causes which the Almighty originates, when in their appointed time He wills that one race of men—as in races of lower animals—shall disappear off the face of the earth and give place to another race, and so on, in the great cycle traced out by Himself, which may be seen, but has reasons too deep to be fathomed by us. The races of the mammoths and mastodons, and the great sloths, came and passed away: the red man of America is passing away.
—General James Carleton, "Condition of Indian Tribes," U.S. Congressional Report, 1867

I am of the opinion that an area as rich as this—with gold, diamonds, and uranium—cannot afford the luxury of conserving a half a dozen Indian tribes who are holding back the development of Brazil.

—General Fernando Ramos Pereira, March 1975

journal entry
Brasilia
September 1993

The Attorney General's office in Brasilia has tried on three occasions to prosecute cases of genocide resulting from violence against indigenous populations over the last ten years, all of them taking place in remote parts of the Amazon. To date no case has ever been successfully prosecuted. What is more unbelievable is that there has never been a successfully prosecuted case of genocide involving any Indian population anywhere in the Western Hemisphere.

I read an article today where the French filmmaker Jean Rouch refers to the camera as a "thief of reflections."

I am eye. I am a mechanical eye. I, a machine, am showing you a world the likes of which only I can see.

—Dziga Vertov, Russian documentary film pioneer, 1922

14

Just after dawn we drive out to the city's tiny airport in Father John's beat-up yellow Volkswagen, passing Brazilian workers on their way to two-dollar-a-day jobs in Boa Vista's shops and restaurants. Through his open window comes a steady gust of warm air pushing back the priest's shoulder-length salt-and-pepper hair. There is no black shirt and white collar for this Church emissary; traditional priestly garb is now donned only for formal Catholic services. He is one of a new generation of "liberation theologians," Catholic clergy who have allied themselves with the poor and dispossessed and, in the process, rejected certain traditions of the Church that they believe distance them from their flock. Padre Giovanni Saffirio, or Father John as I call him, is a quirky but shrewd Italian cleric who is quickly revealing himself to be Catholicism's answer to James Bond. Today's task of frontier espionage is to smuggle us past the military guard at the airport and get us on one of the Church's planes into Yanomami territory.

"It is a bea-u-ti-ful day, isn't it, Geoffrey," says the good Father, his English delivered in a thick Italian accent overlaid by an American intonation acquired studying anthropology at the University of Pennsylvania several years ago. As we talk he slams his fist on the steering wheel, using each of his impassioned gestures to punctuate a point in the conversation. Today's theme is his interpretation of ethics in a frontier region dominated by politics and miners whom he calls "corrupt, tyrranical, and villainous criminals."

"Boa Vista, ha!" shouts this wild-eyed priest over the sound of his old VW rattling down the highway. "This city is the armpit of the world! I hate this place for what it represents."

"So why do you stay here?"

"This is a good question." He pauses, his head bobbing as he contemplates his response. "Because somebody has to fight back. No? Somebody has to help these poor Yanomami."

"John, to be honest, I think there's a part of you that enjoys all this."

"Yes. This is true. I love to break the law," he says, smiling. "Not in the United States, a country that has protected me and where there is respect for the law, but here in Brazil where no one follows the law." *Boom!* Another hand crashes down on the steering wheel. "When you break the law like we are doing. This is a good thing. This I know you understand. Otherwise you wouldn't be here. No?"

"I'm here to cover a story."

"Yes, I know how you journalists respond. 'I am objective, only interested in facts.' You think I have not heard this kind of answer before?"

"I'm sure you have."

"Yes. I've heard it all before," he says, his face suddenly serious. "Don't forget I am a priest. I am the one who takes the confession. There is nothing I don't know about people. Even you, Mr. Geoffrey."

Boom! Again Father John crashes his hand down on the steering wheel and then begins to laugh to himself.

As we drive on I think about what he calls "breaking the law" and what I choose to call "getting the story." From my perspective we are only doing what forty-five thousand gold miners have been doing for the past two years: flying into an area that has been declared by the military a "national security zone" and remains off limits to any outsiders including journalists, aid agencies, and medical relief organizations. Yet, as Father John and I are both aware, the presence of the military has become more pervasive since I first ventured into the gold camps four months ago. They still give the miners free rein, but covert travel in the region—particularly for foreigners—has become more precarious. Several of my colleagues who have recently attempted to smuggle themselves into Yanomami territory have run into trouble. Some have been apprehended by local officials and their equipment has been seized. Others have been robbed at gunpoint by miners and pilots who entrap them by pretending to act as friendly escorts into the area. Gaining entry today will necessitate getting past the military checkpoint at the runway entrance so we can grab a short flight to a village known as Wakathautheri. This settlement of seventy Yanomami sits next to the Catrimani River and the jungle outpost of Father John's group of missionaries known as the Consolatas, an Italian order of Catholics established in Turin at the turn of the century.

Unlike my past three assignments in the Amazon, this trip I will make without the incorrigible Wolf. In spite of all my complaining I will miss him dearly. "Can't go," he told me over the phone when I called three weeks ago from New York. "My girlfriend is having trouble with me. A *lot* of trouble!" he added. There was then a long pause and a sigh. "Too much time out of Rio. My life is becoming difficult. You understand. No?"

The Wolf seeking to mend his ways? This didn't make sense to me. Yet I understood what he was saying. He was being polite. He'd probably had enough of traipsing about the Amazon with a wide-eyed gringo. The "trouble" he really wanted to avoid was the kind I could get him into: trouble with the miners, trouble with the military, trouble he didn't need in a country making its first tentative steps towards democratic rule. I'll probably never know the truth about his "trouble" in Rio but, one way or the other, I'll miss him. His all-night carousing didn't always produce the best results (sometimes there was no sound on the tape), but the Wolf was always entertaining and always there when I needed him to back me up. He had been the right choice for the roughneck gold camps with their castaway characters. We had more than a few tricky moments there, and I know we wouldn't have gotten through them had it not been for the "old shoe."

Vicent, my new soundman, is a character case in a very

different mold: he's a native of São Paolo as opposed to Rio, his behavior more confined and internalized than that of crazy Mario. "If you are in an Indian community," he told me today, "the most important thing is to be yourself. Don't try to be anything else. That will never work." For twenty years Vicent has roamed the Amazon working as a photographer, indigenous rights activist, and most recently an excellent ethnographic filmmaker. His sly grin, green eyes, and wavy brown hair give him the look of a *malandro,* or scoundrel. But he is an individual with a serious past. In the late seventies, he was jailed for aiding the Frano Indians during a period of sporadic conflicts with the government. That action could have easily placed him in the ranks of the "disappeared" of Brazil, those thousands of people who just vanished after being arrested during the military's dictatorship. His years of working with various indigenous communities will undoubtedly make him more at ease with the Indians and, I hope, help us to break through some of the cultural barriers I confronted at the Paapiú airstrip. Without a doubt, I'll miss Mario. But I know Vicent is the better choice for this particular assignment.

We switch cars outside the airport and pack our things into a dented brown pickup truck also owned by the Church. This last-minute crime-novel maneuver adds another layer of tension and intrigue to our venture. And Father John seems to thrive on each and every one. Over the last few days our meetings in Boa Vista have always been held after dark in small out-of-the-way cafes where the good Father personally knew the proprietors: "friends of the Church." Specific details of the trip—even in these trusted locales—were always delivered in a hushed voice followed by an over-the-shoulder glance. He and his fellow Church emissaries have had their share of death threats. Father John doesn't want to take unnecessary chances.

"Don't talk about this trip to anyone," he warned two nights ago when he dropped me at my hotel. "No one can be trusted here."

Early this morning he instructed us to pack our cameras, tapes, and batteries into nondescript bags. The occasional jokes that leavened our conversations over the last few days have become less frequent as the day progressed. We've agreed that if anyone questions us we will say that we are French doctors working with the Consolata missionaries.

When we arrive at the airport checkpoint, the military guard—a disheveled young boy of nineteen with an M-16 dangling from his shoulder—stops the truck. As he glances about the vehicle Father John mumbles a few words of greeting and a brief explanation of our destination. He is nervous, a little frantic; clumsy in his actions in a way that reminds me of Peter Sellers doing Inspector Clouseau. In my conversations with him I've come to learn that this bumbling-clergyman routine is something Father John has consciously cultivated in Boa Vista, a protective cover that works to his advantage in his encounters with the citizenry, many of whom would like to see him and his fellow "communist priests" expelled from the community. And once again it works: the soldier waves us through with a smile. Score one for Father 007. So much for Brazil's National Security Zone. Another victory in Father John's furtive little war.

It is a quick hop to the missionaries' outpost, one hour in a Cessna 206, this time with seats and safety belts—first-class accommodations compared to the gutted gold miners' Cessnas that the Wolf and I flew just a few months back. Father John has assured us that the pilot is "another friend," someone who can be trusted not to tell the gold miners or the military that two filmmakers entered Yanomami territory today. His immediate superior, the bishop Dom Aldo, is accompanying us on this journey. This is not an overnight stay for the bishop; he'll be returning when the plane flies back this afternoon. This is just a "meet and greet" with the local Indians, to see for himself how their life has changed since the miners have occupied their lands.

Dom Aldo is a tall and affable man in his late sixties with silver gray hair, a broad nose, and weary but intelligent eyes, the kind that can pass judgment on you in a quick flicker. He's also got an eerie distanced quality I am having trouble pinpointing. I've never been close to a bishop before. I didn't know what to expect. But there is something a little discomforting about his presence: he seems too "collected." That's the only way I can describe it. Perhaps my unease is exaggerated by the claustrophobic quarters of this tiny aircraft and the bumpiness of our flight. I assume his elevated position in the Catholic hierarchy has put him in closer touch with God and therefore given him a more otherworldly comportment. Maybe, as one assured of his place in the afterlife, he feels more comfortable up here in the heavens bouncing about in these violent wind pockets.

As for me, I am not certain what awaits me in the world beyond. I haven't thought about it much. It is this world that preoccupies my thoughts, particularly when I get this high up in the clouds. Usually I think about what it would be like to suddenly experience engine failure and crash into the forest. Maybe such thoughts are a reflection of my godless upbringing. My current state of existential being operates in a terrain that could best be described as "suspended judgment": I push ahead full speed through life certain that spiritual redemption awaits me but troubled by the knowledge that I can't clearly decipher the passing signposts. In recent years I have let myself be guided more by circumstance than by the hand of God. I find a kind of solace in not really knowing where I am going and what will happen when I get there. Getting to my next immediate destination is my prime concern. My ultimate end is another story, once again sidetracked by the preoccupations of today's pressing assignment.

After an hour's flight we touch down on a soft grassy track cut from the rain forest and still damp from yesterday's heavy rains. As the plane jogs down the runway I look through the murky plastic window and can see a dozen Yanomami men and women standing about like statues waiting to inspect us, the new arrivals, envoys from the white man's world. The landing of a plane in isolated Indian communities is always a special event complete with its own rituals of reception acted out by adults and children alike. The men and women who have emerged from the forest to witness our arrival are now following us to the far end of the airstrip near the six small buildings that make up the Consolata mission complex. As we turn around at the end of the runway the pilot revs the engine one last time, which sends a powerful blast of air sweeping over a group of children; their ecstatic laughter reminds me of great nights with childhood friends caught in a wind tunnel at a local fair.

Stepping down from the small plane, I catch myself staring at the Yanomami who now congregate around us. The Bishop pats a few Indians on the head, shakes hands with a priest, and strides off in the direction of the group of small wooden houses at the end of the airstrip.

Once again I am struck by what I still find odd about the Indians' appearance: their nudity, the small, thin sticks that have been inserted into the chins of the women, the bowl-shaped hairdos and penis strings of the men. The Indians in turn stare at me, a reminder that I am as much an oddity to them as they are to me: too many clothes, too much strange facial hair, and, I can only imagine, too much of an astonished expression on my face. I've reentered terra incognita, an alien if still recognizable land populated by a people vastly different from my own, a people about whom I know so little.

After lunch in the mission house the bishop suggests we pass out *bolachas*, or cookies, to approximately thirty Indians who have gathered in the patches of shade surrounding the mission complex. I hesitate. Vicent refuses outright. In principle, he is contemptuous of missionaries and feels compromised by the bishop's request. However, Dom Aldo is insistent and goes off to get the packages from the plane.

I am troubled by the patronizing nature of this gesture, fearful that it will initiate a strained dynamic of exchange between the Yanomami and myself that will only lead to further problems in the days to come. But I need to remember that the Consolatas have agreed to put us up and act as our translators. We will also require their help in the coming days. Diplomacy is once again required. I think about what happened with Sabastião at Paapiú, about my reckless pride, the problems it caused us, and the pleas of Mario to be more flexible. So when the bishop returns, he and I pass out the cookies. Vicent takes a breather under a nearby tree.

As we dole out the little round vanilla wafers I am having doubts about playing the diplomat. Perhaps I have become an unconscious dupe in a ritual act of Christian proselytizing: the cookie substituting for the Eucharist, the appetite of the Indians a means of gaining access to their souls. *Am I paranoid?* I ask myself as I hand out the little *bolacha* to grown men and women as well as children. The relationship between religious emissaries and Indians is by no means a simple one. For most of the missionaries in the Amazon, particularly the Protestants, the objective is to "break" the culture of the Indians. But Father John has assured me that the Consolatas are a new breed of evangelist. "We are not interested in proselyting anymore," he told me in Boa Vista. "We respect their way of life. Their beliefs. We know that God is talking to them, so we don't try to change them."

I'd like to believe him but I don't know enough about their "mission" to feel comfortable just yet. Besides, among these people every action takes on a complicated dimension, including this paternalistic act of bestowing *bolacha.* Therein lies the problem. The simplest, most well-intentioned gesture can easily backfire, subverting your mission (be it journalistic or religious), even threatening your life.

"Don't play games with fire, don't talk alone with women on the path, and don't leave the day or the day after someone is sick," the anthropologist Ken Taylor told me when I consulted him about entering Yanomami territory. "If you do the first, they will think that you are practicing sorcery, the second, that you are trying to steal their women, and the third, that you are responsible for afflicting that person with the ailment and are then trying to escape," he said. "These are simple things but they can save your life."

Thinking about Ken's warnings, I start to become nervous about my new role as a novice. What would happen if one of these Indians fell ill tonight? They'd come looking for me, but the cool and collected bishop would be safely ensconced in his prelate's chambers back in Boa Vista. Of course he isn't worried about what he is doing. I'm the one who would suffer the repercussions.

journal entry
6/1/89

Here are a few things I need to remember:

It is the Yanomami tradition for a village to separate after it reaches 75 people. It seems that this pattern is changing as a result of contact with the gold miners. Villages are afraid to split up, fearful that if they splinter off in small numbers they'll become too vulnerable to attacks by bands of miners.

Women go into the forest by themselves to have children beginning at twelve and thirteen years of age. They are assisted by their mothers and grandmothers the first time around. They have the children on their own after that.

I saw a Tapir today, something that looks like a pig with a long curling nose. Supposedly it can swim.

The Padre tells me we are one and a half degrees above the equator. No wonder it's so unbelievably hot.

We are lucky to have arrived here when we did, catching a clear day at the start of the rainy season. Showers will come more frequently now, followed by torrential downpours, thick walls of precipitation that come rumbling through the forest sweeping over you in a matter of seconds. It makes everything difficult; filming, eating, even walking become laborious, painstaking chores. Nothing stays dry. Life in the village is also restricted: less visitation, less hunting, and a general reduction in activity as people seek the shelter of the maloca to avoid the heavy sheets of rain that can last for days at a stretch. I did consider postponing this return to the forest—my back has been giving out, contracting into spasms after only a few hours of shooting—but if we had waited another two weeks there is no way I would have been able to get into this part of Yanomami territory. It will soon be closed off for several months. Rainstorms, short ones, are blowing through every day. The airstrip is slowly dissolving into one large, grassy swamp. It is uncertain whether we will be able to fly out as planned. And still this story remains unresolved. No one to date has brought back any images or concrete evidence that, as they're saying in the cities, a malaria epidemic is raging in the forest. Miners claim the rumors are circulated by the missionaries, and call them fanatical alarmists. The Consolatas respond by accusing the prospectors of genocide. Gold and God emerge once again as catalytic forces in the conquest of the Americas.

————————

After dispensing the last of his cookies, the bishop pats a few more Indians on the head, climbs into his plane, and flies back to Boa Vista. As we stand on the airstrip watching the little Cessna disappear in the distance, our new host, the resident priest Padre Guilherme, apprises us of the current "plight" of the Indians. He is a short, intense man in his late thirties, a chain smoker with blond hair, thick black glasses, and the hard, wiry body of a middleweight boxer. He doesn't really speak but hurls words at you in a rapid-fire staccato that I have come to associate with a certain type of impassioned advocate. In listening to his assessment of the miners' recent incursions, I find myself missing the flamboyant sensationalized accusations of Father John. Guilherme's account is a drier, more rhetorical analysis of the culture shock, violent threats, and, he says, increase in disease that have accompanied the miners' recent penetrations into this part of Yanomami territory. He is probably a more reliable source than his fellow clergyman but still one whose accounts will need to be double-checked. He and John do share a characteristic that I am beginning to believe is common to all Italian clerics in the Amazon: a wild-eyed look that seems to proclaim that they will do whatever is necessary to carry out God's agenda.

As we walk the soggy airstrip towards the six small buildings that comprise the Consolata mission, Guilherme describes the gold rush in this area as if he were talking about an approaching army.

"The sounds of the gold miners' boats passing on the river will make the hunters stop dead in their tracks," he says. "You should see them twisting their heads as they try to gauge the distance by the sound of the echo in the forest."

He stops for a moment to light another cigarette, the third or fourth—I'm losing count—that he has smoked in the last half hour.

"How have the miners been getting in here?" I ask.

"They've been gaining entry by truck on the abandoned portion of the Northern Perimeter Highway that ends just over there," he says, thrusting his arm in the direction of a cluster of trees at the far end of the airstrip. I can't see any signs of a roadway but I know from my map that it is supposed to be very close. "It was constructed in the 1970s and shut down within a few years. The Indians were dying from measles and tuberculosis brought in by the highway workers." He pauses for a moment as he weighs what he is about to say next. "There was also a big problem with syphilis and gonorrhea."

"Who is letting them through now?" Vicent asks. "The military or the Indian Agency?"

"The highway checkpoint is controlled by the Indian Agency," he says as he draws on the remaining inch of his hand-rolled cigarette. "They are the ones letting them through. Just last week a Czechoslovakian anthropologist tried to go undercover with a group of gold miners but he was pulled from the truck." Guilherme takes another drag on the cigarette pinched between fingers stained yellow by the tobacco. "They just sent him back to Boa Vista and let the miners on through. That's the Indian Agency that is supposed to be protecting the Indians."

Guilherme drops his cigarette and crushes it into the dirt with his foot. When he looks up he simply stares at us, looking first at Vicent and then at me. We lock eyes for a fragment of a second and I can see him squinting from beyond those big black glasses. He appears to be carrying out a personal ritual of assessment before committing to take us on a tour of the mission.

"So, what is it you want to see?" he says.

I ask him to introduce us to the people of Wakathautheri and we head off in the direction of their village, which sits only fifty yards from the Church's complex.

Similar to the one at Paapiú, this maloca is a large enclosed thatched structure. Ducking through the small opening that serves as a doorway, I can immediately tell that this village is in what anthropologists call a situation of controlled contact between cultures. It is completely different from the chaos I witnessed at Paapiú. These people have obviously been living in a state of peaceful semi-isolation with the missionaries for quite some time. Undoubtedly there have been problems between the Consolatas and the Yanomami, but these Indians don't show any of the trauma that overwhelmed the villagers at Paapiú. On the contrary, there is a semblance of relaxed order to the living environment. Groups of families gather around individual hearths that line the perimeter of this cylindrical structure, while some children are laughing and playing games in the center of the maloca. Three women at three separate fires are cooking in blackened metal pots. But most of the adults are just sitting about in hammocks, taking a break from the bitter heat that has arrived with the clear weather.

Speaking to various villagers, I begin to detect an underlying tension seeping through the conversations. As Guilherme has told us, the nearby presence of a group of miners had become an unnerving fact of life for these villagers.

One man cleaning a turtle for dinner waves for us to come over to him. He calls himself Machadão—roughly, Big Ax. His command of Portuguese consists of a rough mix of nouns thrust up against an occasional verb. It sounds a lot like the way I speak Portuguese. I would guess—by the number of his children and the wrinkles around his eyes—that he is in his mid- to late thirties. I'll ask the priest about that later. Missionaries often get fanatical about recording the births and deaths of villagers, which provides them with important statistical barometers for evaluating the success of their "mission"—and also a means of occupying their time.

"A lot of gold miners come over here. Now I am afraid," Machadão says.

"Why?"

He rips out a large piece of turtle intestine and tosses it to the side. I hope that it is not going to be part of the evening's meal. Father John had mentioned that, on occasion, we might be eating with the Indians.

"Too much coughing sickness," he says in answer to Vicent's question. "Gold miners have a lot of the coughing sickness."

"Do you have coughing sickness now?" Vicente asks.

"Yes, I am afraid," he says. "And with my father. In his time we had much."

Guilherme, who has been playing with Machadão's children, waits for him to finish and then adds his own thoughts. "The leaders here, like that man over there named Carrera"—he points across the maloca, fixing his glasses as they slide down his nose—"are now sending extra men with the women to the gardens because they are worried that the gold miners are going to steal their women."

He translates briefly what he is saying for Machadão, who continues to watch us as he goes about the bloody task of extracting and unraveling the organs and lengthy intestines from the shell of what must have been a giant turtle. Placing a hand on Machadão's shoulder, he continues.

"This man knows what it is like to suffer from his encounters with the white man. In the 1950s his people—they were from another village—they came in contact with a group of rubber tappers in the forest. Soon after, everyone came down with pneumonia. He lost his first wife and most of his family. Only Machadão—" He stops for a moment and asks him a question, then continues. "Yes. Only Machadão, his mother, and his brother survived."

I jot a few notes in my journal, reminders of scenes to shoot, some background on this villager's life, questions to ask in the coming days. As I write I can see Machadão staring at me. Although theirs is an illiterate society, we've been told his oldest son has started taking classes at the mission school. I look up and catch his eye. He gestures with his head to the paper, smiles, and lets forth a high-pitched cackle. He then returns to the work of extracting bits of meats from the turtle, still chuckling to himself. I like this guy. He could become the focus of our work here, his story a way of personalizing what has been happening to these people.

Leaving Machadão, we continue to move in a circle around this large communal structure, going from family to family, introducing ourselves and explaining that we will be filming them over the next few days. Already I can see that access to the Yanomami will be much easier at Catrimani than at Paapiú. But while photographers, anthropologists, and some journalists have been to this area before, the presence of a camera is still rather unique to them. I won't film today. I want to be careful about the way I introduce the camera into their daily lives.

As we greet the various families sitting in clusters of hammocks, Padre Guilherme explains that within the current worldview of these Yanomami outsiders like ourselves fall into a different category than the gold miners. The whites here at Mission Catrimani, he tells us, have been appropriated by the Yanomami. Since Vicent and I are with the missionaries we fall into the category of "their whites," whites owned by these villagers, not to be shared by other communities. We are perceived differently from the gold miners. Those whites want to take their land. And us? We give them cookies.

journal entry
Wakathautheri Village
6/3/89

Today we met Machadão. He comes from the group Waka. Machadão is his Portuguese name, his Yanomami name is never spoken, a custom to ensure protection of the spirit. He is also a shaman, an intellectual in his community, someone responsible for the relationship of his village to the spiritual world and, since the arrival of the miners, with this world.

A rapport was struck up between us right away that probably has more to do with inexplicable, non-translatable, aspects of our personalities than anything else. It can be seen in the pauses between exchanges in conversations. The body relaxes, no longer trying to overcompensate with gestures for the inadequacies of speech. It's in moments like these that nonverbal signals of trust are exchanged. I also look to the eyes when I work with cultures whose languages I don't speak. I search for a quality, a connection. I saw it in his eyes. I think he saw it in mine. I'd like to do an interview with him for our documentary, something that could also be used in some spin-off news reports. Maybe he is someone who could tell us the full story about what is happening here. Maybe though I am deceiving myself. Maybe that's what happened to Padre Calleri?

In Boa Vista Father John told me that the Consolata missionaries had attempted to establish ongoing contact with the Yanomami as far back as 1952. Over a period of thirteen years they sent priests on sporadic missions up various rivers in futile attempts to lure the Indians from the forest. Although the Yanomami in this region had been contacted by the Indian Protection Service in the 1940s, it wasn't until Padre Giovanni Calleri became part of the contact expeditions that the Consolatas began to show some success. This robust Italian priest entered the forest with a head of steam and an unbending will. He worked too hard, often pushing himself from dawn to dusk, frequently going without meals and ignoring the complaints of colleagues who wanted to stop and take a break. In October of 1965, after two weeks of traveling by canoe through Yanomami territory, Father Calleri and Father Bindo Mendelosi landed on the banks of the Catrimani River, claiming it as the site of their Catholic mission. There they set out immediately to contact the Indians by the practice of *atração* or attraction.

This technique, perfected by Brazil's Indian Protection Service under the tutelage of Colonel Rondon, consisted of using objects to lure Indians from the forest. Teams of men known as *frentes da atração*, attraction fronts, spent months at a time in the forest. The objects they brought with them were knives and machetes but also glass beads in bright colors and mirrors. They were usually left hanging from trees strategically placed on Indian paths or at the entrance of an uncontacted village. Steel products were the most prized possessions. They could revolutionize an indigenous community almost overnight. A metal ax in the hands of a Yanomami will cut through a tree six times faster than a stone ax. Knives and machetes perform similar miracles in clearing forests and constructing houses.

It was precisely a miracle that Father Calleri must have thought he was witnessing on the banks of the Catrimani River. Within three days of his arrival a group of Yanomami came to visit. According to Father John, Calleri bestowed upon them more "gifts" of machetes, axes, and "mirrors for the women." This began what the Consolata missionaries referred to as *namoro*, their courtship of the Yanomami. After a few days this initial group of Indians disappeared into the forest, returning two weeks later with a dozen other villagers. There on the opposite bank of the Catrimani River these Yanomami set up a temporary village and garden. In just a few short weeks Father Calleri had succeeded where his fellow missionaries had failed. The Yanomami had been attracted, courted, and finally seduced into maintaining an ongoing contact with the Consolatas. "Before the white men arrived," a Yanomami shaman at Wakathautheri told me, "we sharpened the points of our arrows with rodents' teeth, we cut up our game with bamboo, that's how we lived until we first encountered the whites." As a result of these contacts—first with the Indian Protection Service and later with the missionaries—the Indians had a new time frame introduced into their worldview: events were dated with reference to the introduction of material goods from outside the forest. Their culture had changed, forever.

Meeting the whites transformed not only the Indians' understanding of the outside world but also their relationship with the network of 350 communities scattered throughout this corner of Brazil. Padre Calleri eventually learned that one reason for his success in luring the Yanomami from the forest was that their society was predisposed to the exchange of goods. Such exchanges were, and continue to be, a vital part of the fabric of their culture. When one Yanomami community goes to visit another, gifts of metal objects and ceremonial food are lavished upon the visitors. Such ritual exchanges obligate the visiting community to reciprocate at a later date by hosting a similar feast in their village. These traditional interchanges are part of the way in which alliances between communities are formed. They also open the way for personal relationships to develop, for young people to meet and marry. They are a kind of social adhesive that binds together Yanomami culture.

When Padre Calleri arrived here he probably thought he and his colleagues had stumbled into a missionaries' paradise. Their gifts of manufactured metal objects were extremely popular. Within the first three years of contact, the village opposite the river grew to be five times its original size.

The Indians who relocated there solidified the trading relationship with the priests while excluding other groups who were competing to gain access to these benevolent white men and their seemingly endless supply of valuable goods. This was the beginning of what Father Guilherme called "being appropriated" by the Indians. They weren't stupid. They had their own agenda which came from their culture. They wanted to control for themselves this vital link to trade goods. That was their stake in the creation of this new middle ground. It was an investment, a way of propelling their society into the realm of manufactured objects while bypassing the laborious and painstaking phase of industrialization. When you look at it from their perspective, it was a pretty good deal.

What the good Padre Calleri did not know at the time was that his success with the Yanomami would also ensure his downfall. In October of 1968 this Italian cleric, owing to the breakthroughs he had made with the Yanomami, was asked by the Indian Agency—then under the control of the military—to help make contact with a group of hostile Indians known as the Waimiri-Atroari. They had been killing dozens of highway workers who were involved in a project to connect the port city of Manaus with the frontier town of Boa Vista by a roadway called BR-174. This was in the early stages of the dream scheme to open up the Amazon and the government was determined to push through the project in spite of the violent attacks by the much feared Waimiri-Atroari. Brimming with confidence from his courtship of the Yanomami, Father Calleri accepted the mission to make contact and pacify this unregenerate tribe. Using a small boat specially fortified with protective walls, he went upriver into their territory. After this initial trip he reported that it would take six months to safely make inroads into the hostile society. But the local military commander rejected Calleri's evaluation. Ignoring the historical evidence of the need for a protracted attraction process, the officer convinced Calleri to enter the territory on foot via the roadway that had been partially constructed. "To this day we don't know why Calleri accepted to do such a thing," Father John told me.

In October of 1968 the obstinate cleric and a team of six men and two women flew in a military transport plane to the end of the roadway. There Calleri led his party on foot into the forest, perhaps confident that his experience among the Yanomami had provided him with the key to pacifying the Waimiri-Atroari. On October 31, 1968, he radioed back to a group of nuns at their mission in Manaus. He told them: "Pray for us because if we don't succeed arrows will start flying." They were never heard from again. Fearing the worst, the nuns contacted the local military commander. Two weeks later a team of soldiers discovered Calleri and the others in the forest. They had been bludgeoned and shot at close range with the long deadly arrows of the Waimiri-Atroari, their bloated bodies left to rot in the harsh equatorial heat.

The military response was to close off the area. For several years the project was abandoned. Then in 1974 SUDAM, the government highway department, resumed work on BR-174, this time in conjunction with FUNAI, the newly established Indian Agency. FUNAI started using a more aggressive approach to the courtship process. On a weekly basis they flew over villages in helicopters dropping gifts of machetes, beads, and mirrors. They also set up "posts of attraction" along the rivers. But the Waimiri-Atroari were fiercely resistant. In the first months of 1974 they launched four attacks, killing fifteen Indian Agency employees and highway workers. Then, in December of that year, four more government workers were killed, including the local director of the Indian Agency's pacification effort. Eventually, and at considerable expense, the Waimiri-Atroari were subdued, but not before their population had been reduced from two thousand to three hundred. The roadway, completed in 1976, is often flooded and can only be used at certain times of the year.

The "tragedy of Father Calleri," as Father John refers to it, is that he learned his most important lesson too late. The rules and logic of one society of Indians do not apply to another. The Waimiri-Atroari were not the same people as the Yanomami. There are more than 170 different indigenous groups living in the rain forest north of the Amazon River. Each has its own specific historical relationships with outsiders. Unlike the Yanomami who had been avoiding outside contact for five centuries, the Waimiri-Atroari had a history of violent antagonisms with whites throughout the nineteenth and twentieth centuries. When Calleri's expedition of eight soul-seekers arrived in their territory, the Waimiri-Atroari probably found them indistinguishable from the bands of whites who had destroyed their forests and murdered their relatives in centuries past. Calleri walked straight into an incipient ambush, blinded by the belief that God was on his side. He was not the first white person nor would he be the last to suffer such a fate: reckless hubris seems endemic to whites on the frontier, regardless of whether they are missionaries or gold miners or journalists.

As Father John Saffirio said in speaking of his late predecessor, "It is very dangerous to be a fearless man."

15

journal entry
Mission Catrimani
6/5

Pedro, a local villager leader, says he gave two hundred
bunches of bananas to the gold miners three months ago and
now he is still waiting for payment. He has two wives: one in
Jundia and one here in Catrimani. His father was killed by
Brazilian rubber tappers when he was four. After lunch he
told us the myth of the origin of white people. He and his
friend Joaquim laughed the entire time especially when they
did their imitations of the way white people talk.

   The political roles are complicated here. José, Carrera,
and Pedro are tuxawas who are the village leaders separate
from the shamans who oversee the spiritual life of the
communities. A few years ago Carrera hit his brother, Luis (a
tuxawa) with a machete in a fight over the division of meat.
The son of Luis, José, is now a tuxawa and holds Carrera
responsible for the death of his father. The communities
have been splitting up along these divisions. Family members
and friends from one side have set up a separate village on
the other side of the airstrip not far from here. We might go
over there tomorrow. I wonder if that will cause any
problems with the group we are staying with now?

These days Mission Catrimani is administered by both Father Guilherme and Sister Florence. We met her briefly upon our arrival with the bishop, but she spent the majority of the afternoon separate from us, caring for a few of the Indians at the mission's small medical clinic. Florence, who is also a nurse, is a tall, stocky black woman with enormous hands. She appears to be in her mid-forties. Originally from Guyana, she speaks Portuguese, broken English, and fluent Yanoman. I have already started to think of her as the Amazon's equivalent of Mother Teresa—a dedicated woman of the Church who spends endless hours caring for these inhabitants of the forest. Guilherme, on the other hand, I would describe as Father Workaholic. In the course of a two-hour period his schedule will include fixing the mission generator, instructing Indians on the use of the motorboat, and teaching a class in Portuguese to the children. These tasks are accomplished with the utmost efficiency, the wheels of discipline and progress spinning forward at a rapid clip. In their combined efforts at this outpost for Christ, these missionaries over the last decade seem to have gained the trust of the Indians. And the Yanomami, in turn, have made a lasting impression on the Church emissaries.

"I like the Yanomami, I like to serve the Yanomami and, I would even say, I adore the Yanomami," says Father Guilherme towards the end of an interview we are conducting with him under the shade of a tree on the mission grounds. "I learned their language. I learned to appreciate everything that is theirs and, in this way, I would even say that if I could be born again, I would be born a Yanomami."

When I hear that phrase I shut off the camera for a moment because I can't believe it. To be certain, I lean across to Vicent and ask him to translate the final part of the interview.

"Yes," he says. "He wants to be reborn a Yanomami."

I look back at Guilherme, who is smiling, his body trembling slightly from his constant nicotine infusions. The interview up to now has not been all that unusual, but, knowing these priests, I had expected a guilt-ridden revision of the history of Catholics and Indians in Brazil in which his generation has emerged to make amends for his predecessors. During this past "any Indian who converted to Christianity was a dead Indian," he had told us just a few minutes ago. Now they have opted for "a new form of evangelization. We are here to serve the Indians."

Something, however, is becoming apparent here that Father Calleri would never have expected: Guilherme seems to have been seduced by the very Indians originally seduced by his predecessors. The tables are turning. This priest is dangerously close to "going native." He is, in a way, a benevolent version of Joseph Conrad's Kurtz, the crazed explorer who disappears upriver in Africa in *Heart of Darkness*. Whereas for this missionary the desire to become one with another culture is an attractive fantasy, Conrad's Kurtz is portrayed as living a nightmare where "his—let us say—nerves went wrong, and caused him to preside at certain midnight dances ending with unspeakable rites." Interestingly enough, Kurtz, like Guilherme, had been sent into the jungle with a mission. He was there to write a report for the "International Society for the Suppression of Savage Customs."

journal entry
Mission Catrimani
6/3/89

Got woken in the middle of the night by the most insane raving and chanting I have ever heard in my life. It was the wild child from the village, a boy who looks like he's sixteen but could be thirty. A man but possibly an animal. He is the one who rants and raves during the day walking through the village unwashed, unkempt and whacked out. When we flew into the village he positioned himself under the wing of the plane and sat, squatting and mumbling to himself. Today we started to call him "Pierrot le Fou" after the character in the Godard film.

Last night he stayed in front of our door spinning in circles and screaming the most bizarre primal chant. There is a guttural noise that emerges from his throat that sounds as if his lungs were being torn from his chest with each utterance. He is not a shaman, so there were no justifying ritual associations for his behavior. Vicent and I nervously joked about who was going to go outside and calm him down. Eventually the priest came with a plate of food which did the trick. It seems he gets out of control from time to time and a little nourishment is the best tranquilizer.

I guess it is only by day that Father Guilherme flirts with the idea of becoming an Indian because at night he retreats into the world of the white man. The meals I have shared with the missionaries so far reflect the uneasy and ambiguous relationship that Westerners have with the cultures of the forest. Each night at the Consolata mission the traditions of our world are enacted: Sister Florence does the cooking as well as the dishes, while the Father reads the paper with his coffee after the meal. A BBC radio program runs continuously in the background, drowning out the soft sounds of the forest nighttime.

Throughout the evening various Yanomami men, women, and children pass by, peering through the screen doors and windows, silent silhouettes with their faces distorted as they press up against the wire mesh. Occasionally they will stand there asking for *bolacha, bolacha,* but most of the time they are just staring. You get the impression that your meal is open to the public—that you are part of a stage play revealing how people from outside the forest eat and pass their time. This, of course, is natural to the Yanomami. Theirs is a communal existence. They all consume their food together and sleep in one vast lodging. What are not natural to them are the doors, the screens, the privacy that is enforced here at the mission. Who, they ask, are this man and this woman who spend so much time alone together, who work together, who cook and eat together, yet are not husband and wife? These alien beings have entered their space, their forest, their world, even speak their language—and yet here at the mission, less than a two-minute walk from their village of Wakathautheri, a vastly different set of customs prevails.

Of course, the missionaries are from another culture, one that must be respected even though it has been transported here. The house is not a communal structure. Meals are eaten at a table. Tobacco is smoked, not chewed. And if a Yanomami tries to enter the room, a quick word from Sister Florence sends him away.

The message is clear: the missionaries want to be close to the Indians but a line has to be drawn. The intermingling of cultures is fine as long as it is on the terms of the missionaries. They control the supply of manufactured products, so they make the rules. A balance of power has been struck, less overtly manipulative than the gold miners' but equally clear. That is what bothered me on that first day with Dom Aldo. I can see that now.

Perhaps Sister Florence and Father Guilherme are trying to avoid the fatal mistake made by their predecessor Father Calleri. They are taking nothing for granted, delineating strict limits while keeping in check their own curiosities about the world of the Indians. It is as if they are afraid of going over the line, crossing the blurred boundaries of this now familiar but still alien culture. They are attracted but afraid, two common preconditions of many forms of seduction.

In my experience the fear is shared by most outsiders who enter the territory of the Indians. Be they gold miners or missionaries or anthropologists, they warn themselves: keep one foot always in "your" world, don't allow yourself to be completely overwhelmed by the Indians, don't go too far into their terrain. Getting back might become very difficult. Perhaps this is why Father Guilherme would welcome a second life when he could cross over into their world without hesitation—could start with a clean slate, free of the baggage of his culture, unconstrained by the precedents of his ancestors. Perhaps also he knows that in that other life there could never be someone who would come for him—another priest perhaps—as Marlow had come for Kurtz, trying:

> to break the spell—the heavy, mute spell of the wilderness—
> that seemed to draw him to its pitiless breast by the awak-
> ening of forgotten and brutal instincts, by the memory of
> gratified and monstrous passions. This alone, I was con-
> vinced, had driven him out to the edge of the forest, to the
> bush, towards the gleam of fires, the throb of drums, the
> drone of weird incantations; this alone had beguiled his
> unlawful soul beyond the bounds of permitted aspirations.

16

In the morning we travel with Machadão, chopping our way through the forest in search of a tapir—three and a half hours nonstop through brown, murky swamps, then rivers and soggy paths covered with slippery wet grass, an obstacle course of protruding roots, sharp branches, and fallen trees. Machadão sets the pace, dexterously moving across the terrain, barefoot and wearing nothing but the traditional penis string—the small piece of twine the Yanomami ties around his foreskin and then pulls back around his waist. It hurts just to look at it, yet it also makes perfect sense for their lifestyle. My rain-soaked clothes are extremely cumbersome, making this work even more grueling. I guess I continue to wear them out of habit. I too am not ready to go native.

To cross rivers we have to march waist-deep through strong currents, our equipment held above our heads. We then have to run full speed down narrow, slippery trails in search of game. Already we must have traveled twelve miles. This is easily the most difficult work I've done in the Amazon. Occasionally I am able to grab shots of Machadão as he tiptoes his way through the forest in search of the cunning tapir, a long-nosed beast that somewhat resembles a pig and yet can swim across a river in a matter of seconds. But the weight of the camera seems to be increasing as the humidity sucks away at my energy.

Throughout this trip the Yanomami have been making fun

of Vicent and me, cackling and chanting as we white men stumble through the forest trying to keep up. Our native escorts are following an elaborate system of paths that would have been imperceptible to me in this dense web of vines, trees, and swamp. I can only assume that all the joking is intended to urge us on in the sardonic manner that I am quickly learning is the basis for Yanomami humor, one that finds in the failings of others the basis for comedic relief.

Occasionally we are lucky enough to find footing on a muddy path, but it usually isn't long before we are back waist-deep in the cold, murky waters that seem to dominate this region, an ecological necessity for rain forest preservation but a severe hindrance for hunters or for any filmmakers attempting to accompany them. Miraculously, however, the equipment doesn't get wet and Vicent and I find the energy to keep up.

When we reach a stretch of dry path I take a moment to pull out my still camera for a snapshot of myself. As I push down on the shutter I can imagine the image that will be developed upon my return to New York. I have seen myself in other photos brought back from the Amazon: bearded and beaten and rain-soaked, a vacant, vaguely puzzled look in my eye, as if my soul had been taken from me and replaced—in the split second of a shutter—by something I don't really understand. Upon first viewing, I usually find these snapshots disturbing—a glimpse into a part of myself that I'm seeking but afraid to come to terms with. Usually I toss them into a back drawer in my studio, forgetting almost immediately that I have taken them. Then, months later, they resurface and I am compelled to witness again my own private ritual of self-documentation reminding me that I am drawn to this region because of the sense of escape it provides. But now no sooner have I taken this self-portrait than I have lost sight of Machadão, who has disappeared around a bend in the path. So I step once more waist-deep into the swamp, the Yanomami cackling behind me as I trip over another root in this endless expanse of brown water and thick, clinging muck.

In order to survive as a Yanomami you must be able to hunt, and Machadão is one of the best in Wakathautheri. He has the reputation of being a deadly marksman. The rifle he carries belongs not to him but to the missionaries, a precious item from our world loaned to the hunters on a case-by-case basis. Of the dozen men on this trip, the majority carry bows and arrows. Most of them are dressed in bathing suits also obtained from the missionaries. Only a few wear the traditional penis string sported by Machadão. The quest here is for meat—*nagi*—the preferred source of protein in their culture. A man's honor is tied to his ability to provide it for his family. And Machadão appears to be feeling the demands of his role. When we met him this morning he was nervous and edgy.

"Many days," he told us. "It is many days that my children have not had meat." The Yanomami numerical system does not go beyond two. By my calculation he meant to tell us that it's been four days since they've eaten meat.

"And today, Machadão?" Vicent asked.

"Today I will kill a tapir," he responded with a big smile.

Machadão's wife and children have been subsisting on fruit found in the forest and vegetables from their garden. But, he tells us, they've been asking for *nagi*. The tapir we are trailing was wounded by Machadão the day before but escaped from him just after nightfall.

Accompanying Machadão on this hunt has given me a new sense of respect for these people. This is difficult, exhausting work: survival in this forest means a constant cycle of hunting, foraging, and planting. Most Yanomami villages are semi-nomadic. They move on average every two years, seeking out new gardens and unexploited hunting grounds. When the people of Machadão's village decided to settle next to the missionaries, they broke this traditional cycle, forcing them to travel farther into the forest in search of wild game. And now the arrival of the miners is exacerbating the problem. Local prospectors have been competing with the Indians for wild game, causing severe reductions in an already scarce resource.

After four hours on the trail we finally catch up with the wounded tapir at the edge of a river. Everyone now stops and listens; the hunters' eyes dart about the forest in search of their prey. I glance away from Machadão for a moment to power up the camera. When I look back he has disappeared into the

thick wall of vines and trees that surrounds us. I charge off in
the direction where I believe he has gone, which is into a dense
area of trees and vines. After just fifteen yards I collide into a
bee's nest, providing my Yanomami companions with still more
comic relief: the white man swirling in circles, swatting the
bees as he slips and slides, trying to maintain his footing on the
soft floor of muddy leaves, his cumbersome clothes caught in
the thorny branches of an adjacent tree, cursing to himself in a
series of angry expletives, which, to them, must sound like the
dying shrieks of a bludgeoned pig.

Minutes later we all sit huddled together in the pouring rain,
the Yanomami smacking away flies with their machetes, occasionally looking up at me and laughing as my head swells to the
size of a melon from the bee stings. We are waiting to see if
Machadão returns. In the interim, Vicent and I use our pon-
chos to try to protect the equipment. I think of the shots I was
able to get, wondering whether there will be enough to put a
sequence together.

After a while it is obvious Machadão is not coming back, so
we head home, single-file, on what I estimate will be a two-
hour trek. The jocular banter that accompanied us on the earlier part of our journey has disappeared. Everyone is overcome
with exhaustion. For now there is only the steady sound of rain
hitting the leaves of the forest.

An hour after our return, I see Machadão quickly enter the
village and dart into the maloca. There's no sign of the tapir.
No meat for his wife and children tonight.

journal entry
Mission Catrimani
6/4

There is a kind of exchange going on here. During the day I
move about throughout their village staring at them through
the lens of my camera. At night, I put down the camera and
they stare at me, coming to my window and looking in one
by one, as if Vicent and I are on display for them.

Tonight Machadão and his family came to visit. This is

the third day he has failed in the hunt. I gave them my camping kit. Was that the token gift of the guilty white liberal or simply an attempt to reciprocate in a manner consistent with their culture? Fact is that he's done a lot for me in the last few days. He deserves it.

I've been reading some books about the Yanomami in the missionaries' library. The anthropologists refer to their funerary rites as "endocannibalism." It's a form of cannibalism. *Endo* as opposed to *exto* means they eat their own people rather than others. They don't actually eat the bodies, but they consume the ashes of the pulverized bones after the deceased has been cremated. It is done only in the case of children. When adults die, their ashes are buried near the families' fireplace in the communal lodging. The whole ritual is said to make certain that the spirit has some place to go, so that he or she is not lingering about.

17

In the late afternoon of the next day we do an interview with Machadão outside the maloca. Although the tapir continues to elude him, he is in better spirits today. His wife's brother brought back three turtles from a forage in the forest. It's enough meat to keep the family satisfied at least temporarily. As we set up our equipment, the warm light of the afternoon falls across the forest giving the flora a rich green hue. Above the line of trees in the background I can see the sky, bright blue and streaked with thin white clouds. Most of the villagers are inside the maloca at this time of day, resting and preparing their meals. Occasionally a child appears at the doorway, makes a face, and darts back inside. Machadão has his face and body painted with a bright orange vegetable dye, a preparation not (I trust) for the cameras but perhaps to complement his positive change in mood. "Tomorrow I will go kill the tapir," he says as he raises both arms to mimic the shooting of a rifle.

I have spent three months planning this trip with a view to getting an interview with one or more Yanomami in their own language—thereby, perhaps, illuminating the still impenetrable terrain of their culture, which has remained hidden from the world since the start of the gold rush. Now over the last several days I have observed Machadão closely, trying to determine how he would come across on camera, whether he would be relaxed and forthright in his opinions, whether he could speak about his people from an informed perspective. I am being careful because I know I'll have only one chance for an in-depth interview with one of these Indians. I have very little battery power and I can't keep bothering Father Guilherme to serve as our translator. I've considered approaching other villagers but they don't seem as engaging as Machadão. As a shaman, he is one of the intellectual leaders in the community and it shows in his grasp of Yanomami history and cosmology.

I also thought it would be interesting to interview a woman. But now I realize that to do so would mean crossing a barrier even more formidable: not only of culture but of gender. The problem I face in this community is not so much fear; it's getting them to take the interview (and me) seriously. Lately when I have inquired of the village women about a particular custom or practice, they simply laugh in my face, then deflect any further questions with requests for tobacco and pots and pans, or jokes at our expense.

"You two are both horribly ugly," a woman told Vicent and me yesterday afternoon as we were hanging our laundry outside the little wooden shack where we sleep. "You must be brothers," she added, her body trembling with laughter at the thought that two such horrible-looking creatures could have emerged from the same womb.

This tiny, acerbic comic with sagging breasts, short bangs, and a funny twisted smile was an older Yanomami woman, probably in her late forties but looking sixty. Father Guilherme had pointed her out to us the other day as an example of a female who had two husbands, an anomaly within the Yanomami's male-biased culture. But I guess her unique marital status qualified her—at least in her own opinion—as an expert on men.

"We're not brothers," Vicent told her.

"Well, I am still sorry for you both, because no woman would marry ugly men like you."

"Vicent has a wife," I informed her with the help of Father Guilherme's translation. "But you are right, I'm not married."

"His wife must be old and blind!" she cried out. "And the children must look like rodents!" More laughter, then she pointed to me. "And as for you, I don't think you will have much luck finding a wife."

This was typical of the way our conversations with Yanomami women unfold. They poke fun at us, taunt us with machetes, make suggestive remarks about the lens on my camera, and in general joke at our expense. But they never answer a question seriously. Perhaps if I'd traveled here with a female sound recordist it would have been easier. I've seen women connect across cultures in other parts of the world, and I am certain a female collaborator would have facilitated my access to the women here. However, any woman who accompanied me would be taking a chance with her life and I didn't want that responsibility. There were lots of rumors of Indian women being abducted and raped by miners. The nature of this job was crazy enough. I didn't want someone's safety being unduly jeopardized. It had become clear on my first trip that the miners' camps were violent, very macho locales. When I decided to come here with Vicent, I knew that it would limit my ability to work with the women. But one thing I did not foresee was becoming the brunt of jokes for an entire female population.

This morning I asked Father Guilherme to join us and translate my questions into Yanoman so that Machadão could respond in his own language with maximum fluency. We have agreed that Father Guilherme will give me abridged versions of Machadão's responses. Unless I have any follow-up questions, we'll simply go on down the list of queries I have scribbled on a scrap of paper. I am hoping to touch on a variety of subjects ranging from Machadão's personal history to how shamans perceive the white man and his diseases.

As I set up the shot I ask Father Guilherme to explain to Machadão how we are going to conduct the interview. He points to the camera and the boom pole, explaining the function of each instrument. Machadão follows all this very intently, occasionally laughing as he makes jokes about the way we fuss over the cables and battery bag. At the last minute I decide to add a wide angle to my lens. The shot I have planned is calculated to complement his style: the frame is now

expanded slightly to allow Machadão to use his arms in the
expressive manner he is accustomed to. From what I have seen
so far, Yanomami oral tradition seems to entail one individual
speaking the parts of different characters in whatever story is
being recounted. This traditional oratory is a little more the-
atrical than normal conversation as the narrator takes on the
intonations of all the characters in the tale. But most important
from my perspective, there will be no setups here, no attempts
to position the Indian in accordance with my preconceived
image—at least none that I am conscious of. I see my role as
facilitating the possibility of real dialogue in a debate that has
been dominated by the miners. My camera will act as an electronic mirror seizing Machadão's voice and image and then,
after editing the raw footage, reflecting them back to the world
in the context of documentaries and news reports. For the last
two years the miners have been manipulating the media
through their press conferences. Their images are the dominant
images, the images of the dominant culture. But now a member
of the Yanomami—in his own village and in his own language—will have the opportunity to express his people's
opinion on the changes that have come to them as a result of
this gold rush.

Over here in this direction is where I lived. I lived there
while traveling from the Rio Demini. It is close to that river
that my mother made her home and my father was killed by
warriors from another village who captured my mother and
brought her to the lower stream of the river where we are
now, on the Rio Catrimani. It is on the rapids of the
Piranteira where my new father had his home and he
eventually moved from there. He traveled from one garden
to another, then he moved again and settled in another area.
He finally set up his home on the Rio Pacu. It is there that I
grew up.

In the early days, there were no whites. We did not have
any encounters with them. We did not eat our game animals
with salt. We drank its cooking juices with nothing to add to
the taste. It wasn't until a very long time that my father first

met the whites. It was when I became older. He saw white people near here where we were living. We did not know the whites at that time. Our hands were empty. We had no manufactured objects. This is how we lived until we first encountered them.

The whites had arrived here to collect latex. They visited our community and we returned their visit. It was then that my father caught the flu and he eventually died from it. Most of the generation that I called "father" died from it. That is why I decided to come here to live. We at our village had been visiting with Village Wakathautheri for many years. They had initiated the relationship with us and we then visited each other many times. And later, when my wife was dead, the village headman Carrera called me over and proposed that I take a new spouse. He said to me: "Take a woman from among us! Without a wife you can't help but suffer from want!" He then said to me: "You must be desperate! Take a new wife and settle yourself here."

My youngest brother remained on the Rio Pacu, as well as my mother, but I no longer had a father and that is why I left. That is why I abandoned my community and came to live here. Later, Chagas, my brother-in-law, asked me to go back there but I didn't accept. I told him: "I will not go back to the place where my father and then my wife died from disease!" He said to me: "Come back to the community that is yours!" That is what my brother-in-law Chagas said to me, but I did not accept his words. I told him: "You will live on this site without me because I have abandoned it and I will not go back! I have really settled myself here at Wakathautheri!" I said to him for emphasis: "I will live here indefinitely! My gardens and my children are numerous! And you will have to stay there and live without me!" Only my young brother lives there at this time. It is not far. He comes to visit here often.

Many other people also died. There were large numbers of the men who I had called "father" but they are all dead now. There were no medicines back then. I had much sadness and anger because of all those people who died. These problems

occurred because of a white man called Nonato who wanted
to take one of our women. He asked incessantly for a
woman. He said: "Give me a woman. I must have a woman. I
want to have sex with a woman." When the whites speak in
that fashion I have fear that they will make sorcery with fire
and release the fume of the coughs. I am afraid because it is
this type of anger which could provoke them to cause a new
epidemic of flu. It is when they become angry like that that
the epidemics arrive.

And now we have many gold miners here and they are
living very close. I say to them: "We are not able to go up
the river. Why do you not go back to where you live?" But
they respond: "You cannot stop us from entering this
territory. We are only passing through." This is how they lie
to me.

I tell them: "You are killing all our wild game. Do not
come downstream where we are living." But in spite of my
words, many of them have come to where we live now. They
say to me: "We will not obey someone who is so young. We
will stop coming here only if an old person tells us. You,
however, are too young. We will not obey someone so
young. And once we have left, others, who won't have heard
of you, they will continue to come." But I responded to
them: "You have to stop coming here! There at Paapiú you
destroyed the forest and many Yanomami are in the process
of dying! Who else is going to arrive here? This is what I
want to know!"

I am afraid this is what will happen to us too. This is what
I have been thinking about these days. But they have not
responded to me. At Paapiú they killed the fish in the rivers
and the Yanomami have gone hungry. This is a shame
because the Yanomami at Paapiú are dying. The numbers of
gold miners have become very large. And now very few
Yanomami are still living at Paapiú. I said to the gold miners:
"Don't do the same thing to my territory that you did at
Paapiú!" But they don't respond to me because I am young.
"If you come here without causing any damage, if some of

you don't do anything but pass through here then I will be happy." This is what I said to them.

Then the gold miners responded to me: "If you speak like that, if you refuse to allow us to enter your territory, we will kill you. Don't say anything." This is why I have fear. We can only protest a little bit. They say to us: "The old people did not refuse us entry on this territory. The old people do not speak against us." Then, and this is the truth, they said: "If you, the young, if you speak, we will not listen. If the old speak, maybe we will listen."

This is what they said: "The old people want the manufactured goods that we bring." But I say to the old people: "Do not ask for the goods. The gold miners will only lie to you. They do not have friendly intentions. When there are enough of them, they are going to kill us. They are very ferocious. They have already killed the Yanomami at Paapiú." This is what I say but no one listens.

The old people are hesitant to show their hostility at encounters with the gold miners. This is because they do not know the language of the whites. We do not understand it. We do not understand each bit of their language when they speak to us. The gold miners also ask for women incessantly. And this is bad. I tell them: "Father Guilherme who lives here, he gives us sufficient numbers of things already." I tell them: "I will not approach the other whites." Then they say to me: "Okay, okay. Stay in the forest, there where you live." But another gold miner, far from here, he said to me: "This territory belongs to me also. This forest is also mine. A little of the forest belongs to me. The rest, downstream, you can keep for yourself."

These are the lies that they tell me. And I respond to them: "No, I will not give a little of the forest. This is where I hunt and where I search for game and where I fish. It is also here where at night I light up the river with a flashlight to shoot the fish with my arrows." This is what I have told the gold miners. At Paapiú they destroyed everything. They ruined the earth by digging huge holes in the ground. If they had not done this maybe I could have become friends with them. But they have destroyed all the land and that is bad. If they continue destroying the land then I don't want anything to do with them. I said to the gold miners: "This is my forest and it is I who live here."

The whites, after they have built this road, their numbers have become very large and that has made me angry. If some of them who entered here were content to simply pass by that would be okay. I would be satisfied with that arrangement. As for me I do not want to make friends with them. But if there are other whites, different whites, who want to live here with us maybe I would be friends with them but only if they were like Father Guilherme.

Machadão continues for another hour presenting his vision of the gold rush. Most of it is comprehensible to me, but clearly a more intimate knowledge of the complex fabric of Yanomami cosmology is required. As Father Guilherme translates, I often find myself at a loss for a follow-up to Machadão's responses. Towards the end of the interview, when we start asking some questions about shamanism, he says:

Do you know the evil spirits, Omamari? Do you know the supernatural image of the evil spirits? The spirits that live in the waterfalls, those whose call is "hahahahaaa." They live in the rapids. They have big beards. Like the beard of a white person. Their beards are like this. They dance in the morning. "Hoou reke reke reke!" It's like this that the Omamari spirits talk. They seize the Yanomami and hold them captive here. When they are like an iguana, they carry the Yanomami captured in their mouths.

Machadão is offering me a glimpse at his cosmological vision, but my understanding is limited by the layers of culture that distinguish his society from ours. Yet his comments do recall things I've read in various anthropological texts. For example, the idea that whites "make sorcery with fire and release the fume of the coughs."

The French anthropologist Bruce Albert, who has written

extensively on this subject, says the Yanomami traditionally believed that epidemics were passed into the body of the victim by the fumes of smoke emanating from fires. The perpetrator—a neighboring enemy or local rival—would initiate this act of sorcery by placing magic plants in the fire and then directing the *xawara*, the malevolent fumes, towards the intended victim. But since contact with outsiders, the Yanomami began to reevaluate the way in which these diseases were being transmitted. The trading of metal objects—the gifts of attraction—also started to have an ambiguous significance as the arrival of missionaries and Indian Agency employees gave way to anthropologists and then highway workers and frontier explorers. Missionaries and anthropologists maintained a pacific relationship with the Yanomami. But many rubber tappers, highway workers, and now gold miners competed with the Indians not just for the forest but for wild game and, at times, for women. The encounters between these two groups were often tense and their contacts, with no medical supervision, frequently brought the onset of new and deadly epidemics. During this period Yanomami shamans like Machadão began to theorize that it was the smell emanating from metal objects (particularly objects bestowed upon them by adversarial whites) that was responsible for the transmission of the white man's disease. In their view of the world this theory made sense. They were learning from experience, processing their historical encounters with different whites and correlating them with the onset of new diseases. Such a shamanistic interpretation did not meet the scientific rigors of Western medicine but it provided their people with a cautionary metaphor regarding the consequences of greed for a society who should be satisfied with who they are and what they have. With the fervor of a street-corner Isaiah, Machadão was simply trying to warn his peers of the potential dangers of making deals with the Devil.

journal entry
Wakathautheri Village
6/5

I realized today that I will need two scenes: some shots of families relaxing in hammocks would be good followed by some scenes of women and children fetching water or cutting wood. I also need to explore the forest and I have to remember that there is where the significance of life lies for the Indians. "Urihi" is what the Yanomami call it. It is a place inhabited by supernatural spirits but one which they are also dependent upon for their sustenance. One Indian today gave us a partial list of what they hunt. It included tapirs, two-toed sloths, mazama deer, nine-banded armadillos, three-toed sloths, agouti, squirrels, small caimans, giant anteaters, silky anteaters, macaws and monkeys of which there are several variations including howlers, spiders, white monkeys and capuchin monkeys.

I also learned today that a woman died recently during a festival at the village of Demini. The Indians here at Catrimani and the Indians at Jundia have decided with the help of a Shaman, that another village is responsible, and they are planning an attack against that village. I wonder if they have any intentions of going after the gold miners living down river. Perhaps they already have.

18

"In May I made fifty tests for malaria and thirty-one were positive," says Florence, wiping sweat from her brow as she shuffles about her tiny one-room clinic looking for a needle to give another injection to another Indian in search of more of the white man's medicine. "This was only in the month of May." She pushes down on the hypodermic, thrusting the needle into the arm of an old woman who flinches, cringes, and then lets out a squeaky little sigh. "This is truly the year of malaria."

Florence yanks the hypodermic from the woman's arm with a suddenness that catches me off guard. I step backwards, bumping against a rack of blood samples sitting on a small wooden table. Hearing the sound of the test tubes rattling, I freeze and watch as Florence's head whips around. There's silence for a moment but no breaking glass. Vicent has managed to catch the bottles before they fell. He is now pushing them back, near where she left them, intact on a corner of the table. Florence shoots me a quick nervous glance followed by a smile—a sign, I take it, that I can continue working but that I should proceed with caution, that I shouldn't forget that the fate of whole villages is dependent on the work being done within the confines of this one tiny room.

Along the blue wooden walls of the clinic, old shelves are stacked with an odd assortment of medicines. Another half dozen test tubes sit on a desk to my right—more blood samples to determine if the Indians who visited the clinic today have malaria and, if so, what strain. This clinic is so small that Vicent has moved outside to record sound from the front porch. His boom pole is dropped in through the doorway, carefully positioned to stay out of the way of my shot. But even more than the cramped space, it is the light that is making my work difficult. The harsh sun coming in through the door contrasts sharply with the dark shadows of the clinic's interior. For ten minutes I've come up with nothing but overexposed shots as I have tried to capture Florence's routine of taking blood samples, interviewing Indians, and giving injections. I'm feeling frustrated and claustrophobic, the technological equivalent of a bull in a china shop. My attempts at fluid handheld camera work are proving almost impossible.

An older Yanomami man shuffles into the room, and Florence stands with a hypodermic needle in her hand, her back to me, preparing to take another sample of blood. He's one of the shamans from a neighboring village, a wizened old character with a couple of long gray chin whiskers and baggy bloodshot eyes. Just a few minutes ago he sat outside on the porch bench passing his hands over his arms and chest, letting forth a few feeble chants—attempts (I am assuming) to rid himself of malaria with a traditional cure. Now Vicent sticks his head through the window and raises his eyebrows in the direction of the nurse and the old shaman; he knows a good shot when he sees one. I shake my head, trying to convey my frustration. *Can't roll. No shot. Going to let this one pass.* His eyes widen in feigned disbelief, a not-so-subtle critique that only adds to my concern. I need images like this one—a traditional shaman seeking the aid of Western medicine—to tell the full story of the complex ways in which these two worlds interact. Florence, detecting the problems we are having, asks the shaman to take a step backwards, allowing me to get my shot. He winces and groans as the long thin needle pierces his flesh.

"*Eyyup,*" Florence calls out and another Yanomami woman enters the room with a baby that can barely stand on its own

and a child of perhaps three. The old shaman shuffles out rub-
bing his arm.

Florence is now seated behind her small wooden desk diligently making another entry in the clinic's log. She has just
asked the old man a number of questions about his medical history, giving us time to take a break. I've been able to collect my
thoughts, allowing me to approach this next scene a little differently—to "work the space," as my colleagues say. I've
decided to use the cramped environment and its bad lighting to
tell the story. These limitations can shape the pictures and the
camera moves, the angles, adding another dimension to the
images I am trying to capture—all of this a delicate balancing
act between getting the shot and imposing on the subject. I flip
the start switch on my camera and take a step forward, framing
Florence behind her desk as she makes another entry in her log
book. She exchanges a few words with the young woman who
has just entered. Up close this mother of two looks to be no
more than eighteen and is probably much younger. I have been
told by the missionaries that it is not uncommon for a
Yanomami girl to be married at eleven or twelve years of age
and be bearing children soon after her first menstruation. Still
she looks incredibly young to have borne two children.

Florence scribbles into the notebooks what I assume is the
case history of the young woman. She is, as usual, focused and
intense. To me she is paying little attention, barely glancing up,
a sign that she's finally getting used to the presence of the
camera. The young Yanomami woman looks pallid and
unsteady, rocking back and forth as she mumbles responses in
Yanomany to Florence's occasional queries. The children, their
eyes rolling, stare up at the strange white man before them.
One of them is tugging at the legs of my pants. I see Vicent lean
in through the door and gently pull the child away, allowing me
to concentrate on the work at hand.

"And what about this woman, Florence, what do you think
she has?" I ask as I pan the camera to the young mother, trying
to find a way to add context to the scene.

Florence's high-pitched voice with its Caribbean lilt comes
in on cue: "I think she has malaria because her husband had

malaria, her two children had malaria, and since yesterday she has fever and chills." The words "fever and chills" punctuate the end of my shot as the final frame settles on the young woman, her body shaking, her face twisted into contortions of pain, two thin legs pulled together and bent to the side as she tries to fight off another attack of the chills.

I've finally gotten the kind of image I've been searching for since I arrived here. It is ambiguous and unexpected: no hint of preconceived icons. It manages both to document this world and to conform to the rhythms of life here, an image not stolen but bartered. These people are aware of why we are here and have agreed to participate in this process of documentation. Like any visitor to the village, I will leave gifts of pots and pans and machetes. Their acceptance of my presence as one of the "friendly whites" has given me license to enter their world and to shape it through my images. There is always manipulation involved in this work, it's inevitable. Our images are just sur-face reality. They can never reflect the full experience of their personalities or their culture, nor can they fully capture the pain they might be suffering. Photographers are at best visual intermediaries to the world at large who must be able to fluc-tuate between detachment and involvement. The photogra-pher who shot the famous photo of the napalmed girl in Vietnam is a perfect case in point. He got his shot, then took her in his van to the hospital. Arguably, that shot contributed substantially to our understanding of war and of that war in par-ticular. For me, it is the unreal perspective of the lens that allows me to film things I would not normally be able to witness with my own eyes. I care about this woman, but she is still a subject who must be considered in terms of light, composition, and storytelling. These aesthetic considerations distance me from her world. I need to be able to summon that detachment in order to do my job. I need to focus on the end result: the images that are taken and the side of the story that needs to be told, that I have chosen to tell. I don't second guess the impor-tance of that part of the work, otherwise I wouldn't be here.

In a search for another angle I take a quick step to my left. With my back to the doorway it is easier to take advantage of the bright rays of light kicking in from outside. As I drop to my knees I glance from behind the black-and-white viewfinder of my camera to take a look at my subject in the colors of the real world. The girl's skin is bright yellow. The liver's deadly bile must have already hit her bloodstream; jaundice has set in. Suddenly her body relaxes and she lets out a sigh. Then just as quickly she seizes up again, racked by chills, a bizarre sight considering that the temperature must be hovering around a hundred and four degrees.

Having subjected this young woman to enough of the camera's scrutiny, I pan back to Florence, who is preparing to take a sample of her blood. "What are the range of health problems that you have here?" I ask her as I try to prepare a follow-up question.

"It's the worst problem here, one after another—when you finish something, something else starts," says Florence, struggling with her English. "Maybe the Indians have malaria; when I treat the malaria there appears a cough, then comes bronchitis and if I don't treat that then comes pneumonia."

Florence tells the woman to stand, grabs her finger, cleans it with an alcohol swab, and then pricks it with a pin, letting the blood flow onto a glass slide to be tested later. This procedure is done in one quick, efficient move repeated by Florence a dozen times throughout the day as she tries to cope with this sudden wave of Indians who have descended upon the mission's clinic. According to her statistics for the previous month, she treated three cases of pneumonia, eight cases of bronchitis, and thirty-one cases of malaria, seventeen of which proved to be falciparum, the most lethal strain. These numbers don't include the half dozen Indians who are waiting to be seen outside or the other ten or fifteen who have come and gone in the last few days. And these Yanomami are the lucky ones. They live near a clinic; they have access to a trained nurse and medicines. The few Brazilian Indian Agency outposts in this area suffer from a lack of trained medical personnel and supplies, the latter commonly looted by gold miners seeking remedies for their various ailments, particularly malaria. Before coming here I spoke to other missionaries and anthropologists who recounted rumors among the Indians of more remote villages being hit by waves of malaria. If they are true, then this society of nine thousand could be in trouble.

Malaria is a disease that can destabilize a group in a matter of weeks, a fact well documented in case studies of smaller societies succumbing to sudden epidemics. At its onset the routine tasks of hunting and gardening can become too arduous for villagers. People spend days trying to recuperate in the hammocks, food is therefore in short supply, and malnutrition sets in. One by one the villagers begin to die off. It's the old people and children who go first, the ones whose immune systems have the least resistance.

Diagnosing malaria is relatively simple. Withstanding the disease is another story. The gold miners I've met in the Amazon describe the initial symptoms as a sudden loss of appetite and pounding headaches that feel as if "someone is taking an ax to the back of your skull." Waves of fever interspersed with chills can last for several hours and attack the body over the course of three or four days. Then the face goes pale, the fingers turn white, and the nails become blue. Taking a look at the young Yanomami mother talking to Florence, I see that she has all these symptoms. But there are two more stages that this girl may yet be spared. One is characterized by dry heat and burning skin with the body's urine turning strange colors. And then there is stage three: the killer. That's when the body is drenched in sweat and the urine turns into a thick blood-red liquid. The victim naturally panics. These are signs that the untreated illness has attacked the spleen and the liver, enlarging them, blowing them out of shape, shutting down their vital functions. Then anemia develops, making the victims susceptible to other epidemic strains circulating through their communities. Malaria can also go right for the brain, invading the cerebral tissues, driving people crazy. "Jungle fever," "hill fever," "marsh fever"—you remember those black-and-white movies from the forties and fifties. All those people in pith helmets with mosquito netting draped on cots in the background. Odds are if you are in an infested area long enough, you are going to get nailed by an Anopheles mosquito carrying with it the deadly infection. In the few days since we have arrived I have learned that swatting bugs is a way of life. Throughout the day I find myself constantly wiping splotches of blood off my hands, residue of the dozen mosquitoes I will have killed in the course of a half hour. The Indians have come up with a clever counterattack: they use the flat side of a machete, swinging it swiftly about the body in an efficient rotating motion to kill the pestilent creatures as they land on their bare skin. But even their technique is not proof against the hordes of insects that descend upon us daily. The Indians' bodies are exposed as ours are not. I've seen entire Yanomami backs that resemble one massive mosquito bite. Up close there is an endless series of dots connected to each other in an island of puffy, swelling, reddened skin. Even in spite of my "modern" precautions—bug sprays, mosquito-netted hammocks, long-sleeved shirts—I too am covered with bites. There isn't an inch of exposed skin that has not been attacked. My neck and face are an inflamed and itchy mess. Yet so far I am lucky. I am not showing any symptoms. No ax to the back of the head.

At this time in Brazil the controversy about malaria in Yanomami territory has become a tricky political game of placing the blame: did the miners bring it into the Indians' land, or was malaria endemic to their communities? At the center of the debate is that bloodsucking little creature the Anopheles mosquito, which, usually in late afternoon, injects a "causative organism" known as a plasmodium from the blood of an infected person into the blood of the unsuspecting victim. This insect is an intermediary—an "agent of transmission," as epidemiologists say—between those who have it and those who don't. But also germane to the debate are historical precedents about disease and the indigenous populations of the Western Hemisphere, precedents the gold miners and local politicians are conveniently ignoring.

Since the arrival of Columbus epidemics have been the number-one killer of New World natives. Certainly the conquistadores raped, plundered, and pillaged. And, yes, tens of thousands of Indians were killed in North America during armed fights across that continent. But the most devastating killer has always been simple disease: the common cold, measles, and smallpox. These epidemics have the ability to destroy once-isolated Indian societies, groups that had no prior contact with the infections. The genetic makeup of their people does not provide them with a set of antibodies predisposed to attack the various viral, bacterial, and protozoal agents that come with the carriers of new diseases. Measles erupted in massive outbreaks among indigenous populations in Mexico and Peru between 1531 and 1539, then in Canada in 1635, then in the Amazon in 1745, and in Tierra del Fuego in 1884. Contemporary historians refer to the Spanish conquest of the Americas as the period of Great Dying. During the first one hundred years of the conquistadores' campaign there were fourteen major epidemics in the Americas. After Pedro Cabral, in the name of the Portuguese crown, "discovered" Brazil in 1500, epidemics regularly accompanied the explorers of the Amazon and the frontiersmen and pioneers who colonized the rest of the country. The historical records of Jesuit missionaries in Brazil are filled with horrific accounts of native deaths from diseases imported from Europe and Africa. In the 1550s eight thousand Indians died in the area surrounding the French colony in Rio de Janeiro. One priest estimated in the mid-1580s that of the sixty thousand Indians baptized in Bahia between 1559 and 1583, only three hundred survived. Baffled by the devastation that unwittingly accompanied the arrival of Western Europeans, this cleric wrote "the numbers of people who died here in Bahia in the past twenty years seems unbelievable. No one ever imagined that so many people could ever be expended, far less in so short a time." Such sporadic, deadly epidemics continued over five centuries, striking isolated Indian societies whenever they came in contact with European colonizers. By the time I started working in Brazil in the late 1980s the Indian population, which had been four million strong in 1500, was now hovering at just over 220,000 people.

And among Indian societies throughout the Amazon, death by disease was still the number-one concern.

Epidemiologists say that malaria came to the Western Hemisphere from Africa with the arrival of Columbus and the subsequent voyages of other European explorers and slave ships. Over the last five centuries it has worked its way through the Americas in a pattern of epidemics usually accompanied by several facilitating factors. Foremost among them is the creation of large cleared areas of tropical forest and pools of stagnant water that serve as breeding grounds for the lethal Anopheles mosquito. These are common sights when flying over Yanomami territory today: hundreds of large gold pits filled with water stand out like massive blemishes in what would otherwise be lush green forest. The pits are mined, but abandoned as the prospectors move on in search of other gold deposits. The construction of a hundred new airstrips by gold prospectors in just two years has also drastically multiplied the potential breeding areas for the Anopheles.

However, this is not a one-dimensional story. Placing the blame is more complicated. The Yanomami might also unknowingly be contributing to their own demise. Many villages, attracted by the prospect of trading goods, have in recent years started moving nearer to rivers, placing their people in closer contact with groups of outsiders as well as pools of stagnant water, thereby increasing the possibility of infection. The risk of epidemic has been further enhanced when, with the machetes obtained by trading, they have begun to clear larger plots for villages and gardens. These in turn become expanded breeding grounds for the mosquitos.

While these details might suggest a shared responsibility for the way malaria spreads, its onset per se in Yanomami territory can only be blamed on a government in Brasília that has been unwilling or unable to stop the influx of forty-five thousand miners. These men who have descended upon the Indians' territory are wildcat prospectors acting beyond the supervision of any corporation, paying little heed to medical precaution. Many of them are recent immigrants from the infamous Serra Pelada gold rush where malaria ran rampant over a period of several years. Others come from various gold rush towns in Brazil where the World Health Organization is predicting that malaria will strike as many as one million people in the next year.

What does the historical record show? When the gold rush began in 1987 the government doctors who had worked in this area stated there had not been any malaria reported in Yanomami territory in more than a decade. The last series of small outbreaks dated back to the middle of the 1970s when highway workers entered the Indians' forest during the construction of the Northern Perimeter Highway. There were earlier recorded incidents, usually linked to the arrival of Western Europeans. But there has never been any medical or historical proof to substantiate the miners' claim that malaria has always been in the forest. In fact, most of the medical research done to date—at least what I could find—has contradicted their claims. One expert I spoke to was an epidemiolgoist at Yale University by the name of Dr. Frank Black, a cautious scientist with a soft voice, a man who, he told me, didn't trust journalists. He refused to be interviewed on camera and would talk to me only on the phone. His answers were guarded, evasive. Several years ago he had done work among the Yanomami and several other indigenous groups in the Amazon. He didn't want to get involved in what to him was a political issue. Like many academics who work in the rain forest, he perhaps feared having his research visa refused the next time he applied. But I didn't really need Dr. Black's on-camera assessment, because a careful look at his research reveals significant patterns in the spread of diseases such as malaria through isolated indigenous communities. In a dense medical tract entitled "Evidence for Persistence of Infectious Agents in Isolated Human Populations," Dr. Black and several collaborators document how diseases, after killing off large numbers of indigenous inhabitants, will run their course in small communities and eventually disappear. I'll call it, for lack of a professional term, the "burn-out factor." This is what appears to have happened in the remote Yanomami communities bordering the Northern Perimeter Highway in the 1970s. A disease arrived, it killed off a number of members of the communities living near the roads, and eventually it burned itself out without spreading to other communities. What distinguishes the outbreaks of the 1970s from the ones occurring today is not only the numbers of people entering the forest (there were fewer than a hundred highway workers as opposed to forty-five thousand miners) but the extent to which these prospectors have been penetrating previously isolated communities distant from any roadway or missionary outpost. As Black and his colleagues conclude from their survey of several previously isolated Indian societies in the Amazon, "it has been clear that many infectious agents do not persist in small communities but must be reintroduced from larger populations *at the onset of every epidemic.*" At the rate of two hundred miners arriving daily, the possibility of reintroduction here in Yanomami territory is extremely high.

Sister Florence ushers in a middle-aged woman with three small pieces of wood sticking from her chin, and I scramble to get the last of my shots before losing the afternoon light.

"Where do you think the Indians get these diseases?" I ask Florence as she searches for another clean slide for a blood sample.

"Well, these Indians are from the village of Jundia. And they say the gold miners pass by their villages all the time and then they catch colds, pneumonia, and the other diseases."

Florence herself looks unsteady as she rocks back on the balls of her feet, wiping more sweat from her brow. She has been working since first light and she'll probably continue well into the night. I am beginning to feel guilty about pestering her with these questions after such a long day. I turn off the camera and set it down in a corner of the room. Outside, Vicent is stepping into the mission yard to take a breather.

"How are you feeling, Florence?"

"I'm not certain," she responds. "I think I might have come down with something."

"Like what?"

"Like malaria."

"Are you sure?"

"Yes," she said. "I have not tested my blood but I know too well the symptoms."

At this point the older shaman, still standing by the doorway, asks a question of Florence in Yanoman. As they begin to
talk I join Vicent in the mission yard to discuss our plans for
flying out this afternoon. A minute later Florence calls me over.

"This man is going to do some shamanism," she says.

"On who?" I say.

"On me. When I told him I was sick he offered to help me."

"You believe in shamanism, Florence?"

"Yes."

"Forgive me. But I don't understand. How you can you
believe—"

"—in shamanism?" she says.

"Yes."

"I have seen what they can do. A shaman tells me a baby is
sick and goin' to die then that baby dies. There is nothing I can
do. He tells me the baby goin' to get well, the baby gets well."
She flashes that crazy smile of hers.

"But you also take their cure?"

"They take my medicine and I take theirs."

"You're not supposed to believe in this type of thing."

"But I do," she says.

"Can I film it?"

"Certainly. But hurry on now," she says to Vicent and me. "He
is going to do it right now in the temporary house for the
Indians." She begins to walk away and then calls out over her
shoulder. "We will meet over there. I need to get a drink of
water."

A few minutes later we enter the little maloca as the shaman
begins his preparations for his curing ceremony. Florence, in
her long blue nun's habit, sits beside her naked healer, quiet
and patient. Squatting on the ground the shaman unfolds a leaf
and begins snorting the hallucinogenic powder yakōana into his
nostrils. It is a dark green powder derived from the dried bark of
a virola tree. Taken like snuff, it is considered by the shamans to
be a critical step in contacting the hekura, tiny but powerful
beings who live in the spirit world and control many of the
events in the lives of the Yanomami. As the drug takes effect
the shaman begins a slow, rhythmic chant, shaking his head

occasionally to fight off what I imagine are psychedelic explosions detonating inside the recesses of his brain. After a few minutes of these chants, he rises and begins circling the nun, his melodic incantations now more guttural, his gestures and facial expressions more exaggerated. He appears to have left us and entered another universe. "*Aaaaa—rrrreeeee*" goes the beginning of the chant and then everything else becomes incomprehensible as he communicates with the *hekura*.

At first I keep at a distance with the camera, grabbing mostly wide shots and a few close-ups of his feet as he shuffles about attempting to attract the *hekura* spirit. I am self-conscious about intruding on this sacred ritual, but very quickly I realize that he has little concern for my presence. He is off in the Yanomami cosmos, his entire attention focused on Florence and his interactions with "those whose call is *hahahahaaa*," as Machadão referred to them the other day. It is also common that these rituals are performed in public spaces as villagers go about their daily life. Also, I made a point of telling him before we started that he could stop me if I got in his way.

After about twenty minutes the pace of his chanting quickens and the tone of his voice becomes yet more guttural as if he has summoned up some force from deep within himself. Suddenly he squats beside Florence, grabs her head with both hands, and bursts into a long, high-pitched chant to the spirits. He rakes his fingers over her face and down along her legs, extracting the evil spirits that have invaded her body. Reaching her feet, he cups his hands, lets out an agonized shriek, and rises, extending his arms above his head, unclasping his hands, releasing the spirits back into this world. For the next hour the old shaman alternates between dances and chanting, as he summons the help of the *hekura*. Each of these rites seems more intense than the one before it. Then suddenly it is over. For the first time in two hours I can hear the forest—and faintly, in the distance, the sound of an approaching plane.

Florence steps outside. Vicent and I follow her with the camera rolling. I don't want to miss this moment.

"How do you feel now?" I ask.

"Well, better, the headache is gone," she says. "Maybe it is psychological but I do feel better." As she finishes her sentence the shaman walks past us smiling serenely, something I find hard to believe in a man who has just danced about in a drug-induced frenzy for the past two hours. Somehow I expected him to be collapsed in a corner of the maloca. But then I remember that, like the nurse, he is a trained professional. He has gone through years of apprenticeship to become a shaman. Such tasks are second nature; the side effects are part of the job.

The old shaman, like the other villagers, heads off to the airstrip. We follow them, grabbing our clothing bags and extra equipment on the way.

The pilot is anxious and wants to leave quickly. There are reports of a storm heading in our direction. We say goodbye to the missionaries and the dozen Yanomami who have come down to the runway to see the plane. As we board the aircraft I can see Pierrot le Fou circling in the background near the forest perimeter, talking to himself and clutching his chest.

The plane accelerates down the runway, avoiding several large puddles on the grassy track, picking up speed, then lifting. As we rise above the mission complex I catch a glimpse of a young Yanomami women fetching a bucket of water at the well. She looks up and waves as we soar past her, a wide grin stretching across her face. Then there's just a blur of trees. It all seems to happen in slow motion as the pilot banks due west, lifting us farther above the forest, the cabin humming from the plane's engine, my mind trying to absorb all that I have seen and heard in these last few days.

19

When I wasn't in the Amazon or off on assignment in another part of the world, home was New York City, a rambling Upper West Side apartment on the top floor of a six-story building. On my first days back from a trip to the forest I was always driven crazy by the intolerable city noise outside my window: the empty trucks bouncing along Amsterdam Avenue, my neighbors screaming to friends down on the street, car alarms, ice cream vendors, a plane roaring overhead, and the constant wail of small children—all these sounds intermingled in a nonstop cascade of urban clatter broken occasionally by a flurry of gunshots from another *engagement* in my neighborhood's burgeoning drug war. Then, and only then, there would be a moment of silence followed by screams, slammed doors, and hysterical cries for help.

My neighborhood was called Manhattan Valley, at one time an enclave of Irish and German immigrants but recently it had become home to a five-million-dollar-a-year cocaine trade run by Dominican youths and operating within a three-block radius of my home. The individual dealers used pseudonyms like Chick, Popcorn, Macho, and Joey Tell. They were members of gangs who called themselves the Latin Kings, Purple Top Crew, and Young Talented Children. From my living room window I could look down on the corner of 107th Street and Amsterdam Avenue where they congregated throughout the night, draped over cars and plastic milk crates, stashing their wares between plantains on the vegetable stands as they tried to seduce young girls from the block in front of Pedro's All-Night Market II. This was a community the *New York Times* had cited as the neighborhood with the highest rate of homicide in Manhattan: a free-fire zone where greedy dealers blew each other away in lethal competition for the most profitable street corners in the area. One sick but imaginative thug carried a semiautomatic pistol with an infrared beam that he flashed on the chests of rivals and residents just to let them know that, with one little squeeze of the trigger, their life could be ended. Among the dealers' clientele were desperate urban lowlifes, Hispanic hookers, and "jarhead" New Jersey frat boys, all of them negotiating the street in hopes of scoring enough crack to propel them through the night. These legions of addicts—there could be as many as two thousand each evening—entered the neighborhood with downtrodden, paranoid expressions, their clothes soiled and unkempt from days on a binge. Then minutes after they made their connection, they exited the block electrified, their body parts all ajostle like some hyped-up half-time band leader gone berserk without the rhythmic solace of his baton.

I came to learn that crack or crank or rock—the name seemed to change every time another chemical was added to the addictive concoction—was an indiscriminate drug. Those who fall prey come from all walks of life. Tourists, many of them Japanese, would stumble into this neighborhood looking for some pharmaceutical thrills to enhance their exotic excursions to urban America. I considered warning them about the violent characters they were dealing with, but I always hesitated. I didn't want to become one of the victims of this violent turf war. Corpses on street corners were already a common enough sight. Often in the days following a murder impromptu memorials would pop up in the form of graffiti epitaphs on the sides of buildings or candlelight altars erected in the empty shells of abandoned telephone booths. Messing with the clientele was simply not allowed, an unspoken rule in the uneasy relationship between the community (mostly decent working-class immigrant families) and the dealers (their sons, cousins, and childhood friends).

"Blues out," the peddlers would whisper to me as I entered my building after a long night of editing in my downtown studio. "I got red top if you want it," they would add if their first offer didn't elicit any response.

Not surprisingly, it was the young dealers, those new to the neighborhood and eager to establish an identity, who hassled me the most. Their bosses, smarter and more aware of the local street politics, would often intercede if their "boys" got too aggressive in pushing their wares. "Sorry," they would tell me, a hand placed on my shoulder, signifying our bond as inhabitants of the same tough terrain. "He don't know you live here."

When I asked a young cop one afternoon what his precinct was doing about the problem, he answered the question with a question: he asked me if I had "ever thought about moving out of the neighborhood." This is what it was like in the late 1980s on the forgotten fringe of New York in a neighborhood that had been passed by in the wave of gentrification then sweeping Manhattan. No one cared about us, not even those who had been designated to protect us. Yet this was what I called home, a place to return to between trips to the forest and assignments to Moscow or Tokyo or Costa Rica, a rent-controlled way station for an itinerant freelance journalist unable to spend a lot of money on an apartment where he didn't spend a lot of time. Ironically, it was part of an urban frontier, a terrain not very different from the lawless region I had left behind in Brazil.

But although I was far from the Amazon, its inhabitants—the region's lowland Indians—seemed to be ever present. The impact of the Chico Mendes assassination and the Altamira Gathering had set the stage for a sudden explosion of the Save the Rain Forest movement in North America, Latin America, and Europe. Images and incarnations of Indians were everywhere. There were the Body Shop Indians whose life-size posters adorned the display tables of that chain's cosmetics stores, there were Sting's Indians who appeared with the rock star in layouts in *Vogue* and *Paris Match*, and there were my Indians, the Indians I had photographed in Brazil who now swished by me each day on television monitors as I edited documentaries and news reports for broadcast around the world. And then there were the real Indians: indigenous Amazonian leaders who traveled to New York in search of support for their people.

There were also Indians who weren't Indians but dressed themselves and painted their faces in tribal styles. These were people—almost always middle-class white Americans and a few expatriate Brazilians, also middle-class—who were on a sincere if misguided quest to connect with the indigenous traditions of this hemisphere. They chose facial paint, native dress, and, very often, natural hallucinogenic drugs as their entrée into what they believed to be the consciousness of lowland Indian culture. They were not the first to attempt to span the abyss that separated European and indigenous culture. In the 1960s the hallucinogen peyote combined with a thorough reading of the works of Carlos Castañeda had provided a psychedelic link between the hippie counterculture and the "native experience." But in the 1980s it was the mind-expanding drink ayahuesca that was the drug of choice. This powerful concoction was created by Brazilian Indian societies and appropriated by rubber tappers who in turn passed it on to visitors who smuggled it into the Untied States or consumed it clandestinely during informal eco-tours of the rain forest. These were the days before the Save the Rain Forest movement had become a part of a new era of green marketing and before it was embraced (some would say co-opted) by institutions like the United Nations. It was never a formalized, card-carrying organization but rather an emergent state of global consciousness that informally linked a loose ensemble of international human rights organizations, environmental groups, savvy activist academics, eco-enlightened politicians, concerned celebrities, "green" corporations, and students. A belated passenger on this bandwagon was the mainstream media which slowly began to discover that the public at large were concerned about the future of their planet. In 1989 environmentalism was definitely "in" and a seemingly endless parade of New Age Jeremiahs (mostly academics) appeared on radio and television and in

print with their dire proclamations of an impending environmental holocaust. "We have a decade left to solve the problem
of the destruction of tropical forests" was their common refrain
in the late eighties. "The deleterious consequences of the
greenhouse effect will be upon us any moment if we don't do
something." Sun-block sales were suddenly soaring, recycling
became a household ritual, cosmetics companies scrambled to
release products from the forest, and many of us found ourselves
eating foods whose ingredients had been derived from the forest
and whose profits were purportedly being returned in part to
the Amazon's indigenous communities. During this era the
consciousness of the world had definitely taken a significant
turn and, if the growing number of children's books on the rain
forest was any indication, the impact would be seen for generations to come. Indians were being depicted as central figures in
the push to preserve the planet: "the gardeners of the forest" is
what Sting had called them, people who could turn us down
the path of ecological salvation if we just listened to what they
had to say.

"Turn on *Donahue*," a voice screamed from my phone early
one afternoon just a day after my return from a trip to the
Brazilian Amazon. My friend hung up before I could reply. I
dropped the laundry I had been folding and turned on the TV.
There before me was Raoni seated on a studio stage with a
fellow Kayapo leader named Meguron. Also in attendance were
the rock star Sting, Jean-Pierre Dutilleux, and the ecologist
Tom Lovejoy from the Smithsonian Institution. In brisk cut-
away shots the show's host, Phil Donahue, was seen working his
studio audience. In his overly earnest, slightly acerbic way, he
focused his listener's attention on what was being referred to
with ceremonial flair as the current crisis of the day: the
destruction of the world's tropical rain forests. One potential
solution was offered by the bow-tied environmentalist Tom
Lovejoy, who explained his "Debt for Nature" initiative
whereby the U.S. and other creditor nations could cancel portions of Brazil's crushing debt if they would just agree to desig-
nate large areas of their tropical rain forest as forest preserves.
Donahue listened intently to Lovejoy's proposal, then turned

his attention to Sting and his collaborator the filmmaker-activist Jean-Pierre Dutilleux.

"Uh, does it bother you," Donahue said to Dutilleux, "that we have to use someone with the power and influence of Sting to get on television in the daytime in America?" He paused in mock reflectiveness. "Do you have any idea the chances of a talk show speaking to these issues given the realities of our competitive game right now? How does that make you feel?"

"We've been struggling for this for over twenty years," responded Dutilleux. "I, myself, have been trying to do this for sixteen years. This is the way it works today."

A curious phrase, I thought to myself: *the way it works today*. I thought about how Dutilleux and Sting had gotten to this point in their campaign. Since Altamira they had taken the rain forest issue and given it extensive international exposure in Europe and North America. Their strategy had been to publicize the plight of the Amazon's indigenous peoples by accessing the global institutions of popular culture. In print, radio, and television they simplified the struggle of rain forest Indians by capitalizing on identifiable icons that people like those in Donahue's audience could recognize. Not only did Sting talk about Kayapo territory as a "Garden of Eden" but he and Dutilleux published a glossy book of photographs called *Jungle Stories* in which the rock star often appeared with the Indians seminaked and adorned with Kayapo body paint. This popularizing approach unnerved the anthropologists and die-hard activists who ran such indigenous rights organizations as Survival International in London and Cultural Survival in Boston. To these established activists Sting and Dutilleux represented a dangerous influence on the Save the Rain Forest movement. Their steamrolling attempts to popularize the Indians' struggle were perceived as dangerously close to trivializing a serious cause. These organizations tolerated the efforts of Sting and Dutilleux but they wouldn't lend their names. So in the months following Altamira, Dutilleux and Sting and the rock star's wife, Trudie Styler, set up their own organization, which they called the Rainforest Foundation. As part of their awareness campaign they made public appearances or held concerts in London,

Paris, Madrid, and Rome. Accompanied by Raoni they met with François Mitterrand and his wife, the king and queen of Spain, and Pope John Paul II. The English pop star was at the height of his popularity and Dutilleux, a one-time rock promoter, was maximizing Sting's clout to send a message to people whom the more established groups had been unable or unwilling to reach. These were the people who bought Sting's records, went to his concerts, and were moved by his popular lyrical messages regarding spiritual redemption and a sentimental concern for the fate of the planet. As I watched *Donahue* it was apparent that the Rainforest Foundation had indeed found a way to mainstream a cause that for years had been languishing in obscurity.

"We are far away from the rain forest. What can *we* do to help?" asked a young man in his twenties with the shag haircut of a rocker.

I had been waiting for that one. It's the question most commonly asked at any discussion of the rain forest in the United States. These were people for whom political action has not been a part of life, yet they had within them the kernels of altruism essential for any large-scale social movement. Their souls were ripe for conversion. These were the people Sting and Dutilleux had been intent on reaching. So with the patience and sensitivity of the schoolteacher he once was, the rock star adeptly addressed the young man's concerns.

"This area controls our climate, controls our ability to grow food," said Sting, gesturing emphatically, his hands positioned carefully within the frame of the camera. It was obvious when he spoke that the English rocker was the most polished of those assembled onstage, the one who was in complete control of his telegenic presence, a person for whom all this is second nature. "I think we have to realize it's our problem because we are part of the problem so we have to be part of the solution."

As Sting continued speaking, the camera cut away to the studio audience. The group was mostly white, mostly women, overlit by overzealous technicians presenting us viewers with images of a blow-dried people living in a world without shadows, a land where texture had been replaced by video brilliance, so bright it's unreal. In this world, sound bites replace conversation as part of a chess-game quest to get points across and become part of that culture of the glowing blue box that now dominates most American living rooms, an electronic social space that seems irreversibly part of the fabric of our lives, our postmodern community complete with its own rules, language, heroes, and rituals. Whether we like it or not, television has become our way of spinning myths, the place where we as a culture seek explanations as well as cathartic resolutions. As Dutilleux reminded us, *this is the way it works today*. But what are the consequences? I asked myself as I watched this display of contemporary ritual with its own assortment of ceremonies, icons, and taboos.

Sting as pop star had mastered the art of media manipulation and for this current crusade he had assembled a powerhouse team of indigenous activists and environmentalists. Each individual on stage including Raoni had delivered a sound bite addressing a different dimension of the rain forest issue, the points cleverly orchestrated, building in crescendo to the inevitable big pitch delivered by the band leader himself.

"First of all," Sting said in response to the what-can-we-do question, "I would like everyone to send a little money to the Rainforest Foundation. I think we have a plan that is very concrete. It is not a dream."

The camera cut back to the young man who asked the question. He was nodding. He got the point. Send money. Another mainstream convert for Sting's newfound cause.

The rock star then lectured the audience for a few more minutes about the importance of individual empowerment and the growing need for the consumer to influence corporations to change their ways. This was an act he had polished since Altamira. He no longer faltered in his delivery or displayed that nail-biting nervousness that made you wonder if he really believed what he was saying. He was much clearer about his intentions, more in command of the complexities of the issue.

Donahue interjected his own story about meeting the recently deceased Chico Mendes two years earlier at a Better World Society dinner, an awards benefit for good causes sponsored by the TV magnate Ted Turner. Phil's moment of confessional participation signaled to us that we were well into the cathartic I-wanna-testify part of this daytime television ritual, the part that has been co-opted from our nation's more animated churches or the twelve-step programs of AA, COA, NA, and the like. It is the moment when we as Americans can speak up and be heard, when we can testify in a manner that previously has been the exclusive domain of organized religion. Here, like a preacher's aside at a Sunday morning service, Donahue's personal account served to motivate us all to step forward in imitation of him, our pastoral televisionary. The underlying message was simple. He was moved by Chico's death and we should be too. This was not TV evangelism, but neither was it journalism. It was a new institution, part church revival and part town meeting, a postmodern ceremony that was as much about ritual participation as it was about issues—no different, ironically, from those fireside village rites I have witnessed a half dozen times among lowland Indian societies in the Amazon. There, sequestered in the clearings of that dark green tropical forest, chiefs or shamans or village leaders hold court on the issues before the tribe, the fire's glow contributing its own evocative mood and texture to the event, distinguishing it from both day and night, making it special, giving such a moment an almost sacred dimension. Those assembled (usually men) chime in with respectful additions to the speaker's comments or they voice encouragement for the points he is making. Among the Waiapi Indians, to repeat the last phrase of what has been said is the way to signal support for the position being espoused. In America on daytime television, it is to stand up and make a statement, to declare your opinion before millions of unseen, anonymous others. And yet even in the remote indigenous cultures of the Amazon, the focus of the ritual almost always comes back to the most important and respected member of the community, just as the lens of the talk-show camera never strays far from the host.

The appearance of Raoni and Meguron on *Donahue* wasn't the first time forest peoples had made network television. And Sting wasn't the only "celeb" out there working for the preservation of the fragile Amazon. Jerry Garcia and the Grateful Dead had held a rain forest benefit concert at Madison Square Garden, and Madonna had hosted a concert–fashion show called "Don't Bungle the Jungle." Saving the rain forest was now not only topical, it was hip, and Hollywood was quick to catch on. Members of the motion picture and television community had established two groups, ECO and EMA, both dedicated to the promotion of rain forest issues in film and television productions. In Europe, Danielle Mitterrand, the wife of the French president, had made saving *la forêt tropicale* a top priority, while her husband had infuriated Brazilians with his suggestion that the Amazon could be protected *from Brazil* by establishing "limitations" to the country's sovereignty over the region. England's Prince Charles got involved in the cause when he publicly condemned the gold rush in Yanomami territory.

And then came the movie deals. Robert Redford, a long-standing environmentalist, was developing his own story about Chico Mendes based on a *Vanity Fair* article that had been sold by its author to Redford's company for $200,000. Word of this deal quickly traveled south, infuriating local rubber tappers, who saw it as another gross example of North American imperialism. According to the Brazilian rumor mill, the author had not offered a cent of the $200,000 either to Mendes's Rubber Tappers Union or to his penniless survivors. When the magazine writer attempted to do a follow-up story, he was unceremoniously escorted out of town by Mendes's dirt-poor compatriots. This sad saga of big bucks, good intentions, and ill-conceived deal making didn't get any better when Chico's widow got involved in the movie morass by selling the rights to her husband's story to a Brazilian producer who promised he would make the definitive Brazilian film on Chico's life. The Brazilian filmmaker at "J. R. Pictures" quickly turned around and sold the story to the Hollywood mega-producing team of Peter Guber and Jon Peters, two L.A. heavyweights who made an occasional film of social relevance but were known primarily for such box-office fluff as *Flashdance, D.C. Cab, Who's That Girl?* and *Caddyshack II.* And the machine whirred on. In the pages of *Variety* the names of Hoffman and Pacino were put forward as possible stars to play Chico, while in Brazil the news of the

Chico Mendes movie-rights fiasco—and the deceptive role that a Brazilian company played in it—was a front-page story.

All of this only reconfirmed a nagging anxiety I had about the rain forest cause: that it would ignite the short fuse always smoldering below the surface of encounters between Brazilians and Americans. It also made me think of a story, both surreal and foreboding, that I had heard at the time of Chico's assassination. Within hours of the arrest by the police of Darly Alves da Silva, a woman named Francesca cut her own throat with a kitchen knife on the property of the Fazenda Paraná where she had been carrying on an affair with Darly. The local media attributed her suicide to her fears that her imprisoned lover would punish her because she had been speaking to the police investigating Chico's murder. But a friend of hers, Margarete da Sena, claimed that Darly's mistress had taken her own life because she had been told by the police that "North American ecologists were going to drop an atomic bomb on Fazenda Paraná."

The bomb never dropped but Hollywood deals continued to get made. The American producer Saul Zaentz hired Brazil's preeminent *auteur* Hector Babenco to direct a film adaptation of Peter Mathiessen's *At Play in the Fields of the Lord*. Other movies in the works included *Medicine Man*, *Amazon*, and an adaptation of Payakan's life to be directed by *Blade Runner* director Ridley Scott.

Nor did the Chico Mendes feeding frenzy end with the deals made by Robert Redford and Guber/Peters. More than a year after Chico's death even unglamorous characters like myself continued to be approached by big-name producers, actors, and screenwriters looking to angle their way into a story about his life. But I wasn't about to get involved. Beyond the ethical issue of profiting from a subject's death, there was the practical consideration of being involved in any sort of deal struck over Mendes's body. Such a deal would not only have corrupted my soul but also have tarnished my image in Brazil so irrevocably as to make any future work in that country impossible. Dropping into impoverished frontier communities with a fifty-thousand-dollar camera and a rented car necessitates establishing a bond

of trust not only with your subjects but with the intermediaries—missionaries, anthropologists, activists—all of whom
form critical, often lifesaving links in a precarious chain that on
dozen of occasions got me from New York to Rio to small villages in the interior of the country. These contacts are putting
their reputations on the line for *your* story. They're the ones
who have made a particular community their life's work. And
they are the ones who, long after you're safely back in the
States, will catch hell—or bullets—for the muckraking that
pays your rent and makes your reputation. I wasn't about to
jeopardize the alliances I had forged in the last two years simply
to get involved in the slippery world of Hollywood deal making.

———————

"**Q**uiet down, everyone," said a spry woman with a Southern
accent from a small stage one night in Manhattan. She was
Turner Broadcasting's producer of films from the Amazon and
part of a core group of activists and academics who were accompanying Payakan on his tour through the United States. As the
microphone caught a little reverberation, the crowd settled
into a gentle murmur.

"I want to introduce you to Payakan, chief of the Amazon's
Indians," she said to her audience. As she welcomed him on
stage, the crowd broke into a raucous round of applause pep-
pered with a few strangely inappropriate war cries.

"This is the man who is trying to save the rain forest, and I
want you to help him by buying some of these items," said the
TBS producer.

The last time I had seen her was at Altamira, where she
stood in the Indians' temporary village adorned in Kayapo
facial paint posing for a friend taking her picture. At one hotel
rooftop gathering during this time she was so elated by the
apparent success of the conference that she let out a war cry
and then proceeded to kiss Payakan up and down his arm in
front of a dozen journalists and environmentalists. By then she
had already produced a number of documentaries on this
"Amazonian chief" which were essentially vehicles to place
him at the center of a global movement for environmental

change. Her work had been instrumental in his winning one of Ted Turner's Better World Society Awards for his contribution to environmental preservation. And now rumor had it that she was developing Payakan's life into an animated series for children.

Payakan was becoming bigger than life and this woman was presiding over his transformation. Yet here in the dimly lit club Payakan seemed to have lost the wit and charm that he displayed in Altamira as well as in the documentary films TBS had made on his life. He looked ill at ease in this strange atmosphere, pushing ahead only because he felt it would eventually help his people. The remarks he delivered were rather perfunctory clichés about the need to help the Indians so that they could help us. Then Payakan's filmmaker friend returned to the stage and began to auction bits and pieces of Kayapo regalia.

As the lights came up on the audience, I scanned the crowd. There before me was the avant-garde of a new generation of environmentalists, a legion of scraggly haired kids in their twenties wearing tie-dyed T-shirts, hippie paraphernalia, long skirts, jeans, and baggy khaki shorts. There were also clusters of older people in their thirties and forties. The men, an inordinate number of whom seemed to have ponytails, were dressed in power ties, suits, and suspenders. The women wore skirts with matching jackets, the buttons of their blouses undone a little more than at the office, their feet comfortably sheathed in running shoes after a day on Wall Street and or in Midtown.

As the television-producer-turned-auctioneer cajoled the crowd to up their bids for the traditional headdresses—"Don't you people care about saving the rain forest!" she suddenly screamed, and "Now come on let's s-e-e-e-e some hands!"—I started thinking about her phrase *chief of the Amazon's Indians*. It could be said that Payakan was a chief, although the word has no equivalent in the Kayapo language. The term *chief* is in fact used by the Kayapo and many other of the Amazon's Indians only when speaking to whites. It is our term imposed on their cultures. This shortcut reference to leadership roles is a dangerous misnomer, because it implies a uniform hierarchial structure that in fact does not exist. Yet its malapropos assignation to Indian cultures in this hemisphere is part of the distorted way we have come to perceive them. Hack Hollywood screen-writers have played their part. So have popular figures of speech—"Indian givers," cowboys and Indians (we all know who the bad guys are), "Indian (false) summer," "the only good Indian . . ."—and Indians as sports symbols, including the Atlanta Braves baseball team (owned by Ted Turner) whose fans' "tomahawk chop" has caused consternation among count-less native Americans.

Ironically, we have historically identified as "chiefs" those who acted as point person in the early encounters between their peers and the white man's world. At times leaders in their communities, just as often they are not. But their liaisons with whites give them power and status because they are conduits of products ranging from steel swords to liquor. When I first arrived in the Yanomami village of Wakathantheri it had recently been overrun by gold miners who won over one of the local leaders. This was during a period when the Consolatas had been expelled as part of a government effort to clear the area of foreigners. After the missionaries were reinstated, the miners' influence on the village *tuxawa* named Carrera remained evident. While most of the villagers continued to live with a minimum of clothing, Carrera now wore a brightly col-ored tropical shirt, a pair of pants, a captain's hat, and what appeared to be a doorman's jacket that vaguely suggested mili-tary rank. He had been singled out by the miners in a society where decentralized group decision making was the way of life. Carrera's new status exacerbated long dormant tensions within the community. The village splintered into two factions shortly after the departure of the gold miners. Carrera's rival Pedro, a traditional *tuxawa* who didn't care for the miners, had picked up and formed his own community not far from Wakathau-theri, at the other end of the mission airstrip. Although Carrera had benefited in the short term from his new role, when the miners left he lost his base of power.

As I watched Payakan on stage, I wondered how his life would be changed by his contact with these outsiders, the people who referred to him as "chief of the Amazon's Indians."

The title was not just a distortion but a lie. However, the movement to save the rain forest was in full swing. The headdresses needed to be sold. And no one seemed to be considering the consequences.

20

By the year 1990 those remote, difficult-to-pronounce places the Wolf and I had visited in Yanomami territory—Baiano Formiga, Wakathautheri, Paapiú—were appearing in thick bold print on front pages of major newspapers and magazines. The *New York Times*, *Time*, the *Washington Post*, *Le Monde*, and the *Times* of London had suddenly shifted their attention from Chico Mendes and Sting to the malaria epidemic on Yanomami lands. The initial cases I had documented the previous year had now blown into a widespread epidemic working its way from village to village, wreaking havoc on a rapidly dwindling population of nine thousand endangered Indians.

The story broke when the miners, suddenly reversing their stance that malaria didn't exist, tried to position themselves as the Indians' saviors by flying planeloads of the stricken and dying into the frontier town of Boa Vista. There had been growing criticism of their occupation of Yanomami lands and this last-ditch maneuver was intended to deflect criticism onto the Brazilian Indian Agency FUNAI, the branch of government, presently debt-ridden, that had been charged with the Indians' health care. For years the miners had been decrying the ineptitude of the Indian Agency, proclaiming themselves the most responsible force on the frontier and contending that their legions of wildcat miners were doing a better job of caring for the Yanomami than the disorganized and underfunded bands of FUNAI employees scattered through the forest. "Incompetents," "jackasses," and "clowns" were some of the common epithets I overheard in bars and mining pits when I inquired about this government agency in conversations with miners. When the Cessnas bearing Indians began arriving in Boa Vista, the miners felt they had concocted a flawless plan to strike a severe blow to the credibility of FUNAI. They transported the Yanomami, emaciated and feverish, to a small, run-down, understaffed Indian Agency outpost called Casa dos Indios on the outskirts of town. This wretched halfway house, a circular, prisonlike building for visiting indigenous populations, was quickly overflowing with three hundred disease-ridden Yanomami, most of them collapsed into filthy hammocks, flinching and writhing from the lethal effects of late-stage malaria. Still the miners flew more planeloads of Indians into Boa Vista.

But this bold move, consistent with their entire operation in the forest, backfired almost immediately. What the miners had forgotten was that the world would accept their version of the truth only as long as they controlled the flow of information in and out of the forest. Once the Indians were in the city, the story was up for grabs. Anyone could tell it.

The press went to work. Pitiful shots of feverish and debilitated Yanomami looking jaundiced and confused under the glaring lights of local news cameras began circulating on Brazilian television. They posed a frightful contrast to the sterotypical images of robust and contented Indians living in a pristine forest, a virtual Eden. The plight of the Yanomami became an international cause célèbre when these crude and horrific images were broadcast across Europe and North America. Within a few short days Boa Vista's tiny airport was packed with foreign journalists paying big bucks to commandeer Cessnas, hoping to get a few shots of the dead and dying. As the ever astute renegade José Altino had predicted, "the international press" had proven to be his biggest obstacle.

This sudden explosion of concern for the Yanomami forced Brazil's newly elected president, Fernando Collor de Mello to finally allow international medical teams—accompanied by anthropologists—to enter the Indians' territory. One of the first was Bruce Albert, a tall blond Frenchman who had the cool comportment of a Jean-Paul Belmondo. Albert was not only an expert on Yanomami society (his dissertation focused on the Yanomami's intepretation of disease, funerals, and warfare rituals) but he was one of the few people in the outside world who was fluent in their complex language. As a French national brought up in North Africa and married to a Japanese woman, Albert was also accustomed to straddling multiple cultures. He had also worked among the Yanomam for two decades. Now working temporarily under the auspices of Brazil's ministry of health, the French anthropologist traveled for three months through thirty villages documenting the extent of the deaths in a cryptic culture that forbade survivors from mentioning the names of the deceased. Attuned to the intricacies of Yanomami ways, he ingeniously came up with various methods to circumvent their traditional taboos. He would ask the survivors a series of circuitous questions about each person's fate but that did not force them to openly declare that the person had died. "This man is not living here and he is not living in any other village, is that correct?" was the typical line of questioning Albert would use to confirm a death while respecting Yanomami tradition. "He is not living with the priests and he has not left the forest to live with the white men?" he would add, making sure that he was covering all his bases. Albert's unique skills made him one of the few people who could interpret what had been happening to the Yanomami. And the final tabulations were horrifying.

In the past three years fifteen hundred Indians, or twenty percent of the tribe, had been wiped out by malaria and other infectious diseases introduced—the medical reports asserted— only recently by the invasion of forty-five thousand Brazilian gold miners. In many Yanomami villages up to eighty percent of the inhabitants were suffering from various stages of malaria as well as the anemia and malnutrition that commonly accompanies it. Albert and the medical teams he collaborated with began treating the Indians who showed early symptoms of the disease and whose blood samples had tested positive.

Helicopters were requisitioned from the military to transport those in danger of dying.

Two out of every ten people succumbed for eight out of ten infected—imagine the impact the epidemic had on their communities. What would happen if eight out of every ten people in Manchester, England, or Portland, Oregon, were struck down by a deadly epidemic? Think of them bedridden and convulsive, debilitated by raging fevers as deadly parasites ate away at their brains and livers. This indiscriminate disease affects everyone, so it is just a matter of time before the key leaders— the priests or preachers, the doctors, the local farmers, the town's police—are all infected. Within a matter of weeks, the entire community is a shambles: food is almost impossible to obtain, the rotting bodies of the dead pile up. The family unit crumbles. What makes matters worse is that you may know there is a cure, but it is controlled by the same people who gave you this strange disease, those who live beyond the edge of the world. Sympathetic members of their group—missionaries, a few health administrators—have access to the cure but you are too weak to make the two-to-three-week walk to reach them. You can only wait, and die a slow, tormented death.

"They gave us rice and wheat but then we got sick," a Yanomami man told a *Time* magazine reporter when asked about the impact of the gold miners on their society. "They pretended to be our friends," he continued, "but they are killing us."

21

Davi Kopenawa also had malaria when I met him at JFK airport in April of 1990. He came off the plane smiling but sluggish and dizzy from the effects of a high fever. In stature typical of a Yanomami man, Davi was around five foot four, probably in his mid-thirties, with a roundish face and Western variation of the bowl-shaped haircut customary among his people. His general demeanor was low-key and jocular, yet his eyes were always working the room. This guy wasn't missing a thing.

Davi was accompanied by a thin, intense woman with short brown hair named Claudia Andujar, a human rights activist who had spent most of her life living and working in Brazil. While Claudia was said to be in her late fifties, there was the air of a teenager about her. She had a sprightly walk and a girlish laugh that belied her tragic youth: her father, a Hungarian Jew, had died in a Nazi concentration camp during World War II. Claudia had been brought up by her mother, a Swiss national. She lived in New York as a young woman, then moved to Brazil, where she started working with the Yanomami in the early 1970s taking photographs as part of freelance assignments for magazines. I had always admired her beautiful black-and-white shots. Her work transcended most photojournalists' attempts to record life in indigenous societies. Each shot seemed to bring with it a sense of Yanomami culture and an intimate understanding of their lives. In the last decade Claudia had given up photography and spent most of her time working around the clock as head of the Committee for the Creation of the Yanomami Park, or CCPY, an organization of scholars and activists campaigning for the demarcation of Yanomami lands.

Davi and Claudia's trip to the United States had a twofold agenda: to obtain emergency medical funds for the malaria epidemic and simultaneously to seize the momentum of the Save the Rain Forest movement to force the Brazilian government to recognize Yanomami lands. But their first task in the United States was to tackle the matter of lost baggage. Davi had hoped to bring a few Yanomami bows and arrows to the States as presents, but they were seized by the Pan Am flight crew when he boarded his plane in São Paulo. Now, in New York, Claudia conferred with Pan Am's baggage representatives about the missing items as Davi and I sat together on molded plastic chairs bolted to the floor of the airport lobby.

"*A primeira vez que você tem malária?*"—This is the first time you have malaria?—I asked Davi, hesitantly testing out my Portuguese as we sat pondering one of Calder's enormous but elegant metal sculptures suspended above us.

"No, the tenth time," he responded.

"*Tem muita malária agora na sua aldeia?*" Do you have a lot at this time in your village?

"*Sim, agora tem muita.*" Yes, a lot at this time. "Many of the older generation died from it," he added in Portuguese as he leaned over to take a deep breath. Then a nervous smile inched its way into the corners of his mouth as he winced and let forth a sigh of pain—the malaria was working its way through his body. The drugs—a combination of chloroquin and prima quim—given to him by a doctor yesterday in São Paulo had yet to kick in. He sighed again and took a second look up at Calder's sculpture.

Claudia returned empty-handed. Pan Am was going to get in touch with us in the next few days. Welcome to America.

We drove into Manhattan from JFK on the Long Island Expressway, passing endless rows of two-story houses in Queens

as the black barren branches of city trees zippered by in silhouette. It was a bitterly cold day. Winter had yet to give way to
spring in New York. Fortunately someone (I assume Claudia)
had been wise enough to give Davi a heavy jacket.

"*Por que todas as árvores estão mortas?*"—Why are all the trees
dead?—Davi asked as he peered through the rear windows of
my little rent-a-car.

"The trees here change during the year," Claudia told him.
"They sleep during the winter and come out again in the spring."

Davi had made one trip to France and one to England, both
in the full bloom of late spring, but this was his first exposure to
the colder seasons in the Northern Hemisphere.

"*E o Kenny, onde fica ele?*" And Kenny, where is he?

"*Momentinho,*" Claudia said and turned to me. "Do you know
Ken Good? The anthropologist who ran off with the Yanomami
woman." As she spoke I could detect traces of an Eastern European accent in Claudia's English. It gave her speech a melodi-
ousness, as if the words were filtered through the soft rounded
chamber of a wooden flute.

"I've spoken to him on the phone," I said.

"Davi wants to meet him."

"Okay."

"I think that would be good," she said. "He's been asking
about him since he arrived yesterday from Boa Vista."

I glanced in the rearview mirror and caught Davi checking
my reaction in the reflection as Claudia translated our conversation. Kenneth Good was an American anthropologist who
had broken the ethnographer's taboo by marrying a Yanomami
girl, a member of a village where he had been conducting his
field research. Their liaison had caused problems not only
in the anthropological community but with the Yanomami and
the Venezuelan government as well. Because of their troubles
they left Yanomami territory and settled in the United States.
At present Ken was teaching at a local college in New Jersey
and his wife, Yarima, was adapting to her new role as a suburban housewife.

As we drove I thought about what I had read in different
anthropology texts about women in Yanomami society and

what I had seen in the villages and been told by my anthropologist friends in Brazil. Women were a very important part
of that culture, to be certain. But to what extent they affected
larger Yanomami society was a matter of heated debate in academic circles. Some experts like the American anthropologist
Napoleon Chagnon have claimed that women represented a
scarce resource that created intense intervillage conflicts and
even warfare. This theory has been vehemently challenged by
many of Chagnon's colleagues in Brazil and abroad. They
have countered that contact with white society and the
importation of guns and material objects have actually done
much more to escalate conflicts within Yanomami communities by disrupting the traditional balance of power and age-old
traditions for conflict resolution. Most anthropologists who
have studied the Yanomami acknowledge that the occasional
abduction of women is a part of their culture of warfare. For
this reason women usually go in groups on forays into the
forest, often accompanied by a male member of the village.
This practice is common among many lowland Indian societies. Whether violence against women is much more prevalent in Yanomami society than it is in Western European
culture is the real point of contention in this debate—a point
yet to be proven either way in any kind of objective statistical
analysis.

What was obvious to me driving in from the airport was that
when Ken Good plucked a Yanomami woman out of the
Venezuelan rain forest, it not only sent tremors throughout
Yanomami culture and the academic community, it resonated
deeply within the psyche of my new guest in the backseat.

"Ken lives with his wife not far from here," I said as we
descended into the momentary darkness of an underpass. "Just
across the river from Manhattan. We can give him a call
tomorrow."

Claudia translated as Davi sat motionless, taking in her
words, his eyes locked on the passing sidewalk, searching, I
imagined, for "Kenny," the errant anthropologist roaming
North America with his young Yanomami spouse.

No one spoke again until we crossed the Triboro Bridge, the

image of the Manhattan skyline fluttering by us between suspension pylons like film in a projector suddenly gone out of control.

"*Nova Iorque*. New York," said Davi as he stared out the side window.

I unloaded their bags and hustled Davi and Claudia into my apartment building, dodging a few addicts, their heads snapping back and forth, still flush from a blast of crack. Across the street I saw the early warning signs of every New Yorker's nightmare: workers were setting up jackhammers. They looked like they were going to be staying awhile. In the elevator I considered explaining to Davi and Claudia about the drug-dealing dynamics of the neighborhood but I decided to wait for a more appropriate time. *I'll let them rest—if they can—after the overnight flight. That should provide Davi with enough time to orient himself.* At least that is what I thought.

In the afternoon Claudia slept in the back bedroom, the quietest place in the apartment, while Davi and I sat in my kitchen drinking fruit juice and eating ham sandwiches. The jackhammers droned on endlessly just beyond my window. Davi said he wanted to see pictures of American Indians, so I pulled several books down off my shelf. The first I opened was Dee Brown's *Bury My Heart at Wounded Knee*, a historical overview of the Indian experience in North America. As I turned the pages I read aloud the captions of the photographs, giving rough translations where I could. The majority of the images were portraits typical of the era: men and women, their backs arched uncomfortably (obviously at the photographer's request), staring forward, their eyes locked on the lens of the camera. Some wore the clothes of the white man, while others were adorned in ceremonial dress. All of them, however, seemed to fascinate Davi. The photos, many from the nineteenth-century archives of the Smithsonian Institution, seemed to reflect more about the persons who took them (and perhaps the technology available) than they did about the subjects. These were Indians abstracted from their environment, objects for the perusal of white culture. The photos did not reveal how they had happened to end up in front of the camera. The nineteenth-century photographer Edward Curtis is said to have paid his subjects to sit for him. But

I also wondered what these native men and women thought of the process, and what the white photographers imagined they were accomplishing in creating such lifeless depictions. True, they were working within the technological limits of their medium, but that did not require that their subjects be *taken from the context of their lives.* Even when the images of this era show Native Americans at home, in their villages, it is almost always in set-up poses, adorned in ceremonial dress, very rarely in the customary outfits of daily life. If there was one unifying element to these photos it seemed to be the testament of the subjects' blank stares: the no-win realization that their world was disappearing before them and that there was little or nothing they could do about it.

I've always had mixed feelings about the photographers of this period. I find their images lifeless and controlling in a way that suggests they were practicing the same techniques of manipulation as were being practiced by their pioneer contemporaries. Yet these men with cameras, like Edward Curtis, Eugene Dixon, and the dozens of others who roamed the West at the turn of the century, took great personal risks to give us today the only visual records we have of this time. Was I not doing in Brazil what they had done in the American West? Tagging along on the coattails of gold miners and cattle ranchers, documenting a disappearing culture along a vanishing frontier. Like my predecessors I was taking images from the perspective of the dominant society. Neither they nor I had much comprehension of the complex cultures we were encountering. "The whites told only one side. Told it to please themselves. Told much that is not true," reads a quote from Yellow Wolf of the Nez Percés at the beginning of one chapter. "Only his own best deeds, only the worst deeds of the Indians, has the white man told."

"Qual é o nome dele?"—What is his name?—Davi asked, pointing to a photograph of an Indian man in native dress and braids.

"Kicking Bird," I said, hoping that Davi wouldn't ask me to come up with a translation for that one.

"Kick-ing Bi-rd," he repeated, his English already sounding

better than my Portuguese. He then took a moment to study the stoic face of the black-and-white image.

"*O povo?*" The people?

"Kiowas," I say.

"Ki-o-was," he repeats.

"*Tem muito?*" Are there many?

"*Antes, sim. Agora, não.*" Before, yes. Now, no.

I turned the pages and landed upon the profile shot of a striking, bold-faced Indian man in a feathered headdress. He looked like the archetype that adorned the Indian-head nickels I had grown up with. Davi pointed to the man's photo, then looked at me as I wondered what happened to all those silver nickels.

"Two Moon," I told him.

"Two . . ."

I chimed in. "Mooo . . ."

"Mooonnnn," he said, completing the phrase.

"Which people?" he asked.

"Cheyenne."

"*Tem muito agora?*" Are there many of them now?

"Before, yes. Now, no."

I turned the pages again and this time was presented with an image entitled "Big Foot in death" photographed at the Wounded Knee battlefield. In a snow-covered field a large Indian man, wrapped in layers of the white man's clothes, lies on the ground, his lifeless body frozen and contorted, fingers twisted, his back forming a strange arch, and his eyes—barely visible in this black-and-white print—staring off into the distant sky. This is almost the only photo in the book not shot in a studio. It is also the most shocking. Davi takes more time with it than the others.

"*Qual é o nome dele?*"

"*Pé Grande.* Big Foot," I said, pleased that my scant Portuguese vocabulary would allow me to come up with this translation.

"*Morto?*" Dead?

"*Sim.*"

"*Por que?*" Why?

That's a good question, I thought to myself. Then I took a moment to look at the book.

In the closing chapter of *Bury My Heart at Wounded Knee*, historian Dee Brown focuses in precise detail on the events leading up to the death of Big Foot on a blustery cold day in late December of 1890. The U.S. War Department had recently issued orders for his arrest and imprisonment. He was one of several indigenous leaders charged with being "fomenters of disturbances." The government campaign was intended to prevent Native Americans from practicing the Ghost Dance, an outlawed activity of a Christian-based millennial cult—pacifist in nature—which was attracting great numbers of converts among the survivors of the army's brutal Indian campaigns of the post–Civil War years. Members of the cult were commonly friends and families of victims of the campaigns—in the case of Big Foot's group mostly "widows"—who had come to believe that with the return of the Messiah, an Indian Messiah, they would see restored to them their life as it once had been, on a new earth, "where only Indians would live" and where they could be reunited with the ghosts of their ancestors.

One of the Ghost Dance faith's key proselytizers was a man named Kicking Bear, who traveled among various Sioux communities spreading the word of this new religion. The Messiah had appeared, Kicking Bear told them, and had said that "God made the earth, and then sent the Christ to earth to teach the people, but white men had treated him badly, leaving scars on his body, and so he had gone back to heaven. Now he had returned to earth as an Indian, and he was to renew everything as it used to be and make it better." Native dancing and singing would prepare Indians for the approaching day when God would lift them into the air and a new earth would be created and the buffalo replenished.

The message fell on receptive ears. One leader named Short Bull led a band of three thousand converts into the Dakota Badlands where they danced in the bitter cold snow from dawn until dusk driven by the belief that their efforts would summon the Messiah. But the U.S. government—receiving panicked reports from the region's Indian agents—was not pleased by the newest activity of these unruly people. One Indian Agency official on a Sioux reservation sent an urgent telegraph to Washington saying "Indians are dancing in the snow and are wild and crazy. . . . We need protection and we need it now." The War Department responded by calling for the immediate prohibition of Ghost Dancing and the imprisonment of those practicing it. Sitting Bull was on this list; so was the Minneconjou Indian leader Big Foot. When Major Whitside of the Seventh U.S. Cavalry encountered Big Foot and his Ghost Dancers, they were en route to the Pine Ridge reservation. He instructed them to set up camp on Wounded Knee Creek. The old Minneconjou leader, hemorrhaging from a severe case of pneumonia, complied with Whitside's order. Whitside called for the company's doctor to attend Big Foot and then ordered a portable heater installed in the old man's tent overnight. In the evening Major Whitside's troops camped on a hill overlooking the creek, setting up their Hotchkiss machine guns with the barrels trained on the Minneconjou encampment. In the morning, in accordance with their orders from the War Department, the cavalry called for the Indians to turn over their arms. Most complied, but after an extensive search two Indians refused to give up their weapons. One man named Black Coyote clung to his Winchester rifle, claiming that he had obtained it at great personal expense. When a scuffle started, the first rounds of gunfire occurred. Who fired the first shot is still contested to this day but the outcome is well documented. As Dee Brown relates it:

In the first seconds of violence, the firings of carbines was deafening, filling the air with powder smoke. Among the dying who lay sprawled on the frozen ground was Big Foot. Then there was a brief lull in the rattle of arms, with small groups of Indians and soldiers grappling at close quarters, using knives, clubs, and pistols. As few of the Indians had arms, they soon had to flee, and then the big Hotchkiss guns on the hill opened up on them, firing almost a shell a second, raking the Indian camp, shredding the tepees with flying shrapnel, killing men, women, and children.

"Massacre," I told Davi, putting down the book. I wasn't about to try to explain the sequence of events that led to the killing: my Portuguese just wasn't up to it. I wondered who had taken that shot of Big Foot in the snow. And how long the body had lain there frozen. And what the other photographs were like that had been taken that day.

"*Quantos indios mortos?*"—How many Indians were killed?—Davi asked.

"*Trezentos.*" Three hundred.

"*E brancos?*" And the whites?

"*Vinte e cinco.*" Twenty-five.

In the evening Davi, Claudia, and I went for a meal at the Embarrada Restaurant on Amsterdam Avenue, a simple, clean Dominican establishment with lots of Formica and bright fluorescent lights. In the corner a jukebox blared salsa as a small contingent of waitresses spun about the room in tight jeans and low-cut blouses sharing gossip with neighborhood patrons as they shuttled orders to the steamy backroom kitchen. To get into the restaurant we had to circle around a cluster of young dealers in Timberland jackets and work boots doling out tiny glass vials of blue-top crack in exchange for tightly rolled bills proffered by two anxious young addicts—long-haired, gaunt-looking suburban white boys. Once seated in the restaurant we ordered rice, beans, and chicken as I contemplated how to explain the presence of the dealers and addicts who, particularly in the evenings, were an inescapable presence in this neighborhood. Handing the menus back to the waitress, Davi cut me off before I could begin speaking.

"We don't take drugs," he said, using Claudia as an interpreter to make certain he was being completely understood. "We inhale the *yakōana* powder so that we can go visiting other places with the forest spirits."

The waitress brought a bowl of white rice and the black beans Davi had ordered for a starter.

"These drugs the people take here are destroying people, not giving them knowledge," he said as he lowered his spoon toward the steaming dark beans. "We take our *yakōana* to understand the world, not to kill ourselves. It is not a drug." He smiled, then swung a huge helping of beans into his mouth.

Claudia, who had lived in New York, had obviously spoken to Davi about the trafficking of drugs on the block, relieving me of the sensitive role of cultural interlocutor. Davi's perspective on our "drug problem" was, interestingly enough, derived from a culture in which for the shamans—the spiritual leaders—the consumption of the hallucinogenic *yakōana* was an essential element in their belief system. Davi himself was a shaman's apprentice who had, over the last year, diligently taken part in numerous *yakōana* sessions in a quest for further knowledge about the Indians' complex spiritual world. *Yakōana*, a dark hallucinogenic substance derived from the bark of virola trees, provides for the Yanomami a means of contacting the tiny humanoid spirits known as *hekura* who live inside the chests of shamans or hide out in the tall trees or dark, dank crevices of the Amazon forest.

In his classic *Yanomanö, The Fierce People*, Chagnon wrote at length about the apprentice or "novice":

> An older man or older men instruct the novice in the
> attributes, habits, songs, and fancies of the *hekura* spirits.
> During the period of fasting, the novice must also be sexually
> continent, for the hekura are said to dislike sex and regard it
> as filthy. Novices attempt to attract particular hekura into
> their chests, a process that takes a long time and much
> patience, for the hekura are somewhat coy and fickle, apt to
> leave and abandon their human host. The interior of a
> shaman's body is a veritable cosmos of rivers, streams,
> mountains, and forests where the hekura can swell in
> comfort and happiness. Only the more accomplished
> shamans have many hekura inside their bodies, and even
> then they must strive to keep them happy and contented.
> Once you are on good terms with your hekura, you can
> engage in sex without having your spirits abandon you.

"You people have faxes and telephones," Davi told me later that night as we sat in my apartment. "But we have something better. Our shamanic spirits. Through them we can communicate to other Indians in the Amazon." He gestured widely with his hands. "This is how we know what is happening to our relatives in other parts of the forest."

Since he was a child Davi had been widely exposed to "modern culture," so I found it hard to comprehend that in this day and age he could still believe that he visited other Amazonian societies simply by taking the hallucinogenic *yakõana* shot blowgun-style into his nostrils by fellow shamans. He was not a "Stone Age Indian," as the North American press loved to call the Yanomami. He had been brought up around the New Tribes missionaries and as an adult had been working for the Indian Agency as their contact in the village of Demeni. He had anthropologists as friends, and had traveled to São Paulo, London, Paris, and now New York—which made him as cosmopolitan as me or many of my friends. I thought that when Davi was saying these things, it was certainly a front, you could even say a barrier, a way of protecting himself from the white man, of assuring himself that he was from another world and planned on staying there. Perhaps this stance had been necessary for him to fend off those who throughout his life had been interested in changing his ways: missionaries, Indian Agency officials, misguided anthropologists, even those well-intentioned liberal activists who wanted him to be a mouthpiece for their particular agendas. His culture, Yanomami culture, had suffered tremendously in recent years but its shamans, men like Davi and Machadão, still considered it as strong and compelling and vibrant as it had been in the days of their fathers. Shamanism was the spiritual backbone of their culture, it was a core belief that distinguished them from us.

As I spoke more with Davi in the following days, I realized that these "wild ideas of his" simply reflected the way he looked at the world—that he was just expressing the frame of reference of his culture, a culture in which the assertion "I possess the truth" is a common refrain in day-to-day discussions. What distinguished this apprentice shaman, with his *hekura* spirits and transcendental visitations, from the Second-Coming fervor of the Ghost Dancers was that Davi's beliefs retained all the central tenets of traditional Yanomami cosmology. The Ghost Dancers, on the other hand, had embraced a fusion of their own traditional beliefs and an apocalyptic construct derived from Judeo-Christian tenets foisted upon them by frontier missionaries. They had departed from the spiritual bedrock of their culture and they were lost. The way Davi expressed his vision and the way the Ghost Dancers came to express theirs represented two radically different attempts at adjusting to two very different contact experiences. Although Davi's people had suffered tremendous hardship, they still managed to retain strong roots in their own culture, transformed slightly to accommodate the existence of outsiders. The messianic beliefs of Big Foot and the other Ghost Dancers, however, were a last-ditch attempt by a defeated people to free themselves from the domination, dependence, and devastation that had overtaken them in the nineteenth-century American West. Resistance, treaties, adaptation—all were alternatives that had failed the Ghost Dancers. Their culture and way of life had been destroyed. Awaiting an Indian Messiah was their only remaining option. The Yanomami, however, still retained enough of their culture to preserve their world.

Davi's current path—cultural affirmation combined with political resistance—had been part of his way of life for several decades. His experiences as a child had prepared him for the leadership role he came to play during the gold rush. He had grown up in the forest surrounded by milk-skinned evangelical American missionaries.

The ones who had settled in his community of Demini in the early 1960s were members of the New Tribes Mission, a Protestant group currently based in Florida but, at the time of their members' first sojourns in Yanomami lands, headquartered in Woodsworth, Wisconsin. The New Tribes international headquarters documented the proselytizing efforts of their hundreds of missionaries, in Davi's community and in other backwater parts of the Third World, in a missionary journal with the dubious title *Brown Gold*. This low-budget eight-by-ten-inch periodical resembled a cross between the Jehovah's Witnesses publication *Watchtower* and the mercenary magazine *Soldier of Fortune*. It featured black-and-white snapshots and the rambling prose of its Christian crusaders working among the Yanomami "savages" and "witch doctors." The titles of the articles bristled with apocalyptic and militaristic jargon. One day I called the resource department at the New Tribes headquarters in Sanford, Florida. I asked a pleasant woman named Theresa how they had come up with the title *Brown Gold*. "Well, there's gold gold, and black gold, which is oil," she said, then paused. "But brown gold, that's for tribal peoples; that's what we are after, because we're searching for souls."

According to the back issues of *Brown Gold*, their missionaries were in Yanomami territory so that "the word of the Lord may have free course" and so that God could "do a mighty work in the hearts of these Indians." I had discovered *Brown Gold* in a library in New York when I was helping the anthropologist Bruce Albert with research for a book he was doing in collaboration with Davi on his experiences growing up in Yanomami territory. In one account a missionary wife, a Mrs. Bruce Hartman, sent in a dispatch about the experiences of her husband in contacting a new group of Indians who had suddenly showed up at their outpost:

> Before the Indians left Bruce had several good opportunities to talk to two of the men who had shown the most interest. They both made decisions or professions of faith, as near as Bruce could tell, but he still isn't really sure that they understand and believe enough to be actually saved. Only God knows at this point but, with prayer and further teaching, time will tell. God knows their hearts although it is very hard for us to know whether they have actually been born again.

In another entry submitted by missionaries, a reference to Davi crops up in a description of activities in his village:

Davi still has his problems but continues to show some
growth and is doing well in his reading.

And an account also written in the 1960s by a New Tribes missionary named Keith Wardlaw shares some of his experiences
working with the unregenerate Indians:

> We meet each morning about 6:15 a.m. for prayer preceded
> by about five minutes of instruction in some Christian truth
> pertinent to their needs. Yesterday, it concerned taking a
> wife, disciplining children, and abstaining from committing
> adultery.

The propagation of this "Christian truth" among a people
whose most common expression was "I possess the truth" was not
an easy task. The back issues of *Brown Gold* are filled with frustrated accounts by doubt-ridden missionaries who are never
really certain if in fact they have converted a few new believers
or whether the Indians returned to their heathen existence of
tobacco chewing, polygamy, shamanism, endocannibalism, and
all the other little cultural idiosyncrasies that the missionaries
deemed sinful. In an article entitled "Satan Counter-attack," one
group of missionaries wrote about their efforts to win over the
souls of the heathens in an area known as Toototobi, the region
where Davi was born. Ironically, it was the positive disposition of
the Indians—something one would assume they should be happy
about—that they saw as an obstacle to be overcome:

> Good times and an abundance of food, plus a number of
> other sneaky factors, seem to be detrimental to the growth of
> the Church and the propagation of the Gospel of Christ.
> Spiritual sluggishness, unthankfulness, and a rejection of our
> wonderful God and Savior are the principal earmarks of this
> hour on the Toototobi.

When I first traveled to Boa Vista in 1988 to do research for
my documentary on gold mining on Indian lands, the New
Tribes missionaries were still an active presence in Yanomami

territory. From the Hotel Tropical, I tried for two days to set up an interview by calling the New Tribes office and asking to speak to one of the Americans on the staff. But the timing couldn't have been worse. A climate of heightened xenophobia had recently descended over Boa Vista. The priests and nuns of the Consolata mission had just recently been expelled from Yanomami lands on the pretense that they were foreign saboteurs. The New Tribes Mission—as foreigners also based in this sensitive border area—obviously didn't want to jeopardize their crusade by speaking to a potentially troublesome North American filmmaker. There were long, uncomfortable silences on the other end of the line when I tried to explain that I simply wanted to do an informal off-camera interview on their work with the Yanomami. In subsequent calls, I heard "they're in a meeting," "he just stepped out," "can he call you back?" No return phone call. So I decided to make an unannounced visit to their headquarters in Boa Vista.

I entered the cool shade of a dimly lit office on the ground floor of a small house situated on a quiet back street in the residential section of town. This was the New Tribes Mission Home. From the backyard next door I could hear the piercing, playful screams and laughter of children. Behind a small wooden desk sat a young Brazilian man with short-cropped dark hair. He spoke English with an American accent—a crusader, I assumed, who had been sent north to Florida for a season or two to perfect his language skills and get some first-hand exposure to the center of operations.

"Hi," I said. "I'm here to see . . . Paul." Paul, a Biblical name, seemed like a logical choice for one of their American staff members.

"Paul?" he asked, standing suddenly and looking attentive. *A good sign*, I thought.

"Yes. He's American. One of the program supervisors." I started searching through some papers as if I was looking for something I had written down. "I'm sorry," I added, "I am terrible with names."

"You probably mean Bob."

"Yes, that's right, Bob. Is he here?"

"Do you have an appointment?"

"No, but he is expecting me," I said, assuring myself that this wasn't exactly a lie. Someone had probably told him about my phone calls. Maybe it would have been more accurate to say "anticipating" me, but the young man was already off and down the hallway. Stopping him now would only confuse things; at least, that's how I justified this journalistic intrusion.

Within a few minutes I was shown into a larger office, where I met Bob, who didn't look as if he was too busy or had just led a prayer group or had just rushed in from an urgent meeting on soul saving. In fact this little man with a dour smile and a madras shirt looked bored and a little sleepy. I introduced myself, and said I had only a few questions and would very much appreciate his time for a brief background interview. Neither he nor I acknowledged that he and his staff had ignored my calls over the last few days or that I had lied my way into his office. It was all very polite and formal. Very *norte-americano*.

Bob started off our conversation by acknowledging that he was one of the organization's supervisors—a position that, he took great pains to point out, he "shared" with his Brazilian counterparts.

"Do you think the presence of tens of thousands of gold miners on Indian lands is affecting the Yanomami in your area?"

"The boys don't really worry about this type of thing, Mr. O'Connor."

Okay, I thought. *The boys?* "You mean the people in the village where you have a mission?"

"Yes, you see they are happy with the way things are right now." He paused a moment and looked directly into my eyes. "Have you been speaking with the Catholics?"

He means the competition. "Yes."

"Well, we don't really believe in the kind of position they are taking. We're not civil libertarians."

He means, I'm thinking, *liberation theologists*.

"And as I said, the boys are quite content the way things are."

There it was again. *The boys.* He seemed oblivious to the patronizing tone of his comments. I asked him a few more

background questions about their mission and how long it had
been in existence, interjecting a couple of lighthearted comments about the difficulty of keeping track of the National
League standings or finding "Colonel Sanders" in such a remote
part of the world—these intended to be icebreakers. Yet my
informal asides elicited no response from stoic Bob except for a
deep inhalation, a not so subtle hint that I should think about
finishing up. Perhaps my questions had been too direct, or
maybe he saw me scribble *boys* and *madras shirt* into my little
reporter's notebook.

As our conversation progressed I found myself wanting to
know about Bob and where he got his image of Indian men as
boys, how he and his fellow crusaders came up with terms like
"witch doctor" and "savages." These characterizations had very
little to do with the Yanomami I had known, yet for the last
three decades Bob and his Christian crusaders had taken it
upon themselves to transport such misconceptions into the
forest, along with the multifarious accoutrements of a missionary life including Bibles, toothbrushes, camping stoves,
pots, pans, machetes, and shotguns as well as (and for me the
most disconcerting item of all) a film projector. From what I
understood from a back issue of *Brown Gold*, the projector was
used to show films to the Yanomami. "Bruce Hartman has used
his little projector here very effectively. The story of Noah and
the ark was a real blessing the other night, and four people indicated that they wanted to accept the Lord the following day."
As I worked my way towards the final question, I found myself
trying to picture Bob out there in the forest. *Would he be
wearing a pith helmet?* I wondered. *Who would be working the projector? Did they show other movies?* I guess I thought visualizing
Bob in that context would provide some understanding about
who he was and why he chose to do what he did. I wondered if
he had the same thoughts about me. Most likely he didn't care.

I concluded our talk by asking if there was any possibility I
could visit his area when I returned to do some filming next
January. "That wouldn't be a possibility right now," I was told
as he stood. "It is our policy that only mission personnel are

allowed in the area." I really wanted to know more about the specific tactical maneuvers involved in defending oneself (or one's adopted tribe) from a counterattack by Satan. I thought about staying a few more minutes to try and convince Bob to let me enter the mission. But his body language and avoidance of eye contact told me to save my breath.

————

The history of the New Tribes Mission in Yanomami territory dates back to 1954. The first wide-eyed North American prose-lytizers to enter Davi's region based themselves at an Indian Agency outpost called Ajuricaba. The anthropologist Bruce Albert estimates that the first contact of New Tribes mission-aries with Davi's group occurred on the Toototobi River in 1958 in a place called Marakana. But the first prolonged visit of the evangelical group was in 1960 for a one-month period. Then in 1963 a triumvirate of New Tribesmen—James McNight, Keith Wardlaw, and Bruce Hartman—established a permanent mission on Yanomami lands and moved in with their families.

The *Brown Gold* articles of this era, written primarily by the Wardlaws and the Hartmans using the nom de plume "The Toototobi Gang," carry titles like "Trouble at Toototobi" and "Change of Heart." In a curious entry entitled "On Another Planet" written in 1968, Mrs. Bruce Hartman reconstructs her husband's recent experiences among the Yanomami, beginning the article with an excerpt from one of his letters from the field: "I draw a blank every time I think of writing a general letter or an article. I feel like I have been on another planet for about a year doing things that no one else would understand anyway."

The reader learns from Mrs. Hartman's account that a measles epidemic had broken out and "three different groups were exposed." Approximately one hundred thirty cases were reported from which—"counting babies"—there were twenty deaths. In the bottom left-hand corner of the page there is a photograph of one of the missionaries, a Mr. Jon Enns, with a smile on his face, his large white meaty arms thrown over the shoulders of two scantily clad Yanomami companions (both men). In the background a few other Indians stand wearing an odd assortment of skirts and pants, the details of their faces indistinguishable in the severe shadows of the harsh afternoon light. The photo, we are informed, is from 1964—a good three years before the outbreak of the measles epidemic. The caption written by Mrs. Hartman reads: "No doubt some of them have already passed on to a Christless eternity. How many more?" The article takes great pains to recount the tireless efforts of the missionaries who "worked day and night over a period of weeks" to nurse the Indians back to health. Mrs. Hartman writes at one point that "we know that God never makes a mistake and now that the crisis is passed we can see how the Lord is working in hearts through the things that have happened."

What isn't mentioned is something the anthropologist Bruce Albert discovered in the course of his research: that the missionaries themselves were responsible for the sickness and death that decimated the community. Measles and malaria are epidemics that are transported into isolated indigenous communities; the "carrier" in this case was a daughter of the missionaries. Davi's mother was one of the victims. Perhaps "God never makes a mistake," but in this case someone had conveniently left an important detail out of Mrs. Hartman's letter home. *Is this omission of fact a sinful act?* I thought after I read the article. *How about the inability to recognize responsibility for one's actions?*

There was something surreal, almost kitsch, about the attitudes of these missionaries towards the Indians. I thought again about what the woman at New Tribes headquarters had said about the title *Brown Gold*: "that's for tribal peoples, that's what we are after because we're searching for souls," and about the way Bob referred to the Yanomami as "boys." Showing a Biblical film on Noah and the ark to a group of Yanomami in the rain forest was also an act I found strange in its arrogant assertion of one cultural belief system over another. These little details and others reminded me of the way Milan Kundera described life in Communist Czechoslovakia and what he calls "the aesthetics of kitsch," those "images, metaphors, and vocabulary" that become part of an operative system in a totalitarian world, a system that never questions itself or the duplicity of its failed agendas. It is an aesthetic that simply imposes itself as a

given, as the way things are and should be. I detected an ideo-
logically driven kitsch aesthetic in the New Tribes, with their
Noah film and their insulting titles such as *Brown Gold*. Kundera was writing about Communist kitsch (May Day parades,
slogans, symbols) but, as he points out, it applies to all "faiths,
religious and political." As he says:

> Since the days of the French Revolution, one half of Europe
> has been referred to as the left, the other half as the right.
> Yet to define one or the other by means of the theoretical
> principles it professes is all but impossible. And no wonder:
> political movements rest not so much on rational attitudes as
> on the fantasies, images, words, and archetypes that come
> together to make up this or that *political kitsch*.

I had seen a lot of kitsch during the Save the Rain Forest movement: missionary kitsch, miner kitsch, environmentalist kitsch,
celebrity kitsch, and, yes, journalistic kitsch, all of it swept up
in its own hubris as the image of the Indians was being made
over (as, at times, were the Indians themselves) by self-
described well-intentioned whites who, in one way or another,
had all been involved in the transformation of the world's last
remote indigenous cultures.

"Essa é a casa dos missionários?"—Is this the house of the missionaries?—Davi asked me one morning standing in front of the
imposing edifice of St. John the Divine on Manhattan's Upper
West Side. I had decided to take him around the neighborhood
for a little tour. It was a gray Sunday. Sharp, cold gusts of wind
shot up the concrete corridor of Amsterdam Avenue. Small
groups of Japanese and Italians wandered about with long colorful scarves wrapped around their faces. Occasionally they
stopped and gazed up at the towering gothic columns of the
cathedral which had turned black with city smut. Most of
the tourists, however, simply knocked off a few quick family
snapshots and then headed into the church interior. Working
the crowd was a homeless man, a paper cup extended, with a
downtrodden countenance.

"Yes. I believe they have missionaries," I said in answer to Davi's question.

"But is this the house of the Padres or of the New Tribes?"

"Neither."

He looked at me, puzzled.

"They are Episcopalian, closer to New Tribes than to the Catholic priests in some ways. But different." *Where do you start when you try to explain the numbers of different religions and sects that exist outside the forest?*

We entered the church and stood overwhelmed just inside the portals.

"In my dreams I have traveled to places like this," said Davi as we walked by the various altars that line the sides of the cathedral. I pointed to the tomb of William Thomas Manning, the Episcopal Church's tenth bishop; a funeral effigy was molded in concrete on the lid of the tomb.

"A dead man's body is inside there," I say.

"I understand. But what are they going to do with it?"

"They leave it there."

"But where does the spirit go?"

Where, indeed?

Negotiating subway turnstiles or crossing streets with Davi was one thing, but I wasn't prepared to answer questions like this one. I had tried to make his visit to New York enjoyable, as any host would. On his first day here he told me he liked a certain fruit drink with a picture of a tropical bird on the label, so I made certain there was plenty of *suco do tucano* or "juice of the toucan" around the house. I had considered putting up a hammock in the guest room, but he seemed comfortable using the bed. For the most part his stay went very smoothly, but sometimes his simple requests would have more complicated dimensions.

In one such instance, to my surprise, Davi asked where he could get some hair gel. *Hair gel?* I thought. *Why does this guy who lives in the rain forest need hair gel?* He had seen me using some earlier that day in my bathroom. He now wanted to get a tube to bring back with him to his village. I was perplexed. I was also uncomfortable to think that I would be the one responsible for introducing a new coiffed look to the Yanomami, transforming a once unaffected people with bowl-shaped hairdos into a culture of stylish hipsters. I had seen my role as trying to protect these people, helping them preserve their traditional way of life, not introducing them to the newest trends in hair care. Yet, as I would come to learn, Davi's request made perfect sense from his perspective. The gel, he pointed out, would be useful in ceremonial life, particularly feasts. In preparation for such events the Yanomami adorn their hair with small tufts of white pigeon feathers, traditionally held in place by a friend's or family member's saliva applied to the wearer's head. The interest in acquiring hair gel signaled a smart adaptation of the white man's (in this case, my) cosmetic accoutrements.

Davi was no fool. To selectively assimilate what he could use from us was a key part of his strategy for survival, learned over the years. He had been taught by the missionaries to read, but rejected their religion. As one of the few literate Yanomami also fluent in Portuguese, he had emerged as the sole person from his society who could speak in public forums about what was happening to them. He was now a key player in the fight to refute the gold miners' contentions that they were helping the Indians. Part political activist and part shaman, Davi was uniquely qualified to present the positions of his people. Without him, they would have no credible voice in the outside world. In spite of my initial reservations, Davi was indeed shrewd enough to decide for himself whether or not he should have hair gel. He was simply *appropriating* another product from our world. I was not *imposing* it on him. That, I felt, was an important distinction.

Of course, each step Davi took into our world brought with it the potential for problems in regard to his traditional life back in the forest. He told me that this trip abroad, and the others he had taken, were tasks he did not enjoy. His wife complained bitterly about his absence. When he returned to his village after his journeys he would bring presents for his family, which created jealousies and rivalries with others members of his community. He was perceived by some Yanomami as trying to maintain exclusive access to the white man's manufactured goods. Often it would take months for him to extricate himself from such complex social contretemps. Yet the response he received in the Untied States assured him he had done the right thing in traveling here. People were listening. The plight of the Yanomami people was being recognized in the international arena.

In the course of the next three weeks Davi appeared on NBC's *Today* show and the CBS evening news, and he was profiled in the *New York Times*. He lectured at the Museum of Natural History with former governor Bruce Babbitt, met with the head of the United Nations Human Rights Commission, then traveled to Washington, where he spoke before a packed press conference of Beltway journalists and had meetings with several influential senators and congressmen.

In between Davi's various engagements we made two trips to the home of "Kenny" and his wife, Yarima, in a quiet suburban community located in northern New Jersey. On the first visit Davi was extremely anxious about what he would find. He had heard the stories of the courtship of Kenny and Yarima through the chain of gossip passing from village to village in the forest—"the Yanomami grapevine" Claudia called it. I wondered how the accounts Davi heard in the forest compared to the graphic and brutal version Good gave in his book *Into the Heart*, which documents his perplexed romance with his Yanomami bride. In this account he describes the way he became involved with his Yanomami wife (they were "betrothed" when she was twelve years old) and the circumstances under which he had left the forest with her. I assumed that Davi's version was different. I don't think it had the tone of romance that permeates Good's popular nonfiction account, subtitled *One Man's Pursuit of Love and Knowledge Among the Yanomama*. Davi made it clear to Claudia and me that he disapproved of their union.

In one part of Ken Good's book he describes how he had left Yarima in the rain forest for several weeks after one of his extended stays in her village. It was December of 1987 and he needed to extend his research visa. By this time Yarima had already been given to him as a wife and their marriage had been consummated. Yet upon arriving in the Venezuelan frontier town of Puerto Ayacucho, he started to have trouble with the local Indian Agency officials. They had heard about his liaison with Yarima and some other exaggerated tales about his purported exploitation of the "Yanomama," as they are called in Venezuela. After four months of tense negotiations he eventually got a three-month extension on his research permit and headed back to the village of Yarima's father, where he had left her so that she would be "safer." But Good—even though he had spent more than two years living among the Yanomami— had miscalculated the grave consequences of his extended absence. Not long after he had left the forest the village men began circulating stories that Ken had been killed, which, according to the version Yarima eventually recounted to her husband, is when her trouble began:

> "After everyone thought you were dead, they started to come
> for me. . . . When I went out to the forest to gather they
> came for me. When I went out to bathe they came. They
> never left me alone. My father could not help me. He tried
> to stop them, but there were too many. Sometimes one
> would take me. Sometimes two at the same time. Sometimes
> three. . . . At night they dragged me out of my hammock.
> During the day they dragged me into the forest. They never
> left me alone."

Not only was she raped repeatedly but, in a fight with one of her assailants, a part of Yarima's earlobe was torn, which bled profusely even after crude attempts by some Yanomami women to stitch it together with thread. In his published account Good claims he had no option but to leave the forest and take his wife with him. In his mind she would no longer be safe when he was not there, and the only choice was for them to relocate to the United States, where he would be able to earn a living for them and their child. What Good never seemed to consider was his own complicity in this tragic episode. Among the academic community the case rekindled debate about sexual violence in Yanomami culture. Was Ken's involvement with Yarima the catalyst for such brutal acts, or were rapes a part of everyday life for all Yanomami women? The occasional abduction of Yanomami females during village raiding is a well-documented part of their history. But Yarima's story seemed unusually violent. I couldn't help but wonder what would have happened to Yarima had she been married to a Yanomami man. Would her bond have been respected differently? Would the husband have been separated from his wife for such extensive periods of time? Maybe Ken Good had taken too much for granted. Perhaps he had been mistaken in thinking he had transcended the cultural differences that separated their world from ours. He had embraced their world, but had they actually embraced him? Maybe, as with the late Father Calleri, Ken Good's own hubris had gotten in his way.

Eventually Ken, Yarima, and their child settled in New Jersey, where he had found a teaching position at Jersey City State College. Soon their exotic love affair began to attract national attention, and *People* magazine did an article on them. Then their story was optioned for a movie by Columbia Pictures. The book deal came next. But while living in a small American town might have been the only option for Ken and his family, it also seemed to be an incredible (maybe unbearable) sacrifice for his wife. Their living room was littered with dozens of videotapes that Ken had recorded of life in Yarima's village. She watched these, he told us, throughout the day in order to fight off the intense nostalgia that had beset her since she had left her community. Yarima had also recently gotten a frightfully bad "perm," possibly an attempt to conform to our society's standards for female appearance but one that, in my eyes at least, only seemed to underscore her distance from such standards and from the culture she sorely missed. Yarima was a beautiful woman, and the photographs I had seen of her in traditional dress posed a harsh contrast to the sullen housewife she had become. All this aside, Ken was a caring father and an excellent husband. His love for his wife and children seemed abundant and genuine. In spite of my own misgivings about an anthropologist or any outsider getting so intimately involved with an indigenous culture, my heart went out to someone trying to make a relationship work against incredible odds. Still I couldn't help but think this kind of cultural transgression was going to have serious consequences.

As I thought about this issue, I came up with my own theory as to why Kenny had become an obsession for Davi. This young shaman's life had been devoted to halting the white man's attempts to appropriate all the things of his world. The missionaries who had come to save his people's souls had taken his mother's life. Kenny had taken a woman and thereby denied some Yanomami man a wife. The miners, if the efforts of the Collor government are not successful, will eventually overrun every last inch of his people's territory, raping the land in their quest for precious metals. Davi's people would then have nothing left; their ecological and cultural base would be destroyed; like Big Foot and the Minneconjou a century earlier, the Yanomami could potentially find themselves in a clearing one day performing their own millennial Ghost Dance in a desperate quest for some form of salvation.

After three weeks in the States, Davi returned to Brazil, exhausted but anxious to see his family. He left, however, content with the reception he had received in the United States and the outpouring of concern he had encountered for the plight of his people. Just weeks after his return, Brazil's newly elected president Fernando Collor de Mello arrived in Washington for a series of informal meetings with American businessmen and then-President George Bush. This trip was intended to signal a new era for Brazil. Collor was not resisting U.S. political and financial advice; he was openly seeking it. In recent years there had been a lot of tension on Wall Street and in Washington regarding Brazil's outstanding debt payments. Collor wanted to begin his new presidency with a clean slate and on good terms. But what he didn't realize was that he had arrived in America in the wake of Davi Kopenawa. Everywhere he went Brazil's new president was confronted with questions about the Yanomami tragedy and the ongoing presence of tens of thousands of gold miners on Indian lands. Collor was surprised and embarrassed. When he returned home he immediately ordered the federal police to evict the gold prospectors from Yanomami territory. The army was then instructed to blow up the one hundred airstrips upon which the miners had depended for their invasion. After a three-year hiatus, the Yanomami could once again reclaim their lands as their own and Davi could return to his traditional life as a shaman's apprentice.

In 1993 Yarima, Kenny, and their children returned to her native village in the Yanomama section of Venezuela. They wanted the children to see traditional life, and Yarima wanted to visit her friends and her family. To help pay for the journey Kenny had agreed to take along a documentary team that was interested in recording this latest chapter in their extraordinary romance. When they arrived in the village, Yarima learned that her mother had died. She was devastated. But eventually she came to terms with her grief and returned to the United States with Ken and the children. A month later they made a second trip to Yanomama territory to participate in a census study funded by the Venezuelan government. This time Yarima decided to stay. After days of heated discussions, Ken felt he had no choice but to leave her in the forest. Someone had to get back to the children in the States. Three months later he returned to the jungle with his youngest child to see if he could convince her to return to life in the United States. This time he had more luck. She went downriver with him in a canoe, urged on, Ken says, by her brothers. But at a jungle airstrip near a missionary outpost, she suddenly disappeared into the forest, leaving their youngest child alone on the edge of the runway. It seemed no amount of videotape could replace the experience of actually living in the forest. Yarima wanted the real thing. Ken waited by the airstrip, the plane arrived, and he boarded it with their child and headed back to the United States. According to recent news reports, Yarima currently lives in her native village. She has remarried and has given birth to another child. Ken remains in New Jersey, where he divides his time between raising the children, teaching anthropology, and seeking a buyer for the movie rights to this new chapter of their troubled tale. When the documentary segment on their first trip was eventually broadcast, there was no mention of the dissolution of their relationship, even though it had happened within weeks of the first trip. Maybe that part of the story was too complicated, too real. Maybe it was too easy to go with the kitchified account.

Whenever I hear updated stories about Kenny and Yarima, I think about the way Davi used to react when he returned home from seeing them in New Jersey or at conferences in New York. He was usually sulky and depressed and would go directly to his room. There for the rest of the night he would play cassette recordings of Yanomami shaman chants that he had obtained from Yarima. I remember on his last day in New York we stood on a crowded street amidst the converted residential loft buildings of Soho. The warm weather had finally arrived and New Yorkers were out in the streets embracing the beautiful evening with its deep blue sky. Two lovely young women in flowered dresses strolled by, leaving behind a strong scent of perfume.

"Geoffrey," Davi began, then paused, letting me know that a question was coming. "Why is it that Kenny had to go into the forest and take a Yanomami woman when there are so many women that are already here?"

As if on cue a group of three women came out of a restaurant and walked by Davi and me.

"I am not certain," I told him. And I wasn't.

22

This sleepy town of Rio Maria is strangely quiet even in midday. The air is wet with humidity. Somewhere down the street, out of sight, I can hear a dog wailing and whimpering, someone—some psychopath—beating the life out of it with a blunt object: *whack, slap, whack.* As I pull my camera from the car, a tall, dark-skinned man with a face the shape of a brick steps directly in front of me. The old wooden door to Father Ricardo's enclosed compound rests slightly ajar, just as I left it, only a few short steps away. *Who's the guy?*

It is April of 1992, and my soundman Vicent and I are about to follow Father Ricardo Rezende to a local hospital where a peasant squatter called José Fininho has just arrived, his body pierced by bullets, another casualty in the ongoing land conflicts in the southern part of the state of Pará. This scene will be part of a follow-up story on the good father, who, just like five years ago, continues to be plagued by death threats and assassination attempts as a result of his work as a human rights activist. Today he intends on making an initial inquiry into the circumstances of this most recent shooting in the region's violent land war. It seems José Fininho received three bullet wounds when he was apprehended early this morning by the military police. The area of conflict, Lote Sete or Lot 7, is part of a large estate that has been occupied for several months by a group of four hundred *posseiros*, peasant squatters.

"Onde fica a casa do padre?"—Where is the house of the priest?—says the man with the bricklike face, his breath heavy with garlic. He then takes another step forward. This confrontation has caught me off guard. *Why is he standing so close to me?* My eyes wander down to his hip where I see beneath his T-shirt a large handgun, the pistol grip bulging beneath the fabric. I feel myself go weak-kneed while my Portuguese—poor, but recently getting better—disintegrates into *desequilibrado* or "unbalanced," the only word that springs to mind but one I don't think I'll be sharing with this character, who, I take it, is here to put a bullet in Ricardo. *Will he shoot me on my way inside? I shouldn't have left the door open.* I try to muster some neutral answer to his question in Portuguese while I simultaneously consider running off down the street leaving Vicent and Father Ricardo to fend for themselves. *If I ran would I be a coward? Would this man really kill me?* The truth is that it is only the threat of death that I find attractive in situations like these. Not the real thing. I only want to be close to it, not a part of it. To feel the adrenaline rush of knowing I had been there and gotten away. The exhilaration when the threat passes, when the fear paralyzing my body suddenly subsides, confirming in that very moment that *yes I am alive.* I am ashamed to say that I never expected this flirtation to go so far. I'm not supposed to die here. That was never the intention. I'm the voyeur, not the victim.

"Eu . . . não sabe . . . o padre."—"I . . . don't know . . . the priest"—I say, the words falling out of my mouth in awkward clusters as I step quickly around his large frame and head for the door, my back already tensing to receive an explosive blast of metal bits. I make it into the small compound, close the door behind me, and slip the old metal latch against the rusted bolt.

For the moment I feel safe in the cool shade of the trees and the tall walls of the compound. There's something gothic about this place: the sad countryside town, the cloistered cleric, the murderer with a weapon roaming the streets, the illusion of sanctuary created by the high walls of this little home. It all feels like part of a dark tale from the Middle Ages. *Move away from the door*, I tell myself.

"There is someone with a gun outside," I say to Ricardo as I cross the yard into his house. My Portuguese has failed me completely, so I resort to French, the language in which Ricardo and I share the greatest fluency.

He mumbles a few words to his bodyguard. The man slowly rises and leaves the room, his hand gently touching his small holster, checking to make certain that he's armed. This is done discreetly, probably at the priest's instructions. Ricardo has already told us he feels uncomfortable about having a plain-clothes bodyguard assigned to him by the military police. He objects, he says, to being singled out while so many others are under constant threat of death.

"*Tu veux un café, Geoffrey?*"—Do you want a coffee, Geoffrey?—Ricardo says calmly as if this happens every day. It probably does. He hands me a *cafezinho* and as I grab it I realize I am drenched in sweat, soaked through by the fear and the humidity. No sooner have I taken a sip than I can hear two people approaching, the heavy sound of their feet scraping against the pebbles in the courtyard. Boots, military issue.

"*C'est lui que tu a vu dans la rue?*"—Is it him that you saw in the street?—says Ricardo.

I turn to look over my shoulder. "Yes."

"It is the changing of the guard, the military police," says Ricardo. "He is here for me."

Here for you, but not to kill you.

A wave of laughter passes through the room. Ricardo, always the compassionate priest, puts his hand on my shoulder in a show of empathy, yet he too is having a good laugh.

Usually I can keep fear in check. I do this by preoccupying my mind with a wide range of preparations and precautions— gringo delusions that make me believe I am in control of the situation. But this confused encounter, however ridiculous it might seem, has allowed me to enter the psychological space the good Father occupies daily—to see through my own panic-stricken eyes the manner in which his life unfolds, never knowing from where your assassin will finally appear, whether you will have a chance to look at his face before he takes you out, whether that image will be the last thing you see in your pitifully curtailed life.

As the laughing dies down, the two military policemen enter the kitchen to complete the formalities of turning over the shift. I take a moment to go to the bathroom and collect my thoughts. *How could this have happened? How could things have gotten so confusing so fast?* I run cool water to calm myself and I realize that my former defenses—gringo naivete, hubris, a foolish but stubborn belief in my own immortality—have broken down and I am left, like those who live here, completely vulnerable to terror. I look in the mirror: my face is pale and gaunt, my eyes bloodshot. I'm wired. Too much stress, too many long days on the road. *Why am I doing this to myself?*

In southern Pará nothing is as it seems. I learned that before but now, several years later, it is more apparent than ever. This place is a paradise for a paranoid, where the most minor accident or sudden illness can be easily construed as an assassination attempt: the man emerging from the shadows your killer, the accusations of the town mayor part of an organized slander campaign, the new cook in the local restaurant plotting to poison you. All events resulting in death are suspect because shootings, kidnappings, and murders are never successfully prosecuted in the courts. They are never confirmed or refuted. They exist in a strange state of limbo where they feed the imagination. It was only in the 1980s that a justice system was put in place here and it is a sham. The files of cases constantly disappear, detainees are arbitrarily released, judges' lives are often threatened. Justice is decided by intimidation, and assassination practiced with impunity. It is as if the victims never existed, forgotten in public record, remembered only by people like Father Ricardo Rezende who have worked tirelessly for decades to make certain that with each death there are photos taken, facts documented, testimonies submitted, and pressure—however futile—levied on this chaotic, inept, and, some would say, corrupt justice system.

In the last two decades, more than five hundred peasants, human rights activists, and community leaders have been selectively assassinated in the state of Pará. And for every death there are usually a half dozen unsuccessful attempts against others who remain, and another dozen threats forcing still others to flee. These days Padre Ricardo refers to the telephone as an "instrument of terror" because of the frequency of death-threat phone calls. They come at any hour of the day or night. Sometimes the voice on the other end will simply ask for the "dead man." At other times the message is more elaborate and sinister, the caller reveling in the power of his violent intent, increasing the frequency of the calls to heighten the tension, occasionally bringing friends or girlfriends on the line to participate in the ritual.

One such call, to a local activist and Socialist Party candidate named João Bernardo:

"What's the address of Sebastião, that agitator on the city council?" the caller asks.

"I don't know," says João Bernardo. He has already received four suspicious calls.

"What's his telephone number?"

"I don't know that either."

"You know it. He will die, just like you. You're not involved in land problems, but you agitate a lot around here."

"Here? Where?"

"In Rio Maria. I'm going to kill you."

"Why?"

"Never mind. You're going to die."

João Bernardo left Rio Maria shortly after this call. Others, however, have chosen to stay on. There is another man in town who has received so many death threats that his friends jokingly refer to him as "A.D." for Already Dead. Often Father Ricardo's phone will suddenly go on the blink. He can only receive calls but can't call out. He finds that suspicious, but there is nothing he can do about it. This is southern Pará, a region where the phone company and the court system are equally inefficient and unreliable. Is it part of a plot? That is left up to the imagination.

As I was driving to Rio Maria this morning, I thought about Ricardo's best friend, a man named Father Josimo Tavares, who was shot in the back of the head several years ago while walking into the offices of the Pastoral Land Commission. Just two weeks before he had escaped an attempt on his life when his assassin—possibly the same man who eventually killed him, but perhaps not—riddled his car with bullets, none of which happened to hit him. The man ultimately convicted of his murder didn't know he had killed a priest. "If I had known he was a priest I wouldn't have done it," said Geraldo Rodrigues, his killer. "I am a Catholic," he added from his jail cell. Tavares's assassin was the only man to be successfully prosecuted for a politically motivated murder in this region. Yet he managed on two occasions to escape from prison. The frequency with which accused murderers awaiting trial "escape" from "notoriously lax jails" has become the focus of criticism by human rights groups. But no one knows exactly how they happen, whether bribes or political pressure are involved. Rodrigues, after his second escape in 1990, was recaptured in 1991 and is now serving a sentence of eighteen years and six months.

This story on Padre Ricardo is just one of a series of news pieces I will be doing in the Amazon in 1992 prior to the United Nations Earth Summit. There have been six attempts on his life since he first started doing human rights work in southern Pará in the 1980s. Recently there was a drive-by shooting that strafed the outside of his compound. The threats have become so serious that he now has a twenty-four-hour armed bodyguard assigned by a state judge. His new home of Rio Maria is even more violent than Conceição do Araguaia where I filmed him five years ago. Friends are urging him to leave the area until the death threats subside. Like Chico Mendes, he insists on staying. He doesn't want to give in to the tactics of intimidation.

My report will consist of five days of filming, a look at the work of Father Ricardo and a slice of life on the *posseiros*, those without land who attempt to possess it. The United Nations international conference has intensified environmentalists' concerns about the farming practices of both the large-scale cattle ranchers known as *fazendeiros* and the peasant farmers who work the smaller plots. Ecologists are claiming that the Amazon's soil is weak in nutrients, that the practice of slash-

and-burn agriculture depletes the soil and sends unwanted carbon dioxide into the earth's atmosphere while irreplaceable plants and trees—"the lungs of the world"—are consumed in flames. In recent years environmental concerns have come to dominate the headlines and newscasts. The "greenhouse effect" is being anxiously watched. Holes in the ozone layer have been documented. Planet Earth is in trouble. That's the message being sent from the Northern Hemisphere to the South as we approach the Earth Summit—the UN Conference on the Environment and Development. But many people here in Brazil consider these apocalyptic warnings part of a one-sided, even imperialistic, message: the John Does of this world can have their two cars and air-conditioned homes but the José da Silvas below the equator have got to change their ways.

Driving here from the airport in Maraba, I pulled off the road when I saw smoke billowing up out of a nearby canopy of forest. *Good burning shots,* I thought to myself as I banked up a hill on a dusty road and found an old peasant, a small child by his side, torching a small plot of land. He was no different from the thousands of other peasants I have met on my trips here, just one of the millions who roam this forest with their clusters of ten children and straggly-haired, wafer-thin wives. The young boy standing next to him, presumably his son, looked to be about ten years old. He had no shoes and was dressed only in torn pants and a dirty white shirt. He was sleepy-eyed, sickly, malnourished; perhaps that had stunted his growth. I fired up my camera and walked over to where they were standing, my soundman Vicent trailing behind. The peasant, startled by all the attention, just stood with the torch burning in his hand looking at me.

"Can I take some pictures of you while you work?" I said.

The man listened to my question as if he were a defendant awaiting a judge's sentencing. He had serious and worried eyes. He shot a quick glance at Vicent, then looked back at me. "If you take pictures of me doing this," he said, "then they will see what I am doing on the television in America and they will try to stop me from working my land."

The old man pulled off his straw hat. I watched as his bushy eyebrows pushed up into the worry lines of his sweaty forehead like the bellows of an old accordion.

"How am I going to feed my children then?" he said. "Can you tell me that?"

I stood there for a moment speechless, the gringo caught off guard.

"*Entendo,*" I said finally. Then I trotted back to my air-conditioned car, put away my expensive camera, and drove on to Rio Maria, another concerned citizen brought up short by the paradoxes inherent in the North-South dynamic of our fragile world.

"*A vida é complicada,*" Vicent mused as he turned the radio dials searching for some decent music. Life is complicated.

In Rio Maria one of the Amazon's most high-profile human rights cases occurred just over a year ago in 1991 when a mayoral candidate and the president of the Rural Workers Union, Expedito Ribeiro da Souza, was shot dead on a Saturday night returning home from his union headquarters. The streets, as always, were dark, the lampposts few and far between, their dim yellow light providing only the most minimal illumination. Earlier in the evening Expedito had been watching the news on a friend's television, then he proceeded to the union office to take care of some paperwork. Walking home alone he took his usual route, the sound of the cicadas dominating the air of the town's quiet streets. As he neared his home a boy named Francisco passed him on a bicycle. A few seconds later a man dressed in blue jeans, a white shirt, and a simple gray hat stepped out from the shadows. He first shot Expedito in the back and then, once he fell, the gunman came closer and fired another two shots at point-blank range into his head. Within minutes Expedito's daughter, who had heard the gunshots, arrived. After taking in the bloody scene, she ran home crying out, "Mother, they killed my father! They wanted to shut the mouth of an honorable man." The body was left on the street until someone with a camera arrived to document the murder. This became part of the evidence that Father Ricardo collected. Expedito's wife heard the shots but she never left the house. She said she knew her husband's day had come. The death threats had been going on for too long. She was not surprised that the assassins finally made good on their threats.

Expedito left his widow with ten children and a large batch of unpublished poems. The following day she received another call from a threatening stranger. The man informed her that Padre Ricardo would be the next person to die. In spite of pleas from friends and colleagues he once again refused to leave town. That afternoon he officiated at Expedito's funeral.

I was told before arriving here that Expedito's death had become a kind of obsession for the priest. The two had been close friends. They shared a love of politics and verse. Father Ricardo was determined to see justice served and he was conducting his own personal investigation into the assassination. What struck me about him when I arrived in Rio Maria was the dramatic transformation of his physical appearance: his curly black hair was now gray and receding, his once cherubic features had become furrowed by severe creases across his forehead and along the sides of his face. On the left side of his head just above the hairline stretched a scar from a questionable hit-and-run accident with a truck that had left Ricardo immobilized and near death for several months. Though his coworkers remained suspicious, no one had been able to prove anything about the circumstances of the crash. But perhaps more troubling was the death of Father Ricardo's spiritual mentor, an Irishman by the name of Joseph Hanrahan. Bishop José as he was called by the Brazilians, died suddenly from what was commonly believed to be stomach cancer. No official diagnosis, however, was made, and no autopsy conducted. Ricardo hasn't ruled out the possibility that the Bishop could have been poisoned by a local cattle rancher.

Of course such conjectures can never be included in an official human rights document. There are no hard facts to substantiate them. But they all contribute to a precarious psychological landscape. And very often in southern Pará old suspicions resurface years later when new facts filter in from a *pistoleiro's* jilted lover or a cattle rancher's former maid. People like this frequently show up at the priest's door. Some are guilt-ridden, others just vengeful. In their testimonies to Father

Ricardo they provide detailed accounts of a murder witnessed, a conversation overheard, or a secret carelessly revealed. These unsolicited "testimonies" usually arrive too late for the pathetic courts to take any action, but they become part of the landscape of threat and suspicion. As Ricardo has said, "The practice of terror carries with it a message. It not only deforms the body of the victim but it works to terrorize those that remain alive." Truth here, like everything else, travels on slow and bumpy roads.

We hop out of the truck and enter a small frontier hospital, to be immediately confronted by two military policemen. Father Ricardo negotiates our way past them, allowing us to enter the room of José Moura a/k/a José Fininho, the young peasant who was wounded early this morning. Fininho means "thin man" and it is a fitting moniker. The guy is a human toothpick. He lies on a bed with a handkerchief covering his eyes. Various parts of his body are wrapped in bandages.

"José Fininho?" the priest whispers. "My name is Padre Ricardo. I want to speak to you if you feel up to it."

José Fininho raises his right hand, pulling away the handkerchief and then the white bedsheet. His actions are slow and deliberate. It's as if we are watching Lazarus come to life. The young man has dark brown hair, a thick mustache, and a perfectly round head. His eyes are red and watery. He's maybe twenty-five years old.

"Are you here to give me my last rites, Father?" the peasant asks in a soft, sleepy whisper.

"No. We are only here for a visit."

"I need to tell you something, Father," he says. "I became a Protestant this morning. A minister has promised to get me food. I am sorry."

"That's all right, José Fininho."

"I hope you understand."

"I do."

"There is nothing to eat here in this hospital. He promised me his people would bring me some food."

"I understand."

Suddenly Ricardo turns to his bodyguard who entered the room with us, the giant I mistook for a *pistoleiro* this morning. In a swift Jekyll-and-Hyde moment his voice and demeanor change from the caring compassionate priest to the hard-line human rights activist.

"A moment alone please," he says, punctuating his request with a raised eyebrow—a signal, I take it, that this is one of those times when the priest wants—must have—his privacy.

"Understood, Padre," groans the military policeman as he walks dead-eyed—*this guy never blinks*—out of the room.

Although Ricardo is accompanied by military bodyguards twenty-four hours a day, he doesn't trust them. He believes that some members of the local military police—the very militia group assigned to protect him—have been participating in the violence in this region. Ironically, the ranks of the local militia have swollen in the last nine months, increasing from just five to more than one hundred. Evidence that the government is trying to exert more control over this volatile frontier? Not if you believe Father Ricardo. He contends that many of the military police are moonlighting as hired gunmen for local ranchers, bolstering their negligible salaries with fees paid for murders on the side. In this region there are many *agências de pistolagem* or "rent-a-killer agencies" with names like the Sheik's Clique, Snake-Killer, or the Colonel's Mafia. The killing of a labor leader can bring approximately six hundred dollars, while a priest—a more problematic target in this Catholic society—might earn an assassin the equivalent of two thousand dollars. The going rate for elected officials is four thousand. No bad for a day's work, particularly in a region where the average wage is thirty dollars a month.

Once the guard has left the room, Father Ricardo helps José Fininho to sit up in bed, tilting him carefully as if he were an old clay pot about to spring a leak.

"They shot him in the back of the head and the bullet came out here," says Father Ricardo. "In the front," he adds, pointing to the stitches on the bridge of the young man's nose. There are other gunshot wounds on his chest and rib cage covered only by bold splotches of mercurochrome and held together by a crude assortment of stitches.

"*Você tem muita sorte, José Fininho*"—You are very lucky, José Fininho—says the priest to the Thin Man, who manages to smile despite his injuries. He seems more alert now and perhaps relieved that the priest isn't here to give him his last rites. As I step around José Fininho to get a better shot I almost kick over a large bowl filled with blood and mucus, the drainage from his head wound which now sits on the floor by his bed. A sudden wave of nausea seizes me, a sensation I am able to shake by focusing on my work; the tiny black-and-white images dancing before my eyes conveniently separate me from the unpleasant moment. From this angle I can get an image of Ricardo pointing to the back and front of José Fininho's head. The bullet hole is now clearly identifiable: a round red dot the size of a coin marks the spot where the bullet entered the base of his neck before shooting through his mouth and exiting his nose. Some God—Protestant? Catholic? anyway, some force beyond us all—was clearly looking out for this guy. No one wounded like this should be alive and sitting up in bed talking about it.

I drop to my knees to get close-ups of the other wounds. Here I can see the full extent of his injuries: his hand wrapped in blood-soaked bandages is missing two fingers, while his left breast has been ripped apart by a second bullet, the wound left exposed to the air. I am so close now I can smell the mercurochrome coming off his wound.

After I grab these shots Vicent interrupts me momentarily. He is worried about the sound in the room. The tile walls are creating the effect of an echo chamber. Even the most clear-cut pitch is lost in the space's wild reverberation. To help him, I agree to move the camera closer to the subject, allowing him to position the microphone better.

"Now tell me what happened this morning," says Padre Ricardo as he pulls out a pen and paper.

"One day a gunman came," says José Fininho, "and he identi- fied himself as a Department of Justice official and he told us he would give us only one thousand hectares [2,500 acres] of land. I told him"—José Fininho pauses momentarily, his small brown eyes flicking about as he checks his thoughts—"I told him that we needed three thousand hectares because we were too many families."

"And then what did he tell you?"

"He said okay. Then he came back with two other gunmen and killed one of the peasants who were occupying the land."

"And then two of the gunmen were killed twenty days after the peasant was killed?" asks Ricardo.

"Yes."

"Was it on the *fazenda?*"

"Yes."

The-man-who-got-shot-through-the-back-of-the-head-and-lived-to-tell -about-it reminds me of many of the people I have come to know in the Amazon. They could be characters from a García Márquez novel. Their stories are not one-dimensional tales of woe. They contain ironic moments of comedy and grace, as well as occasional bits of absurd human behavior, all of it offering surprising revelations about what we have come to call the human condition. Vicent and Ricardo and I have just experienced such a moment when José Fininho told us how the bullet passed through his head and came out his nose. He said it was all over before he realized what had happened. We all laughed when he finished his tale—including the victim. Perhaps it was the twisted grin he used to punctuate the story or our own sense of relief that this didn't happen to us. But the laughter, and the release it brought, was undeniable: it ricocheted off the tile walls and spilled into the hallways.

I continue to be reminded of García Márquez, particularly his *Chronicle of a Death Foretold*. It could apply not only to José Fininho but to any number of people in this region, including Father Ricardo. I have always been struck by Márquez's descriptions of the way death creates an aura around those whom it encircles. In some ways his fiction contains more insights into what takes place here than the countless human rights reports that get dispatched from this region. Perhaps this explains why Ricardo has taken to writing poetry, verse being the only way he can comprehend (and cope with) the terror he witnesses here. Maybe it's his way of retaining a sense of truth denied each day by the courts and public officials. I read one of his poems recently and jotted down an excerpt in my journal:

> *On that last night of agony*
> *Fifteen leagues I rowed,*
> *Watched over by the moon,*
> *Pursued by the waters;*
> *I drew from them my comfort,*
> *From love my senselessness;*
> *I buried in the past*
> *That night of agony.*
> *When the rod is broken,*
> *The fish will go free*
> *In the clearest waters,*
> *In the River of Hope.*

While Ricardo, the union leaders, and the *posseiros* have, through their activism, "taken on" the world in Rio Maria, many of the poor in this community have rejected it outright. They are the mystics and millennialists, splinter groups of the Catholic Church, desperate pilgrims who go on crusades through the rain forest in a last-ditch quest for salvation. Some are searching for a mythic "white flag" that will bring them release from this world. Others seek a Heaven on Earth that they believe exists deep in the forest's interior. They are, they say, fleeing the towns and cities because the Araguaia River that runs through this region is about to boil over, an act of God sure to kill all those who have not joined their crusade. These little ragtag sects go by such names as Mary of the Beach or the Society of the Divine Father. They travel in small bands through the jungle, clutching rosaries and praying under the forest's canopy, occasionally trespassing on Indian reserves, most of them fixated on some forgotten saint, too poor to emigrate someplace else, too tired to return to the chaos and violence that awaits them as peons or *posseiros*. Their actions, their beliefs seem crazy, but I wonder. Perhaps their fantastic imaginings have allowed them to see southern Pará for what it might really be: hell on earth.

According to his account, José Fininho was shot early this morning trying to escape from his simple peasant lodging. Before dawn the police had surrounded his mud hut, telling him Hollywood-style to come out unarmed with his hands in the air. But it seems José Fininho had his own movie playing in his head, one that starred James Cagney. First he huddled against a far wall trying to calm his common-law wife and her two children. Then, certain that he was going to be killed, he burst out the front door with gun in hand and was met immediately by a phalanx of militia and local police who laid into him with a series of gun blasts. Somehow he managed to run fifty yards before collapsing against a tree at the edge of the forest, bleeding and in shock. As he was dragged away by the military police, he says he recognized two *pistoleiros* from a local cattle ranch among those who had shot him. He adds that it took nine hours to bring him back to the town of Xinguara where the hospital is located. Along the way he coughed up blood and tried to ease the pain of his mangled hand by wrapping it in a dirty blood-soaked shirt. Before being brought to the hospital for treatment he was interrogated by the police—a procedure, Father Ricardo points out, that is a flagrant abuse of a prisoner's rights.

The priest is diligently writing down José Fininho's testimony in a pocket-sized notebook, occasionally stopping to clarify a detail or get the correct spelling of a name. This is part of his job with the Pastoral Land Commission, a Church organization that documents human rights abuses and provides legal representation for clients with legitimate cases. But I am having some problems with José Fininho's account, and I think Father Ricardo is, as well. The facts aren't adding up. And there is something in the man's eyes. He's not just scared, he's hiding something.

We bring him some food and then leave him in his room as I gather the last images I'll need to make this scene work: details of the nurses at their station, a shot taken from the hallway of him lying in the bed, a couple more close-ups of the wounds:

"money-shots" that will help me sell this story in North America and in Europe.

According to José Fininho's directions, we will need to travel six hours by truck and two hours on foot in order to reach his squatters' community located in the area called Lot 7 on the São José estate, a section of rain forest currently occupied by four hundred *posseiros*. Vicent is not happy. He groans like an old cow when I ask him to get detailed directions from José Fininho. Lot 7 is one of the most contested areas in the region, the site of numerous evictions and not infrequent acts of violence. But if I am going to accurately document this story then I will need to go there. I want to look into the circumstances of José Fininho's shooting, and I need to show the people who represent one side of this land conflict. I need to film in a squatters' camp, interview the people occupying the land, and see them at work. I don't want my report to be simply another sensationalized account, indistinguishable from hundreds of others, of terrorism and murder in a lawless Latin American country. With what I gather in the next few days I hope at least to delineate the factors that lead up to conflicts between *posseiros* and *fazendeiros*, the weak and the powerful, so that viewers can understand how this dispute this morning was resolved as it was, with a man like José ending up in the hospital. These are not random acts. They are part of a culture, a historical trajectory, and larger political forces.

According to José Fininho there is no place to stay over at Lot 7, so we will have to set out in the early morning and return the same day. This will entail at least twenty hours of driving, hiking, and filming in a region that has seen considerable violence in the last several months.

As we are leaving, José Fininho asks Padre Ricardo if we might bring his common-law wife back when we return from this occupied territory. I agree, then grab one more shot of the military guards stationed outside the hospital: two men in fatigues, rifles at their sides, standing guard over a prisoner whom their comrades nearly killed this morning. In a land where you can't trust appearances, I wonder what this little scene really means. And why, if his testimony is true, were there *pistoleiros* with the military guard when José Fininho was arrested?

At two in the morning we wake and drive down to an oil-slicked Esso station on the main road in Xinguara. There we find, loitering among the gas pumps, a half dozen short, dark-haired, somewhat desperate-looking men waiting to rent out their trucks (mostly Japanese) for transport jobs in the area. We negotiate with one *motorista* named Nilton and agree to hire him and his Toyota truck, a sturdy little pale green model, for the day: One hundred fifty dollars plus gas and expenses. With José Fininho's jumbled directions to guide us, we head off into the countryside at first light. For hours we travel crude one-lane roads, bouncing about in the vehicle's cabin like passengers on some whirling bumper car. We cut through patches of thick uncut forest and happen on occasional clusters of cattle. Mostly, however, the terrain is dominated by endless stretches of pasture—some green, some faded by the sun into rough textures of brown and yellow, all of it cordoned off by miles of cruelly constructed barb wire fences broken now and again by a signpost with *fazenda* names like Green Brazil or Big Valley. I'm constantly rolling my window up and down, dodging clouds of dust as I try to protect my equipment from the ever-present yellow silt that lingers in the air, leaving you cotton-mouthed right after a large gulp of water.

After a few hours we pass through a makeshift wooden toll booth signifying that we are leaving one estate and entering the next. In this region the *fazendas* are the size of nations. One estate named Pedro Dotto has four million acres, an area nearly as big as the country of El Salvador. Another, owned by Mario Jorge Moraes, has two and a half million acres, comparable in size to Jamaica. Often in this region the toll posts are manned by the owner's most trusted employees, who in turn are watched over by gunmen with side arms lingering about in the distance. It is common knowledge that inside a *fazenda* anyone—even former felons—can carry a gun. No permit is needed, a situation human rights groups have deemed a "recipe for violence."

Slavery, although formally abolished in 1898, is not an

uncommon practice in places like this. Last year alone, Father Ricardo Rezende's Pastoral Land Commission documented 620 people who had been held captive and forced to work in southern Pará. The men and women, usually from out of state, are hired and transported to this region by labor contractors known as *gatos*, "cats." The workers are lured to the *fazendas* with promises of large salaries for work cutting down the forest. They can spend up to three days in covered trucks in order to arrive at their "jobs," often paying for their own meager allotments of food. Once they are relocated deep in the confines of these mammoth estates they are forced into debt peonage, very often in malaria-infested areas of the forest. Many have been threatened at gunpoint if they complain, or chased by *pistoleiros* into the forest if they attempt to leave. While some have escaped, others are brought back, never to be heard from again. These tales contribute to the rumors that on these lands there are numerous unmarked graves where the disgruntled are disposed of. In the nearby municipality of Ourilandia do Norte two *fazendas*, Santana do Indaia and Santo Antônio do Indaia, were recently visited by Brazil's secretary of labor and the military police. The owners had enslaved more than one hundred workers for a period of three months. The evidence was right at hand, the crime punishable by imprisonment. Yet in spite of the presence of the secretary of labor no arrests were made. No one was charged with a crime of any kind. That's the way it works here.

"The laws exist here in this region," a cattle rancher named Geraldo Tosta told us yesterday, "but they don't work." Tosta, a lawyer, described himself to us as politically "moderate," someone trying to find solutions to the problems in the region. Clean-shaven and dressed casually in slacks and a rugby shirt, he is part of a new generation of smooth-talking ranchers who have realized that the confrontational hardball tactics of the UDR, or Rural Democratic Union, aren't winning them any points in the eyes of the Brazilian press. According to local human rights activists Tosta is not someone who enslaves or kills workers, yet that didn't stop him from blaming the victims and apologizing for the perpetrators. As the head of the newly formed Rural Landowners Union, his job is to protect the interests of his cattle ranching constituents. It's a job he takes seriously. The Brazilian worker, as far as Tosta is concerned, is "lazy and apathetic," and for this reason he says agrarian reform will "never work." With his wife goading him on just off camera, he told us that the "large landowners, acting within their rights, were justified in using this alternative way of doings things." He then went on to say that someday he hoped *fazendeiros* would "stop using force." But that day had yet to come.

After several hours the dirt road ends abruptly before a cluster of bushes. To the left can be seen a small rocky footpath that conforms with José Fininho's description. We unload our equipment and set off on this trail which goes straight into the mountains. After about a half hour we pass several small peasant cottages whose withered and suspicious occupants answer our questions in a broken Portuguese that doesn't sound like any language I've ever heard. Were it not for Vicent I would be completely lost here. He is expert at navigating the Amazon's backwoods. This is an environment where he comes into his own. Somehow he has managed to make sense of José Fininho's cryptic directions which consist of vague phrases like "go left at the big wooden stump" or "cross three little rivers and one big one and then turn left again" or "when you see Jaimundo's old burnt house you will know you will have two more hours." Vicent has spent a lot of time in this region, first living as a teenager with the Kraho Indians, then researching and writing a book about the Araguaia *guerrilha* revolts that occurred here in the 1970s. As we climb the mountain he converses easily with the peasant men and women who speak in a clipped dialect shouted out above the sounds of yapping dogs. We never actually see these people fully exposed, just their tiny heads popping over bushes and out of doorways, probably a self-protective reflex in light of the recent troubles. Even though Vicent is Brazilian, we are still outsiders in this backwoods community. We carry strange gear and, being urbanites, we lack the weatherbeaten look common among these people who spend their lives laboring in the sun. *"É perto"*—it is close— they always add after we ask some specific question about the directions. This is a refrain I have come to learn has no meaning. It exists more as a gesture of encouragement. The peasants have been saying *é perto* for the last two hours as we have stumbled up the mountain following a treacherous path that more closely resembles a dry riverbed.

Finally, in the searing heat of the Amazon's midday, we arrive in a sunbaked village inhabited only by children and women. There are some donkeys tied up at the end of the street but otherwise the town—a cluster of six thatched houses with yellow mud walls—is deserted. This must be Lot 7. I wander about the village trying to figure out why it is so empty. I leave Vicent at a small bar and dry goods store to converse with the local women. On my way out I catch a glimpse of an old man who sits in a chair by an adjacent doorway. He stares straight ahead, his eyes never blinking, a group of flies swirling about his face. If it weren't for the fresh froth at the corners of his mouth I would have mistaken him for dead. He is, however, the only male over ten years of age I have seen so far.

"There is no one here who knows José Fininho," Vicent says when I return from my little scouting trip.

"Come on."

"*Ninguém*, nobody, *nada, personne*."

"This is Lot Seven?"

"Yes, Chefe," he says, flashing me a forced grin.

I look at the emaciated peasant women sitting and standing in the cool shade of this little hut, their black and blond hair greasy and streaked with gray, their skin wrinkled beyond their years, the history of this region written in their tired faces. All of them are clad in dirty T-shirts and skirts; some carry a piece of worn and filthy cloth which they use to wipe the sweat from their brow or wave about to chase away the flies. Many of them have crooked gap-toothed smiles. Others simply stare straight ahead, their mouths locked in a grimace, avoiding contact with my eyes or perhaps simply lost in thought. There is, however, one woman who seems less distant than the rest of the group. She has meaty, strong arms and a broad face. Her name is Flora, she is the owner of this little store. She is the only person in the room who will look us in the eye.

"*Este aqui é Lote Sete?*"—This is Lot 7?—I ask Flora. "*Lote Sete?*" I repeat as I point to the ground.

I admonish myself immediately for doing again the one thing I've always promised myself I wouldn't do: resorting to hand gestures to supplement my badly pronounced Portuguese. I suddenly envision myself as resembling a lone lost tourist in Europe trying to navigate his way out of a back street in Rome or Paris, an amiable guy with a someone-help-me smile. The problem is that we don't have much time here. We will soon have to get back down the mountain. As I scan the room, however, I can see a few heads begin to nod up and down. Signs of confirmation. But it is still only Flora who looks directly at us.

"*Vocês me entendem quando eu falo português?*"—Do you understand me when I speak Portuguese?—I ask the ladies, this time my hands safely thrust into my pockets.

"*Sim,*" says a woman in the front followed by a few other feeble, almost inaudible, grunts which, in my desperation, I take for signs of affirmation. Then in the back of the room a tiny little mouse of a woman with one eye and a shrill voice says *não*, at which point the rest of the group breaks out laughing. Vicent lowers his head, shaking it left and right, making sure I know, if I don't already, that he is *esmagado*, overwhelmed, by the ridiculousness of my attempt to engage these women in conversation. But at least now the mood has lightened. There are a few smiles in the room. I notice Flora has a silver tooth.

"And you say they don't know José Fininho?" I ask.

"No," Vicent says. He makes a clicking noise with his teeth, then nods his head and kicks the dust. Sitting on his wooden stool, he leans over like some heroin junkie about to go down on his last nod into oblivion.

"Strange they don't know him," I say to myself as I look to Vicent for a reaction. He, however, is clearly withdrawing from me. Perhaps it is the absurdity of being stuck up here with a hand-gesturing gringo or maybe it is just the oppressive afternoon heat. I decide not to push him. We're both proud men. The worst type, some say. Better to be a diplomat.

"I also think it is strange," Vicent says finally.

An opening. "Have you asked anyone else?"

"A couple of the women outside." He finally looks me in the eye. "They are all the same. Nobody knows anything."

I take a walk out on the dry clay street and survey the town. The sun now seems softer and warmer in color, its angle against the mud shacks adding texture to what a short while ago had resembled a shadowless lunar landscape. A group of five children are playing in a patch of sun. In the background two stocky mules are tied to a wooden post. I take a quick shot of the street, then another one focusing in on the children before I walk back inside. A few of the women have taken the opportunity to duck out in my absence. Those that remain, I guess, are the curious few and Flora, the proprietor who has no other choice.

"Why do you think they are not talking to us?" I ask Vicent. In my absence he has purchased a soda from Flora and is drinking it. She must bring them up here by donkey. "Did you explain to them what we are trying to do?"

"No."

"What do you mean?" I ask, unable to disguise my irritation. Vicent and I discussed our strategy on the way up the hill. We decided that as soon as we got to the village we would explain to whoever was there that we were journalists doing a story about human rights abuses in this area.

"I told them we were lawyers sent by the priest," he says, then pauses. He looks at the women in the room. "I said that we were here to do an investigation and collect their testimony."

I look at Flora who is the only one in the room who seems to be trying to follow our conversation.

"You did what?"

"I thought this way they would talk to us."

"Don't you think it is obvious that we are not lawyers?" I say.

I look back at Flora who seems attuned to every word. She glances away. She is smart. She can interpret behavior. She doesn't need languages.

"These people aren't stupid," I add, immediately wishing that the words could somehow be sucked back into my mouth.

Gringo arrogance, as I have learned in the past, is a mortal sin in Brazil, a nation that has lived too long in the shadow of the United States. I try another tack.

"Why don't you start by asking Flora if she thinks we are lawyers?"

Vicent just stares at me, then takes another sip of soda.

"Okay," I say. "I'll ask her. *Flora, um momento—*"

"*Flora!*" Vicent cuts in before I can get started. "*Você pensa que nós somos advogados?*"

She stares at him for a moment, then looks at me.

"No." Her response hangs in the air for several seconds, followed by a flurry of old women's laughter, hoarse and breathless.

"What did you think when we first came to this town?"

"A young boy came running to the village shortly before you arrived. He said the military police were returning."

"So you thought we were the military police?"

"Yes."

"So what about now?"

"I don't think so," she says, wiping the back of her hand across the bridge of her nose. "You have these cameras and you are traveling with this American." She pauses a second, considering what she is about to say. "And now you are fighting with each other like a couple of women. I don't think you are military police."

The other women in the room again break into laughter when she delivers this jibe.

"So what do you think we are doing here?"

"I don't know. Why don't you tell us?"

"We are journalists," he begins, then goes on to explain (finally) why we have come and what we want to do. For me this part of the process is perhaps the most rewarding: to see people engaged and, to use that overused word, empowered by someone recognizing that they too *should* have a voice in any public debate on the conditions of their lives, that the realm of television is not solely the domain of the politicians or city people, that they too can share the airwaves. Probably no one is more aware than they that they have been forgotten, that as the poorest of the poor, they have fallen between the cracks of government policies that only give them lip-service alternatives with each of the changing administrations. Former president Sarney promised to find plots of land for 1.4 million people but settled only 115,000 during his administration. The current president Collor is promising to distribute parcels of land to 500,000 but no one here believes him. That's why they have taken to the mountains and appropriated the land for themselves. These uncultivated plots—once they've occupied them for a five-year period—can legally be considered theirs. And that's where the *pistoleiros* come in. They push the people off the land before, and even after, they have had the opportunity to make a legal claim. Violence has become endemic to the region. Just last year the minister of agriculture, Antônio Cabrera, said that "the violence in the countryside is, in its essence, the result of an unjust agrarian structure." In speaking about land conflicts on a recent trip to Brazil, Pope John Paul II warned that "all private property carries a social mortgage." Radical words from a traditionally conservative papacy, but it has been his priests and nuns who have been dying on the front lines here. As far as I can tell, the Protestants have yet to make their way to this remote mountaintop. These people, like the majority of Brazilians, are still Catholics.

When Vicent finishes explaining our presence Flora turns to a young boy standing by the door. *"Vai buscar Anita"*—Go get Anita—she says. Then she turns to us.

"She is José Fininho's woman. She is the one who was there. The only one who can tell you what *really* happened."

Flora then goes on to tell us that the men of the village went off to hide in the bush when they heard of our approach. She sends another young boy to tell them they can return. Minutes later, a small, wiry woman with curly black hair and knobby elbows arrives in the village almost out of breath. She looks to be in her early twenties and is dressed in sneakers, an orange blouse, and a black miniskirt. This is Anita, José Fininho's common-law wife. If her clothing is any indication, she has spent most of her life in towns. How she ended up with José Fininho is another story.

Anita leads us out of the village, and we arrive at a crudely constructed mud hut with a thatched roof sitting oddly alone in a forest clearing as if it had just dropped down from the heavens. This is the home she has shared with José Fininho and her two children from a prior relationship. In her squeaky voice she reenacts the shootout for us, providing background details that José Fininho left out. It turns out he is a thief who has been stealing cattle from the owners of the São José estate. José's rustling put him at odds not only with the landowner but also with the other squatters of Lot 7, four hundred impoverished men and women. For a while José Fininho lived among the other peasants, but then he was banished to this stretch of woods by the legitimate *posseiros* who were attempting to legally claim plots of land. The *posseiros* believed José Fininho's criminal activities would only bring trouble. And they were right. One day the landowner sent a gunman to look for the stolen property as well as the culprit who was taking it. José Fininho saw the man enter the village and he killed him before he had a chance to inquire about the missing cattle. The Thin Man, showing considerable strength, disposed of the body in a nearby ravine. When the landowner sent a second man, José Fininho killed him as well. Why he lingered in the community isn't clear. What *is* clear here is that José Fininho has tried to take advantage of not just the people of this community but the good Father Rezende and me, the gringo journalist.

"He is not a good man," old José Maria tells us later in the day. "José Fininho is trouble, only trouble."

José Maria is one of a dozen men who have now returned to the village, having received word from Flora that it is safe to come out of hiding. He tells us that he has been roaming about this region for decades trying to secure arable plots in between jobs as a peon on local *fazendas*. While José Fininho might be a charlatan, most of the people in this community seem to be legitimately occupying the land, working it in accordance with Brazilian law, hoping one day to claim it as their own.

"The large landowners have everything, am I right?" José Maria says. The words pop from his mouth like marbles spurting in a pinball machine. "They grabbed the land just like we are grabbing it. But they have money so they can put up fences. They make holes and then fortify the area around it. But we pass under the fences and go into the forest."

In less than two hours we work our way around the village interviewing other peasants, filming people at work, taking occasional breaks to quench our thirst or answer the questions of those who have just returned to the community. As night descends on the mountain, we decide to make our way home.

Anita has collected a few bits of clothing and personal possessions, stuffing them into a small bundle. She expects to be with José Fininho for a while. She has arranged for her children to be looked after by her mother. But five minutes down the path she suddenly asks us to wait a moment. As she stands there in the moon's milky blue light her frail body appears to be shaking.

"I am not coming with you."

"Are you sure?" says Vicent.

"Yes."

"Why?"

"I don't know why I am going."

"What do you want us to tell him?"

"I don't know. We lived together but I don't love him. You decide."

And with that she disappears into the night.

———

The following day in Rio Maria we meet Orlando Canuto, a big-eared, razor-thin guy with sad eyes that tell you he's seen it all, too much, more than you'd ever want to imagine. Maybe that explains why at twenty-six he's got the dejected walk of a man in his eighties. Life has been sucked out of him. When I hear his story I understand why.

We've arranged to meet him at his one-story clapboard house on one of the town's side streets. Finishing his coffee, Orlando steps out onto his front porch followed by his twenty-four-hour guard, a policeman recently assigned by a federal judge. With their added weight I can feel the floorboards bend under my feet and I struggle to keep the frame line steady and composed. Their steps produce a faint, hollow echo as they lumber down the porch steps and into the federal policeman's blue pickup truck. For me filming is difficult today. Yesterday's venture has taken its toll. My legs are stiff and sore, my mind groggy from lack of sleep. I adjust the camera's focus ring as I follow them down the steps. Then I quickly change positions to catch them entering the car. I grab a few extra shots of them getting seated, closing the doors, starting the engine. Although this type of coverage has become second nature, I feel as if someone has attached sandbags to my legs. But I've managed to film one really good image, one I know I'll use. It's a zoom out from the federal policeman's gun to Orlando seated in the front seat, his eyes flashing left and right as he scans the street. This is a guy who can't hide his fear. His face tells you he is terrified of dying.

At the modest one-story union headquarters in Rio Maria, Orlando gives us a tour of what I can only describe as their Wall of Ill-Fated Fame.

"This is Raimundo Ferreira Lima," he says, pointing to a photo of a stern man with glasses whose image, unlike most of the portraits, sits behind a glass frame. "He was a trade unionist killed in Conceição do Araguaia. 1980.

"There, also, is the president of the union in Tomé-Açu," he says as he points to a political poster with the photo of a baby-faced man in his thirties. "Benezinno. He was assassinated on July fourth, 1984."

As he shuffles over to other photos, he continues reciting names of victims of assassinations, including Expedito and Father Josimo. Finally he comes to a painting of an older man with glasses, a mustache, and black hair. For the first time there is a flash of emotion in his voice, a little life coming to the surface, stuck there in the quiver of his throat.

"This is my father, João Canuto, the first president of the union, this union. He was killed in 'eighty-five—December eighteenth, 1985."

In a small enclosed back room we set up for a more elaborate interview. Orlando seems uncomfortable on his feet. I sit him down by a window, taking advantage of a technique practiced since the days of Vermeer: soft light spills in from the side, fading off into the background shadows. Once seated, Orlando is more relaxed. He then gives us some background on what happened to his father, João Canuto de Oliveira. In the mid-1980s João became the first president of the union as well as a mayoral candidate in Rio Maria. He was known as a tenacious peasant organizer who had successfully orchestrated several occupations of contested areas of rain forest. It was common knowledge that he was held in bitter contempt by landowners in the region. At the time of his death in December of 1985 he had been representing forty-five families who were in a dispute with the *fazendeiro* of the Canaã estate. These *posseiros* had already been evicted from the land three times. The most recent eviction was in October, when sixty military police accompanied by gunmen forced them from their occupied lands. João Canuto, his son tells us, was an outspoken and confrontational man. He believed the town's mayor, Adilson Larangeira, was secretly acting as a intermediary between the landowners, the *pistoleiros*, and the military police. João went to the local press with his story, which is when the real trouble began. Suddenly the death threats increased and João, fearing for his life, traveled to the state and federal capitals to ask government officials for protection. He refused, however, to back down or leave the area.

Then in mid-December five armed men appeared in front of the union headquarters in a truck owned by the Canaã estate. Accompanied by the trade union's lawyer, João went to the local police station and registered an official complaint against the Canaã estate. One week later he was gunned down while walking home. His killers shot him fourteen times at point-blank range just outside the town cemetery. No one considered the circumstances of his death excessive. Not in this town. Not in comparison to the one hundred forty pieces of lead that were fired into the body of Belchior Martins Costa, a peasant and local activist who had been killed in Rio Maria three years earlier.

Orlando and his brothers were teenagers at the time of their father's death. They didn't much care for politics. They followed their father's case and watched as a familiar pattern unfolded: several arrests were made, the police investigations were never completed, the detainees were eventually released. The boys grew up, married, and started their own families. Orlando eventually moved out of the area to the state of Goiás. In 1990 pressure from Amnesty International resulted in a reopening of João Canuto's case. That is when Orlando's life changed. His brothers, Paulo and José, who weren't involved in politics, started to receive death threats. Then one day Orlando and his brother-in-law Carlos Cabral, a union activist, were picked up by the police in connection with the killing of a man Orlando refers to as "a *pistoleiro* from a local ranch." Hearing of their arrest, Father Ricardo quickly intervened, and, lacking any plausible evidence, Orlando and Carlos were released. Orlando then went to see his mother before he went back to his wife in Goiânia. And "then it happened."

"What?" asks Vicent.

Orlando pauses for a moment, his slack and motionless body leaning against the windowsill. His voice, as always, is a monotone. His eyes dart left and right as if bombarded by the images of a flashback.

"They came to the house and said that they were from the federal police. They arrested us. They put handcuffs on me, with my hands behind. Paulo and José were handcuffed together. They pushed me into the car, then my brothers. They said that we were going to Maraba. During the trip they kept asking, 'How many have you killed?' We answered, 'None.' They asked if we were part of the invasion in Redenção. We said no. 'Yes, you were,' they kept saying. I told them that I had already been arrested on that charge and that I proved in court that I had nothing to do with it.

"They were carrying a machine gun, a 7.65, and three .38s. We left Rio Maria and passed through Xinguara. Before Sapucaia the car got stuck. A wheel had slipped through between two planks of the bridge. They put me outside and forced my two brothers, who each had one hand free, to lift and push the car. We then continued on the road. We passed through Sapucaia. Then when we were near the entrance of the Pontão

Ranch, one of them said, 'Let's go in here to piss.' I knew then that they were going to kill us. Then and there. They got out of the car and pulled my brothers out. I was the last one out of the car. Someone punched me hard on the head, then the driver shot me. The bullet passed through my belly and hit my wrist. At that moment I didn't feel pain. I threw myself against him and then against the other one who was getting ready to shoot me. I ran across the road and bumped into a barbwire fence. I fell over the fence and into the pasture. The bullets passed over me. If I hadn't fallen, I would have been shot. I got up, ran a little more, and fell down again. It's hard to get up when your hands are fastened behind your back so I decided to stay very still in the grass. Not moving at all. I then heard a lot of shots. Two of the men were coming through the fence looking for me. But they closed the circle in the wrong place, leaving me outside of it. I noticed the woods just ahead of me and I ran into the old brush. It's almost forest. I could hear them start the engine of the car and leave. I stayed in the woods a long time. I was afraid they were going to come back again. At eleven-thirty I went to a house near the crossroads. I asked someone to go to the road and get a ride for me because I couldn't raise my arms. They were handcuffed behind my back. The people were scared, so they wouldn't do it. But they offered to cut the chain, freeing my hands. It was midnight. I went out on foot in the direction of Xinguara, through the woods, afraid that the men would catch me. I was thirsty but afraid to drink, in case I might hemorrhage. Eventually, I made it to a gas station in Sapucaia where I hid until my friend Seu Rafael came and got me and brought me to Xinguara."

"And your brothers?"

"Both killed. Shots to the head. Their bodies left on the side of the road."

A year later Orlando's brother-in-law Carlos—he was acting president of the union after Expedito's assassination—was shot in the leg returning home from a meeting with Father Ricardo and some local activists. The gunman had fired three times, the first two bullets passing over his head. The *pistoleiro* had been hiding behind a wall in the town cemetery, the same cemetery in front of which João Canuto had been killed six years earlier. Two years after his brothers' death and seven years after his father's, there have still not been any convictions in the Canuto family murders, their cases "lost" in the disorganized bureaucracy of Rio Maria's court system.

In the afternoon we visit one more time with José Fininho before heading back to the airport at Maraba. This time we slip past the guards with very little problem. We give him some food and explain to him that his wife decided not to come with us. "She couldn't leave the children," Vicent tells him. He takes this news in silence. His eyes, watery, drift off to some spot in the ceiling. He knows we are lying.

"I'm sorry but I can't sit up today," he says after a long pause. "I don't have the strength."

"Can we ask you just one more question?" Vicent asks.

"Certainly."

"You said the other day you were afraid for your life. Do you still feel that way?"

"Yes."

"Why?"

"I am concerned about being sent to Belém and being murdered on the way, in an arrangement made with one of the large landowners." For a second his eyes wander back to the ceiling. "That's common here." He turns and looks at us again. "I was lucky to have the civil police around, which prevented my murder. If they were not around, I would have been killed."

He pauses for a moment and looks to the doorway to see if anyone is listening.

"If I was left solely under the jurisdiction of the military police or the hired gunmen, I would be dead now." His head begins to nod and his eyes water as he bites his lower lip. It is sad to watch a man realizing he will be facing death alone.

Driving from Xinguara to Rio Maria, I watch as a light rain washes over the green fields and I ponder the sociological phenomenon that calls himself José Fininho: cattle thief, gunslinger, con artist. He had killed two men, frontier style, who probably would have killed him had they been given the chance. His wife had left him. He knew no one in town (the Protestants hadn't shown up for two days). Father Ricardo's Pastoral Land Commission refused to take on his case because of his criminal actions. He was in trouble and alone, his fate now solely in the hands of a highly suspect "justice" system. His fatal mistake in his downward spiral apparently was that he acted alone for much of his life. The Thin Man alienated anyone who could have come to his aid at a time like this including—as we saw—his wife. A man alone on the frontier is a man in trouble. José Fininho seems aware of that now.

———

Before leaving Rio Maria I go by to see a plaque in the middle of town that has recently been the focus of contention between the local mayor and the families of eight activists assassinated in the last decade. Father Ricardo told me part of the story and it piqued my interest. It seems just five months ago the Nobel Peace Prize winner Adolfo Pérez Esquivel visited Rio Maria. As someone who had attained international acclaim because of his work on behalf of Argentina's "disappeared," he wanted to show his concern about the violence that terrorized this region. Father Ricardo got permission from the town to hold a reception for the esteemed visitor and unveil a simple three-by-five-foot plaque commemorating the occasion. It read "On this day, December 4, 1991, in the presence of the Nobel Prize laureate Adolfo Pérez Esquivel, we pay homage to the martyrs of the land in Rio Maria." Drink and food were served, the press arrived, the Nobel laureate said a few words and then continued his tour of Brazil. The next day the mayor, Sebastião Emidio de Almeida, and several of his friends went to the site of the memorial and started digging up the plaque. When local journalists arrived on the scene, Mayor Emidio kicked one of the photographers while his cronies threatened and scuffled with the others. Eventually, Emidio and his men succeeded in removing the plaque and they carried it back to the town hall. Word of the confrontation quickly got back to Señor Esquivel, who sent a harsh letter of protest to Mayor Emidio. Fearing an embarrassing international incident, Emidio agreed to replace the plaque. But he rewrote the text.

"I'm not going to tell you what he replaced it with," said Ricardo. "Go see for yourself. It is just down the street."

So here I stand in front of "a gesture of peace" that only added to the insane havoc of this little frontier community. The mayor's version reads: "On this day, December 4, 1991, we pay homage to the winner of the Nobel Prize for Peace 1980, Adolfo Pérez Esquivel, and we thank him for his visit for Peace to our municipality." No mention of those who had died in land conflicts, those "martyrs" Esquivel's visit commemorated. This is the way life unfolds in southern Pará, a land where slavery still exists, where murderers go free, and where the quest for the truth brings with it a price tag of bloodshed.

> *Death will arrive one day;*
> *Only the hour is uncertain.*
> *Often it comes by surprise*
> *And like a bolt from the blue.*
> —Expedito Ribeiro da Souza
> (assassinated 2/2/1991, Rio Maria)

23

Rio de Janeiro, 1992

We've just passed through two roadblocks flashing our press credentials to bored guards in ill-fitting brown uniforms, probably employees of some obscure branch of the Rio de Janeiro police. Driving through the city earlier today we saw dozens of soldiers standing on street corners with machine guns dangling from shoulder straps. Some of them hassled us when we took their picture but the majority of them simply stood there, lockjawed, in statuesque military poses. Tucked away on strategically chosen side roads there were also tanks and armed personnel carriers filled with combat-ready troops. According to my Brazilian friends who were here at the time, this whole scene is eerily reminiscent of the 1964 military coup d'état. But in 1992 the abundance of soldiers in the streets of Rio simply reflects heightened security measures in anticipation of the United Nations Conference on Environment and Development—the Earth Summit. The city, a shell of what it was during its heyday in the 1960s, has also undergone a rapid cosmetic transformation in recent weeks: ambitious highway projects have been completed and new sidewalks put in place, dilapidated buildings have been refurbished, and water once again flows from turn-of-the-century fountains.

Increased security measures might explain the two roadblocks we just passed through, but we've now hit a third one, which appears to be a little different. Three guards with bizarre churlish grins step into the road flagging down our car. They are dressed in baggy blue jeans and shiny synthetic shirts, their hair crudely chopped. One of them pokes his head into the back window demanding cigarettes from my soundman Chris. Another pushes his face up against the front windshield, his bulbous nose and lips pressed flush against the glass, distorting the look of an already strangely contorted countenance. The third man, ignoring me in the driver's seat, thrusts his head into my window and addresses himself to our Brazilian production assistant Maria who sits next to me. *Why did I stop the car?* I ask myself.

"What is your name?" he says to her, his breath stale with nicotine, a little bubble of white froth forming on the edge of his mouth.

"Maria," she says with a small defensive smile.

The man whose face was pinned to the windshield is now off to the left of the road, arms extended, elbows bent, doing a little dance on the grassy edge, some odd version of *Fiddler on the Roof.*

"What's going on here?" I say to Maria.

She pauses a little too long. "I don't know," she says as her suitor suddenly laughs and looks at me.

"Whoa-whoa, big fella," I hear someone say in the backseat. In my review mirror I can see that the third "guard" (I'm beginning to have questions about their status) is rifling the pockets of my soundman Chris for cigarettes. A few fall to the ground, but the man catches one and lights it instantly with a match pulled from his shirt pocket.

"I think it is time to go," says Maria.

"*Com licença*"—With your permission—I say to the man standing by our window as I slowly put my hands on his chest, easing him away from the vehicle. He backs off with quick steps, looking like Charlie Chaplin spinning in reverse in a silent film. The cigarette thief now puffs away as he moves about our car taking photographs of us with an imaginary camera. I throw the vehicle into first gear and accelerate quickly down the dirt roadway, passing a large complex resembling a religious retreat. On the front lawn are more people in ill-fitting clothes, standing about like discarded mannequins, some talking to themselves, others simply staring off into the distance.

"Check out those guys," says Chris, glued to the rear window. Looking back in the rearview mirror I see our three guards crouched by the roadside collecting the cigarettes that fell from our car.

"Is this what I think it is?" I say to Maria.

"The state psychiatric hospital," she says.

As we round the next corner we finally arrive at our intended destination: the Karioca Village, a cluster of three large thatched communal houses, recently constructed, nestled on a ridge of green mountains. This is the outskirts of Rio, an hour's drive from the high rises and beaches of Ipanema and Copacabana as well as the mountainside shantytowns the Brazilians call *favelas*. The Karioca Village is to be the site of the World Conference of Indigenous Peoples, an alternative meeting of native leaders from across the planet scheduled—strategically—one week prior to the start of the official UN conference. We were told earlier in the day by one of the Karioca Conference *representantes* that they expect sixteen hundred journalists and four hundred indigenous leaders. Already the place is packed with camera-toting foreigners spouting forth in a dozen languages. "It's a media zoo," I say to Chris as we unload our equipment from the car. "Roger that, Captain," he responds.

Chris Caris is a sinewy, short-haired, Marlboro-smoking son of Greek immigrants who was brought up in Washington, D.C. His most salient character traits are a love of quasi-military jargon and a predilection for abbreviations—part of his zealous, can-do attitude that has made him an excellent collaborator in the world of shoestring documentaries. He calls himself "C. C." and me "G. O." and has already started calling Rio de Janeiro "R. J." C. C. is here working as my soundman to take a break from his normal job as the production coordinator of our New York office. When we arrived yesterday he insisted on taking a taxi ride by the shoreline, his head swiveling left and right as he whistled "The Girl from Ipanema," another gringo in a tropical

paradise, his head full of illusions created by the strange bits
and pieces of Brazilian culture that through time have managed
to sift up to North America: Carmen Miranda in black-and-
white films, the bodies of murdered street kids on CNN, the
beach with its girls in "dental floss" bikinis, and finally Carnaval: "the biggest and *wildest* fucking party in the world," as a
young American tourist once described it to me on an
overnight flight to Rio.

Never in the history of the world has there been so large a
gathering of indigenous peoples. There are Sarawaks from
Malaysia, Hill People from Pakistan, Apaches and Onondaga
people from North America, Sumi people from the Nordic countries, Aborigines from Australia, Maoris from New Zealand, and
dozens of other "forgotten peoples," as they've been called in the
popular press, including a wide spectrum of indigenous societies
from Brazil. There are those who have arrived here in the
clothing of the Western world but most of these leaders are in
traditional dress. Some are wearing flowing grass tongas, tall elabo-
rately woven headdresses, brightly colored cotton skirts, shorts,
and shirts, ornate necklaces, beads, earrings, and nose rings. They
are here holding symposiums on the "struggles" of their communities, and occasionally giving impromptu press conferences to
international journalists looking for a little background color
prior to the start of the UN conference.

"We are here to speak about the problems of the villages and
to tell the other Indians to continue fighting together," said
Davi Kopenawa to a group of journalists earlier in the day.
"Because if we don't unite, the whites are going to go on dominating our lives and our work."

Davi, whom I haven't seen in two years, has become a veteran of the movement, someone with wide recognition in the
international arena, someone the press seeks out, an acknowledged spokesperson for the Yanomami people. And he has got
something to talk about. Not only did President Collor drive
the gold miners out of Yanomami territory two years ago but
just two days before the start of the Karioca Conference his
government completed the demarcation of Davi's people's
land, thereby officially recognizing their traditional territory.

But as with any of the large conferences I have attended in recent years, there are early warning signs of problems to come. For every indigenous leader here there seem to be at least two or three photographers colliding, cursing, tripping, and shoving, all of them trying to get the best angle, the most intimate exposure. The scene is similar to Altamira, but more extreme: there is more hysteria, more tension. Given the current climate of interest in tropical forests, images of indigenous people are hot-ticket items. These photographers seem to be particularly interested in Brazilian Indians whose elaborate ritual outfits have attracted the largest hordes of image gatherers.

As the day draws to a close I notice a handful of errant psychiatric patients from the local hospital appearing in the crowd of photographers. Among them are the "guards" who confronted us earlier in the day. The patients stand alone, catching the action as their heads pan back and forth, very often engaged in lively conversations with themselves. Somehow they manage to blend into the insanity that has come to dominate this event, and they go unnoticed.

There has been a great deal of tension in Brazil leading up to Earth Summit '92, much of it traceable back to the Woodstock of Amazonia, the Altamira Conference in 1989. That crystallizing event galvanized a generation of Brazilian and international citizens increasingly concerned about the future of the environment. Among their ranks were legions of schoolchildren, journalists, ecologists, college kids, and politicians. All of these groups have in their own way been trying to stop "the threat to our tropical forests." This seemingly innocent phrase triggers a wave of xenophobic fear in the hearts of Brazilian nationalists. The American congressman Robert Kasten—one of a new generation of "green" politicians—declared shortly after the death of Chico Mendes that, regarding Brazil's rain forests, "We need them and we use them—so they're our rain forests too." While those of us in Europe and North America see ourselves as expressing concerns, within Brazil such sentiments are perceived as threats. And the government has been quick to react.

"It is the greatest international pressure that Brazil has lived through in the whole of its history," Brazil's foreign secretary Paolo Tarso Flecha de Lima said in 1989 just one month after the Altamira Conference. The environment secretary Fernando Mesquita—a man booed off the stage in Altamira—was more direct: "There is a real danger of foreign occupation of the Amazon. We are seeing a concerted international effort to hold back development in Brazil."

In 1990 the former president José Sarney—a politician well known for his close ties to the military—took a strongly defensive posture vis-a-vis his adversaries from abroad and what he termed their "international greed." He began lashing out at his foreign critics while reasserting Brazil's control over the region. Environmentalism, Sarney said, was a "Trojan horse" hiding other interests, and statistics on rain forest destruction part of a "campaign of scientific falsehoods." In his speeches he began to use the age-old Brazilian battle cry *"Amazônia é nossa"*—The Amazon is ours. Addressing the high command of the armed forces, he said that "now more than ever" the military had a "mission": defend the Amazon. In 1991 the Brazilian Congress also took action. They began an investigation of a purported foreign plot to "planetize" the Amazon, to quote the country's justice minister Jarbas Passarinho. The message being sent back to the international community was clear: Brazil's politicians—and average citizens—didn't want anyone telling them what to do with their country. It was bad enough that the nation was hostage to North American banks with $121 billion of debt—a legacy of the military dictatorship that had appointed Sarney as part of its transition government. Compromise proposals like Tom Lovejoy's "Debt for Nature" were out of the question as far as Sarney was concerned. "We accept international aid but we don't accept conditions," was how he put it.

But President Sarney's bid to rouse nationalist sentiments could not resuscitate his ailing political career. He was part of the old guard. In 1985 the Archdiocese of São Paolo published *Brasil: Nunca Mais (Brazil: Never Again)*, a thorough documentation of the thousands of people who disappeared and were tortured during the two decades of military dictatorship. In later years, a great deal of public rage was vented against the former dictators and their henchmen who had been given uncondi- tional amnesties as part of their agreement to return the country to democratic rule. Now the electorate wanted to distance itself from the past. With the 1990 election, the nation's citizens ush- ered in a man who came to symbolize the arrival of a new generation: Fernando Collor de Mello, the country's first demo- cratically elected executive official in twenty-six years. Collor was a young, flamboyant *politico* with the slicked-back hair and Teflon manner that defined high-powered players in the 1980s, a man who spoke six languages, wore designer suits, and came from one of the most powerful families in Brazil's Northeast.

Once in office Collor took special care to distinguish himself from his predecessor. Unlike Sarney, he has been sensitive to international concerns, more accommodating to the wishes of *estrangeiros*, foreigners. His quick response to the barrage of questions about the Yanomami after his visit to Washington was just the beginning of a campaign to give Brazil a greener image. Since he took power, he has completely reshaped the country's agenda on environmental concerns. He not only kicked forty-five thousand gold miners out of Yanomami terri- tory and demarcated their lands, but his administration also pushed through the initial paperwork to recognize Kayapo terri- tory. Collor also enticed the UN to hold the Earth Summit in Rio and he appointed a vocal government critic as the country's environment secretary.

But while the new president was scoring points in the inter- national arena, tensions were building at home. Conservative politicians and frontier developers were depicting Indians as obstacles to development, pawns of gringo environmentalists in an international conspiracy to limit the growth of the Brazilian economy. Outspoken Brazilian congressmen believed the indigenous societies' retention of their extensive traditional homelands was holding Brazil back, trapping the country in the Third World. "Civilizing" them or "integrating" them were recommended as the optimal solutions to the Indian question. In 1990 the frontier politician Gilberto Mestrinho, governor of

Amazonas, the largest state in the Amazon Basin, said, "Behind the environmental movement there are economic interests who fear that the economic development of the Amazon would risk investments made in other parts of the world." His recent campaign for reelection included hyperbolic promises to provide every peasant with a chain saw and promote the hunting of endangered species. "In Canada and the United States people use chain saws. Why do our people have to go back to axes?" he asked a North American reporter in Rio. But while Mestrinho and others lambasted international environmentalists, in the run-up to the UN conference Collor's new government was attempting to take a tough stance on environmental issues. It had recently levied million-dollar fines on the illegal activities of two mining companies and a lumber concern in the Amazon, assertive actions that contrasted sharply with the laissez-faire attitudes of the Sarney government. These actions, praised in Europe and North America, were referred to as "absurd exhibitionism" by nationalist critics like Governor Mestrinho.

But it wasn't only the frontier politicians who were outraged by Collor's actions. Shortly before the Earth Summit there was a wave of anti-interventionist journalism in the Brazilian press, much of it critical of the recent role that Indians and the international community had come to play in determining the future of the country's Amazon Basin. Paulo Francis, a popular columnist and TV commentator, wrote a scathing critique of Collor as someone who "gives land in abundance" to the Indians, a people, he said, who "weren't even of use as slaves." The preeminent Brazilian newsmagazine *Veja* warned in the week prior to the summit that "it's time to correct the mistakes of foreigners who talk about Indians, burning, and Amazonia." These nationalist sentiments were echoed by frontier fortune-seekers in the Amazon Basin. In the northeastern state of Amapá, just a month before the start of the summit, I spoke with Antonio Feijáo, president of a local miners' organization that has been vying with Indian groups for the mineral rights to their land. Feigão was also a protégé and ally of José Altino

Machado. "For us, if the indigenous areas continue growing, then they will eventually connect," he told me outside a gold store in the state capitol of Macapá. "So then we are concerned that the UN and the First World countries will intervene here in order to create a state, that is a geographic area and a people, which will be used as a device to create a new nation. And then we will be left with a separate enclave such as there is in South Africa as in the case of Swaziland."

In this current climate of heightened xenophobia Brazil's Indians were increasingly being cast as worthless social drones, the naive dupes of international environmentalists. Gilson Machado, a conservative congressman, wrote during this period: "The image of the Indian using feathers, living naked and useless, and sleeping in grass huts, really belongs in Westerns from the beginning of this century. . . . We should take advantage of Rio-92 and the lessons of the experiences of more advanced peoples so that we can have above all *Ecology with Development.* And as for the Brazilian Indian, all of us who love our land and our people would like to have him properly integrated to true civilization, as in developed nations. We should never agree to see him *eternally dressed in a tanga.*"

This image of the Indian as a pawn and token of a larger international plot was, however, very different from another image that was circulating outside of Brazil and within certain liberal cliques in Rio and São Paulo. To these groups the Indian was not an obstacle to development but a saintly, often child-like, being who was also key in the movement to save the environment—someone who could make the world a better place for a new generation of New Age, sympathetic, ecologically concerned citizens. This 1992-model Nobel Savage was an elaboration on the version that had appeared at Altamira in 1989. The Save the Rain Forest movement had taken on momentum in the intervening years, accelerating the resuscitation of an icon of Western European culture that had lain dormant for several decades.

As repackaged by the environmentally concerned, this new sentimentalized token of eco-consciousness emerged in a wide variety of media incarnations in the weeks prior to the summit. In a Brazilian documentary series on Indians of the Xingú Park, the on-camera commentator told viewers: "The world of the Indian is like a dream. The encounter with the Indian is like a submersion into another time and space, a departure from our civilization, a return to innocence." Championing the cause of the Kayapo, Anita Roddick, founder of the Body Shop Corporation, described Paulinho Payakan as "a new Gandhi"—a characterization, considering its prior application to Chico Mendes, that was now bordering on cliché. She went on to provide the Kayapo leader with a plane while setting up a Brazil nut processing plant in his village of A'ukre. Kayapo products and jewelry were now regular fixtures in her stores, part of the Trade-Not-Aid project she had devised with her husband and partner Gordon. In the weeks prior to the Earth Summit life-size photos of smiling Kayapo also added an exotic element to Body Shop displays in Europe, Canada, and the United States. Brazilian television commercials, even more blatant in their appropriation of the Indian, used images of indigenous peoples as trendy icons in a product pitch. In one Lee advertisement a young white man encounters a group of semiclothed, potentially threatening natives in the forest. He takes off his jeans, trades them for a bow and arrow, and walks off smiling and victorious with the Indian weapons in hand. The tag line: "It's not Lee that is different. It is the others that are the same."

However one views these popularized images—exploitation? cultural appropriation?—they received minor play in comparison to one depiction that turned the noble savage into a virtual deity. This was a cover story in the U.S. publication *Parade* magazine which appeared in April of 1992. The article was part of a public relations effort tied to the broadcast of a rain forest documentary on American television. The magazine's cover carried a color photograph of Paulinho Payakan in extreme close-up wearing ceremonial paint and looking directly into the camera, staring at us, confronting our world with his vision. The story was entitled "The Man Who Could Save the World." The noble savage as ecological redeemer had now reached Christlike proportions. "I Fight for Our Future" read the subtitle accompanying a photograph of Payakan at Altamira, followed by another line that read: "It's a battle Chief Payakan began for the survival of his people, but what's at stake is the survival of us all." The opening paragraph was strangely reminiscent of the prologue to a Disney story:

> Several years ago, a young Kayapo Indian named Paulinho Payakan left his village in the Amazon rain forest of Brazil in order to save it. He ventured to the outside world, warning that if the forest disappears, his people will die. Today he is still standing against the forces of destruction as time runs out. At stake is far more than the fate of a remote Kayapo village. . . .

This depiction of Payakan contrasted sharply with the man I had come to know over the years. Just prior to the release of this article I had seen him in New York, where he was speaking at a conference. He seemed anxious and depressed, but he was someone who had a reputation for violent mood swings. When I asked about his participation at the upcoming Earth Summit, he said he was uncertain if he was going to attend the UN event. He was beginning to question the point of all these trips to North America and Europe. He didn't know what they'd amounted to. The confident, charismatic leader who at one time had been at the forefront of the Save the Rain Forest movement seemed, in just three short years, to have become one of its most embittered refugees. He said he was tired of hearing "promises" to help his people—promises that were never fulfilled. On this trip to New York, Payakan seemed much more intent on escaping our world than on saving it. But that was not a story to interest *Parade*. These current concerns of Payakan were probably too real, too specific, too complicated. What the media at this time wants is a kind of truth that approximates fiction in its blending of fantasy and reality to propagate a cause. The *Parade* article was simply part of a groundswell of attention concerning Amazonia which, it appears, was reaching its apex at the Earth Summit. Environmentalists in Europe and the United States and, with increasing frequency, "green capitalists" and media organizations were in need of heroes around which to focus their causes and campaigns. The bigger the heroes, the better the exposure.

Brazilians are world-renowned for their Carnavals: raucous, Dionysian four-day celebrations that revolve around the parades of samba schools in minute, shimmering, sensuous costumes whose occupants dance through the boulevards of the country's towns and cities immersing themselves in bacchanalian excess just before the arrival of the Catholic Lent. It is a ritual without sanctions, without rules, a time of unlimited possibilities. Carnaval, Brazilians say, helps them to recharge their batteries. The residual effect of this annual event is deeply embedded in the Brazilian psyche. It can manifest itself throughout the year: a party, a soccer match, or some simple celebration can suddenly become transformed into frenzied, cathartic ritual at a moment's notice. That is what has happened on the fourth day of the Karioca Conference: the place has started to get out of control. It has became Carnavalesque.

News stories on the conference have been running on Brazilian television all week. But it must have crossed a threshold because today there is a surge in the number of tourists stopping by to get a look at the plethora of indigenous peoples. Middle-class *mamães* and *papais* with kids in tow are arriving in the village, cameras dangling from their necks, their heads glued to video recorders. All of them seem to be searching for tourist trophies: an Indian necklace or flute purchased for a few cruzeiros, perhaps even a photograph of *la família* with one of *os indios*. As C. C. and I take a break from filming, we watch Brazilian fathers flagging down passing conference participants in traditional dress, mostly Brazilian Indians. Politely they ask the men or women to pose with their wife and children. *"Por favor,"* one man says. "It would make them so happy." If the Indian accepts—which in most cases they do—the father invariably lines everyone up with the Indian in the middle of the shot. And there before us is a socio-

logical centerpiece of Brazilian culture: an indigenous icon captured in a photographic moment, the troubled totem of a con-
flicted culture, a recognizable but very distant cousin. Watching
this scene unfold only reconfirms what has become obvious in
recent days: that the Indian in Brazil has become an object of
contemplation—to some a relic of a distant past, to others the
Achilles' heel of a faltering national economy.

Among today's new wave of Carnaval characters is a strange
cadre of rear-guard gate-crashers. Some of them dress as
Indians. Others call themselves Indians. But neither of these
two groups are, in fact, Indians. They are whites who have
decided to cross over into the world of the indigenous people, a
world "of exoticism and fascination," according to one such afi-
cionado. In this group is Loretta Bartel, a gangly woman in her
late twenties with long, bleached blond hair. She is dressed in a
cowhide bikini top and an ankle-length leopard-skin skirt. Her
face is adorned with two large diagonal swaths of red and blue
paint. The intention, I assume, is to approximate indigenous
facial paint, but it makes her look more like a walk-on character from a *Star Trek* episode than a legitimate participant in a
conference of global indigenous leaders. Originally from
Yugoslavia, she has in recent years made Brazil her home. C. C.
and I have approached her in the midst of her publicity efforts
for the dance group she manages, called Indio Olegui, whom we
filmed earlier in the day.

We introduce ourselves, explaining that we are covering this
event for a documentary for U.S. television. She hands me a
press release for her group. Yes, she says, she would be delighted
to answer a few questions.

"Could you tell us why you are dressed the way you are
dressed today?"

"I am dressed like this for very personal reasons."

"And?"

She shakes her head no. This is sacred ground, I suppose. I
glance down at the opening line of the press release. It reads
"Let me invite you to a thrilling journey to a past we all share."
I try another tack.

"When do you think white people first became interested in the life of the Indians?"

"It started when white women were first kidnapped by the Indians," she says as she pushes her hair back and adjusts the straps of her rawhide bikini top.

"How is that?"

"The European women arrived here and the Indians kidnapped them. Then they took them to their tribes. Then the white men's leaders would send soldiers to bring back the women. But they arrived there and saw how happy the women were, that they didn't want to come back. This is the way miscegenation began."

Okay.

"What do you think lies in store for the future of Indian people?"

"Indian man is strong. Indian man knows what he wants. Indian man has survived all these terrible things for the last five hundred years. He is strong and he will survive."

"Right. Okay, let me ask you another question."

"I am sorry, I have to go with these other journalists," she says, gesturing to a cluster of photographers anxious to do another photo session with their exotic subject. "Please come and see us perform this afternoon."

C. C. and I spend the next several hours filming indigenous leaders in different workshop settings, trying to capture aspects not covered earlier in the week. Later in the day we look for Loretta and her group but they seem to have disappeared. One conference organizer tells us they were asked to leave. In the tradition of Buffalo Bill, I assume Loretta has taken her show on the road.

The next day we encounter "Tall Strong" seated among a group of journalists diligently taking down his every word in notepads. "If you add up the Cherokee people in Oklahoma and the Cherokee in Taos, you probably have well over eight million people," he says. "Because my tribe alone, Atoyak, which is the name of a river in Texas, has about four million people."

In the center of Tall Strong's circle, one lone television camera is focused on him. Next to the cameraman is a slender woman in a flowing white cotton dress, large oval glasses, and a white turban. She is holding a clipboard and occasionally leans over to whisper directions to the cameraman. Tall Strong continues.

"You cannot see an Indian killing just for the fun of it. An Indian does not kill a beast if he doesn't need to. But that doesn't mean that Indians do not raise cattle. An Indian won't kill a tree if he does not need to extract it from the soil."

Tall Strong doesn't converse, he makes pronouncements. His every word is uttered as if it is about to be etched in stone. His hair is short, brown, parted on the side. He is dressed in a light brown three-piece suit with a pale blue tie. It's the look in his eye that is unsettling. It's glazed over in a way I have come to associate with American Jesus freaks and TV infomercial hucksters: an empty look, as if the human spirit has been vaporized from his body and replaced by some synthetic substitute. A tabloid print reporter would have a field day covering the Lorettas and Tall Strongs of the conference. I can imagine the headline: ALIENS INVADE BODIES OF WHITES WHO BECOME INDIANS.

We move about the periphery grabbing various shots of this alien Indian interacting with reporters. At one point he stops his lecture and pulls out both his Brazilian and Cherokee passports. Tall Strong, he tells us, is his Indian name. His Brazilian name is Reinaldo Livio. The proof of his dual identity is in his documents. A German photographer fires off shots of Tall Strong in various poses: Tall Strong smiling, Tall Strong serious, Tall Strong with passports extended before him. Part white man and part Indian, Tall Strong, we are being asked to believe, is a living example of someone who has actually crossed over and *become* an Indian. Why am I so skeptical when all these other journalists seem to be accepting his words at face value? Isn't it possible that he has done what others before him have not been able to do? Could it be that Father Calleri or even Sting could have learned from his experiences? What can Tall Strong tell us?

As I move closer for a better angle of Tall Strong with the photographers, someone grabs my arm, then steps in front of the camera. It is the woman in the white turban, her face "fish-eyed" by the distorted perspective of my wide-angle lens. By her accent I can tell she is from North America.

"You cannot film this man!"

"Excuse me?"

"I said you are not permitted to film this man."

"Okay." I continue filming.

"I have exclusive rights to his life. This press conference was arranged by us for our film," she says as she grabs hold of my arm again, ruining my shot.

I stop and stare at her.

"We are the only ones who can film him."

"I'm sorry, but that's not possible."

"No. I'm sorry."

"Listen, you are in a public space. Look around, there are a dozen other journalists here. I can do whatever I want."

"Sorry. No other television cameras." She steps in front of my lens again. Tall Strong, in the midst of his press conference, glances at us from the corner of his eye.

"Can I ask who you are?"

"I'm not telling you that."

"Okay," I say. "Listen. You find someone from the Conference to tell me to stop doing what I am doing, and until then I am going to continue filming this event." I pause. "Okay?"

"You have no right . . ." she says, her jowls trembling with rage. She stares at me for a moment, silent, her eyes blinking rapidly. Then she turns and disappears into the crowd, leaving me and the reporters with Tall Strong.

By this time I have heard a good deal of Tall Strong's official biography as presented to the press, none of whom seem to doubt that this man is in fact a Cherokee Indian. He is, he says, also "a Tupi Indian from Brazil" by virtue of his one-eighth Indian ancestry. He was born and raised in Brazil but then came to the United States, where he lived for ten years in New York. There he met a Cherokee Indian who "understood that I was an Indian" and introduced him to the Cherokee people, who issued him a passport and made him a "Cherokee citizen."

"Can you explain for us your official status here?" I ask Tall Strong after we pull him away from the other reporters.

"In this particular event, okay. I am a guest lecturer here to talk about the Cherokee nation, our history, and the way we face the indigenous cause nowadays."

"Do you think that, as someone brought up in white society, you can really understand indigenous people?"

"There are several misconceptions about the way the white man is interfering with the indigenous cause," says Tall Strong as he clears his throat, his eyes now scanning left and right. "You are going to find, studying a little bit of history, that in several occasions, the ones who were fighting for the human rights most bravely were not Indians at all."

"Really?"

"Yes. It is proven. In history."

"But what are the qualities that you have that distinguish you and allow you to enter that society?"

"It took me some time to understand what it takes to become an Indian and what it takes to fight for the Indians, but it's so damn simple, it's so easy that I've surprised myself," he says, suddenly elated. "And I've asked myself, Why in the world didn't I jump in this boat before?" At this point Tall Strong laughs to himself and flashes a smile. A photographer behind me takes his picture.

"And what is that simple answer?" I ask, waiting for my photo colleague to move on.

"The simple answer?"

"Yes," I say. "I'd like to know what it is."

"Willingness, that's all. If you want to play tennis and if you want to be the best, what do you do? You learn how to play it and then you get on the tennis court and you play it. And then you can become the best." He smiles again. Eyes no longer flashing. He's concentrated. On a roll. This is what he came here to do. To "use the media today," as he put it.

"But if you sit down and just watch, you are never going to learn. If you want to swim. It is the same thing. Anything in life happens to be the same. Fighting for the Indians is no different at all."

"Anything else you would like to say?" I ask, noticing that his agent/producer has returned, lingering in the background, her image caught in the corner of my frame, once again ruining my shot. I step to the right, adjusting the angle to make certain she is out of frameline.

"No. I think I have said enough," he says.

"Roger that" says C. C. as Tall Strong walks away.

For the rest of the afternoon I keep thinking about Tall Strong's concept of "willingness," his tennis metaphor, and the regret he now feels for not "jumping in the boat before." In the five years I have been covering Brazil, I have met a good number of people who have tried in various ways to cross into the world of the Indians. There have been gold miners and missionaries who lived with them, anthropologists who spent their lives studying them, and activists, rock stars, and filmmakers who have spent countless hours toiling away in apparently sincere efforts to understand and support their causes. In both Brazil and the United States I have met many people like Loretta and Tall Strong, individuals who appear at such events adorned in facial paint or Indian regalia claiming to have some distant link to an indigenous heritage, all of them speaking on the Indian's behalf without questioning the irony and potential pitfalls of inhabiting another culture so very distant from their own. Is it possible Tall Strong has succeeded where others have failed? Has he found a way to transport himself unmolested through that tricky middle ground that exists between their world and ours? *Yes*, I think. *Maybe I have been too hard on Tall Strong.* But then I run into Oren Lyons, one of the elders of the Onondaga people, a group of North American Indians currently living on a reservation in upstate New York.

"What do you make of this guy Tall Strong?" I ask.

"We questioned him and he said he was from the Salagas Nation in Texas," says Oren, a veteran of North American Indian activism. "And we said 'How many people do you represent?' And he said there were one hundred in one group, two hundred in another group, and three million in Texas." Oren pauses for a moment, then gives the camera an exaggerated roll of the eyes. "I mean, it made us suspicious because there's maybe one-point-eight million Indians in the United States, maybe the same in Canada." Oren looks into the camera, shakes his head, laughs, and walks off with several other North American Indians.

Later in the day we get a few more establishing shots of the conference grounds and some interviews with various participants. In the course of filming I notice in the midst of the crowd several more patients from the psychiatric hospital. They are jittery and nervous and among them I recognize, once again, two of the culprits from the roadblock. As before, they are puffing frantically on cigarettes and talking to themselves. But today there is something different about them. Their faces have been painted in broad strokes of red ochre stretching from the center of the forehead down to the tip of the nose. Maybe they too have crossed over the line and become Indians. That wouldn't surprise me. At this point nothing would.

24

"Where's Payakan?" I was often asked by journalists and environmentalists as the Karioca Conference drew to a close. "He should be here," they would say as they walked off, dejected, into the crowds. The big event, the Earth Summit, was just two days away. More than one hundred of the world's leaders would soon be deciding on the environmental and developmental policy of the United Nations for the coming decade. Payakan represented the voice of the disenfranchised, a *symbol* of ecological alternatives, one person whose international recognition would be critical in drawing attention to the fact that indigenous people were being excluded from casting a vote in the official UN decision making.

That Payakan's absence posed a dilemma for environmentalists was easy to understand. For those who had followed the Save the Rain Forest movement for the last several years, it was difficult to imagine an event of this magnitude without him. He was the person environmentalists wanted to see confronting world leaders just as he had confronted the Brazilian government in the past. He was a hero, a fixture in their imaginations. His absence created a strange anxiety in Rio. It was as if you were at the local cinema watching *Rocky VI* without Sylvester Stallone in the lead. Something was missing. It just wasn't the same movie.

The impact of Payakan's efforts was inestimable. Over the

last few years he had been the central catalyst for a series of unprecedented ecological victories in Brazil—and in the process had become a shining example not only for domestic and international environmentalists but for countless other indigenous societies in the Western Hemisphere. This was the man who helped to block the construction of dams at Altamira, who led a successful effort to halt nuclear waste disposal on Kayapo lands, who outwitted the judicial system by shrewdly combating charges of defamation, who campaigned domestically and internationally for the rights of the Yanomami Indians, who helped Raoni to set up the demarcation of Kayapo lands, who created the beginnings of a pan-Indian alliance in Brazil, and who forged an unprecedented, ecologically sustainable economic partnership with the Body Shop Corporation, the first of a new generation of green capitalist corporations that was reaching out to the "peoples of the forest." In recognition of such efforts Ted Turner had recently presented him with a Better World Society Award at New York's Waldorf Astoria, where he had his picture taken with Jimmy Carter—an image (with Payakan in a yellow feather headdress) that received gratifying international circulation, especially in the Brazilian press. And in 1992 the United Nations awarded him its prestigious Global 500 for his work in environmental preservation. So, yes, he is a big draw.

The problem is that so far Payakan isn't anywhere to be seen. He's not even in Rio. At least, not in the flesh. On the opening day of the Summit his image does appear in living color on every street-corner kiosk in town. Brazil's most popular newsmagazine, Veja, is running a glossy cover photograph of Payakan similar in style to the one that appeared recently in Parade magazine.

This time, however, a different message is being relayed. The article is entitled "The Savage," and its cover headline reads: "The symbolic leader of ecological purity tortures and rapes a white student, and then flees to his tribe." Overnight, the Man Who Would Save the World has suddenly been transformed from an environmentalist hero into a violent, diabolical monster. "It is a story to make your skin crawl," write Veja's journalists Laurentino Gomes and Paulo Silber, "documented in the testimonies of five witnesses recorded in an inquiry conducted by the chief of police and in the work of a medical team from the hospital in the city of Redenção."

"I don't believe this for a second!" says an American television journalist as she glances through the article, snapping through its pages like an anxious client in a hair salon. She is surrounded by other international journalists and environmentalists who have congregated at a week-long conference running parallel to the Earth Summit and calling itself the Earth Parliament. This is another of the events where Payakan had been expected. He is on the Earth Parliament's board of advisors, a longtime friend of its organizer Darel Posey, and listed as one of their key speakers.

According to the report in *Veja*, not only has Payakan committed a brutal rape, but he *and* his wife, Irekran, are being charged with acts of "cannibalism" and attempted murder. The article is running with the subtitle "An Explosion of Savage Instinct." Its contents provide lurid, sensationalist descriptions of a purported attack by Payakan and his wife against a "white virgin" named Sylvia Letícia Ferreira. Letícia, as she is known in town, is an eighteen-year-old high school student, a neighbor of Payakan in a frontier community located near Kayapo territory. *Veja* calls Letícia a "Friend of the Indians," a babysitter who on occasion looked after the three young children of Payakan and his wife. "He raped her," the journalists write, "with the help of his wife, Irekran, and in front of his eldest daughter, Maial, five years old." The car in which this brutal and "cannibalistic" act took place is a tiny white Chevette which, according to the *Veja* reporters, looked "as if an animal had bled inside it."

As I glance through the article there are a number of aspects of the reporting that I find disturbing. Most of the prosecutor's accusations are presented as established fact. Nowhere does the story mention that the alleged incident took place in a town in southern Pará notorious for its long history of vendetta, trumped-up charges, and manufactured evidence.

"It's a plot, a conspiracy," the American television journalist tells me when I ask her what she thinks happened. "They've been trying to get to him for years. They killed Chico and they couldn't kill Payakan. So they did this."

The *Veja* story is only the beginning of what appears to be a media blitz. Later that afternoon TV Manchete, the country's second largest television network, runs an interview with the state of Pará's chief of police, Brivaldo Soares.

"He said his wife was to blame for the incident because she was jealous," says Chief Soares, surrounded by a group of journalists, their microphones anxiously bobbing within inches of his face.

"Both took part in the rape, then?" asks one of the reporters.

"Yes."

"Did they force her to take off her clothes?"

"Both used violence to take off her clothes. She didn't want that. He admitted she didn't want that."

Throughout the country, reports such as this one dominate the print and television news. With Payakan secluded in his village, most of the accounts focus on interviews with local Redenção officials or the family of Letícia Ferreira. The Kayapo attending the Earth Summit—including Raoni—give only guarded responses to the leading questions of Brazilian and international reporters.

Then just two days after the initial *Veja* article, TV Globo—Brazil's number-one television network—broadcasts an interview with Payakan from his village of A'ukre. After a long day of covering the events of the Summit, I watch the newscast at the home of Patricia Monte-môr and José Ignacio Parente, friends and colleagues who have provided invaluable help in every story I have done in Brazil. On camera Payakan looks nervous and disoriented. Behind him I can see his lawyer, José Carlos Castro, pacing in the background, the same attorney who represented him in 1988 when he was accused of defaming the nation of Brazil after his trip to the World Bank. In a relatively fluent but still problematic Portuguese, Payakan speaks to the reporter from TV Globo who remains off camera.

"It really happened. We drinking. I drinking, my wife drinking, the girl called Letícia drinking, and the people accompanying, drinking. Everything happened because of the drinking. Now, I'm not afraid or hiding here."

There is complete silence in the living room as we all react to what Payakan has just said. "I can't believe he said that," says Patricia. I couldn't believe it as well. Was this in fact an on-camera confession, the last act of a fallen hero? It appeared to all of us to be a confession. But then, as I watch, I realize we never heard the question that prompted the response. His answer could in fact be interpreted in several different ways. He did say, "It really happened." But *what* really happened?

It is becoming a question increasingly difficult to answer in Brazil. This story—packaged with its bizarre imagery of savages, virgins, cannibals, and demons—is hard to believe and almost impossible to decipher. It's symptomatic of an increasing problem I am having covering stories here. The more I know, the less certain I am of what I am seeing. Somehow in the beginning, in those early years in Yanomami territory, the dimensions of the conflicts between indigenous people and Western European cultures seemed much simpler, more black and white: Indians and gold miners were fighting over land. People were dying. In spite of the miners' denials there were definite historical precedents for the potential impact of con- tact diseases. And there was the undeniable proof of the bodies of the sick and the dying. That story made sense in a very tan- gible way. But this story is different. The exaggerated tale of the "savage" Payakan has gone beyond the dimensions of credible journalism. We now seem to be operating on the level of myth, ritual, and ceremony. Perhaps this new dimension of the story is the inevitable result of the hype and hyperbole of recent years, part of the confusing middle ground that results when our worlds become intimately intertwined in collaborative ventures as simple as harvesting Brazil nuts or as complex as saving the rain forest.

It is the choreography of this breaking news event that first alerted me to the fact that this story has entered a different plane of reality. What I find most troublesome is the way news of the purported rape appeared on the opening day of the Summit, and how the layout and writing of the *Veja* article seems to have been self-consciously created as a counterweight to the *Parade* story.

Who is there to blame for the mess that Payakan now finds himself in? I have asked myself repeatedly over these last few days. Is this the story of an Indian who has gone too far into our world and actually lost his mind? Is it, as the American television journalist suggested, part of some sinister plot conceived in southern Pará and then acted out in collaboration with vindictive media people in Rio? Is *Veja* perhaps right? Is Payakan really a savage? Have I been deceiving myself every time I refer to him simply as "a Brazilian indigenous leader concerned with the environment"? Perhaps this entire story is simply the inevitable result of overinflating the status of a leader—the killing-our-heroes complex resurfacing once again, from Joan of Arc through Gandhi, JFK, Malcolm X, Martin Luther King—and now Payakan?

Whether or not Payakan and his wife are innocent or guilty doesn't explain the severity of this attack in the press and its strange dialectical relationship to the previous press coverage, which had recently approached the level of idol worship. The responsibility for this part of the story, I am beginning to believe, is on all of us who have at one time or another followed or participated in Payakan's rise to fame: environmentalists, journalists, gold miners, anthropologists, loggers, politicians, eco-groupies, rock stars, green capitalists, and—yes—even Payakan himself. Over a period of four years we've all been actors in one way or another in an elaborate, and inevitably destructive, modern ceremony that has brought about his ritual downfall, a ceremony as complex and significant as any currently being acted out in those secluded forest villages lying north of the Amazon River. We, of course, can't see our own rituals taking place because we've come to believe we are divorced from this part of the "primitive world." We live in different times. We consume culture; it doesn't consume us. That's what makes us different from them—the savages, be they noble or violent—those who have not yet entered our civilized modern era—the ones who have yet to be acculturated, miscegenated, saved, protected, preserved. We like to think that we operate in a universe separate from those people steeped in their primitive rituals, a people who ironically have baffled the conquering white man for the past five hundred years. Indians in the Western Hemisphere represent the ultimate "other" in a multicultural society. The ones we've yet to figure out, but whose culture we often appropriate. The ones whose way of life, we tell ourselves, is so vastly different from our own. The savages.

But I have come to believe that we are not so distant from these people as we like to believe, or, as that lone soldier in the New World once wrote, *We are all savages.* I've come to accept the fact that our own lives are steeped in our own dense layers of ritual, myth, and ceremony. We call them sports, politics, the arts, and journalism, but they are part of our ritual expression, our attempts to establish a place for ourselves in this world, to maintain an equilibrium and make sense of the tragedies and mysteries of the human condition. Try as we might to deny it, human beings are ritual beings. We can approximate a dispassionate objectivity but we can never attain it: our stories and our beliefs get in the way. The stories we tell attempt to make sense of our lives, yet they also reflect our collective desires and dreams in our particular moment in history. The Indians' belief systems and ours have evolved over the centuries with different totems, different rituals, and different spiritual leaders or gods. When they become intertwined there is often confusion. We have no common ground for understanding. There is only the precarious middle ground with its patchwork of compromises and ad hoc agreements, surface attempts to bridge the gap between our worlds. When it fails us, we find ourselves at cross-purposes and our peoples in conflict.

As the Payakan "scandal" unfolds, I become increasingly convinced that the UN's Earth Summit is part of a ritual of conflict resolution for the Northern and Southern Hemispheres. In this modern-day ritual, the Indian societies of Brazil are caught at the center of a ceremonial dispute between the hemispheres. The site of this ritual event is Rio de Janeiro, which, like a coliseum in ancient Rome or an African village square, functions as a "decisive meeting place," to use the term of anthropologists. It is the setting of an extraordinary event, a place that by its very nature is separate from the normal rhythms and circumstances of quotidian life. What prompts this ritual is the sense of impending ecological doom that has descended on the nations of the world in recent years. In attendance are the international heads of state—Bush, Castro, Mitterrand, and a hundred others—all there with their political underlings to participate in the formal ceremony of government decision making. But the ceremony participants I am referring to are those multitudes of others who have made the pilgrimage to Rio. There are seven thousand international journalists, tens of thousands of environmentalists, indigenous people from across the planet, the Dalai Lama, and a cast of international celebrities including Shirley MacLaine, Jane Fonda, and Bianca Jagger, as well as several American presidential candidates. This pilgrimage is equal in size to anything witnessed in medieval Europe. And as with those ancient events, these ritual participants have arrived with high expectations, hoping to contribute to a global discussion about our shared ecological destiny.

This ceremony follows a period of rapid change that has disturbed the equilibrium between Brazil and the countries of North America and Western Europe. Power has shifted, and the roles and status of many key players have changed. The environmentalists now have the momentum and want to add to their recent advances. This movement in the press, in politics, and in global environmental policy threatens the economic and political interests of those who want to see the old equilibrium restored, to see a return to the status quo of disenfranchised Indians and unrestrained environmental destruction. On the one hand there are frontier developers and politicians who have the support of conservative and increasingly nationalistic federal legislators and journalists. On the other hand there is an unprecedented alliance of Brazilian and international environmental and human rights groups working with indigenous leaders who have won the support of international politicians, foundations, and celebrities. In the middle are the Indians whose "image" is tied to the preoccupations and agendas of these two dissenting groups from the dominant societies of Brazil, Europe, and North America. These groups, in spite of what they profess, are ultimately in conflict over who the Indian *should* be. Their stated cases represent a desire—or, in some cases, a fantasy—rather than an evaluation that takes into consideration the specific culture of these people and their historical relationship with Western Europeans living beyond the forest. The Indians, with the help of their international "friends," suddenly have achieved a new sense of power. Environmental groups are enjoying previously unavailable access to politicians and world leaders. The Brazilian government, in turn, is experiencing unprecedented international pressure to remedy its lack of environmental safeguards and its neglectful treatment of its indigenous peoples. Frontier entrepreneurs and large landowners—long accustomed to the laissez-faire feudal conditions of the Amazon Basin—are also not adjusting well to the sudden demand for justice and democratic rights on the part of Indians, rubber tappers, and *posseiros*—all the so-called "peoples of the forest." This jarring and sudden sequence of changes, just four years after Chico Mendes's assassination, has hit a threshold, a crisis point, and our societies through the institutions of the media are searching for some form of resolution or, you could even say, ritual sacrifice.

The question of who the Indian is (and in turn what image he projects) has once again become a preoccupation of the white man's world, almost an obsession. In recent years these two opposing camps—through the media, through the courts, through the channels of legislatures in Brazil and throughout the world—have essentially been involved in a ritual dialogue. At the center of that dialogue is Paulinho Payakan, someone who is both a participant in that discussion and a symbol of dispute for the opposing sides. As he has emerged in the *Parade* and *Veja* articles, Payakan is not an actual person but only an image of what these opposing groups feel the Indian should be. Certainly the reporting on who he is and what he does contains factual elements, but it is also infused with allegorical distortions and conscious omissions. Emerging at a certain moment in history this symbolic Payakan—through the ritualizing

process of the media—can no longer just be a Kayapo indigenous leader who, because of his intelligence and his language
skills, has become an intermediary with the world of the white
man. That is not possible during these times of heightened
environmental concerns. Payakan's destiny (in which he is a
willing participant) has been to become swept up in the aspira-
tions and frustrations both of those who seek to preserve the
rain forest and of those who want to exploit its natural
resources. Drawing on clichéd notions from history, these
groups have sanctified him and demonized him in accordance
with their opposing agendas. He is no longer just Paulinho (his
Brazilian name) or Krebenoti (his Kayapo name). Rather he
has become, depending on who is looking at him, the Man
Who Would Save the World or a "savage cannibal." He is
bigger than life, the stuff of Hollywood movies, and part of a
debate that has been taking place for five hundred years, one in
which the opposing moral and ethical forces of the Western
European world have sought repeatedly to define and determine the destiny of the Indian. These are the same forces that
have been at odds since Las Casas first made his scathing critique of Columbus's desire to *subjugate them all and make them do
whatever we want.* They have become part of the allegory we
have been replaying from one decade to the next, from one
century to the next—an allegory that continues to reappear as
the numbers of Indians slowly dwindle. Our "modern world" is,
in fact, no different from the "old world." We've been fooling
ourselves. We in fact have been unable to break free from the
same cycle of wild presumptions that have led to tragic misunderstandings, a cycle started when Columbus arrived on the
shores of the Americas and came face-to-face with those
strange imponderable people he mistakenly called Indians, a
people at once frightening and fascinating, a culture neither he
nor we have ever understood.

Who then are the masters of this modern-day ceremony? Who
are our contemporary equivalents of the shamans, the village
priests, and the elders who control and orchestrate those "primitive rituals"? It is, I believe, "my people" who play this role: that
select caste of journalists, filmmakers, and photographers who

have dropped in and out of this story in the course of four years.
Certainly it is society at large that provides us with our precon-
ceptions of who the indigenous people are. But we are what the
anthropologist Victor Turner refers to as its "ritual authors."
With our pens, laptops, and pictures we take reality and transform it to fit our belief system. In this sense our articles, news
clips, and films are like magic mirrors reflecting back to the world
our vision of who the Indian is. In Rio we bestowed upon
Payakan—through the image we created of him—a ritual aura
(one horrific, the other beatific) separating him from the norms
of life, giving him a grandiose, mythic dimension. And over the
years Payakan—urged on by his friends in the movement—participated in this process of ritualization as well. He often dressed
up for the white man by putting on the ceremonial paint and the
headdress of brightly colored feathers, giving us the exotic image
he knew we desired. In his speeches he distorted his depiction of
his people, leaving out important facts that didn't fit the agenda
of the Save the Rain Forest movement. This role had come naturally to Payakan. It had been part of his upbringing, part of the
middle ground the Kayapo had worked out with the white men.
Through the stories we wrote, the films we made, the pictures we
took, we shaped him into a hero for some, a scapegoat for others,
but always someone bigger than life, someone beyond the ordi-
nary. That is why in the *Veja* and *Parade* cover photos he has an
expressionless face. We need a blank canvas upon which to
impose our own illusions. A smile would have told us too much.
It would have robbed us of the opportunity to project onto him
who we want him to be, what we need him to represent.

Just two months before the start of the Summit I had an
experience that has helped me to understand the way in which
images have come to play a role in the story of Payakan. I was
up north in the state of Amapá visiting an indigenous village
leader by the name of Wai-Wai. Three years earlier I had first
filmed him and his people for a documentary I had done called
At the Edge of Conquest. During that period I did not have much
money, so the editing process was protracted. I would work out
a rough version of the documentary over a period of a few
months, then stop, search for foundation funding, and begin

again a few months later. As it turned out I finished the film just four months before I returned to see Wai-Wai in the frontier town of Macapá. I arrived there hoping to do a follow-up story prior to the start of the Earth Summit. All this time I had been carrying images of him in my head—images that I had shot, selected, and edited into the context of a half-hour documentary. The completed film I believed was a sympathetic but still accurate depiction of the problems he and his people, the Waiampi, were facing in protecting their land from outside incursions. Yet I would come to realize it was still simply *my story* of their lives.

Although I had not seen Wai-Wai in three years, I arrived in Macapá certain that I knew him intimately by virtue of the film I had made. But when we finally met, I was shocked and disappointed. He was much smaller in stature than I had come to imagine him. In the setting of this frontier town he also seemed out of place, clumsy and pathetic. He had worn ill-fitting Western clothes into the city which, in the context of our society, gave him a clownish demeanor. His Portuguese was rough and, I remember thinking, "childish"—a word I had often heard used by the miners when talking about the Indians. That night I remember having trouble sleeping, disturbed by the thought that I too had inadvertently become a dupe of the Save the Rain Forest movement. How could a serious journalist think this way? Perhaps Wai-Wai was not the man I thought he was? Perhaps I had made a dreadful mistake? Perhaps I had *imagined* him?

The next day was April 19, the Day of the Indian in Brazil. To my surprise and delight I saw another Wai-Wai on that day, a person much closer to the one I had gotten to know over the years. He was dressed in his traditional clothes and seemed much more comfortable. He was also speaking through an interpreter in his native language, providing a clarity to our conversation that had been lacking the day before. Perhaps most important, on this day I was also seeing him through the camera. The composed shots and camera angles took him out of the ambiance of this chaotic frontier town and placed him in the context of a defined story, one that allowed me to see him through my perspective, my vision of who the Indian was. He now existed in the confines of a familiar allegory: a David and Goliath tale of a village leader combating a mighty political machine. He was the victim, the underdog, someone the liberal fringe of the white world could sympathize with. I had made my choice as to the way in which I wanted to see him. It was my truth, one that existed in opposition to the frontier entrepreneurs in this region who wanted the Waiapi integrated into Brazilian society and their lands given over for mineral exploration. On that day in Macapá I recognized that I too had been holding up my own mirror reflecting my vision of the Indian back to the world at large. My documentary image of Wai-Wai had become part of "a hall of mirrors" contributing to the ritual dialogue about who the Indian really is, a dialogue we impose on them, a dialogue that seems to have culminated in the vilification of Payakan during the Earth Summit.

25

Pedro Martinez Barros used to brag that he was the one who broke the story of the Payakan scandal to the magazine *Veja*. He was a local politician and a mayoral candidate in the town of Redenção where the incident occurred. He had been running on an anti-Indian platform in a community embittered by the recent decision of the Collor government to pursue legal recognition as Kayapo territory of an area containing the most sought-after mineral deposits and mahogany reserves in the state of Pará. The proposed demarcation, still to be ratified by the Brazilian government, would give five thousand Indians control of ten thousand square miles of pristine forest, an area encompassing four percent of the land in the state and equivalent in size to the country of Belgium. Local residents were enraged, and Pedro Martinez hoped to convert their rage into a successful mayoral campaign.

"It was a very opportune moment," he said of the publication of the *Veja* story on Payakan. "It came right in the middle of Eco '92. It ruined the Earth Summit. And it ruined the Indians, you must understand, because it had just come out in a magazine in the United States that Payakan was a 'man who could save the world.' "

Pedro Martinez, it turned out, was also the uncle of Letícia Ferreira, the alleged victim. His pivotal role in this convoluted and absurd story is one bizarre element in a plot thicker, more surreal than any García Márquez novel. And much darker. Yet although this part of the story contains conspiratorial elements, it is not a simple conspiracy. I would call it a witch hunt in which certain catalytic elements—economic tensions, heightened xenophobia, and intense anti-Indian sentiments—came together in one historical moment of shared hysteria. Its perpetrators were journalists, frontier politicians, corrupt police officials, and the desperate citizens of a local frontier town who were unified by the threat posed to them by an economically and politically empowered Kayapo and one of its preeminent leaders, Paulinho Payakan.

I never made it to Redenção but a journalist friend of mine did. Scott Wallace spent a month in this community in southern Pará in order to follow Payakan's story after the conclusion of the Earth Summit. I returned to the States to start editing news reports I had gathered in Rio. I knew, however, that someday I'd be forced to put together the pieces of this troubling puzzle, particularly since I wanted to make a documentary on the larger question of the indigenous rights struggle in Brazil. That day came several months later when I decided to include Payakan's story in my documentary. So I got together with Scott in New York and he told me what he had discovered in Redenção, a town that ironically translates as Redemption.

Scott had met Pedro Martinez at his house in town about a month after the story first broke in *Veja*. Letícia's uncle was a thin man of medium build with a mustache and short-cropped dark hair. "I was the one responsible for the immediate dissemination of the information," he said. He then gave Scott a breakdown of his plans to have the country's Indian Statute changed. He made it clear that he wanted Indians to be like "common citizens," without any special privileges. "If the laws are not changed, they are going to end up owning the whole city," he told Wallace.

By the time Scott contacted Pedro Martinez no one was denying that some kind of violent altercation had occurred that Sunday night in the countryside near Redenção and that it involved Letícia Ferreira, Payakan, and his wife, Irekran. But the Kayapo leader's newly appointed lawyer had begun to publicly criticize what he called distortions in the media. He claimed his Indian client did not understand the Portuguese word for rape, *estupro*, when he was interviewed by the reporters for TV Globo. He had, the lawyer said, understood it to mean "attack." His client was willing to admit that an assault had taken place and that Letícia had suffered injuries. The extent of these injuries, however, was still subject to debate. Payakan declared to the press and in initial court hearings that he was not the one who had attacked Letícia. It was, he said, Irekran who had gone after Letícia in a jealous rage. In early court testimony he described how Irekran had inserted her hands into the vagina of Letícia as an act of revenge after she had caught him and Leticia "flirting." He later told a local paper that "your alcoholic drinks can affect any human's head—Indian, non-Indian, rich, poor. We were drinking, including the girl drank a lot. We used forty-eight bottles of beer. A lot of drinking shifted the head." When Irekran took the witness stand she admitted only that "with my fingernails I clawed at her with all my strength." Referring to Léticia's claims that she lost her virginity when she was raped by Payakan, Irekran looked Letícia in the eye during her court testimony and said, "I want her to look me in the face and tell me she was a virgin." All these details were reported extensively in the Brazilian press. The story captured the nation's imagination, competing in its lurid subject matter with the most popular of Brazil's television soap operas.

Before and during the trial the person who spoke publicly on Letícia's behalf was her father, Waldemir Ferreira, the brother-in-law of Pedro Martinez. In his conversations with Wallace and other journalists he made no pretense regarding his feelings about Payakan. A "filthy and lying Indian" is how he referred to him. "He says he's an ecologist. A barbaric criminal, that's what he is," he said on another occasion. As for the Kayapo people: "For me Indians are not fit to live in Christian society. They should stay on their reserves among their own kind." Ferreira's sentiments were supported by a number of townspeople who staged a protest shortly after the alleged rape had occurred. "An Indian's place is in the village, a rapist's place is in the jail" read one of their banners which was paraded through town. In one of two interviews Wallace conducted with him, Ferreira claimed he did not learn of the Sunday-night incident until the following Tuesday when his son, Luis, arrived with the news at his two-hundred-acre ranch located thirty-one miles outside Redenção. He told Wallace he went immediately to his brother-in-law's house in town, arriving there late Tuesday night.

"Payakan owes me a big favor," Pedro Martinez said, "because I asked him [Waldemir] what he wanted to do and he said he wanted to kill him. I wouldn't let him do it, so we went to the authorities."

Also assembled in Martinez's home that Tuesday night were a group of politically active local citizens including Manoel Franco, a lawyer and special advisor to Jader Barbalho, the governor of the state of Pará and an outspoken opponent of the plans for the Kayapo demarcation. After discussing the various options available to the Ferreira family, Pedro and Manoel Franco took Waldemir to the home of the town judge that same night. There they arranged for Letícia to appear in court the next day. It was also agreed Manoel Franco would represent the Ferreira family in a $300,000 civil suit against Payakan.

As Wallace points out, what is puzzling about the chronology of these events is that the father, Waldemir, went directly to his brother-in-law's house without stopping at the hospital to see his daughter, a young woman who had supposedly been the victim of a rape, attempted murder, and acts of cannibalism. "I was nervous," he told Wallace in explaining the apparent inconsistency of his actions. "I didn't know what to do."

For Wallace, however, the timing of this gathering as well as the father's apparent indifference to his daughter's well-being raised serious questions about the nature of the charges against Payakan. That nighttime meeting could have been the beginning of a well-constructed conspiracy—or it could equally have been the coincidental intersection of some local members of the anti-Indian lobby. He decided to investigate further by checking the "facts" of the *Veja* article against the statements of people he encountered in Redenção.

One of the key players in the case against Payakan was José Barbosa da Souza, the local police chief. According to *Veja*, Barbosa found the vehicle in question, the white Chevette, "abandoned" in a local gas station two days after the alleged rape. "It was covered with blood from the floor to the ceiling," he was quoted as saying, "as though an animal had bled to death inside." *Veja* also reported that it was Helio Ribeiro de Lima, Payakan's housekeeper, who came to Letícia's aid when he heard her anguished cries for help. It was Ribeiro who said he had seen Payakan holding a piece of wire against Letícia's neck in an attempt to strangle her, an accusation that, with Letícia's testimony, was considered crucial evidence in the attempted-murder charge facing Payakan. The alleged strangulation was described by *Veja* as part of a "demonic ritual." Barbosa was quoted as saying: "The examinations confirm that there was violence and acts of cannibalism that were beyond our imaginations." Yet a month after the *Veja* cover story Wallace met Barbosa in Redenção, where he heard a different version of these events. Barbosa told him that he had never located the car during the investigation. Wallace pushed further.

"Then what about your quote in *Veja*?" the American journalist asked.

"I never saw the car," Barbosa responded.

Chief of Police Barbosa might not have been able to find the car but, with a little investigative work, Wallace did. Following a tip given to him by a young Kayapo in Redenção, he traced the car to Amelton Lopes, known in town by the nickname Borguinho. The Chevette, which had a gray plush interior, came into Borguinho's possession directly from Payakan within seventy-two hours of the incident, a day after *Veja* said that Barbosa had found it soaked with blood "from the floor to the ceiling." Payakan, Borguinho said, had owed him a lot of money. The Chevette was partial payment on their long-standing debt. "The car was in normal condition without any blood or anything," Borguinho said. "And it had not been washed." Wallace, a veteran of bloody wars in Central America, inspected the vehicle but couldn't find any traces of the cannibalistic carnage described by *Veja*. "Not a spot of blood," he told me.

Although Letícia's testimony was extensively quoted in the Brazilian newsmagazine, the authors of the article never questioned the veracity of her allegations and only occasionally used the word "alleged." They did, however, display a great deal of journalistic panache, embellishing the story with gory details straight from the pages of a tawdry gothic novel. "She was biting me all over my body while he was attempting to strangle me," Letícia supposedly testified to Barbosa in the police report regarding the attack by Irekran and Payakan. According to the magazine's writers, three different Redenção doctors had found "wounds spread all over Letícia's body, signs of brutal beatings to the face, the tips of her breasts lacerated by bites." Chief Barbosa was quoted as saying, "It is the most barbaric case I have seen in the ten years of my career in police work." But subsequent medical evaluations requested by the state's prosecuting attorney, Lucia Bueno, clearly refuted the assertions of *Veja*, Letícia, and Barbosa. According to doctors at the Institute of Legal Medicine, Letícia had suffered only "scrapes" and "bruises." Her breasts, they stated, had not been lacerated or bitten. On the question of an attempted strangulation, the same medical examiners concluded that the testimony of Barbosa's key witness, Payakan's housekeeper Helio Lima, could not in fact be true. Lima had been quoted in *Veja* as saying that he had seen Payakan standing with a piece of wire in his hands trying to strangle Letícia. Yet the medical examiners found no sign whatsoever of "strangulation." Helio, a former gold prospector, was a young man in his twenties with short, curly hair and, according to Wallace, blue eyes—one of which wandered off to the side as the result of a birth defect. Not only was his vision impaired, but when he "witnessed" the strangulation he was standing approximately one hundred feet away from Payakan in pitch dark, on a road with no streetlights, and with only the dim beam of a dime-store flashlight to cast any illumination on the distant altercation. When Wallace questioned Helio's brother Edelsen several weeks after the incident, the North American reporter was told that "Helio never saw

Payakan strangle Letícia," that the story had been fabricated. A local farmer named José Raimundo Batista, who came to Letícia's aid that night, also contradicted Helio's testimony. Letícia, he said, had run to his house naked from the waist down. But she suffered only from minor injuries. There were no signs of the bloody carnage described by *Veja*. In the week following the alleged rape, Wallace learned that it was Letícia's parents who convinced Helio to talk to *Veja*. Helio also accompanied Letícia to the courthouse on Wednesday morning, where they both gave their testimonies to the judge. When Wallace tried to interview him a month after the incident, he was told by family members that Helio had gone "into hiding" for fear of reprisals by the Indians.

The state's case against Payakan took almost two years to come to a resolution. There were requests on the part of the defense for a change of venue and a great deal of debate as to whether Payakan and his wife were "emancipated" Indians and therefore fully accountable to the Brazilian courts for their actions. But there was also a serious, unexpected problem facing the prosecution. Lucia Bueno, the state's prosecuting attorney, was having trouble amassing a credible case of material evidence against Payakan. It turned out that Chief of Police Barbosa—*Veja*'s key source and the person who compiled the initial police report—had been arrested one year into Payakan's court case and jailed for being the ringleader of a local gang of bandits. Barbosa and his accomplices had been highjacking trucks and buses in the vicinity of Redenção and robbing the vehicles and their passengers of all valuables. After Barbosa's conviction, the public defender, Rosa C. Rodrigues, moved that the case against Payakan be dropped owing to the "incompetence" of Chief Barbosa. This setback caused further delays.

But the case was eventually tried. The verdict—almost two years after the date of the *Veja* article—came from the presiding judge Elder Lisboa Correa da Costa who, as is customary in Brazil, heard the case without a jury. "There is not enough proof, either material or in terms of witnesses, to confirm that Payakan had raped the student," Judge Correa told reporters. The charges against Irekran were more complicated. According to the judge, "there were evidences of serious bodily assaults against the teen" perpetrated by Payakan's wife. Yet, in accordance with Brazilian law, Irekran was considered a ward of the state, someone who cannot be subject to the codes of Western law. "Because she is free from punishment," Judge Correa said, "she cannot be taken to court."

And what, you might be wondering, ever happened to Sylvia Letícia Ferreira? She married a twenty-one-year-old farmer by the name of Roberto Afonso Cruz one year into the trial against Payakan. Roberto was an agricultural worker and, it turned out, a small-town thug who moonlighted as a thief in one of Pará's most notorious carjacking gangs. While married to Letícia he managed to commit a murder and get captured. He was sent off to jail for nineteen years on convictions of of auto theft and homicide. Several months after the Payakan verdict, Letícia herself was arrested for attempting to help her husband escape from jail. According to the local police she had brought her imprisoned husband "escape tools" (a drill bit and six small saws) sequestered in the false bottom of a thermos. "It isn't true," she told the new chief of police, Aldo Gomez de Castro, who had replaced the now imprisoned Barbosa. "The thermos which I brought was not this one," she was quoted as saying to him at the time of her arrest. Chief Gomez locked her up in a tiny six-by-three-foot cell with just a hammock in which to sleep. "This is a dirty frame-up," Letícia screamed to reporters who had congregated outside her jail cell in Redenção. "My husband is honest. I know our imprisonment is directly linked to Payakan. I am going to request a meeting with the Federal Police in Belém so that that case can be reopened," she said. She was eventually convicted of plotting and attempting to facilitate the escape of her husband. In one of her last public statements a desperate Letícia told a Brazilian journalist, "Just as Payakan raped me, now he is entrapping me."

Her words had little impact. By 1993 Letícia had lost all credibility in the eyes of the Brazilian press; she was but a pathetic footnote to a forgotten tale. But the press had not finished with the fallen hero Paulinho Payakan.

26

The 1992 *Veja* account of Payakan's purported rape, attempted murder, and cannibalistic violence against Letícia Ferreira was only the beginning of his problems with the press. In a series of investigative reports triggered by the accusations, the world at large slowly came to realize that some Kayapo had been involved in gold mining and mahogany contracts while their people were being championed as saviors of the forest. The most shocking revelation of all was that the movement's preeminent hero, Paulinho Payakan, was deeply involved in the sale of endangered mahogany trees to frontier loggers. Suddenly the man who had been branded as both a savage and savior was now depicted by conservatives and liberals alike as an avaricious huckster, someone who had been deceiving not just his foes on the frontier, but his allies in the international environmental movement as well.

Reports critical of the Kayapo's entrepreneurial activities began appearing in high-profile publications shortly after the rape allegations. The initial *Veja* article featured photographs of Payakan sitting in a new car and eating in a plush restaurant with his wife and children. While he was not directly linked to logging activities, a sidebar to that same article described the Kayapo as the "richest Indians" in the country with an income from logging totaling sixty million dollars since 1989. In subsequent articles, *Veja*'s journalists attacked environmentalists—

particularly those from North America—asserting that they suffered from "green blindness" because they did not immediately accept Payakan's guilt in the Ferreira case. In one story entitled "Gigolos of the Amazon," they stated that Payakan's rape charges resulted in millions of dollars of financial loss for "a category of shrewd people who exploit Payakan and other indigenous groups." Among the ranks of these exploitative gigolos, the magazine included "Indian Agency employees, businessmen, professional ecologists, and anthropologists." Over the next two years, more articles and news reports on Kayapo mahogany deals circulated in Brazil and abroad, most of which depicted these former heroes as sellouts and villains.

Prior to these press revelations, only a dozen or so anthropologists, environmentalists, and journalists had been aware of the full extent of Kayapo contracts with frontier entrepreneurs. For the majority of knowledgeable insiders, awareness of the Indians' deal making was limited to a gold contract negotiated by Payakan in 1985. The mining agreement, created under the supervision of the Indian Agency, gave the Kayapo five percent of profits stemming from gold sites located near the villages of Gorotire and Kikretum. Finalized under the threat of a full-scale gold rush, this stopgap measure was intended to be in effect for only two years. But Brazilian prospectors managed to remain in Kayapo territory beyond their deadline, allowing the Indians to eventually increase their revenue shares to thirteen percent by 1991.

While the Kayapo gold contracts of the 1980s had been openly discussed in the public sector, the mahogany contracts—particularly those negotiated by Payakan—had been hidden from the world at large. But in the years following the rape scandal, links between Payakan and the logging community in Rendenção were exposed. During this era frontier loggers and miners became acutely aware that pots, pans, and machetes were no longer sufficient to seduce the Kayapo. The Indians wanted more and got more because they knew they had what the frontier capitalists wanted. The Kayapos' negotiating successes introduced the Indians to an entirely new dimension of middle-ground deal making. By the early 1990s, most villages had received gifts of satellite dishes, Brazilian-style houses, or other expensive modern conveniences from frontier entrepreneurs in exchange for the right to exploit natural resources. And Payakan, in spite of his popular image as selfless crusader, also appeared to be benefiting from such exchanges. The little white Chevette he had been driving in Rendenção was reportedly registered in the name of a logger by the name of Osmar Ferreira, a local businessman with no family ties to Letícia. His *chacra* or bungalow—the scene of the alleged crime—was also owned by Ferreira. In 1993, a young Kayapo by the name of Mokuka, a self-professed "employee" of Payakan, gave a detailed description of the young leader's business activities to the American anthropologist Terence Turner. According to Mokuka's account, Payakan's dealings with Ferreira dated back to 1990, when an agreement was worked out for the logging of mahogany trees near the villages of Gorotire and A'ukre. Payakan's income from mahogany extraction during this period was, according to Mokuka, approximately twenty thousand dollars per month. "Payakan made contracts for A'ukre and Gorotire," Mokuka told Turner, "then he asked me to go in the forest and account for the wood taken out. I took two Indians with me and we did the work for him." While Payakan was selling endangered mahogany reserves to frontier loggers, he also negotiated a contract with the Body Shop Corporation to process Brazil nuts for a new line of hair care products. The English company's "Trade Not Aid" arrangement increased his personal revenues and provided surplus cash and medical services for his community. In spite of the reported success of this ecologically sustainable project, in 1992 Payakan once again negotiated contracts with Osmar Ferreira. He sent other Kayapo to supervise and sign manifests accounting for the number of mahogany trees removed from Kayapo lands. "Payakan said go ahead," Mokuka explained to Turner. "He did it so people wouldn't see him earning money." By 1992 Payakan's income as a key Kayapo middle man had earned him a modest home in Rendenção, a bungalow in the country, two cars, an airplane, and a new set of important allies. When former Chief of Police Barbosa tried to apprehend Payakan for the alleged rape of Letícia, it was the logger Ferreira—intent on protecting his investment—who warned Payakan of his impending arrest.

Payakan, however, was not the only Kayapo actively engaged in carving out a capitalistic niche along the Amazon's frontier. There were probably a dozen other leaders, as well as a new generation of young Turks, who were involved in contractual relations with miners and loggers. Many of them had no direct links to the familial lineages, which for centuries defined leadership structure in Kayapo communities. Their new sense of power resulted from their rudimentary understanding of Portuguese and a basic grasp of arithmetic. They provided a critical link in negotiations with the outside world and, as enterprising intermediaries, these young businessmen quickly gained strong footholds in village life. They provided their fellow Kayapo with badly needed medicines and educational opportunities and unprecedented access to consumer goods from the outside world. They were popular, generous when necessary, and their influence in the villages quickly grew. Older leaders were pushed aside and a power struggle ensued.

The most fanatical of these new free-market converts was Tutu Pombo, a man in his mid-sixties who was considered to be the founding father of Kayapo capitalism. He hailed from the village of Kikretum and was known popularly in the region as "Colonel Pombo." A corpulent and rambunctious villager, the Colonel was often seen at public protests wearing a distinctive multicolored headdress resembling a shower cap plumed with red and blue parakeet feathers. Among international photographers and journalists, his innate sense of vaudevillian theatrics made him a favorite subject of those in search of local color. Many of us at the time naively considered Pombo to be the frontier equivalent of a circus buffoon. We later discovered that he had been a pivotal figure in Kayapo history. Almost singlehandedly, he had opened the floodgates for the mining and mahogany deals that transformed Kayapo society in the late 1980s and early 1990s.

As a young child, Tutu Pombo had been the sole survivor of the massacre of his family by a violent band of frontier pioneers. Adopted and raised by Brazilians, he learned fluent Portuguese at an early age. When he returned to Kayapo territory as a young man, his language skills and his basic understanding of mathematics attracted the attention of local Indian Agency officials. Although he had no familial ties to the traditional Kayapo power structure, he was given the title of "chief" and designated as the village's intermediary for encounters with the outside world. But contrary to the expectations of the Indian Agency, Pombo exploited his new position to broker deals with frontier nut gatherers, miners, and loggers, who in the 1950s and 1960s were anxious to exploit the untapped resources of Kayapo territory. Over the course of four decades, he developed his ventures into a profitable business that, according to the Brazilian press, made him one of the richest men in the country. When the Payakan scandal broke in 1992, Pombo's high-profile status made him the first to be scrutinized by investigative journalists. News reporters in Brazil estimated his combined annual income to be approximately four million dollars, an astounding figure given that most Kayapo still survived by subsistence activities such as hunting, fishing, and the gathering of food from the forest. When Pombo died in 1994, his estate included several cars, three ranches, a hotel, and an airplane, which, with characteristic flare, included a rendering of his profile on the side of the fuselage. Local frontier doctors attributed his death to modern ailments: stress and hypertension, as well as an unhealthy appetite for chocolate and sweets.

journal entry
Megragnotti territory
10/26/92

We were dropped down in a clearing this morning near the border with Bau, the Kayapo area adjacent to Megragnotti. Low forest here, dense with small thin trees much like those of New England. Last night I sat in the Kayapo village of Pukanu watching television. The families were spread out in the village square as if awaiting a display of fireworks. The Brazilian television show *Fantastico* did a review of the week's events: images of the Bush-Clinton presidential debate, anti-ethnic protesters in Germany, the lifting of a space shuttle, all passing by this forest culture that has lived in relative isolation for hundreds of years.

I first entered Kayapo lands in 1992 to do a story on the successful realization of Raoni's two-decade campaign: Megragnotti territory, an area of tropical forest the size of Switzerland, was finally being demarcated. The Rainforest Foundation, which Raoni had established with the rock star Sting, was supervising as well as funding the complicated task of establishing boundaries in this dense tropical forest. For several months, teams of workers armed with chain saws had been traipsing behind topographers through the rain forest carving out a six-meter swathe where no natural boundaries had ever existed. They placed markers and signs along the way, warnings to any trespassers that they were entering Indian lands.

During my one-week stay in Kayapo territory, the village of Pukanu became my base of operations. In this community of two hundred villagers, a dozen large houses made from branches and dried leaves circled the perimeter. In the center of the village was a flat, dusty square, a site for ceremonial dancing, and a men's hut, which served as a meeting place for village discussions. While the architectural design of the village conveyed the appearance of a traditional society, the community was actually swept up in a cultural tidal wave. Empty Coke bottles littered the square. A satellite dish sat prominently in front of a traditional thatched hut. In the men's house, clusters of young boys and girls spent their days transfixed before a television set, watching soccer games, soap operas, and an endless array of commercials. Over the last two decades, Protestant American missionaries had infiltrated the community and were diligently translating the Bible into the Kayapo language while providing medical care for the villages. The Body Shop Corporation had also carved out a niche for itself by establishing a Brazil nut processing plant on the outskirts of the village. Just upriver gold miners operated a mining site that was contaminating the villagers' drinking water with high levels of toxic mercury. Venereal disease, contracted by young men at frontier bordellos, was infecting their female partners in the community, and posed a serious health hazard for the Indians.

The changes taking place in Pukanu were confusing, and often contradictory. In my few short days there, I searched for some kind of context to understand the logjam of cultural forces subverting this community. I had learned enough about Kayapo history to know that these people had consistently defied the pigeonhole classifications of white society. Simple, and by now tired, concepts like "culture shock" and "alienation" couldn't begin to describe the diverse forces tearing at the fabric of their culture. However, while environmentalists, anthropologists, and other sympathetic whites pondered the problem, individuals within the community were attempting to solve, or at least alleviate, it. Throughout this era, Raoni and several other traditional leaders had been actively lobbying to end logging and mining activities on Kayapo lands. His village of Cachoeira-Mentuktire and a second village, Kapot-Roykore, were calling for a return to a more moderate means of contact with the outside world, one devoid of the rampant consumerism that had arrived in this era of frontier deal making. As I got to know some community leaders in Pukanu, I discovered that in spite of the conspicuous signs of consumerism, many of these villagers were bitterly divided over their current situation. "Television is just to see what the white man is doing in the cities," an older leader named Puketheri told us one afternoon. "But bicycles and motorcycles, these things; the people buy them, but I don't like them. I just think about medicines, about getting medicines to help my people, and about getting guns and ammunition to help us to hunt."

I visited village medical clinics and local frontier schools to see firsthand the way surplus cash had been used effectively by the Indians to support social services abandoned by the Brazilian government. But the cash also had less admirable uses: expensive flights to the city to pick up cases of Coca-Cola, cookies, and alcohol, and to allow young men to go whoring. The Indians I met were becoming increasingly dependent on Brazilian foodstuffs like rice, beans, and meat purchased in the cities and consumed in place of their traditional foods attained by hunting, gathering, and slash-and-burn agriculture. Puketheri and a number of traditional leaders were now preoccupied by the precarious future of their people. "The elders have been talking about things long passed in the time of our grandparents. They talk about it all the time and I am also talking about it so that we don't lose it," said Puketheri on one of my last days in the village. "But the young boy who is born into this world today is quickly affected by the ways of the whites. He doesn't know anything else. He just goes about without direction. That is why I continue talking about our culture, so that the Indians will hold onto it."

Between 1992 and 1994 Kayapo commercial activities were the focus of numerous shortsighted press reports in which rain forest experts—many of them former allies of the Indians—declared their critical assessments of recent Kayapo entrepreneurial activities. Shortly after Payakan's rape accusations, the head of a British human rights group claimed that the charges could be attributable to his recent economic activities. He went on to say that "in our opinion, the projects that the Body Shop has run with Payakan are at least in part responsible, in that the company has put him in a position of considerable wealth and power." In 1994, *The Wall Street Journal* ran an article with the title "Kayapo Indians Lose Their 'Green' Image" followed by the subtitle "Former Heroes of Amazon Succumb to Lure of Profit." What these critics failed to recognize, however, was that Payakan and his fellow Indian entrepreneurs were simply doing what the Kayapo had always done: they were trying to get the best deal they could from the white people they encountered. In recent years, social services to their communities had severely diminished while their land was pillaged by outsiders. The time-consuming and exhausting task of safeguarding boundaries had become too much for the Indians. Why shouldn't they profit from their natural resources while pursuing other money-making ventures, such as the sale of Brazil nut oil? The Kayapo sold tracts of rain forest while championing the cause of saving it. From their perspective, this was consistent with their own indigenous *real politick*, developed over the last two centuries and modified to fit the changing conditions of a local frontier society and, more recently, the international community. If a rock star wanted to tour the world with them, if a green corporation wanted to use them as figureheads, if the Pope or the Sierra Club wanted to give them a special commendation, that was just fine. They were willing to play along just as they always had. That was how they had brokered relationships with outsiders in the past. It was consistent with their worldview. From our perspective, they were guilty of questionable ethical behavior. But we in the Western world were also responsible for the outcome of this embarrassing scenario. In our rush to save the tropical forests of Brazil, we embraced the Kayapo as one monolithic entity rather than the fractionalized and complex society they are. The tragic flaw in our plan was that we imposed our vision on them, arrogantly assuming that it complemented the vision they had of themselves. We were deceived, but we also deceived ourselves. Ironically, Sting, a person frequently criticized for his naivete during this era, was one of the few people to admit to his own complicity during this period. "At first it seemed very simple: Let's stop chopping down the rain forest and support these people," Sting told me in a 1993 interview. "But the complexity of the issue, when you take into consideration the whole of Brazil and the Brazilian economy, the poor people of Brazil, and the Indians' needs themselves vis-à-vis the forest, it is much less simple than I originally thought." I interviewed Sting in a New York rehearsal studio the day before one of his annual Carnegie Hall concerts to raise funds for the Rainforest Foundation. "It's really been a learning process," he said as his technicians secured instruments for the next session. "And I've realized that a miracle is not going to happen. What happens is process, long, hard, *boring* process which eventually, I hope, pays off. I mean all we can really hope to do is slow down the process of destruction until people come to their senses."

"Process" did prove to be a deciding factor in changing the course of Kayapo culture in the early 1990s. In fact it was two processes, one from within their communities and one from outside, which reversed the disastrous trends of their troubled society in the mid-1990s. In January of 1994, Brazil's federal prosecutor threatened to enforce constitutional decrees prohibiting the extraction of wood and minerals from Indian lands. Simultaneously, in various Kayapo communities, years of reckless environmental exploitation had taken their toll. There was a sudden increase in problematic pregnancies and a small but significant rise in the number of birth defects that, medical experts believed, could be attributed to the toxic runoff of mercury from local mines. Malaria, which found a breeding ground in stagnant pools of water left by hydraulic mining, was also on the rise. Leaders like Raoni, who for years had been arguing against logging and mining activities, began to gain new support among villages long associated with logging and mining activities. Pukanu closed down its gold operations in 1993. In 1994, a small but significant revolt took place in Gorotire. Young warriors rose up against Kayapo entrepreneurs and evicted three thousand Brazilian gold prospectors at a mining site known as Santido. In December of 1994, federal officials from Brazil's environmental and Indian agencies capitalized on the Indians' initiatives and called a meeting of Kayapo leaders in the nation's capitol. The outcome of this landmark encounter was that the Kayapo agreed to respect constitutional decrees prohibiting mining and logging activities on Indian lands. In January of 1995, federal police—acting on the agreement worked out in Brasilia—entered Kayapo territory, shut down all logging operations, and seized illegally cut trees. In the wake of these radical changes, various villages established intercommunity associations to pursue eco-tourism and a pilot project for "sustained-growth mahogany harvesting." Once again the Kayapo were redefining the middle ground between their world and ours. A new era was in the making. But unlike the earlier idealistic proclamations of the late 1980s, no one was now making grandiose claims about the Kayapos' future. Perhaps our world had finally learned an important lesson. The Kayapo had defied us before. They could easily do it again.

27

"In the early morning the jaguars come out onto the roadway. They look for small animals to eat," says Father John, shouting over the medley of squeaks and rattles coming from our Toyota truck. "This highway was a terrible thing when it was built, but we use it now." We hit a pothole and momentarily rise off our seats as the Toyota veers to the right heading towards a ditch on the side of the road. Father John thrusts his body against the steering wheel, twisting it to the left and straightening the vehicle before we slip off into the forest. "The cost of driving is much less than a plane," the priest adds without missing a beat. "But the ride," he pauses, "it is not so smooth."

I'm headed back into Yanomami territory, to Mission Catrimani to be exact, traveling with my old friend, the crazed Italian cleric. We are driving through dense green tunnels made from overhanging branches as the vehicle propels us farther into the forest, down a roadway which will not arrive at any specific destination, but will simply end because the money ran out. The dictators became weary of their dreams, the forest was far more impenetrable than the planners had imagined, the Indians' immune systems too fragile, and the protests of human rights activists too loud and too far reaching to hide the atrocities that took place in the names of "development," "progress," and "civilization." BR-210, as this roadway is known, is one of the forgotten highways of General Medici's failed plan to penetrate the heart of Amazonia. Like hundreds of miles of abandoned arteries in the forest, this little highway sits in a state of semi-completion. Each year its neglected dirt track becomes increasingly eroded by the constant rains while the forest creeps in threatening to devour it. Today, BR-210 is used almost exclusively by missionaries, Indian Agency employees, the military, and the occasional curious anthropologist.

As the sound of the vehicle drones on, the forest—dense, moist, and green—flashes by on both sides, a soothing hypnotic blur. Occasionally we drive into an area of open savanna, where we are blinded momentarily by the harsh white light of the late Amazonian morning. Then, within seconds, we are delivered back under the shade of the forest's thick canopy with its pleasant, gentle coolness. Bouncing about in the Toyota with me and Father John is my soundman, Francisco Lattorre, a dark-haired, thick-bearded native of Uruguay, who has traveled with me from the States. Every five minutes, he and the priest break into off-key Italian renditions of World War II resistance songs. Their singing is a valiant effort to keep the overworked cleric awake so that we don't drive off into one of the brackish swamps running along the roadway's perimeter. Every hour or so, we stop to get a shot of the mountains or to film a sequence of the truck passing through the forest. Then the humidity soaks its way through our clothes while mosquitoes home in on unprotected parts of our bodies. I've noticed over the course of this trip that Father John has lost his enthusiasm for such endeavors. The days of "Father 007" seem long gone. Maybe that is because it seems his side won. The Yanomami got their forest. It's been demarcated. Most of the miners were kicked out. He even raised enough money to build a hospital for the Indians in Boa Vista. Weariness, however, has taken over. He's looking forward to a new assignment in Toronto: coffee shops, bookstores, and cosmopolitan conversations. He is "happy," he says, "to be leaving this armpit."

We pass two Yanomami communities, Yawori and Rohahipi-itheri, which border the roadway. The inhabitants resemble Holocaust survivors. Gaunt, sickly looking, and dressed only in rags. Their houses are dilapidated. The village grounds are in complete disarray. When we get out of the truck, a number of the Indians surround us. A man asks me to give him my watch, then asks for my silver bracelet, and, finally, a metal necklace (a warning for a penicillin allergy) that I wear on trips abroad. "I need these things," I tell him in Portuguese, only to be met by a blank stare. The man eventually wanders off to inspect the truck. He'll probably be asking for that as well.

Father John unloads a bag of mangos in the roadway, and a large crowd of Indians form around us. There is pushing and yelling as the villagers fight among themselves for the fruit. "There are no older leaders here," the priest comments as he stands watching the Indians jostle for mangos. "No one to give them any direction. That generation died from disease when the Indians came in contact with the highway workers in the 1970s." Here I can see what the term *cultural destruction* really means: no leaders, no rules, no order. Desperation is the dominant social force in the community. I wonder if these people will ever be able to regain what they once had.

Back in the truck, I make a shot list for what we will be filming in the coming days and I think about this, my tenth trip. I came back out of professional obligation, but also compelled by my personal curiosity. I want to see for myself what has happened to Father Guilherme, Machadão, and the other inhabitants of the village of Wakathautheri. I want to see if the world's attention actually made a difference, to see if the sacrifices I made were worth it: the long, difficult journeys, the negotiations, the arguments, the late-night editing sessions, the humiliating pitches to indifferent news editors, the lost weekends, the travel-torn romances, and the continuing obsession that this forest has nurtured within me. If you listen to those who edit the news, freelancers like myself have returned to square one. "No one cares anymore about the Amazon," has become a common refrain in 1995. The Earth Summit in 1992 served as the official end of the story. The United Nations intervened. World leaders took charge. The message was clear: the media can move on to another story. And move on it did. To Central Europe, with its bullet-strafed buildings, bombed-

out squares, and a people caught in the cross-fire of ethnic violence. Those who remained working in Amazonia were, for the
most part, the ones who had been there from the beginning,
along with a few recent converts: the agronomists, the botanists, the anthropologists, the Indian Agency employees, a
handful of journalists, and a dedicated group of Brazilian and
international human rights activists, who for years have toiled
away to make a difference for the people inhabiting these lands.

journal entry
Boa Vista
5/16/95

I read a couple of items in the newspaper about the state of
justice in the Amazon. In the first, it turns out one of the
murderers of the Canuto brothers was, as Father Ricardo
suspected, a former military policeman. The judge gave him
fifty years. Then in the case of Expedito, there were also
some convictions: a *pistoleiro* and a rancher were sentenced
to 24 and 21 years in prison. Their appeals have been
denied.

　　The other item was about the assassins of Chico Mendes.
The father Darly managed to escape, but was recaptured and
sent to a Federal penitentiary in Brasilia. The son, who also
escaped, was later apprehended in southern Pará.

　　It also turns out that José Fininho, the thin man, was found
shot to death in Xinguora after he supposedly "escaped" from
jail. Whether he died as a result of an "arrangement," as he
had prophesied, is unclear. According to Father Ricardo, no
one is investigating the circumstances of Fininho's death. No
one seems to care.

I am calling this my last trip here because the "angles" to this
story are no longer readily apparent. The answers I am now
looking for cannot be found by way of simple documentation.
Maybe I saw too much. Or not enough. Maybe I am afraid to
admit that no matter how long I stay here, I will never be able to
understand this region, that I failed to shed any light on the

forces at work here. But I am not the first to face such a dilemma. Impenetrable, enigmatic, indecipherable: those are just a few of the words that explorers and chroniclers have used over hundreds of years in their attempts to describe this region and its inhabitants. Maybe this is my last trip because weariness has overwhelmed me as well and I just don't want to admit it. Maybe it's time to lift myself from the Amazon's couch and get on with my life. Whatever the case, I've returned here because I feel a need for closure, and that seems to be enough of a justification.

journal entry
5/17/95

Passed through two villages contacted by highway workers in the 1970s. According to Father John, someone was killed there two months ago. An Indian Agency employee named Edevilson shot a Yanomami man named Juliao in a dispute over the sale and transport of twenty bags of bananas. Edevilson told the Yanomami that he didn't have diesel to make the trip back to Boa Vista. The Indians threatened him with "kirima," a ritual threat—the Yanomami version of a macho display of bravado. "Only a threat," reiterated the priest as he told us the story. The Indian agent responded with kicks and punches, then his gun went off. An accident, he claimed. When Edevilson drove away, the Indians shot at his jeep with bows and arrows. He hasn't returned since. The Indian Agency post remains vacant. The people are desperate. The tension here reminds me of the havoc at Paapiú. Depressing.

"We are almost there," says Father John in his lilting Italian accent. "Another few minutes," he adds, then mumbles something incomprehensible about this part of the roadway. I'm now getting concerned about losing the light, as I was hoping to do more filming today. The highway ends abruptly and we turn onto a smaller roadway leading us onto the grassy landing strip of Mission Catrimani. Various clusters of Indians emerge from the little settlements bordering the airstrip. They are splinter groups from the village of Wakathautheri. Undoubtedly they've heard the sound of our vehicle and have come to check out the new arrivals. A woman with a child at her breast and two sticks protruding from her chin steps forward from an overgrown path of tall grass and walks out onto the runway. A small girl follows her and stands by her mother's side resting her head against her thigh. An old man, farther back, wearing only a penis string, stands by the forest's edge holding a bow and arrow in one hand and scratching his leg with the other.

Seeing these people, I feel that old sensation brought on when two vastly different worlds are suddenly juxtaposed. Each of us awestruck by the other. All action seems to slow down as we each try to comprehend the existence of the other, someone so vastly different from that world we call our own.

"There he is," says Father John pointing straight ahead. Through the smudged windshield I can just make out a group of Indians standing outside one of the mission's wooden buildings. Among them is Machadão, the village shaman I met on my first trip here, as well as Pedro, an older shaman who lives in one of the neighboring settlements. With them is Father Guilherme, cigarette in hand, dressed in a striped shirt, white shorts, and sandals. He has retained the stocky look of a prizefighter, but the years have also given him more gray and a receding hairline. "Guilherme has changed," Father John said on the ride in. "He is no longer a priest. He's become a Yanomami." Stepping from the truck I shake hands with Guilherme then clumsily with Machadão and Pedro. I let the camera roll, hoping to use this moment in the film I am currently making.

Machadão appears to be much smaller and thinner than I remember him. But what has not changed is that intelligent energy in his eyes, constantly scanning, absorbing what you say, never missing a gesture or intonation. He begins speaking to Pedro in Yanoman, then lets forth a wild laugh.

"He remembers you from before," says Father John smiling. "He says that you came here with a camera but with another man."

The next morning I survey the mission grounds: more order,

more buildings, less tension. The impending sense of disaster which permeated this community during the gold rush also seems to have dissipated. There is a new medical clinic, a new schoolhouse, a full-time cook, two full-time nurses, and a second priest to assist in teaching and administrating the mission. The Indians have recently destroyed the old maloca adjacent to the mission, and are constructing a new one about a twenty-minute walk from here. Machadão, Father John told me, has left the communal structure of the village and set up his own little hut for his wife and nine children. "We asked them to move their community further away. It was too close," Father Guilherme said. He paused before adding, "For our relationship." The tentative seduction begun by Father Calleri some three decades ago has evolved into something more permanent. A strong bond now exists between the missionaries and the Indians. But the courtship is over. The Indians have acknowledged that the missionaries are a permanent fixture in the forest, and that their lives, particularly those of their children, will never be the same.

Life has improved dramatically for the Indians since 1989, and these missionaries have contributed to the changes. Forty-five thousand gold miners have been evicted from Yanomami territory and there is now an international effort to eradicate malaria and bring medical care to sick Indians in distant villages. Funded in part by the World Health Organization, this program is coordinated by Brazil's National Foundation for Health and unites the work of its own personnel with that of doctors and nurses sent here under the auspices of the Committee for the Creation of the Yanomami Park, Medicines du Monde, Medicines sans Frontier, and various Protestant and Catholic missions based throughout Yanomami territory. It was the domestic and international public outcry which brought the medical relief and millions of dollars of aid that has come with it. Dedicated teams of doctors and nurses have managed to quell the tide of epidemics, but there are still serious problems in the region. In some Yanomami communities, particularly in the state of Amazonas, malaria infects eighty percent of the population. More than half of those infected suffer from its most lethal strain, falciparum. Since 1989, these Indians have lost twenty-one percent of their population to infectious diseases introduced by outsiders. Fortunately, the majority of deaths came at the height of the gold rush and the numbers have dwindled in recent years. For the moment, the Yanomami have avoided becoming another statistic in Brazil's long list of disappearing cultures. But all this international attention has raised suspicions among local politicians. The mayor of a frontier town bordering Yanomami territory stated recently that "Too much benevolence is suspicious."

Although my limited budget will permit me only a few days here, I don't want to start filming too quickly. I'd like for the villagers here to get to know me once again. I'd also like a better understanding of the changes that have taken place before I start asking questions. So I keep the camera under wraps, and wander about the village eating mangos and talking with passersby. Earlier I met up again with the daughter of Carrera, the village leader, and, just as she had done three years ago, she threatened me with a machete. She then said something and broke into laughter as she put away the long, sharp blade. I had no idea what it was she said, but I wouldn't be surprised if was another crack about my resemblance to a rodent.

In the afternoon, Francisco and I set up for an interview with Father Guilherme in the shade of a large tree adjacent to the priests' lodging, a wooden one-level structure painted a rich dark blue. Six years earlier, Guilherme had told me that "If I were to be born again, I would like to be reborn a Yanomami." At the time his comment struck me as odd but innocent. In the intervening years, however, I've learned to mistrust the all-embracing sentiments of outsiders swept up by a desire to help the Indians. The naive and unbridled idealization of the Indian was the double-edged sword of the rain forest movement. Its catalytic energy inspired the public outcry which helped resolve the Yanomami crisis, yet its need for perfect icons created a dangerous dilemma for groups such as the Kayapo who could never live up to the unrealistic expectations of admiring whites. I am now suspicious of anyone who professes a special identification with the Indian. I mistrust their all-encompassing enthusiasm that turns people into kitsch objects and denies them the possibility of ambiguity and imperfection. No one can live up to those ideals, and no one should be subjected to them. So now more than ever, I am interested in seeing if Guilherme's beliefs have in any way been tempered by the changing times.

"I'd never be a good Yanomami," he says when I refer to his earlier comment. "I've realized I cannot be a good one, but I try to be a very good friend of the Yanomami," he adds. "I'm trying to understand all the positive aspects of their culture and, *with benevolent eyes*, I try to forgive the negative aspects of their culture. So my commitment to these people, considering the passion I have for them, is to try to guarantee their survival."

We stop for a minute waiting for the light to change. Harsh beams of the midday sun have been breaking through the foliage, ruining my shot. I've gotten tired of trying to reposition Guilherme under bits of shade so this time we decide to just sit patiently for the angle of the sun to change. As we wait, I think about this priest and the sixteen years he has spent working with these people. He speaks their language, knows their culture intimately, and is considered by most villagers to be their "true friend." Those are not easy accomplishments. Though he has managed to immerse himself in their lives, he is probably right. He will never become an Indian, not in this life and probably not in the next. But to me, his devotion appears to be saintlike and I wonder if his church will ever recognize his efforts. Too far from Rome, too controversial, and, I conclude, not enough of a self-promoter. "The children that are growing up here are like my sons," he tells me as we conclude the interview. "I could die for them; maybe if the situation arose, I could even kill to defend them." The priest pauses for a second and adjusts his black, thick-rimmed glasses, perhaps feeling the weight of his commandment-breaking last statement. "This is because I feel for these people as if they were my own, as if I belonged to them, as if I was adopted by them. We are connected in that we suffer the same problems, the same hardships of existing in such a difficult environment. All this becomes a challenge to strengthen my will to stay here and work with them."

The next morning Father Guilherme tells me there will be a
meeting with the adults and adolescents of Wakathautheri.
Upon "their approval," he says, it will be determined whether I
can film in the village. This sudden introduction of formal pro-
tocol has taken me a little bit by surprise. On my last trip here I
simply approached Carrerra, the village leader, and presented
him with gifts of machetes, fishhooks, and knives. I explained
my intentions and agreed to leave more gifts for the community
when I departed. He contemplated my request, asked how long
I would be staying, and then granted me permission to film. It
was simple. I had done what any outsider would have done.
That, I gathered, was the problem as far as the missionaries
were concerned. In past years the miners had done exactly the
same thing. They gave gifts of food, machetes, and clothing in
exchange for the right to mine the Indians' lands. It now seems
that the missionaries are intent on abolishing the means of
seduction that they and others had used to access and manipulate this culture. They're trying to replace it with a new, more
democratic procedure based on group decision making rather
than the desire and traditional power of one individual.

The meeting takes place in a one-room schoolhouse recently
constructed, Guilherme tells us, in order "to prepare the people
to defend themselves." Those attending are mostly men, but
there are a few adolescent girls and older women. The priest
introduces Francisco and I in the Yanoman language and stands
off to the side to act as a translator when necessary. Carrera is
the first to speak and his tone is surprisingly confrontational.

Por que voce está aqui? "Why did you come here?" he says.

Eu estou aqui porque. . . . "I am here," I say, "because I want
to make a film to show my people how the Yanomami live
today, after the gold rush."

E o outro filme, o que voce fes come ele? "What did you do with
the other pictures that you took here?" asks a young man who is
maybe sixteen years old.

O outro filme. . . . "The other film. . . ." I respond. "That one I
showed it in on television in America and in Ireland, Britain,
Austria, Spain, Australia, and many countries in South America."

Father Guilherme interrupts at that point. He explains that

Davi Kopenawa, who lives in an adjacent village, stayed at my house when he first came to America. He is well known among these villagers, respected for the way he campaigned internationally in defense of their people. The atmosphere changes. The Indians appear to relax. The tone and direction of the questions begins to change. How long will I stay? Do I know Bruce (Bruce Albert, the French anthropologist)? Do I have a woman? How many children do I have? Who is my friend Francisco? Where is the other man (Vicent) whom I was with on the last trip?

I answer each of their questions as best I can. When my Portuguese falters, Francisco jumps in with a quick translation. After about twenty minutes everyone appears satisfied. None of the women have spoken. There are only silence and blank faces. *Tudo bem!* "Okay," says Father Guilherme suddenly. He and Carrera exchange a few words in Yanoman. Rising from their chairs, Machadão, Carrera, and the older men exit the room with the adolescents and women following. The priest turns to me and lights a cigarette. He looks content. "You can film," he says. "Begin anytime." No one had spoken about the fishhooks, machetes, and knives we have brought as presents for the community. At Father John's request, I gave them to Father Guilherme when we arrived. He placed them in a storage room adjacent to the radio shack to distribute or dispose of as he so desires. When will the Indians see them? After we leave, I guess. Maybe never. I don't ask. I am a guest and this is their terrain.

After this formal encounter in the schoolhouse, I better understand Guilherme's cryptic statement about preparing the Indians to "defend themselves." Recent events have necessitated public forums like this one. On July 23, 1993, near Haximu, a remote village near Brazil's border with Venezuela, fourteen Indians were murdered by Brazilian miners in an incident that the federal prosecutor is classifying as an act of genocide. Among the victims were three adolescent girls and seven children ranging in age from eight years to one year of age. In the first reports of this incident, the exact details were shrouded by language and cultural barriers. Initially seventy Yanomami were reported to have been killed. Then within a few days the number was reduced to thirty. Some articles claimed the miners killed the Indians as an act of protest against a recent government eviction of prospectors from the area. Another report stated that the killings were prompted by revenge, that Brazilian miners were seeking to punish the Yanomami because they had served as scouts for the Venezuelan military tracking gold prospectors who had crossed into Venezuelan territory. However, the most realistic assessment of the massacre stressed the fact that problems have occurred whenever whites have attempted to barter for the Indians' resources.

The anthropologist Bruce Albert happened to be in the region when the killings took place. He conducted extensive interviews with the survivors, visited the site of the massacre, and collaborated with the federal prosecutor's office in the earliest stages of the investigation. From the testimonies of the survivors, Albert learned that the Yanomami of Haximu had been involved in an ongoing series of exchanges with prospectors over a period of several months. Following in the footsteps of missionaries and Indian agents, the miners had given the Indians gifts of hammocks, guns, and ammunition in exchange for permission to work in the area. A balance of power had been struck. The terms of this informal agreement, as far as the Indians were concerned, appeared to be clear: the miners were a steady source of material goods for the Indians just as missionaries and Indian agents had been for other communities in the past. But the miners had another vision of this relationship. Their perception of the balance of power was based on their experiences in the gold rush. They were prepared to entertain some of the Indians' requests, but they felt free to arbitrarily dismiss and ignore others. The prospectors acted as if they were still part of a conquering army. They had forgotten that times had changed and now they were outnumbered.

The wildcat prospectors working in this border region had been part of a clandestine group of two thousand men who had managed to remain in Yanomami territory after the 1992 demarcation which had officially made their presence illegal. Working in small bands of ten and twenty, these men no longer commanded the presence of the legions of miners who had swept through these forests in the late 1980s. Not only were they outmanned but—because they had been giving guns as gifts—they had armed a people who were their potential adversaries. Initially they appeased the Indians with gifts, but over time they refused to honor their promises of machetes, guns, and ammunition. Then the ecological damage caused by the miners' presence began to take its toll. The local rivers became brown and filthy from the runoff of hydraulic mining and game animals became increasingly scarce. The people of Haximu began demanding greater compensation for these hardships. The miners responded with more false promises or simply gave the Indians less than they had originally agreed upon. Conflicts arose. The equilibrium between the two groups shifted. The Indians' relationship was transformed from one of dependency to one of independence and open hostility. Then the violence started.

In early July a young Yanomami *tuxawa* (leader) named Kerrero accompanied by another Indian named Devi arrived at a miner's encampment threatening a Brazilian prospector with a shotgun after an argument about an unfulfilled promise of some trade goods. Kerrero fired his shotgun at the man, but there were no injuries. The miner fled into the forest and the Indians destroyed the encampment. Then on July 15, 1993, six Yanomami men, at the request of their village elders, went to another miner's encampment on the Rio Tabocca to lay claim to food, goods, and a gun that they had been promised by a prospector in exchange for the right to continue working in the region. But the miners had been expecting them. They lured the Indians into the forest and killed four of them. Two young men managed to escape. One hid in the forest while the other fled back to the village. The survivor informed the community of what had happened. Village leaders, concerned about the spirits of the dead, sent the young man back to the site of the murders with several other villagers. The bodies of the victims, which had been buried by the miners, were exhumed and cremated. The Yanomami then pulverized the carbonized bones and, according to custom, buried them next to the domestic fires of their families. In the case of children, custom dictates that the ashes be mixed with a banana gruel and consumed by the parents. Consuming the ashes of the deceased assures that the spirits can return to the "world of the dead" located at the back of the sky. If the spirits are not treated in this fashion, they are believed to roam between the world of the dead and our world, causing prolonged bouts of melancholy in the living, a state considered to be worse than death itself.

According to Yanomami tradition, revenge for the dead must be exacted by taking the lives of the perpetrators. So several days later, a group of Indians attacked the miner's encampment killing one prospector and wounding another. The Indians bludgeoned the head of the dead man with machetes, shot his body full of arrows, then stole ammunition and a shotgun from the encampment. In response, various bands of miners in the area organized a vigilante group of fifteen men to retaliate. Over a period of two weeks, the group armed themselves with shotguns and pistols and traveled to Haximu. But when they arrived at the remote village, it was deserted. Frustrated, they burned the maloca to the ground, and set off into the forest in search of the Indians. During this same period, a group of Haximu warriors—still intent on exacting revenge—conducted a second raid against another mining site, wounding one prospector and scaring several others into the forest.

The next battle in this jungle war occurred on July 23, when the vigilante band of miners encircled a temporary village inhabited by the people of Haximu. Most of the men had gone to the neighboring community of Makayu for a festival commemorating the dead. They had left the others unprotected believing that, according to their code of honor, women and children would not be vulnerable to attack during times of warfare. The miners, however, lived by a different code. They surrounded the village and opened fire. Nineteen Indians were there when the shooting began. Five managed to escape. Twelve people were killed instantly. Among the dead were three adolescent girls, six children, and a one-year-old baby. After several minutes of gunfire, the prospectors—according to the testimonies of survivors who hid in the village—completed their work with knives and machetes. Most of the Indians' bodies were desecrated beyond recognition. A young girl suffered severe head wounds and died several days after the attack.

Almost one month later, the prospectors heard on the radio that news of the massacre had reached the outside world. They immediately fled their encampments and returned to Boa Vista. Some were arrested by the federal police. Others managed to escape into hiding in the nearby states of Acre and Amazonas. By this time the Indians had recovered the bodies of the dead and carried out their ceremonial preparations. They burned the corpses and placed the ashes in a gourd sealed with honey, careful to follow the proscribed traditions for containing the spirits of the dead. The final ceremony of ingesting and burying the ashes had yet to take place when Bruce Albert accompanied the federal police to the site of the massacre. What for the Yanomami was considered a sacred and life-preserving act became for the federal prosecutor's office a seemingly unsurpassable obstacle in their attempt to build a case. There were no bodies. No material evidence. Although two of the prospector's cooks and two miners had identified two suspects, the local judge in Boa Vista released those accused within weeks of the murders on grounds that there was not sufficient evidence to hold them in custody. When I did a follow-up story on the massacre in early September of 1993, I interviewed Aurelio Rios, a young federal prosecutor in Brasilia who had been assigned to the case. In spite of the release of two suspects, Rios seemed determined to exact justice for the killings. He was classifying the incident as genocide. If successful, this would be the first proven case involving indigenous people in the Americas. "What proof was there that six million Jews died in German gas chambers during the reign of the Nazis?" he asked rhetorically during an interview in his office in Brasilia late one afternoon. "There were no bodies . . . no records. There was only testimony from the survivors who witnessed what had happened." A successful prosecution of the Haximu case, he said, was a matter "of adapting the law to this other reality."

On December 19, 1996, five Brazilian gold miners were convicted in a federal court of murder and genocide in the 1993 killings of the thirteen Yanomami Indians from the village of Haximu. Each of the miners received sentences of twenty years in prison. To date, only one of the convicted felons, a man by the name of Joao Neto, has been apprehended.

My ancestors who transformed themselves into whites and who were carried away by the floods, it is their land that you inhabit now," Machadão tells me outside the small maloca he has constructed for his wife and children. "Our land is still here. It stops itself here," he says pointing off into the forest to his right. "It is for that reason I do not want the gold miners to try and take from us our land. The gold miners think that we are infants and that we are ignorant. They say to themselves 'I am going to give them objects and I am going to take their land.' This is how they attempt to deceive us, but we are adults. It is only them who take us for children. They think 'The Yanomami are ignorant, we want to take their land,' and that is why they give us presents while lying to us."

It is the morning of our last day here. After a brief but torrential downpour, we have begun interviewing Machadão, the man who over the years has become not only a key informant, but someone I have come to consider a friend, my trusted link to the world of the Yanomami.

"What are your concerns for the future?" I ask Machadão as Guilherme diligently translates my question into Yanoman.

"You the whites, you must stop the gold miners from coming into our lands. This is what I think. I am not friends with the whites except for the Father who lives here with us. It is us who let him live here. He cures us with his medicines. We are friends with him. The gold miners do not possess the medicines. They do not do anything but make us sick and we die."

"There are many whites in the cities who say that the Yanomami should become like them," I say to Machadão. "They say that many of you are already like the whites. What do you think of this idea?"

"The whites stare at the Yanomami because they do not recognize them. The Yanomami appear to them to be a very different people. After having looked and stared, the whites ask themselves, 'Who are these people who act like this?' Then they say that they are like us, that they want to be our friends.

They think that and for that reason they stare at us so as to be our friends. But only the trusted whites are our true friends and that is the way it should be. The gold miners make believe as if they are our friends, but they are not. They are bad. They are only pretending to be friends. They tell us lies. They are pretending. The trusted whites who come to visit us see our festivals and say 'Oh look, this is who the Yanomami are and what they are doing is good.' These people are our true friends."

Interviewing Machadão makes me think about all the changes that have taken place here since the gold rush. I feel good about the work I have done, believing that in a small way I have contributed to the preservation of this culture. At midday a plane lands for a brief stop at the Catrimani Mission runway. Davi Kopenawa is among the passengers. We drink some small cups of cafezinho and talk about his work and the films I have made in recent years. It's been three years since I have seen him, and he has continued to travel extensively in North America and Europe. Today he is on his way to a regional conference of indigenous leaders in a trip paid for by the missionaries. Towards the end of our talk, Davi tells me he appreciates the fact that I have made several films about Indians in the forest. He says he has met many people in the United States and Europe who have seen them. The films, he says, make it easier to explain to people what the Yanomami have been going through in these past years. I walk down to the runway with him and watch as his plane banks west over the forest and heads towards Boa Vista. I walk back to the mission with a renewed sense of satisfaction in my work. I feel more accepted by these people, more relaxed, less the critical outside observer. Three young hunters pass me by with turtles strapped to their backs, and next to the mission medical clinic, a young woman is knocking mangos out of a tree with a long stick. She smiles as I pass and a mango falls to the ground. I begin to toy with the idea of what it would be like to spend several years living among these Indians as Guilherme and Father John have done. The idea is alluring, but carries with it a vague and burdensome feeling. *Is it fatigue or the weight of self-deception?*

In the afternoon, I return to Machadão's maloca to get some final shots which I will need to complete my film. When we arrive, we are told by his oldest son that he is inside the little maloca. When I enter the dark and smoky confines of his home, I squat and take a moment to let my eyes adjust to the light. Then before me appears a primordial image. Machadão sits in his hammock finishing his midday meal. His wife and three small children sit scattered about in various small hammocks holding round gourds of some kind of milky plantain broth. A gray smoke lingers everywhere, and I can taste its ashen fumes. Machadão looks content, rested, and a little surprised to see me.

Posso filmar um pouco com voces depois que voce terminar sua comida. "Can we film a little with you after you finish with your food?"

Certo. "Certainly," he says with a big smile. *Depois.* "After."

Respectful of his privacy, I rejoin Francisco outside in the muddy courtyard and await the arrival of my friend. Ten minutes go by. I check on him again. He has finished eating, but he remains in the dark, in his hammock, relaxed and still smiling. I give a halfhearted wave which he acknowledges with an awkward lifting of his hand. *What now?*

I decide not to press further with my request and return once again to the muddy clearing in front of his hut where Francisco and I make small talk and throw stones at trees in the forest. Five minutes later, Machadão still has not come out. An old woman passes by and I get a shot of her as she wobbles bow-legged down a slippery path towards the new communal village. "Look at that," says Francisco pointing to a parakeet nestled amidst the branches of a nearby tree. I turn and in that instant I hear a twig break. Looking back I see Machadão exit the little hut, bow and arrow in hand. As he leaps nimbly into the forest he glances over his shoulder, and then disappears behind a wall of tropical flora. I stand there stunned. He was simply waiting until I turned my back to escape into the forest.

"Should we go after him?" asks Francisco.

I'm struck dumb by Machadão's vanishing act. Not only have I missed the opportunity to get a sequence I desperately need, but Machadão—with whom I shared a mutual trust, or so I let myself believe—has deceived me.

Francisco and I gather our equipment and head off down the

path back to the mission outpost. We pass the Indians' large communal village and wave to a few Yanomami putting the finishing touches on the roof of the maloca. A few of the men laugh at us. Others smile and wave. As I walk, I consider what has just happened. Deceit was not the issue here. Survival was. Machadão needs to hunt in order to feed his family. My needs, my intentions, they're part of my world—the white man's priorities. That's just the way it is. Conflicting agendas of disparate worlds. An old story. As old as that first encounter between whites and Indians on the shores of the Caribbean. No one has ever been able to get around it. Not even me.

ACKNOWLEDGMENTS

This book could not have been written without the generous help of colleagues, friends, and untold strangers I encountered during a decade of traveling and working in the Brazilian Amazon. I am particularly grateful to Chris Caris at Realis Pictures in New York and to Patricia Monte-Môr and José Ignacio Parente of Interior Productions in Rio de Janeiro, three great collaborators as well as trusted friends who were always there when I needed them.

Alcida Ramos at the University of Brasilia, Terence Turner at the University of Chicago, and Bruce Albert at ORSTOM in Paris provided critical insights during the research and editing stages of this work. Many ideas drawn from their books and articles were adapted by me into this work in my own eclectic distillations. In particular I was influenced by Alcida Ramos's "The Hypereal Indian" and "From Eden to Limbo: The Construction of Indigenism in Brazil," Terry Turner's "Representing, Resisting, Rethinking: Historical Transformations of Kayapo Culture and Anthropological Analysis," and Bruce Albert's "La Fumée du Métal: Histoire du contact chez les Yanomami (Brésil)."

Although this book is based almost exclusively on my personal experiences, I relied on several books for background information, including John Hemming's *Amazon Frontier*, Ricardo Rezende's *Rio Maria*, Eric R. Wolf's *Europe and the People Without*

History, Andrew Revkin's The Burning Season, Napoleon Chagnon's The Fierce People, Shelton Davis's Victims of the Miracle, Sue Branford and Oreil Glock's The Last Frontier, Victor Turner's The Anthropology of Performance, the Instituto Socioambiental's Povos Indígenas No Brasil 1991/1995, as well as various articles including Beth A. Conklin and Laura R. Graham's "The Shifting Middle Ground," Cecilia McCallum's "The Veja Payakan," and Scott Wallace's "Rape and Politics in the Rain Forest." The Ford Foundation kindly provided financial support for the task of putting words to paper, and the Blue Mountain Center provided the environment for its initial genesis.

I had the good fortune of working with Rosemary Ahern, a caring and extremely talented editor whose insights and comments allowed me to create a work that grew beyond my expectations. Larry Schoen and Madeleine Cousineau Adriance read portions of the manuscript and provided many helpful comments and suggestions. Special thanks to Cristina Miranda at Realis Pictures for her excellent research, Sandra Martin, my agent, for walking into my studio several years ago and asking me if I had ever thought about writing a book, Ann Marlowe, for her excellent copy editing and thorough fact-checking, and Kari Paschall at Dutton. Thanks also to Mario Lo Boa, Vicent Carelli, Tito Rosenberg, Maria Byington, Biorn Maybury-Lewis, Dominique Gallois, and Francisco Latorre for hard work and friendship in the field. Finally I am indebted to the Consolata Missionaries, the Rainforest Foundation, Miranda Smith, Stephen Schwartzman, Ken Taylor, Anthony Anderson, Andrea Taylor, David Maybury-Lewis, Davi Kopenawa, Machadão Yanomami, Puketheri Kayapo, Cultural Survival, Survival International, the Brazil Network, the Committee for the Creation of the Yanomami Park, Insituto Socioambiental, Centro do Trabalho Indigenista, the villages of Wakathautheri and Pukanu, and the untold other gold miners, peasants, anthropologists, and indigenous people of Amazonia who generously shared with me their hearts and homes during this long journey. Um grande abraço.

INDEX